Hauerwas the Peacemaker?

Hauerwas the Peacemaker?

Peacebuilding, Race, and Foreign Policy

NATHAN SCOT HOSLER

PICKWICK Publications · Eugene, Oregon

HAUERWAS THE PEACEMAKER?
Peacebuilding, Race, and Foreign Policy

Copyright © 2020 Nathan Scot Hosler. All rights reserved. Except for brief quotations in critical publications or reviews, no part of this book may be reproduced in any manner without prior written permission from the publisher. Write: Permissions, Wipf and Stock Publishers, 199 W. 8th Ave., Suite 3, Eugene, OR 97401.

Pickwick Publications
An Imprint of Wipf and Stock Publishers
199 W. 8th Ave., Suite 3
Eugene, OR 97401

www.wipfandstock.com

PAPERBACK ISBN: 978-1-5326-7148-7
HARDCOVER ISBN: 978-1-5326-7149-4
EBOOK ISBN: 978-1-5326-7150-0

Cataloguing-in-Publication data:

Names: Hosler, Nathan Scot, author.
Title: Hauerwas the peacemaker? : peacebuilding, race, and foreign policy. / Nathan Scot Hosler.
Description: Eugene, OR : Pickwick Publications, 2020. | **Includes bibliographical references.**
Identifiers: ISBN 978-1-5326-7148-7 (paperback) | ISBN 978-1-5326-7149-4 (hardcover) | ISBN 978-1-5326-7150-0 (ebook)
Subjects: LCSH: Hauerwas Stanley—1940-. | Peace—Religious aspects—Christianity. | Race—Religious aspects—Christianity.
Classification: BX4827.H34 H67 2020 (paperback) | BX4827.H34 H67 (ebook)

Manufactured in the U.S.A.   04/13/20

All Scripture quotations contained herein, unless otherwise indicated, are from the New Revised Standard Version Bible, copyright ©1989 by the Division of Christian Education of the National Council of the Churches of Christ in the U.S.A., and are used by permission. All rights reserved.

Contents

Chapter 1 | INTRODUCTION | 1
    Peace in Christian Ethics | 2
    Hauerwas the Peacemaker? | 6

Chapter 2 | PEACE AND PEACEMAKING IN CHRISTIAN THEOLOGICAL ETHICS | 18
    Peacemaking: Conceptual Clarification | 20
    Peacemaking: An Overview | 23
    Developments in Christian Ethics | 31
    North American Debates on Peace and Peacemaking | 54
    Conclusion | 67

Chapter 3 | HAUERWAS: THEOLOGY AND ECCLESIOLOGY | 69
    Themes in Hauerwas's Theology | 71
    Why Is Ecclesiology Important for Understanding Hauerwas's Work? | 83
    Hauerwas's Ecclesiology | 86
    Conclusion | 132

Chapter 4 | HAUERWAS ON PEACE AND PEACEMAKING | 133
    Formation of the Peaceable Body | 135
    From Peace to Peacemaking | 154
    Peacemaking: Peace Lived in Public | 179
    Conclusion | 195

Chapter 5 | WHERE HAUERWAS DOESN'T TAKE US | 197
    Hauerwas's Peacemaking and Lederach's Moral Imagination | 198
    Hauerwas's Peacemaking and Racial Justice | 208
    Religion in Foreign Policy Formation and Analysis | 223
    Conclusion | 267

BIBLIOGRAPHY | 269

Chapter 1

INTRODUCTION

WE ARE IN CLEAR need of peacemakers. Whether the ongoing war in Syria or persistent racism in the United States, the need is clear. The Church follows one who was called "the Prince of Peace" and proclaimed, "Blessed are the peacemakers," but has often lived in ways that belie this reality. Nearing the end of my undergraduate program in biblical studies and with the vision of a vocation of peacemaking beginning to form, I came across Stanley Hauerwas's *Performing the Faith: Bonhoeffer and the Practice of Nonviolence* in the bargain bin at my college's book store. After completing graduate studies in International Relations and nearing the end of two years with the peace programme and seminary of Ekklesiyar Yan'uwa a Nigeria (EYN—the Church of the Brethren in Nigeria), I reread *Performing the Faith*. This work with the Church of the Brethren in Nigeria (EYN) was in the context of a resurging Boko Haram and political violence. The church (and I with it) strained to read and live Jesus's words and the Church of the Brethren's *historic peace church* legacy in such a difficult context. At this time and place *Performing the Faith* spurred me to reengage more focused and extended reflection on a theology of peacemaking.

I was born, raised, and baptized into the Church of the Brethren, one of the *historic peace churches*. My grandfather and father were conscientious objectors as a result of their understanding that a Christian, one who follows Jesus cannot participate in war. We were also active with service efforts such as disaster rebuilding "workcamps." Both the opposition to war and the belief that our faith community was one that followed Jesus in very practical efforts to care for others shaped my understanding of the church. Hauerwas's sharp critique of militarism and nationalism as well as strong assertions of Christ's nonviolence and assertion that to be a Christian necessarily involves formation of individuals and communities resonated with my understanding of Jesus and the church.

This study will assess Stanley Hauerwas's claim that peacemaking is a virtue of the church in which peace exists as a necessary characteristic of the church.[1] Christians are formed by practices of the church and so gain the skills required to live faithfully in the world. Such formation teaches us to be truthful and to be at peace. Peace is not only *part* of this formation; it *is* this formation. Such formation is based on the present existence of peace in the church through Christ. Not only is peace a part of the local and catholic church but war has been abolished through Christ.

Hauerwas claims theology as a legitimate discourse in relation to social and physical sciences. Theology has its primary locus in the church rather than in ahistorical accounts or the university. This claiming of the language of the church creates space for particularity that is often subsumed under the universalizing assertions of the nation-state. With peace as a characteristic of the church, Hauerwas asserts that peacemaking is a virtue of the church and not merely an optional aspect of its life.

Hauerwas raises important questions concerning church, state, war, ecumenical work for peace and justice, political discourse and theory, and assumptions about shared public language. And for the church to sustain its engagement in public life, conflict, and the search for justice, articulating the connection between theology and embodied peacemaking remains a critical task.

Peace in Christian Ethics

Peace in the Christian tradition relates to war, nonviolence, peace, and reconciliation in biblical studies, Christian ethics, theology, and theological ethics. For much of the history of Christianity, peace was primarily discussed in relation to war, reconciliation to God, and interpersonal reconciliation. Many components that are now addressed through the discipline of peacebuilding were part of Christian thinking and life but not held together in the paradigm and discipline of peacemaking or peacebuilding. While the terminology of peacemaking was not extensively used, peace in practice was engaged. This will be differentiated from

---

1. Hauerwas, *Christian Existence Today*, 90.

interior spiritual and emotional peace, and theological or eschatological thinking on peace. While this distinction is not sustained by Hauerwas, within the broader historical discussion this is common.

The nineteenth-century "rediscovery" of Jesus's social ethic, specifically Albert Schweitzer's rediscovery of Jesus's eschatological and ethical significance, provided a critical turn from narrower deliberation on Christian participation or non-participation in war to social ethics that eventually expanded into a more robust understanding of peacemaking. While Karl Barth came to reject many assumptions of European liberalism in the face of the world wars, the Social Gospel as developed in the North American context continues to lead Christians into social and ethical implications of Christianity. Against what he perceived to be idealism, Reinhold Niebuhr, in works such as *Moral Man and Immoral Society* (New York: Charles Scribner's Sons, 1932) put forward a highly influential vision of Christian realism that became the backdrop for much of Christian ethics, including the intentional turn in John Howard Yoder and Stanley Hauerwas.

Peace and Peacemaking

When it is recognized that peace is not simply the absence of violence, more attention is given to the interrelated actions of peacemaking. While much work on peace still addresses war, when and how the use of force is just, work on peacemaking has provided a more nuanced understanding of the causes of the absence of peace and the theology and practices to address these. This focus shifts attention to the responsibility and actions required to realize peace.

A distinction is often made between the theology and the practice of peacemaking.[2] While this distinction makes sense within academic disciplines, it leaves practitioners the task of bridging this gap in teaching and action. I will suggest ways that Hauerwas's work on peacemaking and ecclesiology connect with John Paul Lederach's *The Moral Imagination: The Art and Soul of Building Peace*,[3] as well as issues of racial justice and US foreign-policy formation.

---

2. The distinction may arise primarily in literatures that remain largely separated by academic divisions.

3. Lederach, *Moral Imagination*.

As noted earlier, historically, peace as it relates to participation, non-participation, and the manner of participation in war has been the primary focus of discussions on peace in Christian ethics. This has been true with historic peace churches as well as the rest of Christianity. It is only relatively recently that peacemaking has been discussed explicitly, and then on a limited scale. This mirrors developments in political science and international relations where newer systematic attempts to understand and address root causes of conflict and peacebuilding in post-conflict contexts have led to the emerging, largely interdisciplinary, field of peacebuilding. This project will note the stated motivations and methods of Christian ethicists and theologians for expanding the focus from issues of war and peace to peacemaking.

Peacemaking in the Context of Historic Peace Churches

Though the historic peace churches are frequently categorized together, the Mennonites, Church of the Brethren, and Quakers do not have a single historical point of origination nor do they share all characteristics. Additionally, the moniker *historic peace church* was given in the early twentieth century after a number of groups had already divided from the original groups. For example, the Church of the Brethren, the Grace Brethren, Brethren Church, and Dunkard Brethren all have a historical connection to the first Brethren but varying degrees of continued holding of non-resistance and peace as a core part of their identity. Donald Durnbaugh's *Fruit of the Vine: A History of the Brethren: 1708–1995* and Carl Bowman's *Brethren Society: The Cultural Transformation of a "Peculiar People"* provide valuable historical context on the Church of the Brethren in relation to broader society, other churches, and issues of war, peace, and nonresistance.[4] The three-volume *Brethren Encyclopedia* is a more comprehensive engagement with the various Brethren groups who share the same point of origin in 1708.[5] In a similar fashion, Mennonites, who have a direct historical link to the broader group of Anabaptists, were not the only such group at the time of the Reformation. While Mennonites maintain that peace is crucial, this many-faceted group of Anabaptists included the likes of Thomas Munster, who used and promoted violence, makes problematic a claim of a single unified belief

---

4. Durnbaugh, *Fruit of the Vine*; Bowman, *Brethren Society*.
5. *The Brethren Encyclopedia*.

about peace and nonviolence. Gerald Biesecker-Mast engages in text-based analysis of writings on the dynamics of peace, non-resistance, and Anabaptist relationships to government and other churches.[6]

The commitment to peace and nonviolence stemmed from three primary areas of experience for the Anabaptist strand of historic peace churches. These are the rejection of violence as a response to witnessing violence; the experience of persecution by the church and state due to their religious beliefs and practices, such as adult baptism; and corporate Bible study, which resulted in a desire to recover the church not linked to ruling powers, with Jesus as the center of spiritual and ethical life.

Though peacemaking components existed in the peace churches, the language of peacemaking is a relatively new development. The beatitude of Matthew 5:9, "Blessed are the peacemakers (ειρηνοποιοι)," meant that some form of the idea and language was present through the history of the church, but there have been many ways that Christians have understood their relationship and responsibility to work for peace, resolve conflict, and think about war.

Even as the thinking on nonresistance and participation in the wider society became more varied, peacemaking discourse in the North American peace churches began to generate institutions and actions designed to live out the conclusion that rejecting violence should draw one to build peace. For example, Eastern Mennonite University opened the Center for Justice and Peacebuilding as a way to train peacebuilding practitioners. The Mennonite Central Committee engages in peacemaking and related work in many countries around the world. Christian Peacemaker Teams directly intervene and accompany targeted communities in contexts of violence while On Earth Peace trains in nonviolence and congregational reconciliation. Friends Committee on National Legislation, a Quaker lobby group, works alongside the Mennonite Central Committee and the Church of the Brethren in Washington DC to advocate for policies that support and build peace. Though much could be learned by an analysis of these practical developments, this project will focus primarily on peacemaking in theological discourse.

---

6. Biesecker-Mast, *Separation and the Sword*.

Peacemaking in North American Peace Church Discourse

Harold S. Bender sought to reengage the resources of Anabaptism in a 1944 paper presented to the American Society of Church History.[7] This project continued to animate the work of Mennonite thinkers for much of the next half century. John Howard Yoder is particularly notable in this context. Yoder did more than any other to introduce peace into theological discourse of the second half of the twentieth century. His work continues to generate new work: for example, Cynthia Hess's *Sites of Violence, Sites of Grace: Christian Nonviolence and the Traumatized Self*, and Chris Huebner's *A Precarious Peace: Yoderian Explorations on Theology, Knowledge, and Identity*. Though the work of many subsequent writers can be traced to roots in Yoder, writers such as Willard Swartley, in *Covenant of Peace: The Missing Peace in New Testament Theology and Ethics*, chart directions that utilize but are not dominated by Yoder.

Despite relatively extensive work in several disciplines, a level of disconnect remains between theological and practical peacemaking efforts even when both emerge from similar churches and commitments. This is likely due in part to disciplinary divisions and the emerging independent field(s) of peacemaking, peacebuilding, and conflict transformation in relation to theology, theological ethics, and Christian ethics. Stanley Hauerwas's work relates primarily to this later stream of writing of Christian ethics. When Hauerwas's work on peace and peacemaking ranges outside of theology and ethics, he interacts not with literature on peacebuilding but that of political philosophy.

Hauerwas the Peacemaker?

The Focus of this Study

Hauerwas seldom writes specifically about peacemaking, despite his insistence and extensive work on peace and the virtue of nonviolence as central to the church. This work will focus on how Hauerwas establishes a bridge between peace and peacemaking and on his reticence to suggest methods of peacemaking despite extensive focus on practices embodied in the church. I will assess his work on peacemaking and examine the ways in which it is supported by many other implicitly peace-related aspects of his thinking. I will argue that Hauerwas sees peacemaking not

---

7. Bender, *Anabaptist Vision*.

as a tangential concern, but as integrally bound with his more pervasive themes, such as virtue, narrative, friendship, practical reasoning, democracy, liberalism, Christian ethics, and Jesus.

I will, to the extent possible, follow Hauerwas's methodological approach. In this I will not assess and critique his work in relation to an external or overarching theological or philosophical framework, but according to the internal logics and stated commitments of his work. At points, this will lead to specific critiques such as, given his stated commitment to _____ Hauerwas should _____. Additionally, since his work is functioning within the Christian tradition, writ large, his work is able to be criticized where it fails the broader tradition. For example, if he were aiming to be thoroughly Anabaptist, his acceptance of infant baptism would set him outside this tradition. However, since this is part of the Christian tradition it *may* be justified within Hauerwas's commitments and argument. Part of my assessment will be whether these commitments and assertions hold together. Since this project is in relation to peacemaking in his work specifically, I will assess these commitments in relation to peacemaking and aspects that I understand to be related to this narrower focus. Structurally, my entire project will start broad and gradually narrow to peacemaking in Hauerwas's work and then extend beyond Hauerwas's present writings.

Hauerwas

Hauerwas has often emphasized that he is a bricklayer from Texas and that his ecclesial identity is a composite of a Methodist, Yale Divinity School, and having taught at a Lutheran then Catholic then Methodist/secular university, all while being influenced by a Mennonite. Reading widely, he interacts extensively with St. Thomas Aquinas, Aristotle, Alasdair Macintyre, John Milbank, George Lindbeck, Hans Frei, and John Howard Yoder.

Hauerwas maintains eclectic ecclesial and academic reading habits.[8] He notes that while academics outside of theology in the modern university rarely feel compelled to read theology, theologians must read everyone. This is not a complaint, however; his eclectic reading appears to provide him great joy. Due to these diverse and widespread engagements

---

8. Indeed, Nicholas Healy challenges this eclecticism in the face of Hauerwas's strong claims about authority. See Healy, *Hauerwas*.

in reading and speaking, Hauerwas writes variously on topics such as nineteenth-century novelist Anthony Trollope, radical democracy, or a Catholic encyclical.

At the beginning of his graduate studies he based his thinking in liberal Protestantism, but much of his present work is a reaction to Reinhold Niebuhr, to what he calls "liberal political theory," and to the Enlightenment assumptions that he believes undergird much of this thinking. His critiques of war and the centrality of the church in particular draw heavily on the Mennonite theologian John Howard Yoder.

Why Study Hauerwas?

Hauerwas should be studied because what he writes challenges the church, and the American church in particular, in critical ways. This is not mere criticism but a sustained discussion around the core practices and identity of the church. A not particularly sympathetic writer, Princeton University Professor of Religion Jeffrey Stout, notes his extensive influence in seminaries in the United States.[9] Hauerwas presented the prestigious Gifford Lectures in 2001,[10] and was named "America's Best Theologian" by Times magazine. In addition to a career in teaching at Notre Dame University and Duke Divinity School, he has published extensively.

The work of Hauerwas bears a number of implications for Christian peacemaking. His primary works on peace include *The Peaceable Kingdom: A Primer in Christian Ethics*; "Peacemaking: A Virtue of the Church," in *Christian Existence Today: Essays on Church, World, and Living in Between*; *War and the American Difference: Theological Reflections on Violence and National Identity*; and "The Nonresistant Church: The Theological Ethics of John Howard Yoder," in *Vision and Virtue*.

Christian peacemaking efforts require theological and spiritual resources to embrace the work with endurance and joy. While this difficult work necessitates a substantial biblical and theological backing, it is also engaged in contexts outside the realm of academic theology. Hauerwas brings theology into public debate but also anchors and reenvisions it in the church, specifically in geographically, historically, and ecclesially contingent communities. He redescribes traditional church practices,

---

9. Stout, *Democracy and Tradition*, 118.
10. These lectures were published as *With the Grain of the Universe*.

such as preaching and the Eucharist, to demonstrate their continued value in shaping Christians and providing resources to resist assumptions that distort our common life and worship of God. The generative space he creates in these wide-ranging discussions does not fit neatly in either liberal or conservative, or Protestant or Catholic categories. His writing often feels combative, but its purpose is to gain greater clarity, not simply to defeat opposing views.[11] Some have noted that his wide-ranging engagements and his essay-length rather than book-length format do not allow him to adequately expand arguments. His approach may, however, be more useful for practitioners.

Secondary Scholarship on Peace and Peacemaking in Hauerwas's Theology

Daniel Bell Jr. notes that, considering Hauerwas's reputation and standing as "one of the most prolific and best-known theological critics of war and advocates of Christian nonviolence active in scholarly circles today," he has written relatively little on the subject within his broader corpus.[12] Explicit work on peacemaking appears even less. This relative paucity is reflected in major secondary works that address Hauerwas's writing. Secondary literature has focused on other areas of his work. While these writings do not directly engage with peacemaking, the topics they cover are important for understanding Hauerwas's work on peacemaking. For example, Jeffrey Stout engages Hauerwas on his work on democracy, liberalism, and the church.[13] For Hauerwas, peacemaking comes out of the church's character of peace, which means that it is political; as such Stout's work is relevant to Hauerwas's thought on peacemaking. Similarly, Arne Rasmusson addresses critical issues of theology in practice in public that

---

11. In addition to titles such as "Work as Co-Creation: A Critique of a Remarkably Bad Idea" in *In Good Company: The Church as Polis*, Hauerwas is noted to be a "notorious 'character'" in introductions to books such as *Unsettling Arguments: A Festschrift on the Occasion of Stanley Hauerwas's 70th Birthday*, edited by Charles R. Pinches, Kelly S. Johnson, and Charlie M. Collier, and as a "contrarian polemicist, drawn to exaggerated pronouncements in the passionate service of compelling others to see things differently—or at least in the interest of stirring up a more lively debate." Jones, *God, Truth, and Witness*, 8.

12. Bell, "Way of God in the World," 112.

13. Stout, *Democracy and Tradition*, particularly chapters 5 and 6.

are critical for peacemaking.[14] Eli McCarthy briefly refers to Hauerwas's link between virtue and peacemaking but does not offer a substantial critique or exposition.[15] Mark Thiessen Nation moves closer to engaging peacemaking in "The First Word Christians Have to Say About Violence Is 'Church,'"[16] but remains primarily with the discussion on peace and war. Willard M. Swartley mentions Hauerwas briefly in The *Covenant of Peace*.[17] Richard B Hays critically but briefly interacts with Hauerwas in *Moral Vision of the New Testament*.[18]

Hauerwas's Position on Peacemaking and Ethics in Relation to Ecclesiology and Theology

Hauerwas's thinking on peacemaking and social ethics must be located within his broader theological and ecclesiological claims. Indeed, he would object to the drawing of a distinction between peace and the church in his writing. In "Peacemaking: The Virtue of the Church," Hauerwas responds to the Matthew 18 injunction to go to the one who has sinned against you: "Yet Jesus seems to have been working with a completely different set of presuppositions about what is necessary to be a community of peace and peacemaking. It seems that peace is not the name of the absence of conflict, but rather peacemaking is that quality of life and practices engendered by a community that knows it lives as a forgiven people. Such a community cannot afford to 'overlook' one another's sins because they have learned that such sins are a threat to being a community of peace."[19] For a community characterized by peace and as a forgiven people, particular habits of confronting wrong are necessary. In this Hauerwas demonstrates an *in between* that surfaces in his work. The community lives as forgiven but must sustain practices to forgive in accordance with its state of forgiveness. This peace relating to church bears similar marks in Hauerwas's thought to his claims concerning the centrality and existence of the church in describing and understanding the world.

14. Rasmusson, *Church as Polis*.
15. McCarthy, *Becoming Nonviolent Peacemakers*.
16. Nation, "First Word Christians Have to Say About Violence is 'Church.'"
17. Swartley, *Covenant of Peace*, 75–76.
18. Hays, *Moral Vision of the New Testament*.
19. Hauerwas, *Christian Existence Today*, 91.

For Hauerwas, the continued existence of the church is evidence of God's continued presence. Hauerwas seeks to revive the church's centrality in the lives of Christians and their ethical reasoning. The particularity of the church and its specific repeated practices are not a liability but rather an asset for the continued creation of the people of God in particular locations. The repetition of particular practices creates a people and a time that bears witness to God. Closely aligned to this creation of a people and time is the formation of a community, which is not simply for its own sake, but is the church's bearing witness to the presence of the kingdom of God. Hauerwas maintains, however, that although the church is the embodiment of the kingdom of God, it does not contain or exhaust the kingdom of God.

The church cannot be known in abstract principles but only in the bodies, buildings, and practices of specific congregations. These churches do not exist for themselves or even to make the world more just, but to worship God. Hauerwas often reiterates that the central task of the church is not to make the world more just but to help the world be the world. He does not wish to abandon the world to injustice or violence, but claims that the church's existence does not need to be justified by saying that the church is good for society. Only when it attends to its central task can the church bear witness to peace and justice, which are not gained through coercion or the threat of violence. As Hauerwas repeatedly states, the church doesn't have a social ethic but *is* a social ethic.

For Hauerwas peace is not an unrealized ideal, but is present in Jesus and in the church. Further, the peace is continuing to be made manifest in the people of God.

> The peace Christians embody and seek is not some impossible ideal, as Reinhold Niebuhr would have it. It is not perfect harmony. It is not order that is free from conflict because it has repressed all rightful demands on justice. Rather the peaceable kingdom is a present reality, for the God who makes such a peace possible is not some past sovereign but the present Lord of the universe. Such a peace is thus just the opposite of order, as its institutionalization necessarily creates disorder and even threatens anarchy. In effect the peace of God, rather than making the world more safe, only increases the dangers we have to negotiate.[20]

---

20. Hauerwas, *Peaceable Kingdom*, 142.

The peace that is being made possible is but the adventure to which we are called. Hauerwas's repeated reminder that our calling is never boring challenges us to reconsider the assumption that peace can be equated to quietness, tranquillity, and the absence of conflict.[21] Again he writes, "God's kingdom, God's peace, is a movement of those who have found the confidence through the life of Jesus to make their lives a constant worship of God. We can rest in God because we are no longer driven by the assumption that we must be in control of history, that it is up to us to make things come out right."[22]

Critical to peacemaking in Hauerwas is the notion that peace already exists.[23] As part of his work on peacemaking, he shows the connection between the witness of the church and the church's action as witness in politics. Hauerwas claims on several levels that peace already exists. For example, he argues that we do not need to work to abolish war because war has already been abolished in the death and resurrection of Christ. As part of the community of those who follow the victorious nonviolent Jesus, the church is a manifestation of peace as a forgiven people. As a body so constituted, peacemaking is a virtue of the community.[24] The peace that the church seeks, however, is based on truth rather than power.[25] Additionally, "peacemaking among Christians, therefore, is not simply one activity among others but rather is the very form of the church insofar as the church is the form of the one who 'is our peace.'"[26]

If, as Hauerwas claims, peace is already present how does this become manifest in the Church and broader community? Second to *the already existence* of peace is the need for witness.[27] Witness is the nonviolent performance of the peace received from Christ. This is the case not only for peace but for all theological claims. Hauerwas writes, "Discipleship and witness together constitute Christology; Jesus cannot be known without witnesses that follow him. Discipleship and witness

---

21. Hauerwas, *Christian Existence Today*, 91.

22. Hauerwas, *Peaceable Kingdom*, 87.

23. "I do not want to convince Christians to work for the abolition of war, but rather I want us to live recognizing that in the cross of Christ war has already been abolished." Hauerwas, *War and the American Difference*, xi.

24. Hauerwas, *Christian Existence Today*, 90.

25. Hauerwas, *Christian Existence Today*, 95.

26. Hauerwas, *Christian Existence Today*, 95.

27. Hauerwas, *Peaceable Kingdom*, 12; Hauerwas, *War and the American Difference*, 171–74.

together remind us that the Christ we follow and to whom we bear witness defies generalization."[28] Thus, if Jesus is the peace of God then we, through witness—which is Christology—are the present presence of the peace of God.

Witness takes place both in the form of corporate and individual lives as well as in proclamation. The peace witnessed to is both unity within the church and relation to the world. Unity of the church is less an institutional process of merging structures than something given by Christ: "a unity that only Christ can give."[29] The witness of peace is also a challenge to the violence found in the politics which is our shared public life. "The new politics is a politics of speech—and so also of act. But it begins in the speech of the church, which is a story we Christians believe is not just ours but everyone's. As such it cannot but be a complex story with many subplots. Nevertheless, it begins simply in the meeting of Christ."[30]

The church is a politics. That is, the church is a community composed of people, gathered practices, traditions, and histories that sustain its common life. Much of Hauerwas's writing on peace relates to the politics of the nation-state and war; these will be addressed separately. Hauerwas sees the existence of the church as a counter politics in the face of the nation-state. Hauerwas's writing addresses his particular nation-state of America. This is not because he thinks America is a necessarily pernicious example, but because he believes that no matter where Christians find themselves they should not view this as the ultimate home. Because no nation-state embodies the kingdom of God Christians are called to question the assumptions of the political order.

Hauerwas consistently challenges the assumptions of liberal political theory and practice in which identities are subsumed into the state. He asserts that in the face of American democracy, Christians are relieved that they are free. Liberal political theory succeeds in making religion both private and something that we do not kill or die for. Just as Hauerwas does not support killing for religion, he also opposes the state's claim of the necessity of the "sacrifice" of war.

Hauerwas mounts several challenges to Christians' loyalty to the state. Specifically, he challenges the particularistic claims of the state. He

---

28. Hauerwas, *Approaching the End*, 44.
29. Hauerwas, *Approaching the End*, 100.
30. Hauerwas, *Approaching the End*, 46.

asserts that the state rather than the church is sectarian because unlike the state the church is universal and crosses national borders. He notes that war is part of the nation-state's memory and is its supreme liturgical act. He rejects the inevitability of war and the claims that its sacrifice is necessary. These challenges to the inevitability of war are based on the fundamental theological claims that Jesus has abolished war and God's peace is found in the calling of a particular people.

Ecclesial Communities and Formation of Virtues

The church is a community of peacemaking. Those of us who have been included into the story of the church are formed in the habits of peacemaking. Peace is not merely a good idea, but the result of a life so formed. Closely related to this is *church as sustaining community for peacemaking*. Peacemakers are not heroic individuals, but those sustained by the liturgy and common life that allows for the slow witness to and building of peace. This sort of community has learned the ways of peace that are not built on the presumptions of power or threat of violence.

Hauerwas seeks a closer relationship between theology, ethics, and liturgical practices. This effort is in part linked to his thinking on being church, as a community of peacemaking. It also seeks to shift ethical thinking away from "decision" and toward the people who live in a certain way. He consistently challenges the *and* in theology and ethics. He argues that Christians, particularly those engaged in Christian ethics, must embrace specific theological commitments as integral to their ethical reasoning rather than seeking to "translate theological convictions into terms acceptable to the non-believer."[31] In order for theologians to contribute to ethical discussion, they must write with the assumption of the church as the context. He writes, "It is my suspicion that if theologians are going to contribute to reflection on the moral life in our particular situation, they will do so exactly to the extent they can capture the significance of the church for determining the nature and content of Christian ethical reflection."[32]

From this focus on the church as the necessary context for ethics, which are themselves necessarily theological, Hauerwas develops the characteristics of the church as community that sustains and shapes

---

31. Hauerwas, *Hauerwas Reader*, 68.
32. Hauerwas, *Hauerwas Reader*, 71.

persons who are capable of living cruciform lives of hope. Such lives are virtuous and "ethical" not only in extreme situations of ethical ambiguity but in the mundane circumstances of everyday life. This leads Hauerwas to turn attention away from ethical conundrums and decision making and toward the context in which those ethical decisions are made. This context is a community with a history and stories.

These stories, beginning with the God of Moses, are most fully recognized in the presence of the kingdom of God made visible in Jesus. The community that formed in relation to Jesus continues to embody but not contain the kingdom in such practices as the Eucharist and caring for the sick. Hauerwas is not only retrieving virtue ethics but describing the foundation and context in which virtuous people can exist. It is these people, formed in the community defined by peace and forgiveness, who can patiently bear witness to peace in the face of violence.

Implications of Peacemaking

In my 2009 master's thesis in International Relations, I analyzed case studies of religious actors engaged in international peacebuilding, seeking to understand the countless context-specific approaches to peacebuilding.[33] This project will not attempt to connect the theological ethical work of Hauerwas to such diverse actions but will explore how his work can be foundational for peacemaking within Christian communities. A critical finding of my earlier study was that peacemaking requires sustained creative work in order to be effective. Peace and therefore peacemaking are not additions to be embraced or set aside but are an integral part of the church, which leads to (or results in) greater resilience in acting.

This approach fits with Hauerwas's emphasis on the ongoing, historical life of congregations. Additionally, the improvisation needed for creative peacemaking is found in Hauerwas. Hauerwas's focus on the centrality of peace as a core identity of the church, which the church embodies in its common practices, aligns closely with this type of peacemaking. By reframing core identity and practices as fundamental to an embodied ethic that is displayed through the witness of a counter politics, Hauerwas sets a vision for a community with a cohesive identity but engaged in the broader world in a multifaceted manner.

---

33. Hosler, "Blessed Are the Peacemakers."

Hauerwas strongly and consistently claims that peace is an integral characteristic of Christians and the church. He also posits the necessity of the embodied nature of theology and worship in the everyday lives of Christians. On the few occasions when Hauerwas explicitly discusses peacemaking, he avoids a concrete description of how this might look. While there may be a number of reasons for his reticence, the church members and pastors who seek to live peacemaking in actual historical communities are poorer for the minimal description Hauerwas provides. This project asks how Hauerwas's account of peace joins together with his understanding of the church, virtues, and theological ethics, and how he develops peacemaking from his account of peace. This project will assess how Hauerwas's understanding of peacemaking as a virtue of the church, which is characterized by peace, can be evaluated.

The second chapter broadly describes the landscape in which the work of Hauerwas will be viewed. After outlining a basic understanding of peace and the facet on which I focus, I raise several questions about understanding peace. I briefly comment on peace and peacemaking in the Bible, and on ways peace has been discussed in theology historically. Before returning to a specific look at peacemaking in the North American context, I orient peacemaking within Christian ethics. I propose three streams or traditions that contribute to the development of peacemaking within Christian theology and ethics: the Social Gospel, through *Christianity and the Social Crisis* by Walter Rauschenbusch (New York: Association Press, 1912); the black church and liberation theology; and the historic peace churches, focusing on the work of John Howard Yoder.[34] I emphasize sources on which Hauerwas builds as well as those that he consistently critiques.

The third chapter will discuss several themes in Hauerwas's theology and ecclesiology, including: Christocentrism, the centrality of the church and practices of the body, the centrality of nonviolence, and the importance of ecclesiology. I then turn specifically to his ecclesiology, mapping some broader tendencies and looking closely at worship, witness, a church with a history, a distinct community and peculiar people, a nonviolent church, and a peacemaking community. In part, this will seek to parse his eclectic drawing on seemingly divergent traditions. Of particular interest will be his interest in Anabaptist low-church processes

---

34. The following works by Yoder are particularly relevant to this study: *The Christian Witness to the State*; *The Original Revolution: Essays on Christian Pacifism*; *The Politics of Jesus*; and *The Priestly Kingdom*.

along with his strong view of sacraments and community formation. Central to his thinking on the church is his view of its relationship to politics—or more accurately, his view of the church as a politics in itself. This chapter suggests ways in which these foci could be further developed to support peacemaking.

Chapter 4 provides a close reading of several key texts in which Hauerwas explicitly focuses on peace and peacemaking. The primary texts include *The Peaceable Kingdom,* "Peacemaking: The Virtue of the Church" (in *Christian Existence Today*), "The Nonresistant Church: The Theological Ethics of John Howard Yoder" in *Vision and Virtue,* and *War and the American Difference.* I draw as well on other essays addressing peace, peacemaking, and related issues in order to clarify and deepen the reading of the primary texts.

The fifth chapter explores ways in which Hauerwas's work in ecclesiology and peace creates the space in which he could move more substantially into peacemaking but has not. His work on concrete practices and his strong assertion of the centrality of nonviolence to the Christian understanding of Jesus make peacemaking a seemingly natural step in the progression of his work. I propose three areas where his work could be usefully extended. These include a reading of Hauerwas's themes alongside John Paul Lederach's *The Moral Imagination,* Hauerwas's inattention to racial justice and racism, and Hauerwas and US foreign-policy deliberations.

These chapters place Hauerwas's work within the broader discussions of theological ethics and peacemaking. I also explore the logic and connections internal to Hauerwas's work in relation to these topics and within the broader themes and approaches within these writings. In doing this I will demonstrate what his writing contributes to these fields as well as areas where his work is insufficient. Given the nature of Hauerwas's body of writing, I will draw on a wide range of his texts. Since these are voluminous, however, I will focus in greater depth on key books and essays.

Chapter 2

PEACE AND PEACEMAKING IN CHRISTIAN THEOLOGICAL ETHICS

THIS CHAPTER WILL PROVIDE a working definition of peace and peacemaking while also problematizing these concepts. I will then orient this discussion within Christian ethics. In addition to providing a basic overview of peace within Christian ethics and theology with particular focus on the North American context, I will also start drawing connections between Social Gospel theology in order to broaden Christian social engagement and peacemaking within the larger social contexts. Efforts such as the World Council of Churches' work on just peace propose practices seeking to respond to the multifaceted witness of peace in the Bible (and secondarily the longer Christian tradition.)[1]

This portrait of peacemaking focuses primarily on three strands or traditions of writing that respond to similar questions, concerns, and historical and cultural conditions: Walter Rauschenbusch's *Christianity and the Social Crisis*, and the social ethics and activism that relates to this; the black church[2] (which will include black liberation theology and civil rights discourse and theology); and the historic peace church tradition.

---

1. See "An Ecumenical Call to Just Peace" in *Just Peace Companion*; Stassen, *Just Peacemaking*. I have noted "and the longer Christian tradition" parenthetically because I perceive that while both the World Council of Churches and Stassen are writing within this tradition, they are primarily engaging the biblical texts. They do this in part to get beyond the history of Christian thought often being determined by questions of war and Christians' participation or nonparticipation in war. The biblical witness being much broader than these questions provides a critical foundation for multifaceted peacemaking.

2. Focusing on the North American context. The term "black church" or

Rauschenbusch and the Social Gospel movement challenged Christianity—at least mainline Protestantism—to more fully consider the social implications of the Gospel. A variety of social activist streams emerged from this movement, along with the highly influential critiques by Reinhold Niebuhr. Niebuhr's critique of what he takes to be idealistic pacifism became a major backdrop and dialogue partner for Mennonite theologian John Howard Yoder's explication of an apocalyptic Christological pacifism articulated for the ecumenical community from within the historic peace church stream.

The theological reflection and practice of the black church is a second major stream contributing to this articulation of Christian ethics and peacemaking. Although the complex formation of the black church under the ongoing experience of injustice would require attention much beyond the scope of this chapter, this contribution is a crucial component for several reasons. The civil rights movement is closely linked to the black church, and Martin Luther King Jr.'s articulation and action linking racial injustice with poverty and militarism bring together several important pieces for a multifaceted peacemaking. Additionally, as Reggie Williams demonstrates in *Bonhoeffer's Black Jesus: Harlem Renaissance Theology and an Ethic of Resistance*, Dietrich Bonhoeffer, who has been vastly influential in Christian ethics and nonviolence, was remade as a theologian of resistance during his time in Harlem.

The final stream of theological reflection and church practice considered here is that of the historic peace churches of the Church of the Brethren and Mennonites, which are important to understanding peacemaking.[3] While early Mennonites and Brethren framed "peace" as nonresistance and nonparticipation in the military, this gradually shifted to a more proactive peace position and activist peacemaking. Yoder's response to Niebuhr and the Social Gospel movement occurred at around the same time that the Anabaptist communities were increasingly integrating into the wider society. These as well as other forces generated expanded reflection and action for peace. In part, this greater reflection

---

"African-American church" are often used interchangeably or preferred by different authors. See below for more discussion.

3. I will not refer often to Quakers, who are also typically included in this classification. This is largely due to my focus on Mennonite John Howard Yoder and my personal familiarity with the Church of the Brethren. If this narrowness is justified, it is because Stanley Hauerwas, the central focus of this study, has been greatly influenced by Yoder as well as having greatly influenced how Yoder has been received and engaged in the broader ecumenical community, and increasingly outside the church.

and action for peace occurred while participating in the civil rights movement, while at the same time a variety of denominations, ecumenical bodies, and church councils began to consider what came to be called *just peace*.

In just peace, many facets of these three streams were integrated, and they provide a context for Stanley Hauerwas's writing. Hauerwas regularly states his debt to the work of John Howard Yoder and critiques aspects of the thought of Rauschenbusch and Reinhold Niebuhr and their disciples. Hauerwas spends less time with the black church stream, which is a lack that I will critique, but this stream is a vital contributor to the North American discussion and Hauerwas acknowledges this in several important ways.

Peacemaking: Conceptual Clarification

What is the relationship between peacemaking, peace, nonviolence, and peacebuilding? Is peace merely the absence of violence? Is peace the absence of conflict? If one seeks to remedy one of the causes of violence (say, for example, the corruption that is a cause of the violence of Boko Haram in Nigeria or the environmental degradation by oil companies that disrupts and impoverishes local communities in the Niger Delta) does this count as peacemaking, or is such a remedy simply governance reform or environmental care and corporate accountability? If such governance reform of corruption is not peacemaking, does governance reform that addresses military abuses qualify as peacemaking?

For the purposes of this project, I will work within the bounds of Christian theological ethics. The discussion, then, will be theological but also tied into the concrete practices of Christian communities. Rather than attempt to cover all facets of a possible definition of peace and peacemaking, I propose here a working definition on which to build:

Peace is the presence of wholeness in relationships that are characterized by justice, mutuality, and wellbeing. Peace is not a universal or homogenous experience but is experienced in the appreciation and celebration of diversity and between individuals, communities, nations, and with the environment (non-human world).

Peace is often discussed in relation to war. War is often thought to be the antithesis of peace. Or perhaps more accurately, since war is frequently assumed to be an unfortunate but inescapable reality, peace is thought of primarily with reference to the more normative reality of war. Within Christian ethics and theology, these assumptions are demonstrated by the heavy skewing of writing toward questions of peace and war—particularly in terms of the participation or nonparticipation of Christians in war and, if sanctioned, the manner of this participation.

A second major stream of Christian thought is *spiritual peace and peace with God*. Building from several passages in the Bible that explicitly describe reconciliation between God and humanity, theologians have extensively developed this direction. Peace has also been emphasized in spiritual practices and states of serenity and prayer. Though this direction will not be my main focus, there are good reasons why it should be attended to even within the more action-oriented work of peacemaking. To make peace, especially for long-term engagement, one needs to be at peace (or at least at peace enough to have longevity in the work). This can also closely relate to the work of healing trauma both within the peacemaker and in the community.

Another major stream of thinking is *peace as interpersonal*, focusing on relationships between individuals or at the community level. Much work on mediation and reconciliation deals with this level. Indeed, Matthew 18 has been used extensively as a framework for addressing conflict within certain churches. One such example is the Matthew 18 workshop developed by *On Earth Peace*, an agency of the Church of the Brethren.[4]

The broadest, and perhaps least explicitly developed, stream of thinking is *peace as part of social engagement*. This conception of peace grows out of Rauschenbusch's Social Gospel theology. In this work, there is a growing awareness of two things: 1) social engagement is a necessary element of the Christian vocation; and 2) the social context of a particular social ill is not isolated from other social ills, so that to address one the Christian must also address the others. In this frame, concern for peace does not necessarily assume a strict pacifism or even that questions surrounding a discussion of war must be addressed.

These are the directions in which peace has typically been explored. They are all visible to a degree in my working definition: *Peace is the presence of wholeness in relationships that are characterized by justice, mutuality, and wellbeing. Peace is not a universal or homogenous experience but is experienced in the appreciation and celebration of diversity and between*

---

4. See the On Earth Peace website at http://onearthpeace.org/.

individuals, communities, nations, and with the environment (non-human world). This chapter will expand on this definition, focusing particularly on the work of Stanley Hauerwas.

Before I go too far down the path of defining peace, I will state a few qualifications for this thinking. Canadian Mennonite theologian Chris Huebner problematizes the idea of peace, asserting:

> The peace of Christ explodes that which we take to be given. It radically transforms the world as we know it. It is paradoxically more militant, or at least more militantly disruptive, than the military. The tragedy of Christian pacifism is that its vision of peace has largely become captive to sanitized discourses of humanization. It has adopted the military's search for guarantees, its desire to create passages of safety. It attempts to tame and to bring order to that which is deemed wild and out of control. Like the military, Christian pacifism all too often speaks as if it has a monopoly on peace. Its rhetoric assumes that it occupies a position of ownership over peace. The pacifist speaks as if he inhabits a standpoint that is somehow purified of violence, of sin. Or at least he assumes that he is able to keep violence under control.[5]

This discussion opens up a fundamental question that must be addressed early on: Is peace/peacemaking and peacebuilding a set of technical skills such as mediation, negotiation, political process, or trauma healing, or is it a deeper set of commitments and questions that challenge assumptions around power and contexts of un-peace? While some may grow impatient and desire to simply get on with the slow work of building peace, clarifying assumptions behind the thinking and practice of peacemaking may create foundations and practices that can break the cycle and recycling of un-peace. For Huebner, however, asking to clarify for the purpose of building a better foundation may still fall into the tendency to prioritize technical efficiency and effectiveness. Emphasizing efficiency and effectiveness may be too open to coercive action. Such fundamental critiques are critical for interrogating our notions of peace to uncover the residues of violence and need for control.

Indeed, a further practical question is: Is peace a question for social scientists, politicians, grassroots practitioners, or religious leaders?[6]

---

5. Huebner, *Precarious Peace*, 20.

6. Lederach asks a variation of this question when discussing his focus in *The Moral Imagination*.

Does one discipline or profession "own" the core of peace? What is the fundamental component of peace? If the key is practical, then perhaps some type of political or social-science project focused on the practical organization of society is central. If peace is fundamentally interpersonal, then perhaps a mediator or psychologist can provide a foundational understanding. Such a question may be a form of asking: What is the foundation of peace? This will be considered with respect to Hauerwas and other like-minded challengers of what they see as modernist assumptions of knowledge.

The role of theology as a relevant academic discipline may be useful at this juncture. In *The State of the University: Academic Knowledges and the Knowledge of God*, Hauerwas stakes out a claim for theology as a knowledge in the university but which is also critically located in the church. Though theology is a knowledge of the church, Hauerwas also meets challenges brought by Jeffrey Stout in *Tradition and Democracy*. Perhaps rather than staking a claim to a definitional structure to peace and peacemaking, it is most appropriate in reference to peace and peacemaking to acknowledge context and aims as being from within the church and for the purpose of building up the life of the church toward peacemaking. This is my view, but I believe that it is at least in part also that of Hauerwas.

The purpose of this consideration early on is simply to flag that even in the defining of peace we risk maintaining the habits that undercut the possibility of peace. Indeed, even the construction of such a sentence can be examined for assumptions concerning peace and our relation to it and work for it. One of the questions we must ask, for example, is what this implies about peace being a *gift of God* versus *a product of our cleverness or skill*. These are not questions that I will attempt to resolve now but simply open questions as I move forward.

Peacemaking: An Overview

Biblical Tradition

Understandings of violence, peace, and peacemaking in the Bible are highly contested. Meanings, approaches, understanding and degree of authority, the issue of who within the church structure is entitled to determine meaning, whether there is *one* proper meaning, and the relation of Scripture to church tradition(s) are a few of the hermeneutical questions that shape one's reading of the text. When the issue in question from within Scripture and tradition is *peace*, these questions proliferate. Reading a text relating to peace in the context of the nation-state, nationalism, ideology of empire (implicitly or explicitly[7]), as a part of a racial majority or minority, as a person who is wealthy or impoverished, as a person who self-identifies as straight or gay, or in any other context carries a particular variation of power or oppression that shapes understanding. The following overview of peace in the Bible will not, then, approach a comprehensive consideration, but simply provide a reference point.

The Old Testament/Hebrew Bible

When one is discussing Jesus's teaching on peace in the New Testament, the typical rebuttal is "But what about God's relation to war in the Old Testament?"[8] Certainly, the recorded commands of God to wipe out the enemy and Jesus's command to love one's enemies create certain hermeneutical challenges. There have been many attempts to make sense of the Old Testament injunctions in relation to Jesus's teaching on peace.[9] Some have said that the Israelites misunderstood in attributing these actions to God, while others have posited a fundamentally different God. These are critical issues when seeking to develop a biblical theology of participation/nonparticipation in war, but what is more important for this study is an account that develops an account of peace and peacemaking from the Bible and how this was read in the Church. One significant attempt to focus on occurrences of peace is David Leiter's *Neglected Voices: Peace in the Old Testament*.

New Testament

Certain Anabaptist groups seeking to get to a more basic understanding of the Bible and the practice of the early church often (at least among

---

7. Most American Christians do not think they are living as part of an empire.

8. I once received a letter in response to an article I published on the use of armed drones. The writer identified himself as a "New Testament Researcher" but his arguments to challenge me were based solely on references from the Old Testament.

9. Gregory Boyd proposes a *Cruciform* hermeneutic that reads the Old Testament with particular focus on violent portrayals of God through Jesus. Boyd, *Crucifixion of the Warrior God*.

surviving groups) identified peace as a part of Jesus's life and teaching.[10] Christian groups have often in some way qualified their use of Scripture when discussing matters of war and peace. Much of the subsequent overview examines how groups, theologians, and church leaders engaged in these questions.

Mennonite biblical scholar Willard Swartley has noted that there has been surprisingly little treatment of peace in New Testament theology and ethics.[11] He observes that despite frequent occurrences of *peace* and peace-related words and concepts, many New Testament studies barely mention peace. Some of this may simply be how writers frame their work. For example, work on the relationship between Jews and Gentiles could easily be part of this discussion, but might not be described in those terms but rather as unity or in relation to practicing the law. The former relates more to peace between people and the latter to peace between people and God.

Certainly, the field of Biblical studies is comprised of numerous subfields and has been the subject of intense theological and pastoral work for centuries. In the following paragraphs, I will sketch some of the prominent passages and themes.

Sermon on the Mount

For Christians who emphasize peacemaking and peace, the Sermon on the Mount, found in the Gospel of Matthew, chapters 5–7, has been a key passage. This portion of Scripture includes the verse, "Blessed are the peacemakers for they will be called the children of God" (Matt 5:9).[12] Later, in verses 5:38–48, we read the (in)famous passage on turning the other cheek when struck, and are commanded to "love your enemies and pray for those who persecute you." This teaching alongside Jesus's persistent work of healing and feeding, particularly of those who by their sickness and poverty were on the margins or excluded from the community, conveys a broad view of peacemaking. Additionally, Jesus's forgiveness of those who killed him (Luke 23:34) when held alongside his teaching on forgiveness (Luke 17:4) and his exhortation to confront in order to repair

---

10. See Biesecker-Mast, *Separation and the Sword*.

11. Swartley, *Covenant of Peace*, 4–8.

12. All Scripture quotations contained herein, unless otherwise indicated, are from the New Revised Standard Version Bible.

a relationship (Matthew 18) provides critical foundations and argumentation for peacemaking. Certainly, many throughout church history have challenged the assertion that Jesus's teaching and life support a universal pacifism; however, even a non-pacifist reading of these texts may observe peacemaking as present.

Jesus's Teaching and Life

The life and teaching of Jesus as found in the Gospels are contested on several levels. There are the debates about what these sayings and actions mean, what is the most authoritative, and what is an "authentic" saying or action versus what was added later.

Whereas many ecclesial sources, especially Anabaptists, have sought to prioritize the life and teachings of Jesus in their theology and ethics, this was largely brought into academic theology by John Howard Yoder's *Politics of Jesus*.[13] My working position is that the Bible is the authoritative text with which Christians engage in action and conversation with both the local and broader church ecumenically, globally, and historically. This definition allows a degree of uncertainty (What does authoritative mean?) but also maintains some traditional form without being rigidly literalist (The reading is done in community seeking to follow the Spirit engaged outwardly with their community). There are, however, variations in approaches to professional ethicists and biblical scholars, as Cahill observes:

> In contrast to the typical work of the ethicist, it is striking that biblical scholars develop ethics much more out of a basic conversion or discipleship stance—moral perspective transformed by eschatological faith—than out of concrete moral dilemmas, or even analysis of networks of human relations and actions in their right. Typically, the biblical scholar approaching ethics (unlike the ethicist approaching the Bible) focuses on the fundamental nature of conversion, and poses moral questions out of this standpoint, so that the elaboration of moral rules is at most of secondary importance. When one is deeply engaged with the biblical materials, the absolute urgency of a fundamental transformation of one's life in conformity to Christ overwhelms one's

---

13. Yoder, *Politics of Jesus*.

attention to the particulars of its working-out in day-to-day relationships.[14]

Cahill then notes that for these scholars, assertions are more suggestive than prescriptive.[15] When Scriptures are considered in community, it is a process of discernment and seeking to follow the Spirit through reading, prayer, and action. It is in this space that the specificity often prescribed by ethicists emerges from the text and lived context. There is also a difference in how professional ethicists and biblical scholars divide themselves along disciplinary lines and preaching pastors in the congregation. In the congregational context, there is no sharp division between biblical, theological, and ethical considerations.

These themes continue through the New Testament with the early commentary on the life and teachings of Jesus and the early church's experience and struggle to form as a community. The coming of the Holy Spirit is a vivid early showing of the collapsing of divisions between linguistic and ethnic groups (Galatians 3:28); while the church's going beyond the Jewish community (Acts 1:8) precipitated by Peter's vision before the coming of a Gentile (Acts 10) is a sign of the unity found in Christ. This unity, for the disciples, was prayed for by Jesus (John 17) and is theologized in Ephesians 4. Socioeconomic divisions are challenged in 1 Corinthians 11:17–22 and in James 2, which denounces favoritism. These texts provide a necessary background for a broad approach to peacemaking, although perhaps Romans 12 provides the most substantial explication of such peacemaking. In this passage, we see nonconformity to patterns of the world, which I take, based on other consistent teachings, to have included violence and greed. This chapter is built on the eleven previous chapters of "theology" and includes a quintessential verse on peacemaking: "If it is possible, so far as it depends on you, live peaceably with all" (Rom 12:18).

Emerging Just War Tradition

Theology, that is, the ongoing reflection within the Church and about God and the Church, builds on or reacts to the entire corpus until the time of the writing. My primary interest in this study is peacemaking. In particular, in this background work before I explore the work of

14. Cahill, *Love Your Enemies*, 24.
15. Cahill, *Love Your Enemies*, 25.

Hauerwas in detail I am interested in a cluster of themes that underlie current work on peacemaking, often articulated as *just peace*. In this I am interested in questions of how the church engaged *socially* through meeting needs, responding to violence, and seeking peace.

Writers such as Tertullian and Augustine did not draw a sharp distinction between theology, ethics, and practice. How the Christian lives emerges out of experience of God and the church. Tertullian assumes a position of the church that excludes the so-called necessity of engaging in sanctioned violence of the military. Augustine takes a more divided approach that allows for less of a distinction between the church and the world. Cahill writes, "Their [Tertullian and Origen] pacifism does not consist in nor even focus on an absolute rule against violence derived directly from biblical texts; it is a feature of a multidimensional portrait of discipleship inspired by Scriptures mediating Christ's presence and teaching, but also received within an ongoing community which brings to that depiction its own coloration."[16]

While this study aims to explore the practice of peacemaking rather than questions of war, pacifism, and the just war tradition, the latter need to be acknowledged at several points. Augustine is often considered to have inaugurated just war reasoning within Christianity; Thomas Aquinas develops a more systematic account. For Augustine, questions of war are mixed with other concerns of the Christian life and of the church.[17] He does not allow for killing in self-defense, but only as part of functioning under proper authority,[18] and he exhorts the warrior to be a peacemaker "even in war."[19] Bell notes that "Aquinas certainly shared this understanding of intent in just war as well as the importance of right intent in waging a war justly. But to this he added a notion of the common

---

16. Cahill, *Love Your Enemies*, 41.

17. Bell, *Just War as Christian Discipleship*, 28. Additionally, Paul Weithman writes, "Discussions of politics can be found in a number of Augustine's writings . . . His own treatments of political subjects draw heavily upon ethics, social theory, the philosophy of history, and, most importantly, psychology and theology. It is possible to recover a distinctive set of political views from Augustine's texts. That set constitutes not a political philosophy, but a loose-jointed and heavily theological body of political thought which Augustine himself never assembled." Weithman, "Augustine's Political Philosophy," 234.

18. Bell, *Just War as Christian Discipleship*, 30.

19. Bell, *Just War as Christian Discipleship*, 31.

good."[20] This notion of common good, while still part of the discussion on war, brings us a step closer to the ideas of peacemaking.

Though certain writers, such as John Howard Yoder, have focused on Constantine's legitimizing of Christianity as a shift in the nature of the church, it is a significant point in the development of the church's way of existence and relationship to the empire.[21] Alan Kreider demonstrates the key role of the virtue of patience in early Christian thought, and how, though Augustine engages this virtue, he subtly qualifies and undermines it.[22] The "necessities" of governing emerging from Constantine contribute to this shift and theological reasoning. This possibility, and at times necessity of governing, emerges in Augustine's response to Manicheanism, efforts to restore order,[23] and in his "tendency to focus on inner attitudes rather than external harms."[24] The separation of peace from politics or limiting it solely to war continued to develop.

While the question of rule, and therefore war and Christian participation, became more common and was addressed theologically by writers such a Augustine and Aquinas, it remained part of the whole of theology. Peace is often seen through the issue of war. Matthew Tapie writes, "Most scholars who have commented on Aquinas's view of peace have done so from the context of discussing his teaching that peace, defined as the 'tranquility of order' (*tranquillitas ordinis*), is the aim of just war."[25] Tapie goes on to consider Aquinas's nuanced and scriptural treatment of peace, particularly as it relates to the church.[26] For much of the church, the need to participate in war became an assumed, if unpleasant, necessity. Because of this, and the limited consideration of peace and peacemaking, much discussion has remained lodged in questions of participation or nonparticipation in war rather than on a more dynamic practice of peacemaking. When such a topic is ventured, it has often been seen as a church or spiritual question rather than a political question.[27]

---

20. Bell, *Just War as Christian Discipleship*, 47.

21. Many Anabaptists would say "fall." I use the word *development* here neither negatively nor positively, but simply as a description of the way things changed.

22. Kreider, *Patient Ferment*.

23. Deane, "Augustine and the State," 51–73.

24. Langan, "Elements of St. Augustine's Just War," 178.

25. Tapie, "For He Is Our Peace," 149.

26. Tapie, "For He Is Our Peace," 168.

27. Efforts to break down these distinctions between the allegedly political or apolitical forms of peace will take prominence later on in this work.

The ambiguities of participation in war have been dealt with in a variety of ways, such as distinguishing between what is proper for a lay person, ruler, or clergy person to do as well as if such participation is lauded (as in the Crusades) or requires repentance (as in the Orthodox church).

Anabaptists and the Reformers

The Anabaptists were a diverse group of radical reformers who challenged state imposition of a particular religion and war, as well as other Christians whom they saw as following a compromised tradition. Arising at various times during and since the Reformation, Anabaptists occupied a similar cultural and theological space, but did not necessarily share a common origin. For the purposes of this project, there are several areas of particular interest. The first is an opposition to war and violence by most Anabaptist groups.[28] A second is a razing of hierarchical structures within the church and a challenging of the relationship of the church and individual Christians to political powers and government.

The term *Anabaptist* connotes the centrality of adult baptism.[29] It challenged the practice of infant baptism, which was also tied up in regional political bodies and the state. In Estep's words, "With the introduction of believer's baptism by the Swiss Brethren, discipleship (*Nachfolge Christi*) became a corporate experience. At this point, the Anabaptist vision of the visible church patterned after the apostolic prototype of the New Testament became incarnate in history. Henceforth believer's baptism was to serve as the mark of distinguishing the free churches of the Anabaptists from the territorial churches, the so-called *Volkskirchen* or *Landeskirchen* of the Reformers."[30] This nonconformity to the world,

---

28. Yoder writes, "The revolution of Munster, with which uninformed historians still blacken the Anabaptist name, was not consistent Anabaptism; it was a reversion of the same heresy accepted by Lutherans and Catholics alike—the belief that political means can be used against God's enemies to oblige an entire society to do God's will. It was for this reason that the nonresistant Anabaptists denounced the Munsterites even before the conversion of Menno. Munster attempted, just as did Constantine, to take into human hands the work which will be done by the Word of God at the end of the age—the final victory of the church and defeat of evil." Yoder, *Original Revolution*, 73.

29. "To ignore the role of baptism or to minimize its place in sixteenth-century Anabaptist life is historically unjustifiable. Indeed, understanding the place of baptism in Anabaptist life may well be the key to interpreting Anabaptist views of discipleship and the church." See Estep, *Anabaptist Story*, 201.

30. Estep, *Anabaptist Story*, 237.

along with the attempt to solely follow the words and teaching of Jesus, supported and perhaps even led to the stance of nonresistance to violence and nonparticipation in the military. Carl Bowman observes this shift from nonresistance to the "peace position" in the Church of the Brethren in the twentieth century.[31] He writes, "Between the Civil War and World War 1, the Church of the Brethren was transformed from a small body that backed up its peculiar morality with church discipline to a large, diversified group of missionary-minded Protestants who were hesitant to enforce church principles with 'legalistic' methods."[32] In the face of this new context, the universal draft, and great outward and ecumenical engagement, the church's understanding of nonresistance began to morph toward a broader vision of peace and peacemaking. It was also in this era that the term *historic peace church* began to be used for Mennonites, Brethren, and Quakers.

Developments in Christian Ethics

In this section, I will examine more recent developments in Christian ethics that relate to peacemaking. When one looks at present work on *just peace* and then goes back to find the roots of such writing, it is obvious that it has not emerged solely from explicit conversations on peace but out of a broader discussion of Christian ethics.[33] As will be shown in greater detail, theologians such as Walter Rauschenbusch spent relatively little time on peace, narrowly defined, but did work on many areas of concern typically included in *just peace*. This section will profile specific writers and works as well as suggest ways in which these themes support or detract from thinking on peace and peacemaking.

Rauschenbusch sought to move Christians out into communities and social action. Though he did not address peacemaking in detail, his work lays some of the groundwork needed to move from issues of participation and nonparticipation in war to active peacemaking. He was particularly engaged in issues of economics, poverty, industrialization,

---

31. Bowman, *Brethren Society*, 349–52. Ervin R. Stutzman describes a similar movement in the Mennonite church in *From Nonresistance to Justice*.

32. Bowman, *Brethren Society*, 350.

33. Alternatively called social ethics or Christian sociology in the early years of the late nineteenth and early twentieth centuries. Dorrien provides a brief telling of this history in "Social Ethics in the Making," 393–409.

and workers. On justice seeking rather than typical religious action, he wrote:

> But the point that here concerns us is that a very large part of the fervor of willing devotion which religion always generates in human hearts has spent itself on religious acts. The force that would have been competent to "seek justice and relieve the oppressed" has been consumed in weaving the tinsel fringes for the garment of religion. The prophets were the heralds of the fundamental truth that religion and ethics are inseparable, and that ethical conduct is the supreme and sufficient religious act. If that principle had been fully adopted in our religious life, it would have turned the full force of the religious impulse into the creation of right moral conduct and would have made the unchecked growth and accumulation of injustice impossible.[34]

This sort of social action became part of just peace discussions later in the century in certain circles, denominations, and at the World Council of Churches. The World Council of Churches' *Ecumenical Call for Just Peace* has been framed around several "signposts" or thematic directions, one of which is *peace in the marketplace*.[35] In this document the potential breadth of peacemaking is demonstrated.

Regarding Jesus and violence, Rauschenbusch wrote, "For one thing he would have nothing to do with bloodshed and violence."[36] Rauschenbusch did not, however, assume that Jesus's actions or teaching translate directly. He stated, concerning certain teaching, "These are not hard and fast laws or detached rules of conduct. If they are used as such, they become unworkable and ridiculous. They are simply the most emphatic expressions of determination that the fraternal relation which binds men together must not be ruptured."[37] He went on to note that the "law of love transcends other laws," and that law may need to be broken in order to reach a higher law.[38] An interesting question is whether this qualification opens up the possibility for the use of violence for a proclaimed good end. Thinking back to Huebner, how does the possibility of the use of coercion create the opening for an enforced peace? Rauschenbusch presented a vision of the kingdom of God that grows and progresses: "If the

---

34. Rauschenbusch, *Christianity and the Social Crisis*, 7.
35. World Council of Churches, *Just Peace Companion*, 11.
36. Rauschenbusch, *Christianity and the Social Crisis*, 57.
37. Rauschenbusch, *Christianity and the Social Crisis*, 68.
38. Rauschenbusch, *Christianity and the Social Crisis*, 69.

Kingdom was not dependent on human force nor on divine catastrophes, but could quietly grow by organic processes; if it was not dependent on national reconstruction, but could work along from man to man, from group to group, creating a new life as it went along; then the kingdom in one sense was already here. Its consummation of course, was in the future, but its fundamental realities were already present."[39]

In this vision, progress is easily linked with culture in a way that is notably challenged in a hindsight that includes the world wars. Think of his view of "organic growth" when he states that "Pride disrupts society. Love equalizes."[40] Later on the same page he writes, "All these acts and sayings receive their real meaning when we think of them in connection with the kingdom of God, the ideal human society to be established. Instead of a society resting on coercion, exploitation, and inequality, Jesus desired to found a society resting on love, service, and equality."[41] Rauschenbusch dealt very little with violence, war, or peace. The primary way that he addressed conflict is in economics and industry. For example, he mentioned conflict in labor disputes,[42] as well as a few passing comments on trust, saying, "Trust is the foundation of all higher social life."[43] Though not extensively commenting on peace or peacemaking broadly, the trust and conflict in labor disputes are related.

Not only did Rauschenbusch seek to shift the primary religious vocation into the social realm, but he stated, "The championship of social justice is almost the only way left open to a Christian nowadays to gain the crown of martyrdom. Theological heretics are rarely persecuted now. The only rival to God is mammon, and it is only when his sacred name is blasphemed that men throw Christians to the lions."[44] Given this vocational shift, he asserted that the task of a theologian is to gain a level of proficiency in another social discipline. This allows a person to be effectively engaged rather than making uninformed or naïve ethical claims. Though not focused on peacemaking per se, this sort of discussion, along with more standard debates about war, moves the conversation towards that of active peacemaking. Rauschenbusch

39. Rauschenbusch, *Christianity and the Social Crisis*, 62.
40. Rauschenbusch, *Christianity and the Social Crisis*, 70.
41. Rauschenbusch, *Christianity and the Social Crisis*, 70.
42. Rauschenbusch, *Christianity and the Social Crisis*, 239.
43. Rauschenbusch, *Christianity and the Social Crisis*, 382.
44. Rauschenbusch, *Christianity and the Social Crisis*, 418.

argued that instead of merely lamenting or accepting the fact of poverty, Christians are obliged to address the system. In a similar move, instead of merely debating participation or nonparticipation in war, Christians should address the causes of this violence.

Rauschenbusch noted or approved the convergence of Christianity and a particular civilization. Additionally, he supposed a progress in history that at his writing in 1907 might be almost manifest. This raises the question, If this progress is delayed, waylaid, or not necessarily going to arrive, does this undermine his overall project? Also, how does his conception of the kingdom of God relate to a shift in trajectory in how this is understood? Questions around idealism, relation of the nation state to the church, progress, and eschatology which are present in Rauschenbusch will continue to be reengaged.

The Niebuhrs

The brothers Niebuhr were and remain highly influential. In *Christ and Culture*, H. Richard Niebuhr proposed a typology for Christ's relationship to culture.[45] One of the few public exchanges between the brothers was in *The Christian Century*, on the possibility of the United States' military entry into World War I. After an early period as a liberal pacifist opponent to war, Reinhold Niebuhr took a more "realist" approach. Near the end of *Moral Man and Immoral Society*, he notes the constant tension between the "needs of society and the imperatives of a sensitive conscience." He continues, "This conflict, which could be most briefly defined as the conflict between ethics and politics, is made inevitable by the double focus of moral life." For the individual, the focus is "unselfishness" while for the society it is the "moral ideal of justice."[46]

> Politics will, to the end of history, be an area where conscience and power meet, where the ethical and coercive factors of human life will interpenetrate and work out their tentative and uneasy compromises. The democratic method of resolving social conflict, which some romanticists hail as a triumph of the ethical over the coercive factor, is really much more coercive than at first seems apparent. The majority has its way, not because

---

45. These include, "Christ against culture," "Christ of culture," "Christ above culture," "Christ and culture in paradox," and "Christ the transformer of culture." See Niebuhr, *Christ and Culture*.

46. Niebuhr, *Moral Man and Immoral Society*, 257.

the minority believes that the majority is right (few minorities are willing to grant the majority the moral prestige of such a concession), but because the votes of the majority are a symbol of social strength.[47]

For Reinhold Niebuhr, power is necessary for change.[48] He seeks to break up the notion that nonviolence and violence are intrinsically good and evil. He posits that the connection between goodness and nonviolence is most plausible at the interpersonal level and breaks down as the groups increase in size and complexity.[49] He notes that even nonviolence such as Gandhi's boycott of British cotton results in undernourishment of children in Manchester.[50] "It is important to insist, first of all, that equality is a higher social goal than peace. It may never be completely attainable, but it is the symbol for the ideal of a just-peace."[51] The Niebuhrs, especially Reinhold, remain foundational (or at least frequently responded to) ethical theorists in America today.[52]

---

47. Niebuhr, *Moral Man and Immoral Society*, 4.

48. "Power sacrifices justice to peace within the community and destroys peace between communities. It is not true that only kings make war. The common members of any national community, while sentimentally desiring peace, nevertheless indulge impulses of envy, jealousy, pride, bigotry, and greed which make for conflict between communities." Niebuhr, *Moral Man and Immoral Society*, 16. "The middle classes and the rational moralists, who have a natural abhorrence of violence, may be right in their general thesis; but they are wrong in their assumption that violence is intrinsically immoral. Nothing is intrinsically immoral except ill-will and nothing is intrinsically good except good will. We have previously examined proletarian motives and discovered that, while they are not altogether pure, they are as pure as the motives of collective man usually are; and are certainly not less moral than the motives of those who defend special privileges by more covert means of coercion than the proletarians are able to command." Niebuhr, *Moral Man and Immoral Society*, 170.

49. Niebuhr, *Moral Man and Immoral Society*, 172.

50. Niebuhr, *Moral Man and Immoral Society*, 172.

51. Niebuhr, *Moral Man and Immoral Society*, 235.

52. Gary Dorrien, who occupies the Reinhold Niebuhr Chair of Theology at Union Theological Seminary in New York, writes, "He was the greatest American theologian of the twentieth century. He made a tremendous impact on modern theology and ethics. He was the greatest American Christian public intellectual ever. And he made an important impact on American politics." Dorrien, *Economy, Difference, Empire*, 47.

Dietrich Bonhoeffer's Legacy

In Dietrich Bonhoeffer, there is simultaneously a deepening of the theological concept of reconciliation, such that reconciliation is manifest in Jesus, and a pushing of Christians to engage more explicitly in just causes in the world. He challenges the primacy of narrowly defined "religious" concerns. Further working on the idea of ethics as formation brings the "form of Jesus tak[ing] form in our world" in a way that appears in concrete judgments and action.[53] He seeks to undo the assumption that there are two spheres, that of God and the world. Instead, all is united in Christ: "But the whole reality of the world is already drawn in into Christ and bound together in him, and the movement of history consists solely in divergence and convergence in relation to this center."[54] He asserts,

> *Ecce Homo!*—Behold the man! In Him the world was reconciled with God. It was not by its overthrowing but by its reconciliation that the world is subdued. It is not by ideals and programs of conscience, duty, or responsibility and virtue that reality can be confronted and overcome, but simply and solely by the perfect love of God. Here again it is not by a general idea of love of God in Jesus Christ. This love of God does not withdraw from reality into noble souls secluded from the world. It experiences and suffers the reality of the world in all its hardness. The world exhausts its fury against the body of Christ. But, tormented, he forgives the world its sin. That is how reconciliation is accomplished.[55]

Under the subheading of "The Church and the World," Bonhoeffer quotes Matthew 5:10 concerning "suffering for righteousness' sake" and criticizes Christians who seek to suffer only for "explicit profession of Christ." He asserts that this passage in the Sermon on the Mount "rebukes them for their ungenerousness and narrowness which looks with suspicion on all suffering for a just cause and keeps its distance from it."[56] This broadness and generosity results in the person embracing the situation concretely, without needing to know what such an embrace will fully entail: "The responsible man is dependent on the man who is concretely his neighbor in his concrete possibility. His conduct is not established in advance, once

---

53. Bonhoeffer, *Ethics*, 89.
54. Bonhoeffer, *Ethics*, 195.
55. Bonhoeffer, *Ethics*, 72.
56. Bonhoeffer, *Ethics*, 62.

and for all, that is to say, as a matter of principle, but it arises with the given situation."[57] There is much debate about the nature of Bonhoeffer's decisions to engage in a plot to overthrow Hitler violently.[58] Whereas Bonhoeffer was an advocate of nonviolence, in this instance, he seems to set this conviction aside.

While these are certainly interesting and useful discussions for both Bonhoeffer scholarship as well as the field of ethics generally, what I am more interested in here is his thinking on concrete engagement. He writes, "One must risk looking into the immediate future; one must devote earnest thought to the consequences of one's actions; and one must endeavor to examine one's own motives and one's own heart. One's task is not to turn the world upside-down, but to do what is necessary at the given place and with a due consideration of reality. At the same time, one must ask what are the actual possibilities; it is not always feasible to take the final step at once."[59]

While Bonhoeffer may be similar to Reinhold Niebuhr in his assumption of practical reasoning towards "responsible" action, he seeks to bind all reality together under the sphere of Christ. This does not seem to be present in Niebuhr. Bonhoeffer was a political theologian—deeply concerned to find and describe how following Jesus radically changes and challenges our lives.

Bonhoeffer did not just get like this. He wasn't born into a family of political or theological radicals. He wasn't particularly predisposed to fighting the system or self-sacrifice. He started along this path when he experienced the Black Jesus in Harlem. Reggie Williams tells the story of this meeting.[60] Bonhoeffer grew up during and after World War I, a period in which Germany suffered humiliation and the growth of nationalism. His early theological work sought to establish himself and "acquire as much knowledge as he could, as quickly as possible."[61] During this time he remained largely sympathetic to German nationalism. He did not yet challenge the assumptions of the church that would eventually lead to it largely acquiescing to Hitler's attempted extermination of Jews and others deemed undesirable.

---

57. Bonhoeffer, *Ethics*, 224.
58. See, for example, Hauerwas, *Performing the Faith*, 35.
59. Bonhoeffer, *Ethics*, 230.
60. Williams, *Bonhoeffer's Black Jesus*.
61. Williams, *Bonhoeffer's Black Jesus*, 8.

After finishing his habilitation thesis, Bonhoeffer headed to New York on a fellowship to study at Union Theological Seminary. There, in addition to being unimpressed by American theology and students, he was quickly disillusioned with the Christianity of white American churches. Fortunately, he kept searching, which brought him to Harlem and Abyssinian Baptist Church. This, along with a trip to Cuba while under colonial rule, and his second-semester classes in social ethics, radically reoriented his theology from the abstract to the concrete. Williams writes,

> In Harlem Bonhoeffer learned of a black tradition of Jesus that connected faithfulness to God, and the recognition of suffering, and the presence of Christ as a cosufferer. The ministries that Bonhoeffer participated in at Abyssinian Baptist Church, coupled with the intellectual interrogation of Jesus within the Harlem Renaissance, provided Bonhoeffer with new resources to filter the nationalism from his Christianity and helped to develop him into an advocate of ecumenism [unity between churches], of peacemaking, and of social justice. As a consequence of that black experience with Jesus, his theology became more than conceptual, his Christology become more prominent, and Bonhoeffer become more serious about his faith.[62]

When confronted with deep racism, a creative engagement and reimagining of Jesus by the black church, and a welcome into service in this community, Bonhoeffer's understanding of Jesus was forever changed. As result of this, his writing, witness, and martyrdom have shaped both academic disciplines and the lives of countless Christians.

Black Church Theology and Theologies of Liberation

Martin Luther King Jr. was a prominent writer but is particularly known through his actions as a leader in the civil rights movement. He writes, "Some of us who have already begun to break the silence of the night have found that the calling to speak is often a vocation of agony, but we must speak. We must speak with all humility that is appropriate to our limited vision, but we must speak."[63] Such speaking is far from abstract and is not removed from suffering. Though King was strategic, he also raised

---

62. Williams, *Bonhoeffer's Black Jesus*, 107.
63. King, "Time to Break the Silence," 231.

fundamental questions about the nature of society. Particularly later in his work, he also began to link the civil rights work for racial justice with poverty and militarism. In "A Time to Break Silence," he states, "We must rapidly begin to shift from a 'thing-oriented' society to a 'person-oriented' society. When machines and computers, profit motives and property rights are considered more important than people, the giant triplets of racism, materialism, and militarism are incapable of being conquered."[64] Though King is known for nonviolence, this linking of issues is similar to peacemaking.

For King, nonviolence challenged the "giant triplets of racism, materialism, and militarism" as well as being strategic. Though nonviolence was used as confrontational direct-action, King also hoped for reconciliation. He writes, "A genuine revolution of values means in the final analysis that our loyalties must become ecumenical rather than sectional. Every nation must now develop an overriding loyalty to mankind as a whole in order to preserve the best of our individual societies."[65] This action for the purpose of gaining power and changing policy and actions was not a hesitant acquiescence or feeling that such power was necessarily problematic. He asserts, "There is nothing wrong with power if power is used correctly.... What is needed is a realization that power without love is reckless and abusive, and love without power is sentimental and anemic. Power at its best is love implementing the demands of justice, and justice at its best is power correcting everything that stands against love."[66] Such power, to be used rightly, is used with love for justice. For this reason, despite violence in opposition he remained committed to nonviolence:

> And so I say to you today that I still stand by nonviolence. And I am still convinced that it is the most potent weapon available to the Negro in his struggle for justice in this country. And the other thing is that I am concerned about a better world. I'm concerned about justice. I'm concerned about brotherhood. I'm concerned about truth. And when one is concerned about these, he can never advocate for violence. For through violence you may murder the murderer but you can't murder murder. Through violence you may murder the liar but you can't establish truth. Through violence you may murder a hater, but

64. King, "Time to Break the Silence," 240.
65. King, "Time to Break the Silence," 242.
66. King, "Where Do We Go From Here?," 247.

you can't murder hate. Darkness cannot put out darkness. Only light can do that.[67]

Theologies of liberation come in many forms and emerge from marginalized communities. While there have always been religious communities and theology in oppressed communities, the liberation theology movement began with Peruvian Catholic priest and theologian Gustavo Gutierrez.[68] This was not, however, a unified movement. James Cone notes in his preface to the 1986 edition of *A Black Theology of Liberation* that at the time of his first writing he "was completely unaware of the beginnings of liberation theology in the Third World, especially in Latin America."[69] In his 1973 work, Gutierrez began to formally develop a theology of liberation from Latin America. While I will not give a comprehensive overview of Gutierrez's work nor of the various streams of liberation theology, I will briefly note some common themes and variations in the North American context, with primary focus given to the black church and black theology.

Black theology is, of course, not one thing.[70] There is, however, a consistent and conscious engagement with the injustice faced by African Americans and the African American community. J. Kameron Carter observes this in Cone: "James H. Cone's theological interrogation of New World Afro-Christian faith pioneers in the history of American theology. Its groundbreaking nature lies in its attempt to uncover the theological significance and political promise of black faith and existence given the racist practices and dispositions of America and, indeed, of modernity."[71] This consideration and interrogation addresses not only racist political/cultural manifestations such as mass incarceration but also deeper strains and origins of race in the theological imagination.[72] While this is certainly not the only topic engaged, it is, because of the historical context, a part of the theological/ethical reflection process.[73] This is minimally the case

67. King, "Where Do We Go From Here?," 251.
68. Gutierrez, *Theology of Liberation*.
69. Cone, *Black Theology of Liberation*, xii.
70. Such a term may not usefully indicate particularity but might reinforce that theology (without "white" being named) is normative while "black" theology is an irregularity or not the standard and normative account.
71. Carter, *Race*, 157.
72. Jennings, *Christian Imagination*.
73. For example, M Shawn Copeland considers the "homosexual body" in *Enfleshing Freedom*.

because blackness is an ever-present reality in the United States.[74] While it would be problematic to separate out or consider as a community black theologians and ethicists generally, to the extent that there is an extended self-referential consideration of the context of the black community in relation to the church and theology, this can be useful.[75]

A central concern is engaging the system of oppression theologically and ethically, which is to say engaging the oppression for the sake of transformation.[76] In the opening lines of *A Black Theology of Liberation*, Cone asserts,

> Christian theology is a theology of liberation. It is *a rational study of the being of God in the world in light of the existential situation of an oppressed community, relating the forces of liberation to the essence of the gospel, which is Jesus Christ*. This means that the sole reason for existence is to put into ordered speech the meaning of God's activity in the world, so that the community of the oppressed will recognize that its inner thrust for liberation is not only *consistent with the gospel but is the gospel of Jesus Christ*. There can be no Christian theology that is not identified unreservedly with those who are humiliated and abused. In fact, theology ceases to be theology of the gospel when it fails to arise out of the community of the oppressed.[77] For it is impossible to speak of the God of Israelite history, who is the God revealed in

---

74. "It is . . . worth saying explicitly, that 'white' and 'race' and even 'black' are in this text not merely signifiers of pigmentation. In other words, their referent is perhaps only secondarily to color. Rather, they signify a political economy, an *ordo* or a social arrangement, what Irenaeus calls an *oikonomia*." Carter, *Race*, 8.

75. The risk is that theology done by white folks is seen simply as theology, and as such, normative, while theology done by black folks is seen as black theology, and as such, a side or novelty theology. The reverse may be also true that if an African American is not so designated then they will be assimilated into structures of whiteness.

76. Carter asserts, "Indeed, [Cone] is innovative precisely in his introduction of history, particularly that of the dispossessed, into the heart of American theology." Carter, *Race*, 172.

77. "Many of the early Latin American liberation theologians were either foreign born and/or European educated, which actually contributed to their ability to mount a Marxian social analysis of oppression that was also able to cast a critical and revelatory light on the ways in which the Christian churches and theology contribute to social injustice. In many respects, like the political theologians, the liberation theologians spoke *on behalf of* the poor; they did not themselves generally belong to the category of the oppressed non-person however much in solidarity they were with them." Hewitt, "Critical Theory," 464.

Jesus Christ, without recognizing that God is the God *of* and *for* those who labor and are over laden.⁷⁸

Black theology and spirituality arose from locations of oppression and active repression.⁷⁹ Such a context was not incidental or simply a "problem" to address among a number of other concerns. M. Shawn Copeland writes,

> Slavery exacted a perverse intellectual, spiritual, psychological, and physical toll . . . Moreover, on many plantations, the enslaved people were forbidden to worship, to invoke the Spirit. Again, they risked abuse, assault, even martyrdom to withdraw to secret places in the woods and gullies to commune with the Author and Source of Freedom. In seeking freedom and resisting domination, in striving for literacy, in cultivating counter discourses and practices, in fixing themselves within the realm of the Spirit, the enslaved people nurtured a sense of themselves as subjects of freedom.⁸⁰

Not only did church practice and spirituality grow within active repression, but the accompanying theological and ethical reflection grew from the same soil.⁸¹ Naturally, this theology reflected this situation. Rosetta Ross notes, "Womanist scholars present what may be called a 'ritualized' understanding of Black religious women's persistent work to preserve and enhance Black life every day . . . [This is the] 'ritualized mundane.'"⁸² Though this theology from *within* the community supported the community, theological reflection as a whole has not been nearly so positive. J. Kameron Carter notes that theology's participation in the formation of the modern racial imagination renders it a questionable endeavor for those not part of this formulation.⁸³ He writes,

---

78. Cone, *Black Theology of Liberation*, 1.

79. Carter (*Race*, 160) notes that "Cone is acutely sensitive to the problem of abstraction in theology."

80. Copeland, *Enfleshing Freedom*, 38.

81. "In illuminating the nature of God and moral responsibility of humans, Thurman's ethics move in two concentric circles. The compact inner circle is the inherent relatedness of inclusive community. Thurman rules out laws, principles, norms, or fixed ends and the like as models for moral agency; ethics emerges from mystical consciousness which obligates individuals to transform the social environment." Cannon, *Black Womanist Ethics*, 21.

82. Ross, *Witnessing and Testifying*, 13.

83. Carter, *Race*, 8.

> The perennial though increasingly invisible theological problem of our times is not race in general but whiteness in particular. The modern racializing of bodies in social space is unintelligible, apart from how Christian identity was reimagined during the Enlightenment and how both the content and the disposition animating Christian theology shifted. Christianity was severed from its Jewish roots, lopped off from the people of Israel to facilitate Western conquest.[84]

He continues,

> Theology must do its work no longer under the preconditions of the 'forgetting of being.' Rather, it must do its work in company with and out of the disposition of those facing death, those with the barrel of a shotgun to their backs, for this is the disposition of the crucified Christ, who is the revelation of the triune God. The question that must be addressed, then, is this: What does it mean to speak with theological imagination *from within* crises of life and death rather than in scholastic universes and out of the disposition of scholastic reason in the mode of the religious, the disposition whose condition of possibility turns from the painfully real worlds?[85]

As a result of repression of efforts of literacy and formal education as well as general marginalization from academic discourses, there are fewer explicitly theological writings that are broadly acknowledged as theological and ethical sources. To address this paucity, Katie Cannon reaches back to literary resources of moral reasoning that are not typically considered in dominant ethics. In so doing, she asserts that ethical practice in written form existed though necessarily outside the standard sphere due to the numerous controlling practices and mechanisms enforced on the community. Not only does Cannon draw on unconventional sources of ethics, but she closely attends to the historic experience in her work. She recounts the "moral situation" of black women from 1619 to 1900 and then in the twentieth century:

> The moral situation of the Black woman in contemporary society is still a situation of struggle, a struggle to survive collectively and individually against the continuing harsh historical realities and pervasive adversities in today's world. The determining existential circumstance in which the Black woman finds herself

---

84. Carter, *Race*, 372.
85. Carter, *Race*, 377.

in the 1980s is little better than the situation in the 1880s. The Korean and Vietnam wars, Federal government programs, civil rights movements, and voter-education programs have all had a positive impact on the Black woman's moral situation, but they have not been able to offset the negative effects of the inherent inequities which are inextricably tied to the history and ideological hegemony of racism, sexism, and class privilege.[86]

Such writers create context-based theology and ethics outside the dominant structures.[87] Cannon writes, "In dominant ethics a person is free to make suffering a desirable moral norm. This is not so for Blacks. For the masses of black people, suffering is the normal state of affairs."[88] Suffering, then, is the context for ethics and theology. Not only does this suffering require response, but one can draw parallels between the suffering Christ and the suffering community. In *The Cross and the Lynching Tree*, for example, Cone explores such parallels, as well as ways in which this imagery has been taken up by black artist, poets, and theologians.[89]

> The combined force of the inherited tradition of race, sex and economic discrimination imposes on the vast majority of Black women a severely disadvantaged status. Black women in their development, analysis and appraisal of various coping mechanisms against the white-oriented, male structured society do not appeal to fixed rules or absolute principles of what is right or wrong and good or bad, but instead they embrace values related to the causal conditions of their cultural circumstances. The cherished assumptions of dominant ethical systems predicated upon both the existence of freedom and a wide range of choices

---

86. Cannon, *Black Womanist Ethics*, 66.

87. Since many of these writers are in some manner working within institutional educational and church structures it may be more accurate to say, "working outside dominant discursive structures" or "outside or not completely in line with the texts of dominant structures."

88. Cannon, *Black Womanist Ethics*, 3.

89. "The lynching tree—so strikingly similar to the cross of Golgotha—should have a prominent place in American images of Jesus's death. But it does not. In fact, the lynching tree has no place in American theological reflections about Jesus's cross or in the proclamation of Christian churches around his Passion. The conspicuous absence of the lynching tree in American theological discourse is profoundly revealing, especially since the crucifixion was clearly a first-century lynching. In the 'lynching era,' between 1880 and 1940, white Christians lynched nearly five thousand black men and women in a manner with obvious echoes of the Roman crucifixion of Jesus. Yet these 'Christians' did not see the irony or contradiction in their actions." Cone, *Cross and the Lynching Tree*, 30–31).

have proven to be false in the real-lived texture of Black life. Thus, Black women have cultivated a set of ethical values that allow them to prevail against odds,[90] with moral integrity, in their ongoing participation in the white-male-capitalist value system. The best available literary repository for this underground treasury of values is the Black woman's literary tradition.[91]

Within the context of multi-layered oppression that includes but is not limited to restricted access or exclusion from many "normative" streams of moral discourse, black women have improvised and built spaces for such exploration. According to Cannon, "Throughout the various periods of their history in the United States, Black women have used their creativity to carve out 'living space' within the intricate web of multilayered oppression."[92] It is not that black women did not participate in moral reasoning, but rather that they did so through means and modes not privileged by the arbiters of dominant ethical and theological practice. In the work of Zora Neale Hurston, Cannon documents the demonstration of "quiet grace" and "unshouted courage" exemplified and at times problematized in Hurston's characters: "They are living human beings 'who overturn the normative moral structure of the oppressing society.'"[93]

This tradition of ethical and theological reflection from and about contexts of suffering continues on through works by Kelly Brown Douglas and James Samuel Logan.[94] Focusing on the US criminal justice system, racialized mass incarceration, and police violence against Black bodies, Logan writes,

> By continuing to imprison millions of people under intolerably cruel and dangerous conditions, the United States has effectively put its own racial, ethnic, and class-based apartheid into place. As authorities continue to stigmatize, scapegoat, and

---

90. "The concept of 'making a way out of no way' articulates black women's relationships with God as they navigate the reality of their lives in the pursuit of wholeness and justice. No one womanist theologian directly points to 'making a way out of no way' as a theory of salvation. Nevertheless, an examination of 'making a way out of no way' reveals that this concept is a construction of salvation that brings together the different emphases of various womanists without denying their particularities." Coleman, *Making a Way Out of No Way*, 12.

91. Cannon, *Black Womanist Ethics*, 75.

92. Cannon, *Black Womanist Ethics*, 76.

93. Cannon, *Black Womanist Ethics*, 127.

94. Douglas, *Stand Your Ground*; Logan, *Good Punishment?*

disproportionately 'disappear' Black, Latino/a, Native American, poor, mentally ill, drug addicted, homeless, miseducated, and other prisoners from the nation's democratic hopes, they unravel some of the important gains of the Civil Rights era.[95]

M. Shawn Copeland, while still arguing strongly for liberation, writes, "With the expression *mystical body of Christ*, I want to reaffirm salvation in human liberation as an opaque work, that is, a work that resists both the reduction of human praxis to social transformation and the identification of the gospel with even the most just ordering of society."[96] Copeland's approach to theology prioritizes suffering but does not make it the only consideration. In her view, "this 'shouldering' summons us to take intentional, intelligent, practical steps against 'the socially and technically avoidable sufferings of others.' For Christian solidarity repudiates every form of masochism and any assent to suffering for its own sake. Solidarity affirms life—even in the face of sin and death."[97] While the community need not intentionally embrace suffering since the suffering is already present, solidarity in suffering "affirms life" and is necessary.

Latin American Influences and Liberation

The black church and black liberation theology are not the only sources of liberation theology in North America. Cuban-American liberation theologian Miguel A. De La Torre establishes a framework of liberation ethics before showing how this methodology works through a series of case studies on global, national, and business ethics. His theological ethical method, with its strong emphasis on communal discernment through study of the Bible and the necessity of lived theology, strikes me as similar to that of Anabaptists. He writes:

> For those who struggle within oppressive structures, the personhood of Jesus Christ as a source of strength becomes crucial. The life and sayings of Christ, as recognized by the faith community that searches the biblical text for guidance to life's ethical dilemmas, serve as the ultimate standard of morality. While Eurocentric theology, and the ethics that flow from it, has a tendency to abstract the Christ event, those on the margins

---

95. Logan, *Good Punishment?*, 97.
96. Copeland, *Enfleshing Freedom*, 102.
97. Copeland, *Enfleshing Freedom*, 101.

recognize that Christ remains at work in the United States today.[98]

De La Torre pays a great deal of attention to social and geographic location. This recognition and the commitment to justice closely links ethical and social commitment to the possibility of rightly understanding the text. As he states, "Ethics begins with our own surrender, with our own self-negation. Those who benefit from power and privilege of social structures can encounter Absolute only through their own self-negation by crucifying their power and privilege."[99] As a result of the centrality of location for rightly engaging the task of ethics, he challenges the social location of the ethicist, particularly for white ethicists with the economic privilege and stability of full professorships.[100] Even with "good" politics or social concern, the social location undercuts the possibility of ethical reflection by those who are not oppressed. He asserts,

> Praxis leading toward a more just social order was the first casualty of abstract ethical thought. Even though such abstract deliberations may be sympathetic to the plight of the oppressed they still fall short by failing to alleviate the root causes of disenfranchisement. To some degree, Eurocentric ethics has become a matter of explaining what is ethical. But for those doing ethics from the margins, the question is not to determine some abstract understanding of what is ethical, but, rather, in the face of de-humanizing oppressive structures, to determine how people of faith adapt their actions to serve the least among us.[101]

For De La Torre, ethics is a practice based in the margins.[102] This is not simply a technical fix to assure some sort of greater democratic representation in the field of theology but also reflects the reality of God. God suffers with the suffering and sides with them; but God's reign is found also in the present. De la Torre claims, "God's reign is not in some far-off distant place disconnected from the trials and tribulations here on earth. No. God's reign is a present-day social, political, public, and personal reality evident among God's people. While not negating some

---

98. De La Torre, *Doing Christian Ethics from the Margins*, 7. Though Anabaptists such as Brethren and Mennonites originated in Europe, their marginal status influences theological method.

99. De La Torre, *Doing Christian Ethics from the Margins*, 18.

100. De La Torre, *Doing Christian Ethics from the Margins*, 25

101. De La Torre, *Doing Christian Ethics from the Margins*, 26.

102. De La Torre, *Doing Christian Ethics from the Margins*, 36.

form of final reward in the hereafter, the gospel message is primarily for the here-and-now."[103] Theology, then, is not simply an intellectual task but an active one. He notes, however, that getting a Christian into a position of power may not bring adequate change because the structure itself needs transformation.[104]

Of course, the church and theologies have long history of asserting or seeking political influence on theological grounds and many of these projects and aims have not aligned with De La Torre's vision. As a way to implement the practice of *ethics from the margins*, De La Torre proposes what he calls the hermeneutical Circle for Ethics. This consists of five steps: 1) Observing: historical and interpretive analysis; 2) Reflecting: social analysis; 3) Praying: theological and biblical analysis; 4) Acting: implementation of praxis; and 5) Reassessing: new ethical perspectives.[105] He describes the shift in this method from that of Eurocentric approaches.[106] This is part of the stream of greater engagement on social issues and justice, as well as a challenge to the assumptions of the inherited tradition.

Social Change and Justice—Detractors and Descendants

Before moving to a more explicit focus on peacemaking in North America, I will draw some connections and observations relating to the three traditions being considered here: Rauschenbusch, along with his disciples and detractors; black church and liberation theology; and peacemaking in the vein of the historic peace churches. I will also note some

---

103. De La Torre, *Doing Christian Ethics from the Margins*, 42.

104. De La Torre, *Doing Christian Ethics from the Margins*, 43–44.

105. De La Torre, *Doing Christian Ethics from the Margins*, 69.

106. Terry LeBlanc's work with the North American Institute for Indigenous Theological Studies (NAIITS) to develop indigenous Canadian theological training institutions in order to undo the communities' reliance on Western traditions of inquiry, epistemology, and theology is an interesting example of a material effort to structurally change the situation of aboriginal Canadian Christian theological resources. See http://www.naiits.com/. De La Torre writes, "Besides analyzing the effectiveness of the course of actions being taken, the process of reassessing also creates systems of ethics. As we have seen, Eurocentric ethics is deductive, being with a 'truth' and moving toward the application of that 'truth,' subordinating ethics to dogma. Doing ethics from the margins reverses this model. After praxis, as part of the reassessment, the individual returns to the biblical text with the ability to more clearly understand its mandates." De La Torre, *Ethics from the Margins*, 69.

questions that have been raised about the subject and methodology of ethics in America. This is intended to suggest ways in which the division between theology and ethics or divisions between social engagement, justice advocacy, and peacebuilding will play out and move toward resolution throughout this project. This section will be somewhat different in approach to the preceding and following sections but will, nonetheless, contribute to a greater integration and assist in leading into the following chapters.

Many writers, consciously or not, take up parts of the project of Social Gospel in a revised form. Other writers, including Stanley Hauerwas, challenge activist theologians and ethicists to be more explicitly theological and rooted in the church.[107] While activists may indeed be concerned with the basic questions of defining justice theologically and questioning the relation of Christians to the State, they are often impatient or dismissive of the "neo-Anabaptist/neo-Traditional"-inflected critique of the (perceived) assumptions behind activist theology. The activists often assert that raising these questions in the manner that the neo-Anabaptists do undercuts efforts to seek justice by questioning Christian engagement in public life or political action. In one of the more intense rebukes, Jeffrey Stout challenges what he refers to as Hauerwas's and MacIntyre's "New Traditionalism," claiming that they "undermine identification with liberal democracy" through a "rhetoric of excess."[108]

There are many variations and internal disputes over the nature and manner of the work of social engagement. David Hunter questions various types of efforts of seeking to change the world but does not suggest reactive disengagement. After sifting through a number of articulations and theories of change by activists on the left such as Jim Wallace of *Sojourners* and those on the political right, Hunter proposes what he calls "faithful presence."[109] While I do not disagree with this idea, he does not seem to include work at the policy level in this possibility.[110] It may be

107. Hauerwas writes, "When the content of such ideals [such as love and justice] is spelled out . . . we begin to suspect that the language of the kingdom is being used to underwrite ethical commitments and political strategies that were determined prior to the claims of the centrality of the kingdom for Christian ethics." Hauerwas, *Against the Nations*, 111.

108. Stout, *Democracy and Tradition*, 118.

109. Hunter, *To Change the World*, 255–73.

110. While it may be understandable that those not engaged in this work see it as somehow different from other, slower or more local forms of organizing, much of the work of shaping or influencing policy still rests on the skills of practical

that he simply does not include any "good" examples of this work, but it seems that he intentionally omits this. Though this is an unfortunate gap, Hunter's work is a useful attempt to constructively motivate for "justice" and "peace" while also asking substantive questions of the assumptions behind such work.

The question of how to engage the public sphere pulls this stream of work together. In "Social Criticism with Both Eyes Open," Stout observes that despite methodological, philosophical, and theological differences, a number of apparently vastly dissimilar writers come down at almost the same spot when engaged in actual social criticism.[111] He notes this not to discount these differences, but to suggest moving forward and getting on with social engagement and critique. Also in this vein Gary Dorrien includes chapters such as "Imperial Designs: Neoconservatism and the Iraq War" and "The Obama Phenomenon and Presidency," which engage in implicit theological social and political commentary. The concern of Hauerwas is that such work takes on a particular political position as a primary reference or starting point.[112] The counter-challenge is that Hauerwas (as a white male working in an elite university) undercuts attempts for justice for the oppressed by challenging the terms of democracy and justice.

Other writers bring notable challenges to these approaches to theology, ethics, ecclesiology, and politics. They tend to position themselves in opposition to "liberalism" and the assumptions of modernity that are said to hollow out the life of the church. They seek to provide (or urge others to provide) "thick" descriptions of liturgical acts that constitute the Church as a politics that is not necessarily separated from "the world"

---

reasoning, relationship building, coalition formation (which includes the practical reasoning and relationship building), and attending to the formation of certain virtues as individuals or organizations (which establishes as a trustworthy partner a reliable source of information, and the ability to negotiate compromise and upholding values). Hauerwas and Coles write about the "politics of micro-relationships." The full quote reads, "Make no mistake: Christianity and radical democracy are revolutionary. Yet we are convinced that there are no revolutions (only historonic returns to the same or the worst) that would be above and beyond—rather than through—the fine grains of the politics of micro-relationships and small achievements." Hauerwas and Coles, *Christianity, Democracy, and the Radical Ordinary,* 4. Of course, much of policy change is also the process of forming power and seeking to "rule" but even these achievements, which may in fact be theologically problematic, are surprisingly reliant on basic forms of organizing.

111. Stout, *Ethics after Babel,* 266–92.
112. Hauerwas, "Reality of the Church," 122.

but does not assume that the nation-state or America are the primary referents for ethics. Hauerwas would assert that though civil rights leaders such as Martin Luther King Jr. utilize these political categories, their context of the black church undoes these criticisms.[113] These topics, and Hauerwas's engagement with them, are key to his framework for peace and peacemaking.

I read this work of Hauerwas and the broader related group as arising out of greater awareness of the significance of context but also the desire to engage *theologically*. There seems to have been an emergence of a greater awareness of context and a re-valuing of Anabaptist and Catholic sources by those outside and, perhaps, inside, these communities.[114] At around the same time, liberation theologies and those influenced by them were breaking open the theological and ethical field: Gutierrez's *Theology of Liberation* was published in 1973; John Howard Yoder's *Politics of Jesus* came out in 1972.

Another significant direction in this work is the assertion that there is more to the story than a series of contextually free-floating propositions about God that can and must be believed apart from a community of practice. James McClendon writes on the first page of the first volume of his *Systematic Theology*, "Surely, it will be said, the salvation of the world must rest on some better foundation than tales about an ancient nomad and stories of a Jewish healer?"[115] This points to stories as the starting point of ethics and theology. These stories are not simply illustrative, but are the formative storytelling of the community. The interwoven reflection on Scripture, story, and action from within an embodied community is what constitutes theology. Kallenberg states that "postliberal theology in the vein of McClendon and Hauerwas reminds us that claims about God *are* claims about God. However, in order for these claims to be intelligible, they must find a home in the context of practices

---

113. Hauerwas writes, "But as King well knew, nonviolence is not just an 'ideal' but must be embedded in the habits of a people across time in order to make possible the long and patient work of transformation necessary for the reconciliation of enemies. King was a creature of the African American church." Hauerwas, *War and the American Difference*, 94.

114. Hunter calls at least some of this group (he does not give a comprehensive list of those he includes) neo-Anabaptist. While his description may be correct, I have included a re-examination of both Anabaptist and Catholic themes in my description because of the strong emphasis on liturgy, "high" church themes, and potentially stronger roles for clergy. See Hunter, *To Change the World*, 150.

115. McClendon. *Systematic Theology*, 17–18.

(for example, confession, worship and witness) which give to all forms of Christian language their sense."[116] Lindbeck defines post-liberalism as follows: "The function of church doctrines that becomes most prominent in this perspective is their use, not as expressive symbols or truth claims, but as communally authoritative rules of discourse, attitude, and action. The general way of conceptualizing religion will be called in what follows a 'cultural-linguistic' approach, and the implied view of church doctrine will be referred to as a 'regulative' or 'rule' theory."[117] While these two quotes seem to differ in terms of the so-called "objective" truth claims, they are similar in that these claims of doctrine are true *in* the community, which is not the same as saying they are *not* true *outside* that community.

The framing of narrative became, somewhat ironically, a topic of substantial theorizing. This gave rise to, or was a product of a loosely related cadre of "post-liberal" theologians. These theologians and ethicists engaged common questions with similar approaches as articulated in George Lindbeck's *Nature of Doctrine: Religion and Theology in a Post-liberal Age*. This narrative is both the narrative of the biblical text as well as that of the particular community. Kallenberg notes, "The impasse that resulted from modernity's assumption that ethics must be done either from 'the bottom up' or 'the top down' was surmounted by Wittgenstein, who labored to show that language and world were internally related; one cannot begin from either the top or the bottom. One must begin in the middle of a particular, concrete community whose identity constituting form of life is determinative for the proper application of the means by which ethics and theology take place at all, namely, their common language."[118] Mary McClintock Fulkerson explores how the practice of participant observation research can be paired with theological reflection to help describe such a community.[119] When this approach is used in sermons, for example, I suggest that it might tend toward an anecdote that is as much to get and hold people's attention as it is to provide a thick description. Jennifer Hosler's work, "Stories from the Cities," could be one such example.[120] Since she is both a pastor and community psychologist doing official research on the particular community, she is trying to

---

116. Kallenberg, *Ethics as Grammar*, 233–34.

117. Lindbeck, *Nature of Doctrine*, 4.

118. Kallenberg, *Ethics as Grammar*, 247.

119. Fulkerson, "They Will Know."

120. Hosler, "Stories from the Cities," http://www.brethren.org/messenger/articles/stories-from-the-cities/?referrer=https://www.google.com/

accurately convey the good and difficult parts of each congregation while also reflecting theologically. Such descriptions exemplify this approach once it gets beyond theorizing.

In this orientation the church and its theological task, the imagery of language and grammar becomes key to developing the cultural linguistic community of "church." The church then becomes a community with a body and tradition that *takes up space*. The occupation of space is not, however, an imperial mission to recapture what was lost to secularity but rather an effort to become a visible body. This is a winding back of assumptions of invisibility of the "true" church that arose out of the growth of Christendom as an official religious-political construct.

As such, liturgy becomes a forming act that constitutes the body. Christians are trained bodily through worship in what is at times called discipleship but more generally ethics. This world of discourse then seeks to shift the subject of ethics out of methods or points of decision to the broader question of formation, which some call virtue.

Such forming allows for the possibility of an alternative political imagination. In addition to shifting ethics from decision to formation, the formation of the community is emphasized. This community, while not political in the sense of party politics, is nonetheless a political body or space. William Cavanaugh provides one such example.[121] From the concrete community, which exists as embodied reality of reconciliation with God, comes the possibility of the Christian political imagination. Church as political community; church *as* politics. According to Cavanaugh, "'Political theology' and 'public theology' have assumed the legitimacy of the separation of the state from civil society, and tried to situate the Church as one more interest group within civil society. None of these models has fundamentally called into question the theological legitimacy of the imagination of modern politics."[122] The Christian political imagination is, then, a reimagining of the assumptions around what counts as political space, which structures dominate this space, and what the 'proper' role of the church is in relation to this space. For example, Cavanaugh "focus[es] on the Eucharist as an alternative imagining of

---

121. Cavanaugh, *Theopolitical Imagination*. It could be noted that a number of these sources function more at the intersection of theology and political theory rather than ethics proper. Cavanaugh quotes from Benedict Anderson's *Imagined Communities: Reflections on the Origin and Spread of Nationalism*, on his first page. This is a text I read in a political theory class in my master's program in international relations.

122. Cavanaugh, *Theopolitical Imagination*, 3.

space and time which builds up a body of resistance to violence, the body of Christ. This is the body that is wounded, broken by the powers and principalities and poured out in blood offering upon this stricken earth. But this is also a body crossed by resurrection, a sign of the startling irruption of the Kingdom into historical time and the disruptive presence of Christ the King to the politics of the world."[123]

In a manner similar to Cavanaugh, Copeland considers the Eucharist in relation to racism. "Eucharist," she writes, "radiates from the trajectory set by the dangerous memory of the audacious rabbi from Nazareth . . . Racism opposes the order of the Eucharist."[124] Worship and theology, then, can both challenge and shape the work of ethics and social change. These considerations problematize as well as deepen efforts of social action within the life, theology, and ethics of the church. In the context of peacemaking broadly defined, these questions are directly relevant to working for a peace that is wider than the absence of violence or conflict.

North American Debates on Peace and Peacemaking

Turning now to more explicitly peacemaking discussions within the limited context of North America, we see that there are several streams of discussion around peace and peacemaking. One could be called practical peacemaking—a subset of social concern. For example, if Christians should help feed the hungry and people are hungry because of ongoing civil war or low-intensity violent conflict, then in order to feed the hungry, Christians also need to build peace. This position, while challenging the assumptions of the use of force, is not necessarily pacifist. Two important works in this realm are Glenn Stassen's *Just Peacemaking*,[125] and Lederach's *Moral Imagination*.[126] Whereas Stassen's work has significant biblical and theological components, there are other skill-based and highly practical resources such as Mennonite Conciliation Service's manuals.[127] Works like Stassen's, and to a lesser extent,

---

123. Cavanaugh, *Theopolitical Imagination*, 7.

124. Copeland, *Enfleshing Freedom*, 108–9.

125. Stassen, *Just Peacemaking*.

126. Lederach, *Moral Imagination*.

127. Schrock-Shenk, *Mediation and Facilitation Manual*; Fisher et al., *Working With Conflict*.

Lederach's, are important for this study. Skill-based or non-theological studies will be used primarily to inform readings of other works. The final chapter, however, considers *The Moral Imagination* as a possible practical extension of Hauerwas's work.

A second stream of discourse reflects on issues of participation and nonparticipation in war and how such participation is conducted. This is the area most typically assumed to embody thinking on peace and typically includes consideration of just war theory and pacifism. Much of Yoder's work falls into this category. Where this stream is most relevant for this project is in Hauerwas's *ad hoc* critiques of the United States' relationship to war, which I will argue are a form of peacemaking *as witness*. As such I will focus on the role that this argument plays or the strategy of resisting war that Hauerwas uses more than an analysis of how his argument holds up against just war theory and other pacifist writing

The third stream involves fundamental theological questions around war and peace. The work of Chris Huebner on Yoder in *A Precarious Peace* is one such example. Huebner's work examines how our epistemological method does or does not embody the peace we profess. This tries to get below what is typically assumed to be our practice and beliefs on peace.

John Howard Yoder

John Howard Yoder was perhaps the most influential theologian for peace and an approach to ethics explicitly based on Jesus in the last century. In so doing, he built up the capacity of the church for peacemaking and Anabaptist ethics. Yoder also used his power as an influential theologian and figure in the Mennonite Church to sexually manipulate and abuse women for several decades.[128] In this way, his life dramatically undermined the possibilities that his work suggested.

I will not attempt to summarize all the recent work within the Mennonite Church to grapple with both these realities. It is critical before moving on, however, to lay out how I will approach Yoder's work without minimizing the consequences of his actions. My basic approach is this: Yoder's work is no longer *his* work but that of the church. As far as it is deemed useful for the building up of the life of the Church, it will be used as the property of the church—a gift received in spite of wrongs

---

128. Goossen, "Failure to Bind and Loose."

committed by the giver. I take this approach because I believe that the church and the work of the gospel of peace would be further damaged if this body of writings were removed from our lives.

The work of Yoder is extensive and influential. *The Politics of Jesus* is his most widely known work and was game changing in the world of Christian ethics.[129] In it Yoder asserts "not only that Jesus is, according to the biblical witness, a model of radical political action, but that this issue is now generally visible throughout New Testament studies, even though biblical scholars have not stated it in such a way that ethicists across the way have had to notice it."[130] Yoder addresses how New Testament studies of the day were increasingly pointing to a much more radical portrait of Jesus, assumptions about the kingdom of God, peace and war, and ethics. He asserts that he makes no innovative claims or arguments but is simply pulling together common themes in research which are beginning to point in this direction.[131] Yoder's social ethic is based in the New Testament witness and the ecclesial community. It is articulated in a way that is radical, but grounded in Scripture and the church. For Yoder, peace is central but is embedded in the life of the community rather than at the point of ethical decision.

Mark Thiessen Nation notes that more recently Yoder's work has not been widely used by Mennonites interested in peace. Beginning in the 1990s, there was a surge of Mennonite writing on peacemaking, but relatively little that engaged with Yoder's work. Thiessen Nation conjectures

---

129. When I first read Yoder's *Politics of Jesus*, I was surprised that it was considered to be so significant. I am unsure if this is because his work was thoroughly absorbed into the theological field by that time or because the Church of the Brethren congregation I grew up in was largely unfazed by larger academic theological discussions or because we were largely assuming the Anabaptist approach he was suggesting. I suspect it was some of all of these.

130. Yoder, *Politics of Jesus*, 12.

131. Yoder states, "The case I am seeking to make has to do not narrowly with the New Testament text but with the modern ethicists who have assumed that the only way to get from the gospel story to ethics, from Bethlehem to Rome or to Washington or Saigon, was to leave the story behind. I shall be looking more at the events than at the teachings, more at the outlines than at the substance. The next pages present soundings rather than a thorough survey. Nor is it the intention of this paper to be exegetically original. At no point do I mean to be hazarding unheard of textual explanations. All that I add is the focusing effect of a consistent, persistent question. It is because I claim no originality at this point that I may dispense with some of the pedantic paraphernalia which would have been helpful or needful if I were making claims never heard before." Yoder, *Politics of Jesus*, 25.

that the minimal engagement with Yoder could be because Yoder was seen as promoting a model of faithfulness over responsibility, which engendered withdrawal.[132] Nigel Biggar references Arne Rasmusson's assertion that Mennonites have allowed mainstream Protestantism to define both responsibility and what it meant to be Mennonite.[133] This critique is similar to that levelled by Jeffery Stout against the "New Traditionalists."[134] It is also likely evident in Gary Dorrien's not even mentioning or citing Hauerwas in *Economy, Difference, and Empire*.[135]

Yoder asserts that it is critical for Christian thinking on peace to firmly rest on eschatological foundations. He defines eschatology as "a hope which, defying present frustration, defines a present position in terms of the yet unseen goal which gives it meaning."[136]

> Jesus' interest was in man; the reason for his low esteem for the political order was his high, loving esteem for man as the concrete object of His concern. Christ is *agape*; self-giving, nonresistant love. At the cross this nonresistance, including the refusal to use political means of self-defense, found its ultimate revelation in the uncomplaining and forgiving death of the innocent at the hands of the guilty. This death reveals how God deals with evil; here is the only valid starting point for Christian pacifism or nonresistance. The cross is the extreme demonstration that *agape* seeks neither effectiveness nor justice, and is willing to suffer any loss or seeming defeat for the sake of obedience.[137]

In Yoder's work, peace is founded in theological claims, which are substantive statements of the presence of God's kingdom rooted in the biblical witness. Here, he focuses on eschatology: "Effectiveness and success had been sacrificed for the sake of love, but this sacrifice was turned by

---

132. Yoder is also seen as too sectarian for civil rights era Mennonites. See Dula and Huebner, *New Yoder*, xi.

133. Biggar, "Is Stanley Hauerwas Sectarian?," 146–50.

134. Stout, *Democracy and Tradition*.

135. This omission of reference to Hauerwas's work may simply be incidental given the differing approaches between Dorrien and Hauerwas. Given Hauerwas's prominence, however, it seems likely that this, while not necessarily an intentional insult, is a result of largely different approaches and is not a neutral omission.

136. Yoder, *Original Revolution*, 53.

137. Yoder, *Original Revolution*, 56.

God into a victory which vindicated to the utmost the apparent impotence of love."[138]

This then becomes the basis for the formation of life through discipleship rather than a rule-based approach.[139] Since much criticism of pacifism hinges on responsibility to one's neighbor to protect in the face of an attack by another neighbor, Yoder clarifies background assumptions and challenges them: "Divine patience" does not equal complicity in guilt.[140]

While particular themes emerge and reemerge, Yoder's work is dispersed and specifically addressed particular needs or concerns. As discussed below, Huebner notes this *ad hoc* nature of Yoder's work. He assesses this as an intentional methodological choice, which as a methodology seeks to embody the very peace discussed.[141]

Considering the significance of Yoder's work on peace and nonviolence for the broader church but the relative minimal use by Mennonites writing in peacemaking, it seems useful to highlight how certain Anabaptist theologians utilize his work in this area. Two examples are *A Precarious Peace* by Canadian Mennonite Chris Huebner and *Sites of Violence, Sites of Grace*, by Cynthia Hess, who was raised in the Church of the Brethren. Both of these writers give strong focus to Yoder's understanding of the ecclesial community and formation of identity in relation to ethics and nonviolence. Huebner carries on Yoder's project by challenging certain approaches to pacifism:

> The first shortcoming privileges the *what* at the cost of the *how*. It focuses on the content of Christian pacifism, understood as an autonomous ethical position, and fails to appreciate that epistemology and method are equally implicated in the question

---

138. Yoder, *Original Revolution*, 57.

139. Yoder, *Original Revolution*, 57.

140. Yoder, *Original Revolution*, 61–62.

141. If, however, the method of work supports or undermines the position, how then does Yoder's work stand up under his sexual exploitation of numerous women? Perhaps it could be argued that the *ad hoc* form of writing is an approach woven through the writing in a way that is different from how Yoder's life can be in some way separated from it. Huebner writes, "He claimed that the peace of Christ involves a rejection of the possessive logic of security and control. A key part of Yoder's theology is his critique of the Constantinian project of outfitting history with handles to move it in the right direction . . . [and that] his conception of epistemological patience is related to his notion of the Body of Christ as a scattered, diasporic body." Huebner, *Precarious Peace*, 117–18.

> of peace and violence... Christian pacifism becomes only one answer to some kind of basic question (e.g., When is it permissible to go to war?) that admits a spectrum of different answers, both violent and nonviolent. But fails to pay adequate attention to the sense in which the questions themselves are not morally neutral but have significant implications for *how* the debate is conducted. In other words, the spectrum itself might need to be called into question... The second shortcoming, by contrast, tends to focus on the *how* at the cost of the *what*. Such an approach takes the character of pacifism for granted and concerns itself with epistemological and methodological questions. It begins with the gospel message of peace as a given and concentrates on developing a medium that will more effectively spread the word.[142]

For all Huebner's talk of being sure to keep peace concrete, these assertions, if embraced, would render problematic efforts to concretely live peace. It may be that this is the point, to make peace precarious, or at least to destabilize our assumption that we know what peace is. Peace is more than a formula or technical process. While this is an important move it may be that too much uncertainty (or precariousness) in the practice of peacemaking will invite paralysis and inaction rather than courageous Christ-like peacemaking. His description of how Yoder should be read points toward what concrete practice might entail. He writes,

> Just as *The Politics of Jesus* is an attempt to display that the doctrine of Christology cannot be abstracted from the life of disciplined imitation of Christ as sustained in ecclesial practices, Yoder's work as a whole is to be read as a series of thick descriptions of social practices, such as baptism and communion, forgiveness and community discernment, that collectively define a particular stance or way of life called church.[143]

Huebner's extension of Yoder's stance on peace resists generalized approaches to peace in which a clear prescription can be produced that will definitively establish peace. If this is the case, then how does one get from the desire for peace to having the necessary skills to work for peace? Though this question can be addressed more thoroughly later, my hunch is that a handbook of peacemaking would present an array of skills which, when embodied and embedded in theologically-derived communities,

---

142. Huebner, *Precarious Peace*, 104–5.
143. Huebner, *Precarious Peace*, 108.

would provide contingent and suggestive guidance towards practices that *might* result in a context-specific peace. This type of situation, which in some way was equipped by a compendium of peacemaking skills embedded in theologically robust communities, can act as a witness to one possible way towards peace for other communities. Framed in this way, universal assumptions are avoided while at the same time intentional actions towards peace may be engaged. This is articulated as *witness* in Huebner's reading of Yoder. "Witness," he states, "is the most important medium for expressing the message of Christian pacifism. The truth of Jesus can only be witnessed to by way of invitation and example, and is best understood as an exercise of gift-exchange."[144] The notion of *gift* indicates openness to both receiving and giving.

This freedom and openness relates both to the process of peacemaking and to ways of knowing. Huebner observes Yoder claiming that nonviolence is linked with epistemological closure whereas the Radical Reformation allows for fallibility and vulnerability.[145]

> One of the great contributions of Yoder's work, however, is to illustrate the sense in which Christian theology, including much that sees itself as pacifist, is often complicit in such a violent attempt to impose order on the contingent world. Moreover, this violent tendency toward mastery and control is not merely a political or economic phenomenon but is involved in the production of knowledges and theories as well, as Yoder's rejection of methodologism so helpfully shows. One of the main tasks of peacemaking in a globalized world is to be especially attentive to these matters . . . [The peace of Christ] resembles a delicate and nuanced art more than a mechanistic program. The peace of Christ cannot be bureaucratized and domesticated, just as it cannot be finally secured. Rather, peace can only be given by way of witness.[146]

In Yoder's work, ecclesiology and patience become a method in contrast to the logic of violence and speed.[147]

Cynthia Hess brings Yoder's work into conversation with literature on trauma healing.[148] While not framed as "peacemaking" per se, trauma

144. Huebner, *Precarious Peace*, 109.
145. Huebner, *Precarious Peace*, 110.
146. Huebner, *Precarious Peace*, 112.
147. Huebner, *Precarious Peace*, 126–27.
148. Hess, *Sites of Violence, Sites of Grace*.

healing is a critical component of both inner peace and community and societal recovery from violent conflict. The work of Glen Stassen, on the other hand, moves toward concrete proposals for building a just peace. Stassen takes a three-mode, "trilingual," approach in describing actual contexts of peacemaking practice, biblical and theological reflection, and just peacemaking theory. First, his work is substantively biblical with particular focus on the Sermon on the Mount. In his words, "The Sermon on the Mount is not about human striving toward high ideals but about God's transforming initiative to deliver us from the vicious cycles in which we get stuck. . . . [It] describes specific ways we can participate in new initiatives that God is taking. They are not harsh demands but methods of practical participation in God's gracious deliverance."[149] Stassen pushes to move the conversation beyond typical pacifist and just war theory discussions of participation or nonparticipation in war into proactive efforts to build peace and seek justice before coming to the brink of war. He describes feeling deep frustration when the Society of Christian Ethics resolutely declared that the invasion of Iraq in 1990 was not just but "did not urge itself or the people or the Congress or the president to take any clearly defined conflict resolution initiatives. Because we had no clear model of ethics of peacemaking on which to base our debate, but only two models of the restraint of war, the points that were made in oral debate about peacemaking initiatives did not have a clear paradigm with which to resonate."[150]

Stassen develops a Christian ethic of just peacemaking but then demonstrates how to move the theory into the broader public discussion. This is particularly useful in the face of Hauerwas's concern about Christians adopting a stripped-down or de-theologized vocabulary.[151] Though on this Stassen seems to take a more constructive approach, I believe they are basically in agreement. Stassen demonstrates that human rights discourse, for example, originated out of Christian theology; he aims to reclaim it to build deeper Christian support without assuming exclusive origin or credit for the church. This rooting of Christian action in theology before moving to a broader public discourse provides a lasting foundation without narrowly limiting common action.

---

149. Stassen, *Just Peacemaking*, 37–38.
150. Stassen, *Just Peacemaking*, 17.
151. Hauerwas, "Naming God," 79–93.

Importantly, Stassen consistently focuses on concrete steps and actions. He gives particular attention to what he calls *transforming initiatives*: human rights and democracy. In addition to creating a framework for just peacemaking, he narrates historical events in peacemaking and international relations, describing how the theories and ideas of just peacemaking can be seen in the initiatives and actions of churches and parties.

Democracy, Racial Justice, and Reconciliation as Forms of Peacemaking

As noted earlier, the line is often faint between peacemaking and other activity addressing the causes of conflict, violence, or non-peace. One could further ask if the person addressing poverty, racism, or political corruption needs to articulate their work as peacemaking or simply value the same things and have the same or similar goals of peacemakers to hold such a designation. One such area that I will briefly consider, because of its prominence and its part in reducing or providing an alternative to political violence, is democracy.[152] Cavanaugh, for example, discusses democracy as an example of practical reasoning and ordering of public life without resorting to unfettered coercion or violence.[153] The larger political context of democracy or other political arrangement is specifically relevant when thinking of movements or churches organizing for peacebuilding, against war, or for justice. This is also a critical point in which questions of public theology, theological politics, and religion in public life become explicit. Jeffrey Stout's *Democracy and Tradition*, Cornel West's *Democracy Matters: Winning the Fight Against Imperialism*, and Coles and Hauerwas's *Christianity, Democracy, and the Radical Ordinary* raise questions and propose ways forward regarding the role of religion in public space. On Hauerwas's part, this seems to be in part a response to Stout's criticisms of where he accuses Hauerwas of reactive blanket condemnation of many efforts to build democracy. Both *Radical Democracy* as well as *Performing the Faith* include attempts by Hauerwas to respond to Stout.

---

152. It will also become clear later on that "democracy," or at least American Christians' commitment to it, will come under criticism by Hauerwas.

153. Cavanaugh, "Politics of Vulnerability."

I take this to be similar to Stassen's effort to urge peace rhetoric to take on specific concrete forms. Rather than simply protesting the possibility of going to war, it is critical to work towards alternatives. Such alternatives may be specific peacebuilding initiatives or a focus on processes of governing more justly and towards peace. In Stassen, we see peacemaking—just peace—given concrete form both theologically and in specific practices. Cornel West offers numerous strands of social criticism that, though not specifically framed as peacemaking, include many of the same components. For example, he writes:

> Much of the future of democracy in America and the world hangs on grasping and preserving the rich democratic tradition that produced the Douglasses, Kings, Coltranes, and Mobleys in the face of terrorist attacks and cowardly assaults. Since 9/11 we have experienced a niggerization of America, and as we struggle against the imperialistic arrogance of the us-versus-them, revenge-driven policies of the Bush administration, we as a blues nation must learn from the blues people how to keep alive our deep democratic energies in dark times rather than resort to the tempting and easier response of militarism and authoritarianism. . . . To confront the role of race and empire is to grapple with what we would like to avoid, but we avoid that confrontation at the risk of our democratic maturation. To delve into our legacy of race and empire is to unleash our often-untapped democratic energies of Socratic questioning, prophetic witness, and tragicomic hope.[154]

In this passage, critique of several aspects of violence functions as witness against violence in order to reveal and stop it. These elements, as Derek Alan Woodard-Lehman observes, are the violence of empire, racism, militarism, and authoritarianism.[155] Though his critique is aimed at deconstructing systems of violence rather than peacemaking, it fits within a framing of peacemaking that is not simply the creating of calm but the establishing of justice and wellbeing. Through the work of Cornel West and Miroslav Volf,[156] we see that reconciliation and racial justice have similar methodological relationships to the framework of peacemaking.

The connection between the enslavement and continued repression of Africans and African Americans as well the violent displacement of

---

154. West, *Democracy Matters*, 21, 41.
155. Woodard-Lehman, "Body Politics and the Politics of Bodies," 295–320.
156. Volf, *Exclusion and Embrace*.

Native Americans is linked through the *doctrine of discovery* by Navajo activist and theologian Mark Charles.[157] Cherokee theologian Randy Woodley maintains a strong critique of systems of injustice, but also explicitly reflects on peacemaking through a comparative reading of the biblical idea of *shalom* and what he terms the *Harmony Way*. He states: "In their nature as constructs, shalom and the Native American Harmony Way have much in common. Shalom, like Harmony Way, is made up of numerous notions and values, with the *whole* being greater than the sum of the parts. Both are meant to be a way of living life in concrete ways that include more than all the terms found within the construct."[158] He continues,

> The task of creating communities where shalom is lived out may not be easy, but we can know whether or not we are successful in our efforts. How can a community tell if it is practicing shalom? Fortunately, a consistent standard is given throughout the sacred Scriptures. Shalom is always tested on the margins of a society and revealed by how the poor, oppressed, disempowered, and needy are treated.[159]

Woodley observes that "the Law as interpreted by Jesus here is completely consistent with living out shalom. Many Native Americans understand the wisdom of living out shalom because it is a parallel concept to the harmony way of living out what was given to our own people."[160] Though he does not articulate a natural theology, Woodley asserts, "The Harmony Way is embedded in the created order and is meant to be lived out *on* earth by all creation. The Harmony Way, or shalom, is revealed deeply in Jesus's life, even as a baby, with many of God's creatures surrounding him at his entrance into the world."[161] This *shalom* or *Harmony Way*, though a state of being which embodies peace, is not as narrowly action-oriented as peacemaking. Though it is broader than a set of activities, the actions embraced in these two states are necessarily connected to both outward and inward processes of peacemaking. In this vein, Woodley notes, "According to [John] Mohawk, the path to better health, wellness, or well-being for Native Americans is decolonization. But

---

157. Charles, "Transcript of Homily at Call to Action 2016."
158. Woodley, *Shalom and the Community of Creation*, xv.
159. Woodley, *Shalom and the Community of Creation*, 15.
160. Woodley, *Shalom and the Community of Creation*, 18.
161. Woodley, *Shalom and the Community of Creation*, 44.

decolonization in and of itself is incomplete because it fails to remove the systemic relationships embedded in colonialism and neocolonialism."[162] Though certainly not comprehensive of Native American writing or even Native American Christian theologians, Randy Woodley's work highlights a number of critical facets for this project, including geographically, culturally, and historically embedded theology and ethics; concern for the broadness of peace which necessarily includes justice, wellness, and right relationships; and engagement with the biblical text to elaborate a theology of peacemaking.

Eli McCarthy offers a Catholic effort to engage nonviolence and just peace through US policy.[163] McCarthy sets out to examine nonviolent peacemaking in relative isolation from more typical questions of participation or nonparticipation in war and just war consideration. Within the context of Catholic social teaching, he seeks to build a framework for peacemaking that is more theologically robust than considerations of nonviolence as a strategy and more active than ethical rule prohibitions against participation in violence. McCarthy's work is needed in the effort to demonstrate the inseparability of theology and social engagement in the church. Though McCarthy does not overtly discuss democracy, his policy advocacy in light of Jesus and Catholic social teaching functions within the context of US democracy.

Wider Debate: World Council of Churches

The World Council of Churches (WCC) has published two documents, *Ecumenical Call to Just Peace* (ECJP) and the *Just Peace Companion*,[164] which are relevant to this section on North American discussions of peacemaking. The WCC includes many US-based communions; as such, it is a potentially major force in Christian discussions on peacemaking. In the ecumenical advocacy and policy community, issues such as war, peace, poverty, the criminal justice system, and food are intentionally linked by some to connect issues of resistance to war with peacebuilding, human need, and environmental degradation in the framework of *just peace*.[165]

162. Woodley, *Shalom and the Community of Creation*, 92.
163. McCarthy, *Becoming Nonviolent Peacemakers*.
164. World Council of Churches, *Just Peace Companion*.
165. This is particularly true of Michael Neuroth of the Justice and Witness

The ECJP starts with the assertion that "Just Peace embodies a fundamental shift in ethical practice. It implies a different framework of analysis and criteria for action. This call signals the shift and indicates some of the implications for the life and witness of the churches."[166] While building a case for the necessary connection between justice and peace, the document recognizes the challenge involved, and frames this work as a journey towards this vision. The ECJP frames the work in four realms: "peace in the community," "peace with the earth," "peace in the market place," and "peace among the peoples." While the ECJP challenges assumptions about war and the use and misuse of the just war theory it does not absolutely reject the possibility of the use of violence.[167] Paragraph 22 states, "There are extreme circumstances where, as a last resort and the lesser evil, the lawful use of armed force may become necessary to protect vulnerable groups of people exposed to imminent lethal threats." It continues, however, "Yet even then we recognize the use of armed force in situations of conflict as both a sign of serious failure and a new obstacle on the Way of Just Peace."[168]

The final section consists of "Just Peace Practices." Topics covered include peace education, interchurch and interreligious peace works, "gender, peace, and security," "indigenous matters," and "from issues to practices." The final section discusses the International Ecumenical Peace Convocation (IEPC), which brought to a close the World Council of Churches' *Decade to Overcome Violence*. In reflecting on this gathering,

---

Ministries (Washington, DC) of the United Church Christ; Eli McCarthy, the director of Justice and Peace for the Conference of Major Superiors of Men; and the Church of the Brethren's Office of Peacebuilding and Policy, which I lead. For Neuroth this is part of seeking to reengage the UCC's official self-designation as a Just Peace Church in the 1980s. Additionally, Neuroth was a presenter in a workshop on the "US Churches' Response to Just Peace" that I organized on behalf of the National Council of Churches of Christ in the US at the World Council of Churches' 10th Assembly in Busan, South Korea, in 2013.

166. World Council of Churches, *Just Peace Companion*, 1.

167. I have wondered if the ECJP is really a paradigm shift or simply a concerted effort to make the use of lethal force truly the last resort as prescribed in just war thinking. I tend to believe that the latter is the case; the shift is that just war criteria tend to be used only when needed to make a decision about military engagement, whereas the ECJP attends to the contexts out of which this need to decide arises. Whereas just war theory is used to discern action when A is attacking B, the ECJP asks, what are the conditions around A and B? At times, these conditions include war or possible war, but more often they are economic, environmental, or justice/injustice based.

168. World Council of Churches, *Just Peace Companion*, 6–7.

this section highlights several initiatives discussed at the IEPC that linked concrete actions of churches and NGOs to the foci of the ECJP. In this it broadens just peace beyond conflict resolution and even conflict transformation to include issues of poverty and environment as well as what has been more strictly considered issues of peacemaking.

Conclusion

My portrait of peacemaking has focused primarily on three strands or traditions of writing. These are not comprehensive of the work in Christian ethics generally or in the United States, but they have been both highly influential and relevant to the focus of this project, peacemaking in the work of Stanley Hauerwas. These traditions were Rauschenbusch's *Christianity and the Social Crisis*, the black church and liberation theology (which include black liberation theology and civil rights discourse and theology as well as a small sampling of other liberation theologies), and the historic peace church tradition.

The Social Gospel challenged Christianity to pay greater attention to social issues. Though the church has always included traditions of charity and service, the Social Gospel advocated greater engagement in systems of injustice and violence. From this emerged a variety of social activist and analysis streams, as well as the critiques of this theology and US foreign policy by Reinhold Niebuhr and his disciples. Niebuhr's critique of what he takes to be idealistic pacifism became a major backdrop for Mennonite theologian John Howard Yoder's apocalyptic Christological pacifism. Though the historic peace churches and Anabaptist churches traditionally read Scripture in community and in relation to the early church, Yoder intentionally engaged Niebuhrian thought and the ecumenical movement. As will be seen later, Yoder then gained a wider audience through the work of Stanley Hauerwas.

The black church stream of theological reflection and lived theological practice is a second major tradition that contributes to my analysis of Christian ethics and peacemaking. While I cannot do justice to the breadth of this tradition here, it is a crucial stream of reflection in the North American context. Not only was the civil rights movement closely linked to the black church, but Martin Luther King Jr.'s linking of racial injustice to poverty and militarism brings together several important pieces for a multifaceted peacemaking. Additionally, as Reggie Williams demonstrates, Dietrich Bonhoeffer, who has been vastly influential in Christian ethics and nonviolence, was remade as a theologian of resistance during his time in Harlem.

The final stream of theological reflection and church practice is that of the historic peace churches. While early Mennonites and Brethren framed peace as nonresistance and nonparticipation in the military, this gradually shifted to a more proactive peace position and activist peacemaking. In part, Yoder's response to Niebuhr and by extension to the Social Gospel movement, combined with a greater integration of these faith communities into the broader society in the mid-twentieth century, helped to generate reflection and action for peace. In part, this integration occurred while participating in the civil rights movement. During the same time period a variety of denominations, ecumenical bodies, and church councils began to consider what came to be called *just peace*. In just peace, many elements of these three streams have found an integrated articulation.

Chapter 3

HAUERWAS: THEOLOGY AND ECCLESIOLOGY

> Trained by my father to labor for bricklayers, I helped build the church in which I could not be saved.
> —STANLEY HAUERWAS, *HANNAH'S CHILD*, 2

> The pacifism of Hauerwas is squarely rooted in his ecclesiology. To be pacifist is to be the church.
> —HARRY HUEBNER, "AN ETHIC OF CHARACTER," 192

IN CHAPTER 2 I described the broad background for peacemaking within Christian theology and ethics. In this chapter, I turn toward the main subject, that of the work of Stanley Hauerwas. While the goal is to assess his work on peacemaking, this must first be located within his broader project. More narrowly, attention will be given to his ecclesiological framing and to his work on ethics. Hauerwas goes to great lengths to erase the division between ethics and theology. Given this approach, separating peacemaking from ecclesiology and other parts of his theological ethics may be futile. Similarly, to Hauerwas, Emmanuel Katongole notes that much of this practice of discussing the potential connection between theology and ethics is largely an effort to secure the "relevance" of theology.[1] To Hauerwas, such an effort reinforces the assumptions of modernity that are problematic.

In the following passage, we observe not only Hauerwas's emphasis on the centrality of the church in theology, but also his assertion of church as politics: "Indeed, we believe in the strongest sense that outside the church there is no salvation, for the church offers us participation in light of a people that is an alternative to the world's violence. We know of no way of being saved other than a way which is ecclesial, in effect, political. Therefore, we are really about challenging the assumption that salvation is somehow *extra* political."[2] Hauerwas's theology is the persistent work of demonstrating not only how the church occupies public space but is itself political. This statement is more fundamental than that the church is a body of people who represent a subset of civil society.[3]

---

1. "It is interesting to point out how modern philosophers (and theologians) in discussing the problem of the relation between religion and ethics are, in effect, inquiring about the *relevance* or *usefulness* (if any) of one's religious convictions to the moral task. The fact that this assumption is shared by theologians no less than philosophers is an indication that the 'politicization of religious conduct' does not happen solely as an 'external' domination of religious institutions by hostile moral-political goals. There is as well an inner transformation on the part of Christian self-understanding. Having lost the Constantinian political monopoly, religious beliefs and institutions themselves begin to 'work' differently and thus betray another kind of dynamic based on another system, an order which they no longer have power directing, but whose protection they now take to be their moral and religious duty. The contemporary expression of this inner transformation is manifest in theology's often-apologetic quest for 'relevance' by uncritically underwriting the *humanum*, whether in the form of social and political strategies for peace and justice, or a personal quest for meaning or happiness." Katongole, *Beyond Universal Reason*, 12.

2. Hauerwas, *In Good Company*, 62. When he says that there is no salvation outside the church, does he mean that the church has a monopoly on or is the (arbitrary) dispenser of salvation? Such an understanding seems to allow coercion which Hauerwas would, if he fully embraced Yoder, reject.

3. "From a theological perspective the church is not simply another NGO, though it is part of civil society. NGOs are essentially voluntary organizations called into being to serve a particular role at a given time in society, and generally composed of like-minded people. Once their purpose has been served, and sometimes once their founder or leader is no longer involved, NGOs tend to dissolve or are disbanded. The church, on the other hand, is a community of very diverse people who have been baptized 'into Christ,' that is, they participate in an organic life that exists beyond themselves or their own choice, and for a purpose that derives from God's purpose in the world. . . . This understanding of the church is . . . a theological one, but it is essential for the church's own self-understanding, that is, in order for the church to understand its particular and peculiar role in society. The church exists both as a means to an

Rather, the church is in some way a self-contained politics. As a *politics unto itself*, it is not separate from the world or the broader politics outside its own walls and polity.[4]

This chapter is divided into two main sections. I begin by considering major themes of Hauerwas's theology. This section will not be a comprehensive review but a consideration of central themes: Christocentrism, the centrality of the church and the practices of the body, and the centrality of nonviolence. These themes are critical to understanding the broad shape of Hauerwas's theology. They are also particularly relevant to his ecclesiology and peacemaking. The end of this section will suggest key ways in which more explicitly ecclesiological thinking develops from this broader theology.

The second section deals with major themes within Hauerwas's ecclesiology. Hauerwas insists that the church cannot be defined outside of its practices. He asserts that there is no noncontingent church that is known apart from the way that it exists in the world. These themes include worship, witness, a church with a history, distinct community/peculiar people, a nonviolent church, and a peacemaking community.

Themes in Hauerwas's Theology

For Hauerwas, theology is reflecting on and living peaceably in the presence of God as a community located within the ongoing narrative of Jesus and the people of Israel. This people is the church, which is called to witness to the ongoing work of God. Additionally, this people is formed through the reading of the text, common prayer, liturgy, and going out in mission to bear witness to God's peaceable kingdom. This community forms a politics that stands as a challenge to the violence of the world but is not entirely separate from this world.[5] R. R. Reno asserts that the

---

end that has to do with God's justice and *shalom*, and as an end in itself, that is, as a community in which human divisions are transcended in the 'unity of the Spirit.'" De Gruchy, "Democracy," 450–451.

4. By *politics unto itself*, I mean it is a political body whose identity and constitution is not contingent on the state for validity. By *polity*, I mean the institutional structures of denominations and communions as well as the bylaws of individual congregations.

5. "The question of the distinctiveness of Christian ethics—or as I have put it, the insistence on the significance of the qualifier—also involves questions of the relationship of the church to the world. Indeed, how the task of Christian ethics is to be conceived is as much an ecclesiological issue as an issue having to do with the nature of grace, creation, redemption." Hauerwas, *Peaceable Kingdom*, 60. Hauerwas goes on to

challenge to the presumption of the necessity of violence is Hauerwas's most basic and recurring conflict.[6] Additionally, because Hauerwas refuses to separate theology from ethics, he does not present theological discussions separately from discussions of ethics and discipleship.

For Hauerwas, even the most foundational points of theology on *God* or *salvation* are fundamentally political and necessarily bound up with the church. Michael Baxter notes, "Hauerwas counters the assumption shared by both liberal and conservative Christians that salvation is about the religious meaning and eternal destiny of individuals. 'Rather, salvation is being engrafted into the practices that save us from those powers of the world that rule our lives making it impossible for us to truly worship God.' In short, 'The church's politics is our salvation.'"[7] As such, all of Hauerwas's theology is to some extent political and ecclesiological.[8] But asserting that the basic theological point of God is wrapped up in the (nearly profane) church, which can only be known through board meetings and potlucks,[9] seems circular. For if there is no foundational

---

note that, though distinct, this is not a license to assume superiority or dominance. On several other occasions he comments that he is essentially for theocracy (albeit a nonviolent one). These seeming affirmations of theocracy are used for shock value to challenge the assumption that Christians are *necessarily* for democracy and that democracy is a manifestation of a "Christianizing" of the nation-state.

I initially included "or should not be" but then considered that Hauerwas would say that even those communities that intentionally separate themselves from "the world" are still functioning in relation to "the world" to which they are responding.

6. "Christian power meets resistance. Being trained through Jesus' story means adopting the practices and habits of a new city, and this cannot help but create a conflict between the church and the world, for the world seeks to put us to its own malign purposes. A great deal of Hauerwas's work focuses on particular scenes of this conflict, which are many. Materially, this diversity of conflict is unified under a general scheme of violence and peace. Worldly powers, for Hauerwas, are not the most visible and potent in injustice or oppression. Instead, worldly powers show their true face in the presumptive necessity of violence. Secular power must threaten in order to be effective. In contrast, the defining practice of the church is peace-making, and precisely because of this, the density of the church necessarily collides with the social 'realities' that require menace in order to maintain power." Reno, "Stanley Hauerwas," 310.

7. Baxter, "Church as *Polis*?," 133. Internal quotation is from Hauerwas, *In Good Company*, 6.

8. Hauerwas writes in *The Work of Theology* (171), "I assume every theology, even theology done in the speculative mode, has been produced and reproduces a politics. If theology is done faithful to the gospel it will not only be political but it will be so in a particular way."

9. An example of narrating a church's experience can be found in Hauerwas, "Ministry of a Congregation," 123. In this essay, Hauerwas notes, "One of the essential tasks

notion of God or at least the possibility of attaining access to such a being, but merely people who are clergy (usually white, almost always men) or theologians (also disproportionately skewed in this direction) who decide these things, then one should give up hope in a discovery of truth. Though a legitimate concern, Emmanuel Katongole observes:

> However, one must note the self-referential aspect within this understanding of religion as a tradition is significant: A "religious experience" is only possible within the space of religious language and practice. The circle, however, is not vicious but hermeneutic, which, as we have noted, points to the necessity of training and initiation. However, it is such hermeneutic circularity that makes intelligible Hauerwas's contention that "outside the church there is no salvation." For, away from the particular tradition that offers a training in the language of, and the particular skills that are associated with, the stories of God, one would not know what "salvation" is all about. Without these concrete practices and specific language one would not even "see" that one is a "sinner," who thereby needs to be "saved." Thus, the full critical force of Hauerwas's apparently conservative claim ("Outside the church there is no salvation") is to deny that "God," "sin," "salvation," etc., are natural categories, and to affirm how these categories are arrived at historically through participation in given cultural-linguistic way of life.[10]

Hauerwas focuses on practices. This focus ranges from the forming of virtue through liturgy to a discussion of parallels between jazz improvisation and the Christian life to consideration of how lives are shaped by narrative.[11] For him these practices are not practices in general, nor is "narrative" in the abstract significant. Both, however, are closely related to the goal of shaping a more faithful church. (This formation of the church, particularly the creation and construction of the peaceable body, will receive extended treatment in chapter 4.) Nearly all Hauerwas's writing includes some stated connection to practices and these are almost always

---

the theologian-ethicist performs is to help congregations like Broadway appreciate the significance of the common acts."

10. Katongole, *Beyond Universal Reason*, 207.

11. On the central place of ethics, Hauerwas writes in *Peaceable Kingdom* (55): "I wish to show that Christian ethics is not what one does after one gets clear on everything else, or after one has established a starting point or basis of theology: rather it is at the heart of the theological task. For theology is a practical activity concerned to display how Christian convictions construe the self and world."

related to the church. This church is Christocentric. All Hauerwas's theology, then, is based in Jesus but necessarily passes through the church.

Following is a discussion of several themes that are critical to understanding Hauerwas's theology: Christocentrism, the critical nature of the church and the practices of the body, the centrality of nonviolence, and ecclesiology. The aim of this section is to provide a summary of Hauerwas's theology that will serve as a foundation for his ecclesiology and peacemaking.

Christocentrism

Hauerwas's work in general and his ecclesiology specifically is Christocentric[12]—though he would likely challenge such a characterization. As he notes, the early church's "Christology" "did not consist first in claims about Jesus' ontological status" but relied on telling his story.[13] Implications were certainly drawn, but they were not abstracted from the story nor was the "essence" of the story the main feature.

In his Christocentrism, Hauerwas has claimed affinity with Barth and Yoder.[14] However, his approach in imitating Barth's "confident

---

12. "There can be no separation of Christology from ecclesiology." Hauerwas, *Community of Character*, 37. Hauerwas claims great affinity for Yoder in these matters. Carter writes, "Yoder's approach to the church's witness to the state needs to be understood in terms of Barth's ecclesiology. It is a development of Barth's Christocentric method and creative appropriation of Barth's method of analogy in Christian ethics. Yoder's development of themes in Barth's theology in a believers' church direction is one of Yoder's significant and original contributions to Christian social ethics. Yoder's appropriation of Barth at this point allows him to offer a third way besides the usual alternatives of either a doctrine of the state that is not specifically Christian because it is not derived from a Christocentric account of the church, or the inability of Christians to say anything to the state at all, which is the charge of irrelevance often made against those in the believer's church tradition. By understanding the church as an eschatological community, a new society in the process of being redeemed with an exemplary role as the foundation of its witness, it is possible to draw analogies from the nature of the Christian community to the will of God for human community in general." Carter, *Politics of the Cross*, 214.

13. Hauerwas, *Peaceable Kingdom*, 73–74.

14. "Hauerwas often positions himself on the side of Barth and diametrically opposed to Niebuhr, specifically culling from Barth the Christological center of theology that engenders the finality of Christ's lordship over history." Morgan, "Lordship of Christ," 61.

theological speech"[15] may be a more determinative influence.[16] He writes, "Yet one of Barth's great virtues was the courage to say what he knew needed to be said before he figured out how to defend it."[17] A number of pages later he continues, "For Barth, the denial of natural theology, as well as the discovery of the Christological center in theology, was of a piece with his opposition to Hitler."[18] Hauerwas challenges what he sees as the incessant "throat clearing" of modern theology bent on sorting out the methodological challenges of doing theology in modernity. Both the moving forward in doing theology (rather than lingering in methodological considerations) and a Christological center, provide the substance and weight to challenge the presumptions of the nation-state bent on war.[19] Here, both the content and approach may be embraced for practical, that is, political aims. Though shaped by his reading of Barth, Hauerwas is not defined by him. As Douglas Gay notes, the "crucial area

---

15. "The *Church Dogmatics*, with its unending and confident display of Christian speech, is Barth's attempt to train us to be a people capable of truthful witness to the God along who is truth." Hauerwas, *With the Grain of the Universe*, 176. The concepts of witness and truthfulness return in Hauerwas's work on peacemaking. Witness plays a key role in the framework of church as politics, and truthfulness is a central impetus for confronting sin and the subsequent peacemaking. See Hauerwas, "Peacemaking." Commenting on the founding of the journal *Modern Theology*, Hauerwas writes, "Ken, I think, rightly sensed twenty-five years ago that a more confident theological voice was then in the making and that the new journal he was inaugurating was required." "'Writing-In' and 'Writing-Out,'" 63.

16. To verify such a statement would take considerable work. I take his strongly worded and rhetorically jarring approach to be an attempt to challenge perceived reticence and equivocation or qualifications in theology. He has said of pacifism that he states his commitment to nonviolence publicly so that he can be held accountable for this commitment. Hauerwas, *Against the Nations*, 60. This confident theological speech may in large part be a spiritual practice of attempting to strengthen himself as much as (perhaps more than) an aggressive challenge to the church. If this is the case then his strong wording is not so much judgement on others as a practicing of Christian speech.

17. Hauerwas, *With the Grain of the Universe*, 144.

18. Hauerwas, *With the Grain of the Universe*, 170. Might this relate to Reno's assertion of Hauerwas's "brick-like character" of theology?

19. "The worst betrayal of the task of theology comes when the theologian fears that the words he or she must use are not necessary. The result too often is a desperate shouting. One of the reasons that I so enjoy Barth is that there is nothing desperate about his theology; rather it is the joyful celebration of the unending task of theology." Hauerwas, *Working With Words*, xi.

in which Hauerwas wants to push beyond Barth is ecclesiology, where he believes Barth is insufficiently catholic and insufficiently Anabaptist."[20]

For Hauerwas, Jesus is central. This approach is similar to Barth's. One scholar asserts that Barth's "whole theology is basically an impressive elaboration of Christology."[21] In his consideration of Hauerwas in relation to Barth and Niebuhr's interactions, Morgan notes that whereas Barth's orientation is Christological realism and Niebuhr's is political realism, Hauerwas occupies a complex middle in which ecclesiological concerns drive his work.[22] Barth (whom Hauerwas reads in part through Yoder's lens of Christological nonviolence) is not concerned for the survival of the church because of his strong view and centrality of God.[23] Hauerwas dominates this work with the church's relation to liberalism. Morgan notes,

> There is an important question here about whether the gathering of Hauerwas's church rests on a desire to provide a stable alternative to contemporary political needs. If this is the case, then a tension arises in Hauerwas's critical appraisal of Barth and Niebuhr vis-à-vis his own constructive task. Can he take seriously Barth's account of the finality of Christ's lordship while also putting it in service of establishing an anti-liberal ecclesial politics in response to the Niebuhrian problem of theological accommodation? Can Christ's lordship be theologically capitalized for such purposes, or will Hauerwas have to take Barth more seriously in order to move past an ecclesiology often presented in his writings as an alternative to that problem?[24]

20. Gay, "Practical Theology," 14.

21. Morgan, "Lordship of Christ," 57.

22. "In his 2001 Gifford Lectures, Hauerwas repositions their Christological concerns as ecclesiological concerns, which is emblematic of how he indexes contemporary Christian ethics to the same impasses explicated in the 1948 exchange between a Niebuhrian anxious survivalism and a Barthian Christological freedom." Morgan, "Lordship of Christ," 61.

23. Morgan, "Lordship of Christ," 65. Since Hauerwas came to Yoder's work somewhat later he would have read Barth prior to Yoder. That Hauerwas found Yoder compelling may have been in part due to his appreciation of Barth's Christological focus. However, following his Yoderian conversion to Christological nonviolence, Hauerwas read Barth through the lens of Yoder. At present, I am unaware of any accounts of Hauerwas reflecting on this. Hauerwas does comment ("Dietrich Bonhoeffer's Political Theology," 35) that his having previously read Bonhoeffer was likely why Yoder's *Politics of Jesus* had such a profound influence on him.

24. Morgan, "Lordship of Christ," 65.

If Hauerwas's theology at least in part prioritizes a desired practical outcome, "establishing an anti-liberal ecclesial politics" over Christology, it must be asked, How much do practical desired outcomes drive the project and is Hauerwas's project still Christocentric? Are these theological points then employed simply as a tactic of rhetoric?[25]

For Hauerwas, then, Christology may be practical, but this is not due solely to its practicality or tactical use. For Hauerwas, *incarnation* as a theological category is not a dominant theological lynchpin. As such, the story of Jesus and the community that formed around this story and became part of this story[26] means that Jesus is the center and the center is simultaneously theological as well as inherently ethical.[27] Not only does Hauerwas elaborate his understanding of peace through Jesus but claims that history must be read through Jesus. He writes, "In modernity it has been very hard for theologians to resist the presumption that their task is to provide more determinative accounts of the truth of what Christians believe, accounts that are more basic than the beliefs themselves. Thus my observation: if you think you need a theory of truth to underwrite the conviction that Jesus was raised from the dead, then worship the theory—not Jesus."[28] Jesus, however, cannot be best understood from historical research that isolates Jesus, but as part of the story of the church.[29]

In chapter 5, "Jesus: The Presence of the Peaceable Kingdom," of *The Peaceable Kingdom*, Hauerwas says that all chapters to this point were preparation for this chapter.[30] These earlier chapters include the "qualified

---

25. Does this edge toward an ironic use? If so, does it undercut truth claims or is it simply part of using the language of Christianity? If this is the case, then what would seem to be orthodox theological statements may take on an entirely new hue or meaning. See Kallenberg, *Ethics as Grammar*, for an extended discussion of this.

26. Hauerwas writes, "I will suggest that Barth is not sufficiently catholic just to the extent that his critique and rejection of Protestant liberalism make it difficult for him to acknowledge that, through the work of the Holy Spirit, we are made part of God's care of the world through the church. Barth, of course, does not deny that the church is constituted by the proclamation of the gospel. What he cannot acknowledge is that the community called the church is constitutive of the gospel." Hauerwas, *With the Grain of the Universe*, 143.

27. Though as discussed later neither Hauerwas nor the early church distinguishes between discrete disciplines of *ethics* or *theology*.

28. Hauerwas, *Cross-Shattered Church*, 144.

29. Hauerwas, *Peaceable Kingdom*, 73.

30. Though this chapter is not out of the ordinary, its orientation within this work is significant. While similar chapters occur elsewhere, in most cases these are parts of collections of essays, which, while not consistent in theme, are not part of a

nature of Christian ethics," the focus on narrative, "historic nature of human agency," and sinfulness, which began to frame the centrality of the "moral significance" of Jesus's life.[31] Their significance is not in simple mimicking of specificities of Jesus's existence but a deeper imitation of him.[32] That we do not know him apart from accounts of the disciples and the early church is not only *not* a problem, it is in fact *required* given the "demands Jesus placed on his followers," which means he cannot be known "abstracted" from their response.[33] Furthermore, not only is the kingdom of God central to Jesus's proclamation, it is made present in him.[34] This exposition then leads to further chapters explaining social ethics as located within the community (church) and witnessed in the "marks" of church: "These rites, baptism and the Eucharist, are not just 'religious things' that Christian people do. They are the essential rituals of our politics. Through them we learn who we are. Instead of being motives or causes for effective work on the part of Christian people, these liturgies *are* our effective social work."[35] In this, Hauerwas continues to lay out a nearly seamless connection between these marks of the church and the centrality of Jesus as a continuation of the story of Israel embodied in the story-formed community. This community is formed and sustained in Jesus through practices that continue to engraft persons into the ongoing life of the church. The life of the church is itself in relation to all that is not the church through politics of reconciliation.

Centrality of the Church and the Practices of the Body

Before moving to an extended analysis of his ecclesiology, it is necessary to orient the centrality of the church and practices of the body within

---

book-length treatment and as such their placement is less instructive. This is largely because Hauerwas has written few works of a length that sheds light onto his larger structures of thought. Given this scarcity, it is important in such works to attend to the way that these structures are arranged.

31. Hauerwas, *Peaceable Kingdom*, 72.

32. "Mimicking" picks up on the way that themes and practices of imitation are at times discounted, since it is of course obvious that Christians cannot imitate all facets of Jesus's life. However, without particular practices or all practices reduced to an allegedly more spiritual core, the material shape of Christian discipleship is lost.

33. Hauerwas, *Peaceable Kingdom*, 73.

34. Hauerwas, *Peaceable Kingdom*, 85.

35. Hauerwas, *Peaceable Kingdom*, 108.

his broader theology. In Hauerwas, church and the body are the primary location of the action and understanding of the kingdom of God. Belief in Jesus and nonviolence needs not only to be affirmed, but known, understood, and rightly responded to through practices of body.[36] The *body* is neither simply the individual Christian's body nor the corporate body of Christ, but both of these. These physical practices of the church are found in the Eucharist and worship, but also in less narrowly-defined practices such as *witness*. Samuel Wells, reflecting on Hauerwas's work, writes, "The world has been saved. Its destiny does not hang in the balance, waiting for the church's decisive and timely intervention to tip the scales. The church must not talk or act as if God were dependent on its faithfulness or initiative. The church does not make the difference. The church lives in the difference Christ has made."[37] Because the difference has already been made, the church need not act coercively to either "make the change" or ensure its institutional survival. This in turn allows for freely living rather than anxiously striving for significance or control. According to Hauerwas, because the church is thus free from the need for coercion, it can bear witness and demonstrate a politics that is radically separate but not unconcerned with "the world."[38] Since Christian ethics is theology, then any statement regarding the world by necessity bears practical implications. Hauerwas writes,

> From my perspective, the only reason to be a Christian is that it makes you part of a people committed to telling one another the truth. I have always presumed that such people have no reason to think that we have nothing to learn from people who

---

36. Timoteo Gener explores a variation of this: "The vitality of Christian witness relates integrally to Christology since the point of biblical Christology is discipleship in context. The first Christians' path to faith in Jesus as the Christ may actually be called discipleship-in-context Christology, or missiological Christology/ies." Gener, "Christologies in Asia," 60.

37. Wells, "Difference Christ Makes," 18.

38. This designation of "the world" is carried in biblical themes and has been a major component of Anabaptist identity. Hunter (*To Change the World*, 160–62) notes, however, that the distinction of "the world" may overdetermine Hauerwas's and neo-Anabaptist vision and lead them to seemingly have little positive to see in the world. Rather than seeing the world as the site of violence, it should also be seen as the point of God's creation, grace, and humanity's exploration of beauty even when not within the church. At a number of points Hauerwas speaks with great admiration of novels and baseball, so though the short form of "world" may in the end sound dismissive and negative, I do not believe it is nearly as thorough as it would seem from a focus on particular phrases in Hauerwas.

do not share our faith. So, of course, Christians will discover commonalities with those who are not Christian. What I have objected to is the assumption that what we may find we share in common can be insured by a theory in a manner that removes the necessity of actually getting to know those who are different. Commonalities may exist, but you will only discover that they do so by looking. I fear too often Christians have assumed an imperialistic position by declaring that they and their neighbors are essentially the same before they have looked.[39]

In this statement Hauerwas shows a hand that is often obscured. Whereas he often writes as if the church is a beleaguered victim of liberalism or the nation-state, I suspect that he is *at least* as concerned, if not more, that the church (as if there were one and only one way of functioning) not betray the nonviolent Jesus by acting from an imperialistic position. In fact, the popularity of Hauerwas's work as recounted by Stout may in part hinge on his engagement with the changing status of the church, which, at least in the United States, is losing is preferred social standing.

In the quotation above, Hauerwas is challenging both the priority and genesis of the idea of commonality. He does this with many strongly stated facets of his work (e.g., justice is a bad idea—which Yoder viewed as maximizing "the provocative edge of the dissenting posture"[40]). Rather than locate the beginning or foundation of theology in an otherwise discernible theory, Hauerwas pushes Christians to base theology in the church. In this Hauerwas is less an anti-foundationalist than he is a challenger of the notion that the foundation can be located in an independently verifiable foundation that is equally accessible to all rational

---

39. Hauerwas, "Making Connections," 84.

40. "For his part, Yoder sees Hauerwas as maximizing 'the provocative edge of the dissenting posture with titles like *Against the Nations* or *Resident Aliens*.' Therefore, the for/against distinction is not without merit, especially since Hauerwas tends to use what has been termed contrarian language, making use of sweeping denunciations, especially of movements. However, in my view, Yoder and Hauerwas view the relationship of the church to the nations in very similar ways, although Hauerwas's language makes it more difficult than necessary to see this. In fact, use of such language makes Hauerwas easy to mark for those searching for the stench of sectarianism. The difference between Hauerwas and Yoder cannot be characterized by saying that one is for and one is against nations. The similarities between the ecclesiologies are far greater than any dissimilarities." Doerksen, "Share the House," 190.

individuals.⁴¹ He calls this "beginning in the middle."⁴² In "The Church's One Foundation Is Jesus Christ Her Lord or In a World Without Foundations All We Have Is the Church," Hauerwas attempts to explore this by presenting three sermons as a method of such a foundation. He begins by asserting, "For in a world without foundations all we have is the church. That such is the case is no deficiency since that is all we have ever had or could ever want."⁴³

Hauerwas asserts that theology and ethics are one and that the Christian life is political. It is political and is mediated through the church. In an effort to remove the *and* in "theology and ethics," Hauerwas consistently seeks to undermine the linguistic division between ethics, theology, and the possibility of separating these from the church. One may ask, however, if Hauerwas's antagonism towards articulations of causation and sequence (i.e., worship *leads* ethics) renders compelling his work toward an undivided Christian life? Or does it simply create confusion by blurring an important distinction between theology/worship and practice/ethics?⁴⁴ Hauerwas is intent on breaking down these distinctions so that all of life is rendered *more political*. Hunter asserts that this tendency of what he calls "neo-Anabaptists" is overdone and in the end unhelpful.⁴⁵

41. "Yoder thinks that Christians often make the strategic error of thinking that they can persuade people who reject the lordship of Jesus to accept the lordship of God the Father by means of a doctrine of creation that does not speak of Jesus Christ . . . Yoder stresses the necessity of beginning with 'the confession of rootedness in historical community,' but he does not see this as a handicap for Christians because everyone else must do the same thing, too. There is no such thing as a 'scratch' from which one can begin. In a postmodern situation, Christians are at no disadvantage in this regard. But we are so used to being in the position of power that it *feels like* weakness to admit that our social ethics arises out of our historical community." Carter, *Politics of the Cross*, 208.

42. Hauerwas, "On Beginning in the Middle," 50–71.

43. Hauerwas, *In Good Company*, 33.

44. Critics' consistent assertions that Hauerwas advocates withdrawal from public life due to his focus on the church being the church might be a sign that his stance generates confusion.

45. "In some respects, neo-Anabaptists politicize their engagement with the world even more than the Right and the Left because they cast their oppositions to the State, global capitalism and other powers in eschatological terms. To literally demonize such powers as the State and the market as they do means that they draw much of their identity and purpose in the here and now through their cosmic struggle with them." Hunter, *To Change the World*, 164. While I do not doubt that there are cases of overreliance on oppositional identity, Hunter may miss part of the purpose of the critical

I turn now to the centrality of nonviolence in Hauerwas's work. This is a more specific case of the church's political nature. Hauerwas's attempt to get past what he sees as false divisions is also relevant for the consideration of nonviolence and its relation to the Jesus and the church (as discussed above) and peacemaking (chapter 5).

Centrality of Nonviolence

For Hauerwas, not only is Christian theology understood through Jesus, but nonviolence is integral to understanding Jesus.[46] Nonviolence is related to peace and peacemaking but not synonymous with them, though Hauerwas tends to use the terms interchangeably. That it is Christocentric means that nonviolence is based on Christ and is at the center of Christian thought and life rather than an idealized commitment or a pastime of the notably saintly. His dictum that "war is abolished in Christ" challenges both the conservative and liberal assumption that "you can get your doctrine of God straight without thinking about war."[47] Disavowal of the use of violence by Christians then allows for the possibility of peacemaking, since there is no other option but to figure out whatever conflict may lead to the assumption that violence is necessary.[48] This peace, along with forgiveness, is possible by virtue of already having been accomplished by God, as well as the Christian's needing to *accept*

---

edge of at least certain neo-Anabaptists. Whereas certain just-war-theory-touting churches, church practitioners, and theologians hold that this theory has adequate traction to actually limit and guide the use of force by the United States, Anabaptist social analysis often detects that the state is not using just war theory in good faith. When one accounts for the enormous expenditure by military contractors to convince Congress to use their products (at times including actual advertisements for missiles in the Metro station closest to Capitol Hill) as well as the enormous cultural investment in the myth of redemptive violence in entertainment, the notion that we come at considerations of the legitimate use of military force with an open, unbiased, and uninfluenced mind seems unjustified.

46. Samuel Wells asserts of Hauerwas's work, "The difference Christ makes is this: peace." Wells, "Difference Christ Makes," 19.

47. Wells, "Difference Christ Makes," 84–85.

48. The limitation forces an imaginative reconsidering and search for solutions. As Hauerwas states: "Creativity in moral life, far from implying an escape from the constraints of habit, transforms what is into what ought to be by displaying through the virtues the implications of our obligation to witness to God's rule . . . Put starkly, moral obligations create the necessities that empower imagination." Hauerwas, "On Keeping Theological Ethics Imaginative," 55.

forgiveness. This accepting as well as dispensing of forgiveness is a necessary dispossession of power.[49]

Christian nonviolence in relation to the nation-state is both a prerequisite and an outcome of forgiving and receiving forgiveness, which then plays out in the "virtue of peacemaking." This peacemaking is the central focus of my entire project, and is a practice, virtue, and reality of Christians formed in the way of Jesus. It is the purpose of this project to assess whether these assertions can be sustained in the discourse of the life of the church lived out in the face of violence. Nonviolence is central to Hauerwas's thinking in that it is an integral element of Christian theology and life. It is not merely a strategy for getting what one wants without violence, but is a Christian virtue deeply embedded in the Christian's life. Though not primarily a strategy, nonviolence also has practical implications that invite Christians to find ways to work collaboratively with others to strengthen capacities, practices, and even institutions in building peace and reducing violence.[50] Peace, peacemaking, and nonviolence will be examined in greater depth in chapter 4; it is adequate here to note their centrality without fully exploring Hauerwas's meanings or the implications for his assertions.

Why Is Ecclesiology Important for Understanding Hauerwas's Work?

The concluding section on the major themes in Hauerwas's theology will consider the centrality of ecclesiology in relation to his broader theological vision.[51] Since the rest of this chapter will focus specifically on

---

49. Hauerwas, *Christian Existence Today*, 93. Hauerwas also writes, "Thus, within a world of violence and injustice Christians can take the risk of being forgiven and forgiving. They are able to break the circle of violence as they refuse to become part of those institutions of fear that promise safety by the destruction of others." Hauerwas, *Against the Nations*, 117.

50. See Hauerwas, "Taking Time for Peace." On Yoder and Volf, Sider writes, "The church embodies the memory in God's work in Jesus by institutionalizing processes and practices of forgiveness and reconciliation and thereby activating charity, both in the sense of a capacity to receive the other as gift and in the sense of a pouring out of oneself for the other. Eschatology and ecclesiology intertwine as the 'conditions of possibility' for practices of charity by creating, sustaining, and shaping the memory of redemption." Sider, *To See History Doxologically*, 134.

51. Douglas Gay asserts, "Hauerwas places ecclesiology at the center of theology and his work seeks to defend and display the claims that the church is epistemologically,

ecclesiology, this section will simply orient ecclesiology within Hauerwas's theology and set the stage for the more detailed discussion that follows. Due to Hauerwas's insistence that theology be done for and within the church, as well as his insistence that Christianity is not a set of beliefs, but is embodied practices rooted in ongoing narrative of the church, ecclesiology becomes the basic assumption and locus for much of his work.[52] This does not mean that explicitly or solely ecclesiological discussions occupy a substantial portion of his writing, but that strands and assumptions of his ecclesiology are woven throughout his writing. Indeed, his work would be incoherent if ecclesiology were removed; it is entirely rooted in a community that gathers in the ongoing narrative of Israel and Jesus Christ.[53] For Hauerwas, without such a community, virtue cannot be demonstrated, worship is too abstract, peace is diminished to processes (such as conflict resolution or mediation skills) or simply a cessation of violence, and rootless individuals are unable to resist the allure of the nation-state's mythology. It is not so much that Hauerwas is anti-foundational in his thinking, it is simply that the foundation is the church as part of the ongoing narrative of Jesus rather than a particular set of independently verifiable principles.[54] This foundation is not simply

---

axiologically (ethically) and politically prior to the world." Gay, "Practical Theology of Church and World," 5. Hauerwas himself comments on various attempts at finding a center of his work: "The list goes on, but the truth is that there is no center to my work unless you count work itself the center." Hauerwas, *Work of Theology*, 25. While it may be true that there is no predetermined center in the form of a systematic structure, there are certainly themes that come up more frequently and consistently than others. There are also themes, such a racism, that are strangely absent from his work. I will critique Hauerwas later for the paucity of discussion of racial injustice. Of course, Hauerwas might reply that he has simply responded to requests. This is true in part, but on many occasions he has taken a request to address a particular topic, and reframed it or reoriented it in a direction that he views as more important to address at that moment. In this he shows himself to not be fully limited by limited requests.

52. I originally wrote "foundational assumption" but then thought that might insert unnecessary confusion given Hauerwas's non-foundationalism. Of course, he *does* have a foundation—it is just the church, rather than some allegedly a-theological, universally verifiable foundation.

53. Wells's thesis #10 on Hauerwas's work states: "It is not possible to separate Jesus from Israel." Wells, "Difference Christ Makes," 16–17.

54. This final phrase needs reconsidering. Katongole states, "What is perhaps even more problematic about the posture of fideism (e.g., Barth's and Kierkegaard's unapologetic theology) is a form of faith-foundationalism. As foundationalism, fideism shares the formal strategy of reason-foundationalism of the classical rationalists (deism and liberal Protestantism). Both classical rationalists and fideists respond to the

for the purpose of providing the means for theology understood outside the church, but is the necessary location of that theology. He writes,

> We assume that—no matter how orthodox it may be—theology divorced from the practices of the church cannot help but be ideology. In short, all theology must begin and end with ecclesiology. The very assumption that theology could be an autonomous discipline done for anyone was the result of Constantinian Christianity, which assumed that what Christians believe, anyone would believe on reflection. We decisively reject that presumption, believing as we do that theology cannot escape into "thought" but remains rooted in the practices that constitute the church as a community across time.[55]

In this we see a critique not only of rootless theology but of the notion that such a theology—if it is to remain orthodox—is even possible. While this notion of "orthodox" so understood may need to be interrogated, Hauerwas would follow Katongole's assertion that this circularity is not vicious but hermeneutic. As such, orthodox is known only *in relation* to the community that determines what counts as orthodox. This discernment or regulation has happened through an array of practices, texts, and liturgies that, though originating in the church, now stand as a semi-autonomous (that is, self-supporting) rule for consideration of right belief and practice. Such a structure certainly *can* and often *does* contribute to the coercive muting of particular voices.[56] When, however, the practices are performed with openness to the Spirit, this process is far from static or simply determined to maintain the status quo. Of course, there is no unified body that legislates this for all Christians.[57]

---

dialectical challenge of modernity by constructing a foundation. They only differ both in materials they use to construct their foundations and whether people get access to that foundation basically through 'reason' or 'faith.'" Katongole, *Beyond Universal Reason*, 184.

55. Hauerwas, *In Good Company*, 58.

56. These concerns are woven into the institutional and corporate memory of Anabaptist bodies that are part of an ecclesial stream variously considered to be heretical, dangerous, suspicious, or peculiar.

57. I purchased Wesley Granberg-Michaelson's *From Times Square to Timbuktu: The Post-Christian West Meets the Non-Western Church* at the 10th World Assembly of the World Council of Churches in Busan, South Korea. While an older ecumenical body, the WCC includes fewer than 350 of the 40,000 or so denominations in the world. Many of the member communions are much larger and more established than many non-WCC members, but the non-legislating nature of the WCC, as well as the breadth of the rest of the Christian world, means that even such a venerable institution cannot enforce particular standards.

Hauerwas's theology aims to be Christocentric, critically linked to the church, and necessarily nonviolent. These three components cannot be understood in isolation, but are fundamentally linked in the life of the church. In his view, then, theology cannot be done apart from ecclesiology. I turn now to a closer examination of Hauerwas's ecclesiology. I will propose several themes and characteristics of his work while also considering how he goes about describing the church.

Hauerwas's Ecclesiology

Introduction

All of Hauerwas's theology attempts to be in relation to the church or to reflect on how it *should* be in relation to the church.[58] As such, his ecclesiology and ecclesiological assumptions are either explicitly or implicitly related to his other areas of focus. Various reflections on or around the church are arguably the organizing framework of his work[59]—although asserting an overarching system to Hauerwas's work is somewhat problematic given his organizational and (anti-) methodological stances.[60] Nonetheless, the church is either assumed or named in nearly all his writing. Even without explicitly saying so, Hauerwas writes for the church in such a way that the church, and thus ecclesiology, is never far away.[61] He challenges the idea that the church can be known apart from its actions, practices, and material presence.[62]

Hauerwas asserts that the church cannot be known abstractly but rather by what it does. While I posit that Hauerwas prioritizes *doing*

---

58. This strong first statement can be somewhat qualified by asserting that this has shifted during Hauerwas's decades of writing. Early on a more general account of "community" was present. This "community" was not, however, distinct from the church; the framing was simply a marginally more general conception of community.

59. Hawksley, *Ecclesiology of Stanley Hauerwas*, 5.

60. Hauerwas has said, "Thus my observation: if you think you need a theory of truth to underwrite the conviction that Jesus was raised from the dead, then worship that theory—not Jesus." Hauerwas, *Cross-Shattered Church*, 144. His "methodology," then, is more a commitment to continual but non-systematized reflection rather than a strictly delineated method.

61. Hawksley, *Ecclesiology of Stanley Hauerwas*, 13.

62. To the question "Where is this church you describe?" Hauerwas notes churches and examples that otherwise do not seem particularly remarkable (*Hannah's Child*, 221, 254).

and *being*, this is roughly parallel to his writing on the individual level of virtue.[63] Much of his work on virtue is modeled after apprenticeship in which one learns on the job from a master practitioner.[64] In the case of virtue, it is not simply getting the action correct, but also the internal disposition and motivation, and the way the action is done.

This is parallel to Hauerwas's thinking on the church. Here, the discussion of the relationship between theology and ethics is at the forefront. Hauerwas rejects the notion of setting a condition from which another condition or action arises. He continually attacks the notion that one can or needs to get one's theology straight before moving to ethics.[65] This plays out in particularly interesting ways in his formulations of "the political" and the church as political.

The Political Body

The church, according to Hauerwas, is a political body. "The political novelty that God brings into the world," he states, "is a community of those who serve instead of ruling, who suffer instead of inflicting suffering, whose fellowship crosses social lines instead of reinforcing them. The new Christian community in which walls are broken down not by human idealism or democratic legalism but by the work of Christ is not only a vehicle of the gospel or the fruit of the gospel; it is the gospel."[66]

This "political novelty" points to an assumption in which *political* would seem to indicate that the church will be engaged in public life in some manner. In Hauerwas's thought, indeed, even in this quote, the "politics/political" he envisions is not a politics based on issues of governance, violence, money, or popularity. Cavanaugh takes this point further, writing,

---

63. Though virtue is primarily present in the body of the individual, Hauerwas would assert that it remains a community endeavor. Hauerwas affirms a comment to this effect by Jennifer Herdt. Hauerwas, *Approaching the End*, 163. Jennifer Herdt's comment is found in "Virtue of Liturgy," 536–37.

64. Hauerwas, *Approaching the End*, 161.

65. In this, his view is similar to McClendon's in *Systematic Theology: Ethics*. Hauerwas comments on this in discussion of seminary curriculum: "The assumption, for example, that students should take 'systematic theology' before they take ethics invites the presumption that theology is in some sense more basic than ethics." Hauerwas, "How 'Christian Ethics' Came to Be," 47.

66. Hauerwas, *War and the American Difference*, 167.

> The eschatological "not yet" means that history of the drama so far needs to be told hopefully but penitentially, with room for marginal voices and conflicts. The story is not told in an epic manner, as if the church were made to rule. As the embodiment of God's politics, the church nevertheless muddles through. God is in charge of all of history. The church's job is to try to discern in each concrete circumstance how best to embody the politics of the cross in a suffering world.[67]

In urging embodied politics, Hauerwas challenges the notion that politics only happens in the capital city. What should be noted is that though public policy recommendations by the church are not the *sole* role of the church, this form of work is nonetheless important.[68] People often seem to assume that there is a sharp division between local ministry and service and what goes on in the Washington DC political scene.[69] And some appear to think that there is no ambiguity in working for the state, as if one's narrow role is not contributing to the larger whole,[70] which in the case of the US is an empire with designs on hegemony. I take Hauerwas to often sound more ambivalent than he is on the manner of political engagement. His projected ambivalence seeks to break American Christians free of the idolatry of the state. While strongly affirming local "politics" of the congregation, he assumes that the church will collaborate with others on larger issues but will not wholly buy into a particular movement.[71] So while the church and Christians are engaged in public life, there remains a primacy of the church and a hesitation or tentativeness

---

67. Cavanaugh, "Church," 405.

68. On a number of occasions Hauerwas has made brief remarks indicating his assumption that such engagement will happen.

69. Being a pastor at a local congregation on Capitol Hill within sight of the United States Capitol and living in a neighborhood not far away forces the qualifier "political scene" since there is much more to Washington DC than Congress, the State Department, or the Pentagon (which incidentally is not in the District of Columbia proper).

70. Yoder makes the point that the early church could work for the government or even military because not all facets were involved in violence. This, however, requires limited participation. In Hauerwas's interpretation, Yoder asserts that to assume the options are either "unqualified support" or "no participation" is to misunderstand the relationship. Though this is the position of the Church of the Brethren, I remain unconvinced, however, that such discrimination is likely or that the barriers between various parts of the military are as impermeable as this implies such that participation in one part is separate from other parts.

71. In this, greater discussion by Hauerwas on how this plays out on the street would be useful.

towards nation-state politics. Hauerwas would be in general agreement with Marsha Aileen Hewitt when she states:

> The term "political theology" is by its nature ambiguous and potentially misleading, for at least two main reasons. The first rests on the assumption that there is something distinctive or uniquely different about a theology that is "political," as if some or most theology were not in any case "political," the idea that theology is apolitical is blind to the inner contradiction between repressive and emancipator impulses within theology that become visible through critical self-reflection. It ignores the fact that theology, like all cultural forms and theories, is mediated through human action and experience, generating its own forms of social organization and power hierarchies, and is thus inevitably political.[72]

As Hewitt says, theology is necessarily political rather than political being the exception (with exceptions being politics being the specific topic of reflection or theology being a tool for mobilization).[73] Political in this use is not, however, the tool of a political party.[74] This is at least partly in opposition to conventional uses of "political." While preparing for a session entitled "Congregation as Site of Public Witness" at the Church of the Brethren's 2016 Annual Conference, I began to wonder if the insistence of using "political" as a descriptor by theologians such as Hauerwas may be a less effective tactic in non-academic conversations with Christians and ministers. If theology is for Christians in churches and "political" is not a theologically necessary term, then energy expended to

---

72. Hewitt, "Critical Theory," 455.

73. "In one way or another, all political theologies at the end of the twentieth century can be read as so many attempts to come to grips with the death of Christendom without simply acquiescing in the privatization of the church. Nevertheless, Christian political theology has strangely neglected the topic of church." Cavanaugh, "Church," 393. In this Cavanaugh is commenting on theologies that are specifically and intentionally *political* theologies. Hauerwas asserts that all theology is political. Of course, he would also strongly criticize much of the church for buying into the "Enlightenment assumption" that religion is private, thus surrendering space to the nation-state. As such Hauerwas seems to assert that all theology *has the potential* to be political or that it is *in fact* political just not always recognized. The latter of these is closer to his position, which may be analogous to an eschatological present but not yet.

74. How to engage without fully engaging is not fully clear. Likely this is where the discerning community and practical reason would come into play. See Ryan, *Politics of Practical Reason*, and De La Torre, "The Hermeneutical Circle for Ethics" in De La Torre, *Doing Christian Ethics from the Margins*.

re-imagine this word may be better used to describe the ways the church can be more outwardly oriented without reference to the word "politics." Of course, some of the church's work may indeed be in reference to politics as contained in capitals, governance, laws, taxes, campaigns, and policy. If this approach were to be taken then perhaps "public" is a more helpful term to explore in congregations. This is, of course, not taking into account distinctions between public and political theologies—which would also be largely irrelevant descriptors for those who are not specialists in such distinctions. Hunter notes that, "As with the Christian Right and Christian Left, the neo-Anabaptists make no distinction between the public and the political. Indeed, Cavanaugh argues that many efforts to distinguish the public from the political fail because so much of the public is subsumed by the state—its laws, policies, and other instrumentalities."[75]

Hewitt goes on to note that both critical theory and political theology hesitate to align too closely with concrete programs or movements:

> Strategic politics are constructed on ideological scaffoldings that do not easily tolerate too much critical self-reflection, which is understandable from a *strategic* point of view. Ideologies and their adherents tend to demand and enforce conformity, marginalizing or obliterating dissent for the sake of preserving their goals. The logical and inherent tendency of ideology is to curb critique rather than cultivate it, with the result that its underlying premises and values cannot be subject to serious critical scrutiny from within or without. Ideology is not universal, but rather is a set of ideas that corresponds to a particular set of social relationships and cultural forms. In this sense, ideology regulates not only human action, but also *what can be thought.* The critical theorists knew this, which is another reason why they refused to align themselves with social programs or political movements.[76]

For Hauerwas, there is a diminished line between politics and theology and a notable hesitation to align with particular movements as well as broader non-church political commitments or theories (stating the church does not have a political theory). Arne Rasmusson compares what he calls political theology with theological politics, attributing political theology to Moltmann and theological politics to Hauerwas. He

75. Hunter, *To Change the World*, 163.
76. Hewitt, "Critical Theory," 464.

observes Moltmann endorsing social and political movements while Hauerwas is much more circumspect and oriented toward the church.[77] For Hauerwas a role of theology is criticism,[78] in much the same way Hewitt describes critical theory.[79] Another, perhaps primary, task is formation. This formation is a politics but is not typically aligned with a particular political party or movement. Virtue is embodied in the church and Scriptures.[80] Hauerwas gets at a description of church-politics in the following passage:

> Ministers should be the most political of animals because, in contrast to much of what passes as politics in our time, those in ministry cannot help but be about the formation of people who can know they need one another to survive. To ask those in ministry to take seriously your political responsibilities may well entail a radical reorientation of what those in ministry do. That is particularly true if you believe as I do that we are living at the end of Christendom.[81]

Hauerwas's work maintains a significant focus on the formation of Christians as well as the political significance of the church.[82] Samuel

---

77. "Moltmann's political theology makes the politics of the world primary. The consequence is that political issues he discusses are already given by the social and political conflicts of the contemporary world. The question becomes on which side the church should be on. In contrast, Hauerwas's theological politics makes the church the primary locus for its politics." Rasmusson, *Church as Polis*, 331.

78. Hauerwas engages Yoder on social criticism in "The Nonresistant Church," in *Vision and Virtue*, 216–18.

79. This is similar to Yoder who asserted, according to Carter, that "The witness [to the state] is *ad hoc* in four ways: in the sense of not being systematic, in the sense of dealing with only one issue at a time, in the sense of usually taking a negative form, and in the sense of arising out of its own life as example." Carter, *Politics of the Cross*, 209.

80. How is this simply not another party, which is theocratic? If it is not a party, then how is it not simply the formation of disparate individuals? To this question I imagine Hauerwas would say that it *is* like a political party—one that has refused violence and models another way rather than seizing power.

81. Hauerwas, *Work of Theology*, 113.

82. Describing Hauerwas on this topic, Reno writes, "Christian power meets resistance. Being trained through Jesus' story means adopting the practices and habits of a new city, and this cannot help but create a conflict between the church and the world, for the world seeks to put us to its own malign purposes. A great deal of Hauerwas's work focuses on particular scenes of this conflict, which are many. Materially, this diversity of conflict is unified under a general scheme of violence and peace. Worldly powers, for Hauerwas, are not the most visible and potent in injustice or oppression.

Wells maps a trajectory through Hauerwas's early work on character through virtue, narrative, community, and church. These themes emerge as ways to address challenges that arise out of his earlier account of ethics. In fact, they are listed in a generally chronological manner related to the development of Hauerwas's thinking. While it is not the case that each theme is strictly limited to a period of writing, the particular terminology of character as an early topic fades from his usage or morphs into consideration of virtue. I will now turn to the formative and political facets in the closer consideration of worship, moral formation in liturgy, and witness.

Ad Hoc Approach

Hauerwas does not orient himself in relation to the field of ecclesiology in general but rather engages specific themes, writers, and events that could be viewed as being within the scope of ecclesiology. He does not engage in any sustained way with particular themes or writers that would typically be included within a discussion of ecclesiology. Much of his work is occasional essays in response to a request to speak or a specific work. In these instances, his work is in opposition to or in response to an event or work (e.g., United Methodist Bishops' statement on nuclear weapons).[83] To do this Hauerwas draws on a range of sources from Catholic and Anabaptist theology to the philosophies of Wittgenstein and social theorists. This eclectic approach likely arises in part from the primacy of his commitment to the church rather than to an academic discipline. Because of this, he is uninterested in furthering any academic discipline

---

Instead, worldly powers show their true face in the presumptive necessity of violence. Secular power must threaten in order to be effective. In contrast, the defining practice of the church is peace-making, and precisely because of this, the density of the church necessarily collides with the social 'realities' that require menace in order to maintain power." Reno, "Hauerwas," 310.

83. In a review of *The Work of Theology*, Sarah Morice Brubaker observes that Hauerwas disproportionally engages with white male writers. She notes that though the academic fields that Hauerwas primarily engages are disproportionately white and male, his citations and interlocutors are even more disproportionately represented than these fields. Brubaker, "*Work of Theology*, by Stanley Hauerwas." Because Hauerwas reads and responds widely, this skewed engagement is even more notable. Gloria Albrecht provides an important challenge to Hauerwas's seeming hyper-awareness of social location (or at least his making much of being from Texas) and his seeming obliviousness to his particular social location. Albrecht, *Character of Our Communities*.

in particular. The *ad hoc* nature of this tactic makes it difficult to summarize and situate his work within the broader field. Here as elsewhere, I will seek to allow the shape of Hauerwas's work to remain visible while examining it in relation to that of others.

Though Hauerwas speaks forcefully in a way that seems to assume commitment to the authority structures of the church, he himself seems bound only by the local congregation or the broader church tradition and history rather than within one set of ecclesial structures from one denomination or communion.[84] In *Approaching the End*, he attempts to address the question of why he has not engaged in official ecumenical dialogue spaces given his concern for the unity of the church. In this book, he states that his bigger goal is to change the questions rather than assume that ecumenism as defined by formal institutional channels is how the work is necessarily done.[85] In this, however, as in a number of other topics, he skirts the issue and answers a different question. Douglas Gay writes,

> It is however, undoubtedly one of the most fascinating things about his work for many who read him and arguably has strong resonances for a third or fourth "ecumenical generation" audience in the churches, who have strong "post-denominational" instincts. While he is deeply concerned about disunity within the church, he has little to do with formal ecumenical activities, acting more as an ecumenical entrepreneur—setting up unscheduled meetings and forming unholy alliances without waiting for ecumenical protocols to give him permission.[86]

Hauerwas does not intentionally or extensively align himself within the ecclesiological debates at large.[87] Rather, he pulls out particular

---

84. It has been noted that though he makes strong claims of the church and not the university being a place of non-policed thought he has functioned almost exclusively within and supported by the university.

85. This approach mirrors in a way the interim report of 21st Century Ecumenism Committee report of the Church of the Brethren's 2016 Annual Conference. In it they observe that much of the energy and action in ecumenical action now happens at the local level. See "Unfinished Business."

86. Gay, *Practical Theology of Church and World*, 48–49.

87. "I should also acknowledge that I was never particularly interested in the movements concerned with the institutional unity of mainstream Protestant denominations. I am not sure why I was uninterested in those attempts to overcome theological and ecclesial differences in the past, but I must admit that I just did not see any reason to think, for example, that the joining of mainstream American denominations

strands as useful. For example, he draws on the work of John Howard Yoder when framing discussions of the broader purposes and life of the church, but not on the quintessential Anabaptist topic of baptism. Rather than engage in ecumenical discussions seeking to produce a common understanding of the practices of the Eucharist or baptism, he is more likely to discuss how baptism interacts with political understandings and practice.[88] And though Christian unity is a central concern, he does not enter into more official ecumenical dialogues or other more formal deliberations such as those resulting in the World Council of Churches paper on *Baptism, Eucharist, and Ministry*.[89]

Later in the same chapter, however, he asserts that in the new context of reduced social and political power of the church, theology must be done from below. "In particular," he states, "I suspect that theology needs to be much more concrete and specific. When you are in survival mode you do not need an 'atonement theory' if you take seriously that through the church, and in particular the Eucharist, we are made participants in Christ's very life. In such a circumstance churches may well discover that what was thought to be church dividing turns out to be less significant than they thought."[90] This position of minimal social and political power has been the reality for many Anabaptist groups throughout history. As generally marginal ecclesial communities that were at times brutally repressed by both other churches and various governments, these groups often developed theology and practice from reading the Bible as a community rather than through highly educated theologians or church structures.[91] It is not clear how Hauerwas's two statements relate. While it

---

would be interesting from a theological point of view. I suspected that the theological differences that were once thought so important that they could not be compromised in the interest of unity, only to be considered later to be no obstacle to the merger of churches, meant that these were churches that had given up the importance of theology for discerning what we believe to be true." Hauerwas, *Approaching the End*, 101.

88. Consideration of ecumenism a mode of Hauerwas's peacemaking will be considered at the end of chapter 5.

89. See "Baptism, Eucharist, and Ministry."

90. Hauerwas, *Approaching the End*, 119. It could be suggested that Hauerwas's engagement with Anabaptist and peace church theologies influences him toward the concrete. For while these churches originated in Europe and then migrated to the North America, they grew (at least initially) on the margins. This marginal status created a greater need for thinking concretely.

91. On a different theological topic (Christocentric hermeneutic) but making the same point, Boyd writes, "Indeed, we will see that certain Anabaptist leaders were moving in this direction, though their wrestling with violent divine portraits remained

may be the case that the possibility of ecumenical unity at the structural level is more likely because of a general dismissal of the importance of theology through disinterestedness that is corrosive to witness, this leaves unanswered, why this disinterestedness? If it is in fact because Christians have simply gotten over arguing for points against one another and are now ready to recognize their essential unity, then the loss may only be in the assumed value of academic theologians. If this disinterest is a result of essential unity it would also seem to challenge his comments on the importance of theology and theological education and the role of theologians,[92] for certainly a "theologian on staff" at either a university or church presumes a level of luxury beyond survival.[93] Even if one were to say that such a role is not necessarily a staff position, the typical practice of seven years to get through university and then seminary or even more for a PhD is a luxury that assumes a number of social contexts. Mennonite theologian Thomas Finger notes,

> Eventually, survival often came to depend on cultural isolation, sometimes under overlords who offered protection in exchange for clearing swamps and forests and then farming. Gradually these descendants, mostly called Mennonites, won respect for their practical Christianity: their industry, thrift, honesty, and increasingly their pacifism. Relatively few, though, attained more than a practical literacy. Many of their writings—sermons, letters, devotional thoughts—were unsophisticated and occasional.[94]

This quote perhaps takes us even further and we should observe that the question of unity on the national/international/denominational level is a question of such privilege that asking it isolates one from the vast majority of "embedded" congregational theological reflection. In this respect,

---

underdeveloped owing to the intense persecution they suffered." Boyd, *Crucifixion of the Warrior God*, 95.

92. Hauerwas notes in "Communitarians and Medical Ethicists: or 'Why I am None of the Above,'" that "No one anymore really believes that an incompetently trained priest might threaten his or her salvation, since no one really believes that anything is at stake in salvation; but people do think that an incompetently trained doctor might in fact do them serious harm." Hauerwas, *Dispatches from the Front*.

93. Historically, for the Church of the Brethren, even a paid pastor was unusual. As churches have diminished in size in the last decades, this practice of not having a paid pastor is now reoccurring.

94. Finger, *Contemporary Anabaptist Theology*, 10.

Hauerwas's aloofness feels artificially dismissive because of disinterest, and would likely appear glaringly elitist to much of the global church.[95]

Hauerwas's work is simultaneously very concrete and disengaged from typical "practical" questions.[96] This is, in fact, part of my critique of his work on peacemaking that will be discussed in chapters 4 and 5. For all his talk about practices and embodiment, Hauerwas's assistance in the practicalities of peacemaking and nonviolence is notably thin. His approach is to consider the fundamental assumptions that undergird practices, but not propose a detailed implementation. In this, his work is more political philosophy than a how-to manual. In response to a pastor's urging him to be more concrete in *The Work of Theology*, Hauerwas asks, "What are you waiting for? If you think the Christian people should be against war you need to think about how to preach that. If you think the church needs to be distinct, what does that mean for your budget?"[97] Hauerwas may feel that this does not fit within his ecclesial vocation of theologian. In this view, the pastor or person working in the congregation might be the correct person to explore practical implications. A second possibility could be that he believes any attempt to describe how a particular point of theology may play out in a congregation must be so generic as to render the exercise more or less meaningless. It could even be argued that such a practice would actually be detrimental to the degree that it limits in some contexts what might be actionable in other contexts. This could be why Hauerwas occasionally describes and re-describes theologically a particular community but shies away from general prescriptions. In this, Hauerwas practices observation similar to the "supernatural sociology" described by Izuzuquiza.[98]

---

95. Such a statement though moves closer to the arguments for Christians to be "responsible" and engage in X political/public activity. While I certainly think certain types of engagement are critical (it is officially in my job description to work to further develop the Church of the Brethren's "public witness"), this gets at the need to question assumptions around who defines "responsible" and how such work is carried out or what it entails. Being "responsible" either in the broader public life or ecumenical discussions does not mean that all forms of participation must be embraced at all times.

96. Douglas Gay asserts, "What is most distinctive about Hauerwas's approach is that he takes three central questions of the European Enlightenment—how do we know, how should we live and how should the world be organized politically—and argues that the church is central to how these questions are to be answered." Hauerwas, "Practical Theology of Church and World," 8.

97. Hauerwas, *Work of Theology*, 120.

98. "Milbank has effectively argued, social sciences and methodological strategies are not neutral. If we can still use those sciences, we cannot do so in a naïve way.

Hauerwas claims a connection to Anabaptists as noted in chapter one. In particular, he has been shaped by reading John Howard Yoder. From this reading he has claimed to be a "high church Mennonite."[99] In addition to not being part of an actual Mennonite community, his method is different from many Anabaptist communities because of the breadth of his sources. Many Mennonite theologians might consult a similar breadth of sources, but such persons are Mennonite more because of their participation in a Mennonite community than because of the books they read.[100] As such, the ecclesial identity of *Mennonite* is prior to the theological vocation. In this, Hauerwas's challenge to university theologians writing for other theologians becomes relevant.[101] For example, his use of Aristotle and MacIntyre to sustain an account of virtue appears to be a variation of the traditional Anabaptist vision of discipleship. Anabaptist thinking on discipleship, however, emerged from the community reading together and in order to follow Jesus rather than from a theory or philosophy.[102] This may be why some find Yoder to be groundbreaking, but I thought on my first read that he was simply straightforward.[103]

Supernatural sociology will tend to privilege some methods over others (for example, qualitative methods will usually be more fruitful than quantitative ones). Likewise, it will privilege some approaches that the dominant discourse tends to discard (for example participatory action-research)." Izuzquiza, *Rooted in Jesus Christ*, 60.

99. Hauerwas often says, "I am a high church Mennonite, which makes me Methodist." In explanation, he states: "For I believe Methodism had the potential to be the form of evangelical Catholicism that maintained such continuity with the great confessions of the church because such confessions are integral to sustaining a disciplined community capable of living as a free church." See "Whose Church? Which Future? Whither the Anabaptist Vision?" in Hauerwas, *Church as Polis*, 66.

100. Gregory Boyd is one pastor who has claimed to be Anabaptist. See Boyd, *Crucifixion of the Warrior God*, 15.

101. In an instance where he allows that theologians may write for theologians, he still asserts that theological writing cannot only be addressed to other theologians: "Too often specialized vocabularies are used to intimidate anyone who is not an academic theologian. There is a place for theologians to write primarily for other theologians, but if theology is genuinely a church discipline I do not see how it can be so restricted." Hauerwas, "How to Be Theologically Ironic," 148.

102. In chapter 13 of *Covenant of Peace*, Mennonite scholar Willard Swartley lays out a New Testament engagement of discipleship and imitation of Jesus.

103. I first read Yoder as an undergraduate at Moody Bible Institute, while studying with Professor Michael McDuffie. Having grown up in an evangelical Church of the Brethren congregation and served with Eastern Mennonite Mission, both the assumption of Christian nonviolence based on the Bible and the outward mission orientation of the church were part of my basic assumptions.

Yoder's work feels rather traditional for some, but others have found his work provocative and a generative conversation partner.[104] In *Waiting for Godot in Sarajevo*, David Toole considers Yoder alongside Foucault as an example of postcritical theology.[105] This raises the question of the intention of Yoder (and Hauerwas) as well as how this relates to the larger tradition, both the body as a whole and ministers. This consideration is of particular importance for ministers. The Anabaptist traditions were largely marginal. While not always actively oppressed, they, as well as their ministers, tended to be rural, residing outside the social and academic centers of power.[106] If Yoder is taken up by postcritical theorists, is he treated as an outsider or as part of their inquiry? If as an outsider, is this because he occupies a space similar to these Anabaptist ministers who have been socially marginal? If this is the case, it would be more accurate to describe him as *pre* rather than *post* critical, or at least representative of such a group. A further question is whether these postcritical writers are using him coercively or ironically?[107]

104. See Dula and Huebner, *New Yoder*.

105. The opening note on the series *Radical Traditions: Theology in a Postcritical Key*, which includes *Waiting for Godot*, states, "Far from despairing over modernity's failings, postcritical theologies rediscover resources for renewal and self-correction within the disciplines of academic study themselves. Postcritical theologies open up the possibility of participating once again in the living relationship that binds together God, text, and community of interpretation. *Radical Traditions* thus advocates for a 'return to the text,' which means a commitment to displaying the richness and wisdom of traditions that are at once text based, hermeneutical, and oriented to communal practice." Toole, *Waiting for Godot in Sarajevo*.

106. In the Church of the Brethren before 1950, most "free" ministers had eight or fewer years of formal education. Fitzkee, *Moving Toward the Mainstream*, 70.

107. Peter Dula and Christ Huebner discuss this usage by "New Yoder" scholarship in the introduction to *The New Yoder*. They note that this new work rarely engages with Yoder's sources of Scripture and sixteenth-century Anabaptism (xix). So, if it is true as they note earlier (xvii) that Yoder demonstrated that Anabaptists were "one of the original colonial others" and that his work comes out of this context rather than philosophical work, then the question arises, why do these writers feel justified in "using" Yoder for their own ends apart from what he intends?

Obviously, Yoder himself, as a white male North American, European-educated polylingual professor, was not remotely the epitome of marginalization; however, the usage seems suspect given the stated commitments of such post-colonialist writers. Hauerwas notes of using Yoder, "That someone like Coles, a political theorist, can write so insightfully about Yoder makes clear that Yoder is beginning to have an effect in the 'wider world.' That 'effect,' as these essays exemplify, is to show that Yoder cannot be understood as a 'representative Mennonite' because the politics of Jesus is not something peculiar to Mennonites or even Christians." See the Introduction in

Determining Hauerwas's relation to the Anabaptist community matters, in part, because of his ecclesiological commitment to being embedded in an actual church community. While I do not need to push this question very far, I note it simply to emphasize that to "be" Anabaptist—or Mennonite or Brethren (the latter having historically referred to themselves at times as a "peculiar people")—requires more than simple affirmation of a distinctive practice or doctrine. This is relevant to clarifying what it means to be part of the community and is a part of asking what the community is and what action is part of it. This is where the issue of ecclesiology leaves the academy and is evidenced in church practice.

In an essay considering Bender's "Anabaptist Vision," Hauerwas writes, "For example, 'voluntary church membership' was a prophetic challenge against mainstream Christianity, but once Christendom is gone the call for voluntary commitment cannot help but appear as a legitimation of the secular commitment to autonomy . . . That is why I emphasize the importance of practices, which may of course involve 'doctrine' as well as 'called membership,' since practices provide the material specifications that help us resist the endemic character of modernity, bent as it is on turning faith into just another idea."[108] This approach of apparent appropriation but at times reworking of the idea of practice beyond the original idea is somewhat curious. For Hauerwas, on many occasions, has written that the purpose of theology and the role of the theologian are not to innovate but to faithfully pass on.[109] The dramatic reworking, which at times seems to render the idea wholly different, seems to belie this claim. It appears at times that an ecclesial identity or parts of a tradition are taken up simply to make a larger theological point.[110] Additionally, as

---

Hauerwas, *Mind Patient and Untamed*, 12. I find this statement curious and incongruent with other assertions of non-universality by Hauerwas. This may be part of Hauerwas's claim that while we cannot simply state a universal or assume it, we may find interesting connections once we start to interact.

108. Hauerwas, *In Good Company*, 73.

109. "Whatever else might be said about Hauerwas's understanding of tradition, it is never a cozy, uncritical, and 'faithful' passing on of a 'deposit' or form of life. On the contrary, any adequate tradition 'must accept *creative tension* to be a permanent feature of its way of life.'" Katongole, *Beyond Universal Reason*, 150.

110. As an aside, one may raise the following question: Does Hauerwas form part of the Anabaptist tradition? One cannot be part of Anabaptist ecclesiology without being part of an actual community of practice. However, it is not clear what it might mean to define a community as Anabaptist. One option is that this designation could be reserved for congregations that are part of denominations that historically emerged from Anabaptist movements and which actively presently embrace the label of

Katongole observes, there are times when Hauerwas takes on an element of a writer's position seemingly without significant examination.[111] This somewhat erratic approach is a feature of his intentionally nonsystematic approach to theology.

By asserting a Christological ethic of nonviolence at the center of the church, Hauerwas is claiming that nonviolence is central to theology, that ethics are formed around Jesus, and that nonviolence in the church must be lived and results in peacemaking. Such an ecclesiology relies on actual communities to produce not only the body but the reflection.[112] These foci, learned from Yoder, make Yoder's history of sexual violence a devastating self-critique.[113] This is also why Sarah Morice Brubaker's

---

Anabaptist. There are, however, many congregations, which, though formally within these historical structures, do not embrace the moniker Anabaptist either as a name or in their practices. In the reverse, there are congregations that embrace these practices but are not rooted in the historical ecclesial stream that bears the label. To further complicate things there are those individuals who embrace Anabaptist values and practices and aspire to these for their congregation or denomination but this aspiration is not mutual. Additionally, since Anabaptist ecclesiology is made up of several practices that are not uniform across historically Anabaptist bodies, many individuals and churches may embrace only a subset of these. At a minimum, Anabaptists historically were those who practiced adult baptism and not infant baptism. This might be considered a cornerstone practice, except that there are presently a host of other bodies that rely on adult rather than infant baptism and do not also carry other "typical" traits, such as nonviolence or minimal formal hierarchy. Hauerwas as an individual embraces some of these and has been substantially influenced by the work of a theologian from within the historical Anabaptist stream.

111. "Perhaps what should be noted here is that this failure may point to a general limitation within Hauerwas's work. His readiness to claim affinity with other authors, but without engaging their work in sufficient detail, may leave him open to the charge of eclecticism. Moreover, by not taking time to critically engage these adopted positions, he risks inadvertently bringing on board aspects that sit uneasily with his own positions." Katongole, *Beyond Universal Reason*, 178.

112. Kallenberg writes, "Hauerwas's failure to accommodate liberals by translating the gospel into terms they can already understand is not an instance of fideism because the gospel can be more powerfully and clearly displayed in the actual life of the church, enculturation into which constitutes the whole salvation. Of course, the absence of such a church would severely weaken Hauerwas's position." Kallenberg, *Ethics as Grammar*, 159.

113. Though Yoder's sexual exploitation and misconduct with women over the years does not form a significant part of my discussion, it is undeniable that his behavior undercuts the credibility of his work. In many ways, his actions seem to belie his work on nonviolence, ethics, accountability and community. This raises a dilemma: Yoder's actions undercut his work, but this work has been very valuable for theology, theological ethics, ethics, and peacemaking. This opens up many significant questions

review of Hauerwas's *The Work of Theology* is so biting.[114] For all Hauerwas's talk of friendship as a major theme within the church, his neglect of extensive engagement with writings outside his white maleness calls his work into question. A fundamental characteristic of Anabaptist thought is that it is never just a *thought* but also a community. This community includes the work of those tasked with reflecting on both the text and the community.

The facets of the Anabaptist communities' ecclesiology emerge from their joint reading of Scripture in relation to particular historical and ecclesial contexts. Anabaptist ecclesiology is less an overarching theory that holds the community together than a set of practices developed from within the community. *Recovering the Love Feast: Broadening our Eucharistic Celebrations*, by Church of the Brethren pastor Paul Fike Stutzman, is one such work. This work anchors the "Love Feast" in the New Testament and church history and shows how this practice helps to form the community.

For Anabaptists, ecclesiology is "low" in the sense of elaborate and vertical church hierarchy. The place of the church in both theology and practice is quite high; the church is, in fact, the central location of the experience of God. Whereas for some Christians, the celebration happens at the point of the Eucharist, for Anabaptists it is in the meeting of the community. This is in conscious reflection on Jesus's words, "Where two or three are gathered, I am in their midst" (Matt 18:20). Thomas Finger notes, "Since the church heralds the new creation's fullness, Anabaptists can call it, with liberation theologians, an eschatological sacrament: a visible, present sign of what God finally desires for all humanity."[115] The community then embodies its theology and practices. Peacemaking is one such practice, and will be addressed at length in chapter 4. While the discussion of Hauerwas's relationship to Anabaptists may simply be a question of formal membership, it is more relevant as a consideration

---

as to the basis of authority in theology and ethics and in the church, and how much this relates to the character and actions of the writer. Given Yoder's positions, one would say that this connection is important. My basic approach is as follows: 1) processes of accountability and conciliation should happen within the academy and churches in which these abuses occurred; 2) the writings penned by John Howard Yoder are not "Yoder's work" but the property of the broader church; and 3) insofar as this work remains a fruitful source for continued reflection it should be used with due recognition of the ambivalence of the legacy of Yoder's actions.

114. Brubaker, "*Work of Theology.*"
115. Finger, *Contemporary Anabaptist Theology*, 253.

of Hauerwas's assertions of material/embodied/lived ecclesiology and his participation and relation to actual historically contingent church bodies. Given Hauerwas's strong critiques of subtle forms of liberalism, nationalism, and other alleged theological blunders, his participation in particular practices or institutions is significant.

As noted earlier, Hauerwas does not establish an overarching ecclesiology but assumes the centrality of the church. He emphasizes several themes throughout his work. These include *worship, witness, a church with a history, a distinct community/peculiar people,* and *a peacemaking community.*

Worship

Hauerwas places the life of the church, particularly core practices of worship, at the center of his ecclesiology. He frames the church as a *political body*, and in this gathered community, worship is central.[116] It is simultaneously training through repetition and the sending and embodiment of peace.[117] Through worship, which is necessarily about God and not people, the church is re-formed in a politics which comprehensively reframes the world (including the church).[118] Hauerwas asserts that beauty

---

116. "Worship is the time when God trains his people to imitate him in habit, instinct, and reflex... The people who expect God to communicate in worship learn to discern his voice in in the shopping queue or the news bulletin... Above all, worship trains God's people to be examples of what his love can do. Worshiping God invites him to make the life of the disciple the theatre of his splendor." Hauerwas and Wells, "Gift of the Church," 25.

117. Hauerwas is similar to Yoder in the relationship between worship, ecclesiology, mission, and eschatology. According to J. Alexander Sider (*To See History Doxologically*, 195), "Yoder argued the Gospel as promise. That promise, to be led where Christ leads, is of its nature open-ended, such that Yoder did not picture eschatology as the closure of borders or, much less, the radical expansion of borders that assimilates otherness into the purity and unity of the holy city. Rather, Yoder though eschatology demanded the continual opening of the people of God onto new horizons of encounter with otherness—imitating the fusion of the Epistle to the Hebrews of the images of city and camp in the wilderness. Eschatology funds mission, being sent out in praise and with no other purpose than to go outside the camp. Eschatology does not mean that Christians, who believe in the last things know how to steer the course of history towards those last things."

118. In a response to a response to the 9/11 attacks, an "estranged friend recently wrote... that I disdain all 'natural loyalties... To this I can only answer, 'Yes.' If you call patriotism 'natural.'" Hauerwas, "September 11, 2001," 184.

In an essay considering this statement alongside Hauerwas's repeated references

is *necessary* for combating the trivial. If worship is to be significant, it must be beautiful.[119] This is naturally embedded within a narrative and is part of the ongoing story of the church. That beauty matters is simply an indication that worship matters.[120] The long process of forming and refining the language of reflection on God means that the Christian's language is made more significant.[121] As such, worship is not *for* the people but nevertheless does not leave them unchanged—or, perhaps, even unscathed.

While it is difficult and perhaps impossible to separate out liturgical moral formation from worship, I will make an attempt to do this below. Since worship is a fundamental piece of Hauerwas's ecclesiology, I include a description and analysis here. I address liturgical moral formation as part of "forming a peaceable body" in chapter 4. Though this division could be challenged, the formation of the peaceable body needs

---

to Pleasant Grove, his birthplace, Boersma writes, "I do not mean to suggest that a strict disavowal of natural loyalties is what's actually taking place in these memoirs. Stanley Hauerwas is and remains Hannah's child. He cannot—and I think he does not want to—escape the claim that God has laid on the realities of his mother's prayer, of the brick and mortar from his home town, and of the many ways in which Hauerwas, perhaps at times despite himself, has found something of a true home." Boersma, "Realizing Pleasant Grove," 314.

Hauerwas attempts to challenge what he perceives as American Christians' presumption of the primacy of national loyalty while also seeking to embed Christian existence within the materiality of the church and "normal" life. An Orthodox contribution from an ecumenical conference moves in the same direction: "The liturgy ... has the power to fashion us into persons who are able to recognize justice and injustice when we see it and to stimulate us to live justly, to denounce, diminish and even defeat injustice." Calivas, "Experiencing the Justice of God in Liturgy," 293.

119. Hauerwas, *Performing the Faith*, 161.

120. In *Enfleshing Freedom* (18), Copeland writes, "Beauty is consonant with human performance, with habit or virtue, with authentic ethics: Beauty is the living up to and living out the love and summons of creation in all our particularity and specificity as God's human creation in all our particularity and specificity as God's human creatures, made in God's own image and likeness." While affirming this strong place of beauty, saying, "Beauty nourishes and restores interiority and incites a longing for what is true," she asserts that this is weighed down by racial control. She writes, "But within a white, racially bias-induced horizon, such a depiction of beauty erases blackness; the black body *cannot* be beautiful. In this bias-induced horizon, the black body is repulsive, hideous; it encodes the demonic, the disposable, the lost, and the vacant." Though Copeland does not come into conflict with Hauerwas on the importance of beauty, she does challenge a claim that does not actively examine notions of beauty and who asserts them.

121. See Hauerwas, *Working With Words*, for a collection of experiments and reflections on "learning to speak Christian."

to be included in chapter 4 in order to adequately portray and assess Hauerwas's work on peacemaking.

Hauerwas is keen to oppose descriptions of worship that make a human-centered process central to the act of worship. He might, however, allow that a common good for the larger community is that in gathering as a community for worship, the church increases the well-being of the extended community. Whereas Hauerwas would highlight the formation value of such gathering, he would strongly assert simply that the church gathers to worship God. Though worship may serve a human function, it is not primarily for this purpose. It must be theocentric rather than anthropocentric. Worship is for God.[122] In addition to the gathering church's apparent community-building value there are a number of ways that "Jesus's values" or theological concepts (such as the Trinity) may inform public, community, and/or family life. Kathryn Tanner notes in a similar manner, "If one looks at the full economy and avoids isolated attention to the Trinitarian persons, Jesus' relations with the Father and Spirit do not appear in any obvious way to be the model for relations *among humans*. They are, instead, the sort of relations humans are to have with the Father and Spirit, as human beings come to be united with Christ, through the Spirit, and share his life."[123] While this relationship brings changes, these are based on the life of Jesus. Worship is thus not primarily functional in terms of effects on humans but is necessarily formative—even though God is the focus, not humans.

Hauerwas describes liturgy in worship as a habit-forming practice.[124] Because of this emphasis on theology happening in the congrega-

---

122. Tanner considers the uses of the Trinity in political theology. "Contemporary theologies of the Trinity exhibit both these general reasons why all theology tends to be political theology. Theologians are enlisting support for particular kinds of community—say, egalitarian, inclusive communities, in which differences are respected—through arguments over the Trinity. They are enjoining a political fight on cultural grounds: the meaning of the Trinity is where political disagreements over the shape of church life, and over the social and governmental policies Christians should endorse, are engaged." Tanner, "Trinity," 320.

123. Tanner, "Trinity," 329.

124. Through a process of participant observation with Good Samaritan United Methodist church, Fulkerson challenges post-liberal assertions of churches as linguistic, and considers broader forms of habituation. In "They Will Know" (277), she writes, "The hybridized story of welcome—Christian neighbourliness—habituating persons into postures of welcome, even reciprocity with those who are radically different is, perhaps, a thin beginning of a full account for its apostolicity, holiness, and catholicity . . . However, I commend it as theologically significant because it does two

tion, he often includes sermons in his books. He considers the sermon to be the real locus of theological reflection. Hauerwas and Wells write,

> Thus Christian ethics is the study of how God meets the needs of those who call upon him in need and expectation, thus enabling them to fulfill all righteousness. The attitude of Christian ethics should be one of intercession, from an experience of need. But heaven is open, and prayers can be heard. God is intimately concerned with the destiny of his people. God makes his people new through the power of the Holy Spirit. Christian ethics is about how God makes people who are capable of fulfilling all righteousness; it is about how people are shaped to live good lives before him. God gives his people Jesus—who is everything they need. Christian ethics names the ways in which the Church inherits and embodies what God gives his people in Jesus.[125]

In the essay "Suffering Beauty: The Liturgical Formation of Christ's Body" found in *Performing the Faith: Bonhoeffer and the Practice of Nonviolence*, Hauerwas considers what he indicates might be seemingly "transcendental" notions and connections around truth and beauty. Indeed, in this piece he explores connections not easily articulated. He begins by describing an informal meeting that took place while lecturing at Viterbo College in La Crosse, Wisconsin. A nun at a small abbey expressed urgency for people to commit themselves to the life of prayer. While affirming that it was good for young people to be in the streets struggling for justice in the civil rights movement, she stated, "It is good that many feel this way. But God needs our prayers. So please pray that God will send us vocations so that we may continue to pray for God's world."[126] Hauerwas notes thinking that this has to be right. He continues, "Worship is not what we do to motivate a passion for justice. Worship, which from beginning to end is prayer, is justice."[127]

> Drawing on what I learned from the Benedictine sister in La Crosse, Wisconsin, I have been unsympathetic with attempts to explore what, if any, relation may exist between liturgy and

---

things. First, getting the skill to expand one's notion of neighbour (the stranger), such that this graciousness becomes a 'body memory,' is a mark of uniqueness, and it is uniqueness that, unlike doctrinal marks, can 'travel,' i.e., occur in different locals and contexts, look different, and require different liturgical and mission forms."

125. Hauerwas and Wells, "Gift of the Church," 16.
126. Hauerwas, *Performing the Faith*, 152.
127. Hauerwas, *Performing the Faith*, 152.

ethics. Elsewhere I have argued that the politics that creates the "and" between liturgy and ethics reproduces the politics of modernity that privatizes what makes the church the church, namely, the worship of God. That Christians now must try to understand, for example, how prayer may or may not be related to the moral life indicates something has gone profoundly wrong with the practices that are meant to shape the Christian community.[128]

For Hauerwas worship is, at minimum, *part* of what it means to be a Christian. In this he appears to be reacting to uncertainty (or perhaps a false modesty or impulse toward a generic pluralism) over the place or value of the church in society and in relation to other religions.[129] It is in this space that what should be the secondary values of church as a community group or as good for community cohesion displaces what Hauerwas as well as traditional orthodoxy name as *the* reason for church: worship of the Triune God as displayed in Jesus through the calling of the people of Israel. He asserts, "When liturgy becomes a motivation for action that does not require the liturgy for the intelligibility of the description of what we have done, then we lose the means as Christians to make our lives our own."[130] Though his view of the formative role of liturgy does not challenge its value as a motivator of practices (such as service or peacemaking) that help create the common good—Hauerwas objects to the bypassing of liturgy's central role.

In Hauerwas's strongly worded challenges to accounts of "justice" or "democracy," some have understood him to be promoting withdrawal from public life. Hauerwas has regularly flaunted the accusation that he is a "tribal, sectarian, fideist" and has dismissively asserted that he is no longer interested in responding to such ill-placed criticism.[131] Commenting on the tendency for critics to assume that for Hauerwas moral formation displaces public service, Jennifer Herdt writes,

> This task of moral formation is never concluded; one can never say, "okay, now that we've taken care of that task, we are ready to go out and be publicly involved." So it is understandable that

128. Hauerwas, *Performing the Faith*, 153.

129. See Mark Ryan's account of Sabina Lovibond's response to Jeffrey Stout's critique of Hauerwas and the need for justification of positions in public in *Politics of Practical Reason*, 166–77.

130. Hauerwas, *Performing the Faith*, 153.

131. Hauerwas, *Work of Theology*, 267.

critics might conclude that the task of moral formation has essentially displaced the task of public service. Actually, Stanley's emphasis on liturgy as the primary site for Christian formation should itself help to correct this impression. For the rhythm of gathering for worship and being sent out is not postponed until one is ready, fully formed, wholly virtuous. Rather, Christians are sent out, resting in God's sustaining grace, and are gathered back in again to confess their failures and be reformed and kneaded again into the Body of Christ.[132]

Hauerwas also comments on the problem of academic specialization that fragments theology and the church. Such a fragmentation disempowers Christian educators from thinking they can engage with liturgy because liturgy becomes housed in a guild. He states, "Fragmentation is the social condition that creates the politics that makes intelligible the question: 'What is the relation between liturgy and ethics?'"[133] It is for this reason that he thinks of what he does as *theology* rather than the narrower label of *theological ethics* or *Christian ethics*. In this, liturgy, like ethics, is open for discussion since in the life of the church these are hardly separate spheres.

For Hauerwas, "ethics and liturgy but name different ways of specifying the practical wisdom of the church about the everyday practices necessary to constitute the life of the church across time. The virtues are the way Christians talk about the moral formation necessary for our being timeful people."[134] By timeful, he means embedded within time. This is a people not abstracted from their history or trying to set up camp in ahistorical bureaucratic structures to shield from the uncertainty of existence. Such practical wisdom builds the possibility in the community to respond well and consistently in the face of either the tedium of "normal" life or the urgent decision that is often thought to be the crux of ethical practice.[135] Kallenberg concludes, "If liberalism bases decisionist ethics on a prospective conception of the self, then Hauerwas eschews

---

132. Herdt, "Truthfulness," 29.
133. Hauerwas, *Performing the Faith*, 154.
134. Hauerwas, *Performing the Faith*, 156.
135. Particularly in his earlier work, Hauerwas often challenged the notions that ethics rides on singular urgent questions. See Kallenberg, *Ethics as Grammar*, 11–47, for a comparison of Wittgenstein and Hauerwas's use of the therapeutic role of philosophy and ethics.

decisionism entirely because of his eschatological understanding of the self."[136] The formation that Hauerwas seeks to describe is Christians who *are* and act *justly* but that these are so inseparable that the designation "Christian" covers this description of someone who is a certain way and does certain things. In this context these actions and attributes cannot be separated into distinguishable categories or display cases. As such, to be Christian is to be just and to be Christian is to be nonviolent. Of course, even a cursory sociological and historical study indicates that this is at least as much aspirational as it is fact. This relationship between the described and the aspirational is explored in greater detail below. The important point here is that the division between liturgy and ethics does not hold, nor do the general divisions between aspects of church life remain meaningful, under Hauerwas's critique.

In the final section of his essay, "On the Beauty of Goodness and the Goodness of Beauty," Hauerwas wades into the relationship of beauty, liturgy, and truth. He notes, "Of course, it may be objected that to suggest that tacky worship produces tacky people or tacky people produce tacky worship comes dangerously close to suggesting that moral and liturgical practice is a matter of taste. So let me be as clear as I can be. Moral and liturgical practice is a matter of taste. The problem is not that they are matters of taste, but rather the modern assumption that taste is but a matter of subjective opinion."[137] He goes on, "Liturgy is the source of the word-care necessary for our lives to be beautiful and good—beautiful and good because by the constant repetition we have learned the habits necessary to speak truthfully."[138] Why is this the case? Is there any way to test such a hypothesis? Of course, Hauerwas would not want to try to subject such an assertion to quantification; however, it is a bold claim that is not self-evidently true. It could fall into the same category of critique that Hauerwas brusquely brushes off from Healy,[139] but again, it may not. For while I have found such statements compelling, I easily imagine that repetition can become unheard rote repetition or simply archaic phrases embedded into one's speech rather than resulting in formation in the way Hauerwas suggests. Now *unheard* might mean that the language and cadence has become embedded in one's soul. Despite this, the challenge

---

136. Kallenberg, *Ethics as Grammar*, 114.
137. Hauerwas, *Performing the Faith*, 161.
138. Hauerwas, *Performing the Faith*, 162.
139. Hauerwas, *Work of Theology*, 267.

of positing or not positing "What causes what?" emerges. Hauerwas continues, asserting: "Liturgy is quite literally where we learn to suffer God's beauty and so suffering discover we are made in God's image. Through worship we discover the truth about ourselves, making possible lives of goodness otherwise impossible."[140] This statement and essay are replete with such impressive and poetic assertions. While I find it compelling, I recognize that this is due in part to my particular milieu and ecclesial experience. I grew up and went to college within a church tradition that lacked elaborate or particular liturgy and became attracted to liturgically beautiful worship towards the end of college and during graduate school. This difference, as well as the prescribed prayers at a time when my spiritual practice lacked the resources to generate prayer, led to an appreciation of high church worship. This was also during a time when it was a trend for some evangelicals to migrate toward liturgical practices and churches. This migration was also part of Hauerwas's journey. Though I still appreciate such services, I am now, as a minister, much more interested in beauty through simplicity and spontaneous, flexible worship services.[141]

This personal reflection certainly does not disprove Hauerwas's views, but it may slow down unqualified acceptance. For the purpose here, Hauerwas's assertion of the centrality, embodied nature (linguistically, materially, and as a corporate body), and forming capacity establish the practice of worship within Hauerwas's work but also mark it as necessary for understanding his writing on ecclesiology and peacemaking.

Witness

For Hauerwas, witness, often described as mission, is a primary mode of relating to the world as well as inside the church.[142] Witness is the proc-

140. Hauerwas, *Performing the Faith*, 164.

141. Michael Budde considers the way that worship may challenge global media and markets by being one of the few places where Christians step outside the deluge in "Collecting Praise."

142. Though he retains a division between "the world" and the "the church" in nearly all statements, he undermines his thinking by saying that peacemaking is not limited to those within the church, witness is both inside and outside, and the kingdom of God is not contained solely within the church. Given his strong ecclesial focus and linking of salvation with the counterpolitics of the church, there is certainly an *appearance* of distinct realms. Indeed, if he were to read "that there is certainly the appearance" he would likely say, "There *is*." However, by his consistent assertion of

lamation of the Gospel of Jesus. He asserts that the church *is* mission and is *in* mission.[143] In 1974, he asserted that the most vital concern should be the type of community the church forms.[144] This is in contrast to an emphasis on institutional forms. The content of the church's "doctrine, liturgy, and communal form will not let it forget that it exists only as mission to the world."[145] The *only* in this is notable. This mission is part of the focus on Christian speech that he later saw as a key practice and characteristic of the church.[146] For Hauerwas, truthful speaking is essential in both Christian speech and mission. *This* mission is an adventure that cannot be controlled and is done by a people that are simultaneously bound to a place but also free. In Christendom and in the time of the apparently powerful church it was difficult to embrace this uncertainty, outward orientation, and mobility.[147] In this, the church can both critique and model an alternative, but since this cannot be controlled, the church can be free of the pretensions of being in control. While in control and with power, any call to join in with worship and the body carries the strong potential to sound ominous, threatening, or coercive. When disempowered, or at least not overly powerful, the church is left to witness rather than dictate.[148] As Hauerwas states,

---

non-limitation of most practices or virtues to the church he (intentionally?) undermines the epistemological certainty and the power of "the church" to judge the world. Certainly, Hauerwas would allow for judgement but would say that this judgement is *at least* as strongly aimed at the church.

143. See Hauerwas, "Sent," and "Beyond the Boundaries."

144. Hauerwas, "Nonresistant Church," 197–221. In this, the church as a politics also shows through his account of mission. The church is a community that takes up space, bears witness, and is on the move. See Hauerwas, "Beyond the Boundaries," 157; "Witness," 37–66.

145. Hauerwas, *Vision and Virtue*, 216.

146. In *Working with Words* (x), Hauerwas writes that "The theological task requires that we speak of God, but the God to whom and about whom we must speak defies the words that we use. This defiance seems odd because the God about whom we speak is, we believe, found decisively in Jesus of Nazareth, very God and very man. Yet it seems that the closer God draws near to us the more we discover that we know not how to say 'God.' The same is true even when we invoke the Holy Spirit who draws us into God's very life."

147. Hauerwas, *War and the American Difference*, 174–75.

148. In his sermon, "Sent" (168), Hauerwas writes, "God is whittling us down. We are a church that is quickly losing its power and status in the world as we know it. Those losses may well mean that whatever witness we are capable of making will be a witness without protection. The witness of those who have come before us must serve as a reminder that to be without protection is the condition necessary to learn to live

> The political novelty that God brings into the world is a community of those who serve instead of ruling, who suffer instead of inflicting suffering, whose fellowship crosses social lines instead of reinforcing them. The new Christian community in which walls are broken down not by human idealism or democratic legalism but by the work of Christ is not only a vehicle of the gospel or the fruit of the gospel; it is the gospel.[149]

After considering Yoder's claim that unity is experienced locally, Hauerwas comments,

> It certainly seems to be the case that locality means difference. Difference can threaten unity, but unity cannot be catholic without difference. Yoder is well aware that locality can tempt Christians to identify the church with a given society or assume some way of being church in one context to be necessary for all churches. The only safeguard against these temptations is to demand that the church be in mission. For it is through mission that the church finds that there are different ways to worship Jesus. The difference moreover, is not right or wrong. It is just different. But these differences must be tested so that Christians moving from one Eucharistic assembly to another Eucharistic assembly can have confidence they are worshiping the same God.[150]

As one who found a vocation through the felt call to work in international missions and who has remained significantly engaged on international issues through the church ever since then, this resonates deeply. However, it is not at all clear to me how mission is a safeguard against a prioritization of one culture over another, at least in any immediate or automatic sense. Willie James Jennings asserts that the dislocation from particular geography experienced by European Christian missionaries is a form of displacement that significantly contributed to the racialization of theological discourse. He writes that this displacement has yet to be reckoned with within the tradition:

> From the moment Acosta [an early Catholic missionary] (and all those like him) placed his feet on the ground in Lima, the Christian tradition and its theologians conjured a form of

---

at peace with one another. For if we fail to live peacefully with one another the witness we bring will not be a witness to the gospel of Jesus Christ."

149. Hauerwas, *War and the American Difference*, 167.
150. Hauerwas, *Approaching the End*, 111.

practical rationality that locked theology in discourses of displacement from which it has never escaped. The metaphor of 'feet touching the ground' is an important one here. Acosta stepped into a world, the Indias Occidentales, that was radically altered and that in turn would alter the way he perceived the world. More specifically, it would not alter the creedal substance of his doctrine of creation but the way in which its logic would be performed. The ground on which Acosta was to stand was disappearing and reappearing in a new way.[151]

Jennings also considers the theological and biblical translation work of John William Colenso, sifting through the multidirectional nature of translation, both of texts and cultural logics. He maps the complexities and unintended consequences of even attentive language acquisition and relationships.[152] Breaking theology and the Bible free from locational identity and translation is neither neutral nor straightforwardly empowering and anti-colonial.[153]

Jennings challenges Lamin Sanneh's and Andrew Walls's assertions about the nature of mission, and the resultant cultural relativism, challenging ethnocentrism that is similar to Hauerwas's claim above that mission is a safeguard to prioritizing one culture over another.[154] The positive effect of crossing cultural borders may be the case in large ecumenical gatherings such as the World Council of Churches 10th Assembly. Whereas in this context we gathered for worship that drew intentionally on the various churches and cultures present, it seems like the result is often more like cultural hegemony through globalization or imperialism rather than greater appreciation. Even in this intentional space, English was the predominant language. This was practical given the current global linguistic state of affairs, but nonetheless may be linguistically imperialistic.[155] Though going out in mission is indeed critical for such

---

151. Jennings, *Christian Imagination*, 71–72.

152. Jennings, *Christian Imagination*, 126.

153. "Colenso's universalism was the other side of his colonialism. His ability to conceptualize a God who was not only beyond but in some sense opposed to the strictures of Jewish identity draws life from colonialist abilities to universalize the earth, that is, to free it from the strictures of particular ways of life. Of course, missionary life is by its proper nature boundary crossing, but his universalist vision reduces the power and presence of the very things it claims to grasp, the particularities of African peoples." Jennings, *Christian Imagination*, 146.

154. Jennings, *Christian Imagination*, 158.

155. Hauerwas has on several occasions noted that the possibility of the use of

exposure to difference, I, along with many others critical of American, white, and male dominance, am less optimistic about such encounters. In such cases, it is at least as likely that understandings of the Gospel, Christ, and the church may be assumed to be neutral (or biblically-based), but are largely products of this dominant culture. To learn another culture takes a great deal of time and may be impossible.[156] Jennings's critique goes even deeper, but he allows that even in the case of missionaries in the midst of the colonial period the negative effects were not immutable but some effect was inevitable.

Witness cannot escape social location or the reality of power. Location, then, shapes the rhetorical approach or assumptions. The following quotation relates both to ecclesial presumptions as well as rhetorical styles or argumentative approaches. Though the rhetorical approach is apparently different (with Hauerwas writing a book titled *Against the Nations* and Yoder following with *For the Nations*), the ending point is quite similar. Hauerwas considers why this may be the case, saying,

> John [Howard Yoder] can be for the nations because he was never intellectually and ecclesially tempted to be in control in a way that that would capture the imagination. But I have to be against, because I come from a tradition that has thought that there is no alternative to being in control. Of course that is not quite true. When I say I come from such a tradition, I do not mean to say that I come from a tradition given my class and ecclesial background. It is only the pretension of a Yale education that would have given me that presumption of being in control.[157]

violence and urgent calls for justice often end up being the basis for violent intervention. Chris Huebner explores this in relation to Yoder and Paul Virilio connecting speed with violence in *A Precarious Peace*. Given institutional constraints and the intentional character of the WCC, such linguistic decisions were likely well-justified. It is the two quickly writing off such concerns on the basis of practical necessity that signals a problem. What is deemed a "necessity" is typically the purview of those with power. The definition of necessity, then, is not a neutral or risk-free assertion.

156. This is not only the case with the church; it happens in many other structural forms of globalization. Rory Stewart describes his post-diplomatic service trek across Afghanistan in 2002 in *Places In Between*, 247–48. He comments that, while acknowledging all the negatives of nineteenth- and twentieth-century colonialism such as overt racism and suppression, many of these administrators lived for years in the same spot and grew knowledgeable of the culture and language while present-day expat experts on development or peace demonstrate a newer "more enlightened" assumptions of universals. Hauerwas's "Taking Time for Peace" is relevant to these concerns.

157. Hauerwas and Huebner, "History, Theory, and Anabaptism," 393–94.

Additionally, beyond going to Yale, being a white American man teaching in a major university would certainly lend itself to Hauerwas's assumption of being in control. The necessity of awareness and accounting for location is a key component of the breaking open of church and theological leadership. Even when incomplete, this awareness and expanding participation runs parallel to several other streams of the humanities and social sciences, such as community psychology. More importantly, it moves closer to the biblical vision of Revelation 7:9 and the "great multitude . . . from every nation" before the throne of God.

Hauerwas describes the church in geographical and spatial terms. At some points, he frames the church as *polis*; at other times, he asserts that the church is *mission*. Nathan Kerr presses him on this image of *polis*, arguing that Yoder, when not seen through the lens of Hauerwas's interpretation, takes the church in a more constructive direction:

> Whereas for Hauerwas apocalyptic becomes essentially an ecclesiological strategy for establishing the church-as-*polis* vis-à-vis the modern liberal nation state, for Yoder apocalyptic remains principally a tactical process of negotiating the ordinary (secular) contingencies and particularities of the everyday world and seeking from within them to articulate the truth of the gospel, the divine inbreaking of God's Kingdom which is the very historicity of Jesus of Nazareth.[158]

It is this uncertainty that requires witness rather than control.[159] The theme of joining in with God's eschatological work rather than being the locus of it recurs throughout Hauerwas. In the first footnote of "Beyond the Boundaries: The Church is Mission" (in *War and the American Difference*), he notes that this language and focus was in part a response

---

158. Kerr, *Christ, History and Apocalyptic*, 131.

159. Kerr continues, "A *sociality of dispossession*. This is what the liturgy of Christian mission commits us to. And yet, there is no way theoretically to anticipate what this sociality will look like; as Yoder puts it, 'The only way to see how this will work will be to see how it will work.' Such a sociality is only discoverable as we are *bound* ever anew to the world via that pneumatic gathering which constitutes our participation in that ongoing Christic inbreak that is God's apocalypse. Constituted by mission, 'church' is entirely the operation of God's apocalyptic *action* in Christ, and its 'peoplehood' the diasporic *work* of the Spirit. As under exile, such a 'peoplehood' is bound to appear as tenuously ad hoc, its fleeting presence being only 'for a time', and so at its best politically *irrelevant* and at worst dangerously *ineffective*. And yet such might be the surest sign that one has, by God's grace, been delivered over to that mode of engaged and embodied action whereby alone we pass from ideology to doxology." Kerr, *Christ, History, and Apocalyptic*, 195–96.

to challenges to his language of *polis* in *In Good Company*. Though his observations lack Jennings's detail and critical edge, his assertions that the church is a local endeavor and "culturally disruptive wherever it finds itself" reach towards similar concerns.[160] Jennings's account carries more weight regarding the development of "race," but Hauerwas's framing, along with his consistent challenge to the nation-state, means they are moving in a similar direction. This said, I maintain that Hauerwas—for all his concern for the particular—does not adequately account for his own particularity and its shaping influence on his writing.

Witness in the ecclesiology of Hauerwas is based on proclamation and the church as mission. This outward orientation means that the church is necessarily political though also nonviolent. While Hauerwas asserts that such witness and mission is essential for the appreciation of particularity, I have noted a limitation in his failure to fully recognize his own particularity. In spite of some questions, however, I believe that witness is an important part of Hauerwas's ecclesiology and will be a critical component of the church's peacemaking.

A Church with a History

An important facet of Hauerwas's ecclesiology is his assertion that the church, and Christians, exist *with a history*. A common refrain from Hauerwas is "Who told you the story that you should have no story except the story you chose when you had no story?"[161] In this question, he seeks to challenge the notion of ahistorical choice and freedom that he sees as pervading American Christians' assumptions about church and faith. For while American Christians may assume such freedom from history, they are nonetheless located within a particular history and set of historically contingent assumptions. Hauerwas aims to uncover these assumptions and reposition Christians within the story of Jesus. In so doing, he acknowledges particular histories (in his case, that of being a Texan and a bricklayer), while reminding the church as a whole that it is part of the story of God.

By way of example, Hauerwas offers a Pentecost sermon largely in the form of a retelling of the stories of Babel in Genesis and Pentecost in the Acts of the Apostles. Here, Hauerwas demonstrates the churchly

---

160. Hauerwas, *War and the American Difference*, 170.
161. Hauerwas, "No Enemy, No Christianity," 33.

practice of writing a sermon built with narrative and describes the church as part of the history of God. He writes,

> In this transformation [Pentecost] of the disciples we see the central theme of the Gospel. To be a disciple of Jesus it is not enough to know the basic "facts" of his life. It is not enough to know his story. Rather, to be a disciple of Jesus means our lives must literally be taken up into the drama of God's redemption of this creation. That is the work of the Spirit as we are made part of God's new time through the life and the work of this man, Jesus of Nazareth.[162]

He continues,

> The unity of humankind prefigured at Pentecost is not just any unity but that made possible by the apocalyptic work of Jesus of Nazareth. It is a unity of renewed understanding, but the kind of understanding that is not created by some artificial Esperanto that denies the reality of other languages. Attempts to secure unity through the creation of a single language are attempts to make us forget our histories and differences rather than the unity made possible by the Spirit through which we understand the other as other. At Pentecost God created a new language, but it was a language that was more than words. It is instead a community whose memory of its savior creates the miracle of being a people whose very differences contribute to their unity. We call this new creation *church*. It is constituted by word and sacrament, as the story we tell, the story we embody, must not only be told but enacted. In the telling we are challenged to be a people capable of hearing God's good news such that we can be a witness to others. In the enactment, in Baptism and Eucharist, we are made part of a common history that requires continuous celebration to be rightly remembered. It is through Baptism and Eucharist that our lives are engrafted onto the life of the one that makes our unity possible. Through this telling and enactment we, like Israel, become a people who live by distinctly remembering the history of God's redemption of the world.[163]

Through the narrative telling of history Hauerwas seeks to locate the church within this history of God and form Christians as people who recognize their place within this history.

---

162. Hauerwas, "Church as God's New Language," 148.
163. Hauerwas, "Church as God's New Language," 148–49.

For Hauerwas, the theologian's task is not to be innovative but to be faithful. As such, he asserts along with Harold Bender that theology cannot be done separately from history.[164] However, the question would seem to be open as to which story the theologian is to be faithful. Since there are many stories that are claimed as truth or as appropriately told, it is crucial to acknowledge that one speaks from a particular frame. Hauerwas does this, but he often seems strangely reluctant to engage in the stories of the church and of Christians outside of white male America. Douglas Gay notes, "Among those most appreciative of Hauerwas, there is a kind of bafflement about why this perennially loud theologian/ethicist is so quiet on the subject of violence and discrimination against women, poverty and systemic disadvantage within and beyond America and the ongoing struggle with racism in American life."[165] Hauerwas should not be reticent to engage in such stories, given the extensive work that has shown how whiteness and white privilege deeply shape perceptions and thinking. Though the telling of the story of God may sound relatively particular, there are many and various strains within the life of the church—particularly when the church is involved in the perpetuation of violence against theological, ethnic, racial, sexual, gender, or political heretics—that make such a telling complicated. To tell this story well, the theologian must be eager to listen to those without the power or authority to shape the history to their benefit. I will take up this concern in greater detail in chapter 5.

Of course, history is not just God's deliverance of the Israelites from Egypt, the self-baptism of eight theological radicals in 1708 (which gave rise to the Church of the Brethren as well as related present-day denominations), or the declining membership of American mainline Protestant denominations in the second half of the twentieth century. History also takes place in the less concrete realm of ideas and arguments (which are at times about the history of such "concrete" events). To hear well one must listen well. Hauerwas, though well read, seems prone to focusing his reading within particular demographics.[166] Additionally, his writing feels at times offhandedly critical or perhaps critical to subtle implications in

---

164. Hauerwas, *In Good Company*, 70.

165. Gay, "Practical Theology of Church and World," 51.

166. This is, to some degree, based on who responds to him and who is writing on similar topics. I noted this challenge while working on this paper. Such a dynamic certainly takes intentionality but is also part of white dominance.

word choice that he perceives but which the writer in question may be unaware.

Izuzquiza offers a similar critique of Milbank: "Milbank's *way of arguing* is not without difficulties. He practices a 'hermeneutics of suspicion' that gives the impression of interpreting authors out of their actual intentions and forcing them into his own framework. This negative and dangerous approach leads him to extrapolate the position of authors studied and sometimes to misrepresent them."[167] When reading Hauerwas, I get the impression (sometimes confirmed by his own words) that something makes him "mad as hell," but also that even his sharp criticisms have the good of the of the church in mind, and are not made with the intention of gaining political or academic points.[168] While this is more laudable than nitpicking to score points, such an approach, especially given his claim of the centrality of the scriptural text, must be considered in light of the "fruits of the Spirit," such as kindness and gentleness (Gal 5:22–25). Hauerwas would likely consider calls to tone down his criticism "democratic policing" or unfounded liberal niceness. Paying attention to his own particular power and assumptions of who merits substantial engagement—whether positive or negative—should fall within his concern for virtues found in the fruit of the Spirit and his stated interest in people interrogating their own assumptions. Additionally, the exercise of patience that Hauerwas calls for in political change would seem to be relevant for theological discourse.

That the church has a history and is part of a story emerges clearly in Hauerwas's focus on narrative.[169] While early in his career, Hauerwas appears to have been interested in narrative in general,[170] he later asserts that he is not interested in narrative generally, but in the particular narrative of the church.[171] In the *Peaceable Kingdom* he is already strongly

---

167. Izuzquiza, *Rooted In Jesus Christ*, 46.

168. Hauerwas states in *In Good Company* (12) that the point is not to score points but to foment a revolution.

169. Narrative as part of the formation of the peaceable community will be addressed in greater depth in chapter 5.

170. The editors of *The Hauerwas Reader* make a similar observation. They note that the "Church as God's New Language" (1986) "signals a significant shift for Hauerwas in the mid-1980s, distancing him from formal appeals to the notion of narrative (or, for that matter, character) and emphasizing the material significance of the Christian narrative in the lived experience of the church" (142).

171. "I have increasingly become convinced that rather than talking about narrative as a category in itself, we are better advised to do theology in a manner that

asserting the narrative basis for theology. Even here, he does not see "narrative" as a thing on its own that somehow circumvents the need for reflection; rather, this reflection is embedded in a story and refers to a story. This poses a challenge to the notion of abstract ideas, which by Hauerwas's account, are not *more basic* but simply isolated from their narrative framework. "Doctrines, therefore," he asserts, "are not the upshot of stories; they are not the meaning or heart of the stories. Rather they are tools (sometimes even misleading tools), meant to help us tell the story better. Because the Christian story is an enacted story, liturgy is probably a much more important resource than are doctrines or creeds for helping us to hear, tell, and live the story of God."[172]

The assertion that the church is *with a history* is a pillar of Hauerwas's ecclesiology. As such, Christians cannot "just make it up," but neither are church practices iron bound or static. *With a history* provides an orientation, formation, and guidance in the complex task of worshiping God rightly, bearing witness, and as we will see—peacemaking. It is within the repetition of practices and a retelling of the story of God that Christians and the church are made part of a politics that outstrips the nation-state and that allows a unity based on appreciation of particularity.

Distinct Community/Peculiar People

Hauerwas has often claimed that the role of the church is not to make the world more just but to be the church. He seeks to establish the church as primary,[173] rather than assuming the primacy of political questions and

---

displays what we have learned by discovering the unavoidability of the narrative character of Christian convictions." Hauerwas, "Narrative Turn," 140.

172. Hauerwas, *Peaceable Kingdom*, 26.

173. Peter Dula rightly notes ("Response," 19–20) that, "to say the church's first task is to be the church is not to say this is the church's only task. The church's participation in struggles for justice and freedom and dignity and respect and peace are taken for granted, rather than excluded; the point is that if the church is to know what it is doing in such struggles it must be imbued with the difference Christ makes." Hauerwas and Sherwindt write, "Indeed, when the content of such ideals is spelled out, as we see in the case of Rauschenbusch, we begin to suspect that the language of the Kingdom is being used to underwrite ethical commitments and political strategies that were determined prior to the claims about the centrality of the Kingdom for Christian ethics.... The Kingdom of God is the hope of the people whom God has called out among all the nations. The question of ecclesiology, therefore, precedes strategy for social action. Without the Kingdom ideal, the church loses her identity-forming hope; without the church, the Kingdom ideal loses its concrete character. Once abstracted from the

frameworks grounded in the nation-state.[174] His claim should be considered in relation to his response to accusations of sectarianism.[175] He has assiduously asserted that although the church should be the Christian's primary reference point,[176] in no way does this mean that Christians should be separated from the world, nor that this is even a possibility.[177]

There are a number of ways in which separation might occur. For example, would different ethical norms and practices around war for reasons of faith be considered separation? Is a national holiday

---

community it presumes the Kingdom ideal can be used to underwrite any conception of the just society." Hauerwas and Sherwindt, "Kingdom of God," 130–31.

174. "Hauerwas therefore offers us a kind of 'political theology' but not as we know it. It is a strange hybrid of Catholic and Radical Reformation political theologies." Gay, *Practical Theology of Church and World*, 32. Hauerwas gives a generally positive read of Wolterstorff's "Jesus, the Justice of God," 99–116. Though some have perceived that Hauerwas is unwaveringly negative toward "justice," he is more accurately concerned with practices and discourses that prioritize and affirm justice in a particular time and place. Hovey, in "The Public Ethics of John Howard Yoder and Stanley Hauerwas," asserts a substantial difference between Yoder and Hauerwas on the point of relation to "the world" and uses of non-Christian concepts such as freedom, liberty, or justice.

175. The challenge given to him by those who accuse him of being sectarian is the requirement (which is assumed impossible for Hauerwas given his commitments) to translate to outside the community. Kallenberg writes in *Ethics as Grammar* (133), "Hauerwas has taken his cue from Wittgenstein in order to correct the sorts of misunderstandings that plague the modern academia. The pattern of human social interplay, or forms of life, that frames the grammar of the Christian community's language is at the same time the form of that community's canonical narratives. Thus, an incommensurability of language-games between rival communities is simultaneously a fundamental difference of stories. The distance between languages is not bridged by some form of translation (a case of semantics without syntax) but by human capacity to become bilingual. The centrality of the community for this tutoring process implies that salvation is therefore political in nature: outside the church there is no salvation."

176. Though Gloria Albrecht's description of Hauerwas's church and its "political commitments" to the trivial are generally accurate (see *Character of Our Communities*, 56), she does her argument a disservice by omitting Hauerwas's repeated caveats that, though the Christian's primary vocation is not politics as usual, the Christian should remain engaged in these cooperative efforts to work for peace. For example, Hauerwas writes, "I do not wish to be misunderstood. I am not suggesting that those who would be faithful to God should give up trying to make the world safe from nuclear destruction. Let us continue to tie ribbons around Washington. Let us continue to try to find ways to help our political leaders discover the means to end the constant spiral of nuclear buildup." Hauerwas, "Taking Time for Peace," 257. Though Hauerwas has made such statements throughout his career, he has done more constructive work on this sort of action since the late 1990s.

177. On a related point, he asserts a distinction between the kingdom of God and the church.

commemorating a war an example of separation? Does separation entail building an entirely separate and self-contained economic and political system? Hauerwas presumes that the theology (and ethics) of the church necessarily puts it in opposition to certain practices of the state, but that this does not entail an absolute prohibition in engaging the state in dialogue or advocacy, or as an employee. This engagement with the state is, however, not absolute, but may entail selective nonparticipation.[178]

Hauerwas consistently challenges theologians and social ethicists who think the primary focus of their reflection is America and how to make it work. Ugandan priest Emmanuel Katongole likewise challenges the limited imagination often in play when considering Africa and its politics. The following lengthy quotation is a demonstration of the potential of building on the foundations laid by Hauerwas. Katongole writes,

> Yet these recommendations [of how to make politics work better] do not pay sufficient attention to the possibility that politics in Africa, and the nation-state in particular, have not been a failure, but have worked very well. Chaos, war, and corruption are not indications of a failed institution; they are ingrained in the very imagination of how nation-state politics works. To put the argument differently, while Christian social ethics in Africa have focused on providing strategies for revising, improving, or managing a failing institution, they have paid very little attention to the story of this institution: how it works and why it works in the way it does.[179]

He continues,

> In short, my frustration with social ethics in Africa is not about its failure to come up with practical recommendations for improving the nation-state institution and its politics; indeed, there are too many of those. My greater frustration is with its failure of imagination, with the assumption that the nation-state is the only possible structure for modern social existence in Africa. In the case of Christian social ethics, the failure to imagine other forms of social structure outside the nation-state is fundamentally self-defeating, because this failure undermines the central claim that Jesus is the Savior and Lord of history. To assume that the only way that Africa can be saved is through nation-state modalities, and that the church can only contribute to this process by helping nation-state politics, is ridiculous, especially

---

178. Hauerwas, *Vision and Virtue*, 203 and Hauerwas, *Performing the Faith*, 173.
179. Katongole, *Sacrifice of Africa*, 2.

in Africa, where the church has far more credibility than the corrupt nation-state institution. Even more ridiculous is the idea that the church can only make claims about Jesus as Savior by qualifying that his salvation is only "spiritual." The salvation promised by God to God's people, to which the birth, life, death, and resurrection of Jesus is witness, is not merely spiritual: it is a concrete social, material, political, and economic reality that is ushered into existence by God's revelation in history. The failure of Christian social imagination is a failure to imagine and live in this new reality, which in 2 Corinthians 5:17 St. Paul refers to as God's "new creation."[180]

Though Hauerwas has zealously challenged the focus on America and the nation-state as normative, it is not always clear who would be included in the group of offending ethicists and what the parameters are.[181] This is similar to his approach to the "liberal."[182] While his criticisms may be useful, his definition has been questioned.[183] With a relatively all-encompassing statement he more easily knocks down what may really be a straw man.[184]

For Hauerwas, the church is a politics.[185] By this he means that the church is a body that cannot be known apart from its practices. As

---

180. Katongole, *Sacrifice of Africa*, 59.

181. Hauerwas, "How to (Not) Be a Political Theologian," 172, 174.

182. Hovey observes that though Hauerwas attacks Constantinianism, as does Yoder, it is liberalism that gets more of his attention. He writes, "Yoder and Hauerwas are certainly both opposed to Constantinianism, that is, the presumption that the church must take responsibility for making history come out right by aligning itself with state power. It was on this assumption that the church resorted to violence in the name of securing a future for itself and lost its critical edge and distinctiveness. For Hauerwas, however, the more persistent enemy of the church is liberalism. Liberalism is the modern belief that reason is grounded in rationally *qua* rationality and is therefore the reason of any clearly thinking person." Hovey, "Public Ethics of Yoder and Hauerwas," 207.

183. Stout, for example, asserts that Hauerwas's "heavy-handed" use of the term as an "all-purpose critical instrument continually reinforces that total rejection [of 'the world'] is required." Hauerwas, *Tradition and Democracy*, 148.

184. Stout challenges MacIntyre on this front, observing that he gives "liberalism" both much less time as well as much less specificity than other traditions he considers. See Stout, *Democracy and Tradition*, 128.

185. "Like Bishop Taban and Angelina Atyam, Maggy's Maison Shalom is driven by an ecclesiastical vision. Maggy's life and work exemplify not only the story of God that shapes the future, but that the task, gift, and art of crafting this new future is what it means to be a church. That is why, in final analysis, Maggy's Maison Shalom is primarily about proclaiming the gospel, which is the ministry of the church—it is not about programs or projects; it is about mission." Katongole, *Sacrifice of Africa*, 190.

quoted above, he also makes a strong link between salvation and the church. Though on the surface, he appears to closely mimic the traditional Catholic position of no salvation outside the church, he subtly shifts this meaning. For Hauerwas, the church is a visible body in a place with practices and a language, but these boundaries are rather permeable. This is particularly evident in his statements that the kingdom of God is not bound within the church.[186] His assertion that salvation is found in the church starts to sound like salvation is embodied in people and practices in history, but is not claimed or controlled by one body or set of bodies. Salvation is found through participation in the church, but is not dispensed by the church. In light of this, Hauerwas's transgressing of ecclesial boundaries takes on a new, less "consumer preference" dimension. He writes, "We know of no way of being saved other than a way which is ecclesial, i.e., political. Therefore, we are really about challenging the assumption that salvation is somehow *extra* political."[187] Additionally, he asserts that the "voluntary" membership in the church turns out to be a good Constantinian strategy.[188]

Hauerwas seeks to demonstrate "that in order to find a common good that can sustain a common morality we need the church—a church, Rahner rightly argued, that must recognize and learn to live as a worldwide communion."[189] He begins by challenging the notion that globalization entails a weakening of the nation-state. In the face of globalization, which has largely resulted in the expansion of options for the consumer, he comments on MacIntyre's assertion that the discovery of the good through practical reason is a local affair. If this is true, the particular practices necessary for the discovery of the common good are undermined by the processes associated with globalization.[190] He follows MacIntyre in asserting that genuine political process through practical reasoning takes place at the local level. As such, the "bigness" of globalization can be seen as corrosive to politics. In this sense, globalization, although thought to

---

186. Hauerwas, *Against the Nations*, 119.

187. Hauerwas, *In Good Company*, 62.

188. Hauerwas writes in explanation, "The voluntary church cannot develop the disciplines necessary to distinguish the universalism of the gospel from allegedly universal presumptions of a democratic social order." Hauerwas, *War and the American Difference*, 156.

189. Hauerwas, "Worldly Church," 136.

190. Hauerwas, "Worldly Church," 137.

generate greater connection, actually serves to make people simply individual consumers.

In the face of such fragmentation, Hauerwas asserts that "as Christians we will best serve God and our neighbor by seeking to form a common life in the world as we find it. That may well mean that we must attempt to develop institutions, such as a university, that makes it possible to engage in the kind of exchanges MacIntyre thinks necessary for the development of practical reason. What we cannot fear or try to repress in the name of peace is conflict. Christians, particularly Christians in diaspora, owe one another as well as their neighbor truthful judgments that come only by having our convictions exposed by those who do not share them."[191] This characterization of politics shifts from what is often assumed to be a confrontational struggle for control to a process for the organization of public life. It is not that this organization of public life is without conflict but that the conflict is at least potentially constructive.

Though Hauerwas wants a space for continued church existence, he is less convinced that the protections provided by the state are sufficient. He writes, "I simply do not believe that the 'guaranteed right of the freedom of the church' insured by democracies in itself should lead us to think that democratic societies and states by being democratic are less omnivorous in their appetites for our loyalties than nondemocratic states."[192] In this he continues to assert a difference between the church and the nation-state on the desire of protection of the church. Though for protection, this is less "protection" guaranteed externally by the state but rather an internal church defense against encroachment of the state.

Stout believes that Hauerwas has undercut commitment to democracy. While this may be true, it misses the point.[193] For both Hauerwas and Stout, the desired state would be something like justice and peace for individuals as part of a community of virtuous living embedded in and acknowledging its historical contingence. At the present time, democracy might be the best present political mechanism for reaching this more

---

191. Hauerwas, "Worldly Church," 146.

192. Hauerwas, *Against the Nations*, 127.

193. How would one measure the empirical validity of this? There might be mechanisms for doing so. If, however, we take as true Hauerwas's assertion that we can never really know our motivations, then even if we were to determine that people are moved by his ambivalence toward democracy, it would be hard to determine if he is simply giving voice to what is otherwise happening, or if the articulation of his view is a causal factor.

basic goal. For Hauerwas, however, the church responds to concrete social conditions; it does not provide a theory of the state.[194] Engaging with Hauerwas on the topic of a social ethic and political theology for Africa,[195] Katongole writes, "This shift in the understanding of politics from bureaucratic forms of management to concrete social engagements, from an exclusive focus on power and management to everyday practices, also involves a shift in the site of where the most interesting forms of politics happens—New York, Yaounde, Kampala—to villages, grassroots communities, and congregations—in a word, to local places where Christians and others face the challenges of everyday life."[196] Katongole asserts that the "problem" with African politics is that the social imagination needed to challenge the assumptions of the imported system of nation-state or other markers is lacking. He notes in particular the church of Rwanda's inability to challenge the labels of "Hutu" and "Tutsi."[197] In a similar vein, Cavanaugh states, "The liturgy we perform in our churches is an enactment of true reconciliation of the world in Christ. It is, therefore, a profound challenge to the politics that claims that we are essentially individuals whose reconciliation is always tragically deferred. The liturgy is more than symbolic. The communal body of people that is formed by the liturgy is meant to embody the politics of reconciliation, the politics of Jesus, in the world."[198]

Cavanaugh also notes, as does Hauerwas, that the church is more universal than the state since it spans the globe. This liturgy binds Christians across the more limited bounds of the nation-state. Ironically, rather than Christians then being those who separate and are thus "sectarian," the state is the true sectarian. The sectarian state might ask me to kill

---

194. Summarizing the position Yoder takes in *The Christian Witness to the State*, Hauerwas writes, "This cannot mean that the Christian's criticisms of the society and the state depend on some 'theory of the state' found in the gospel. The Christian does not have a special Christian theory for the legitimate state, but rather simply accepts the fact that the state exists. Because of this the Christian witness to the state will always express itself in terms of specific criticisms to concrete injustices." Hauerwas, *Vision and Virtue*, 209. See also Hauerwas, *State of the University*, 152.

195. "For Hauerwas the task of Christian social ethics is not one of simply providing theological recommendations in light of the given political or economic interpretation of reality. Rather, it is to uncover the political interpretation of the church in general and Christian convictions in particular." Katongole, *Sacrifice of Africa*, 119.

196. Katongole, *Sacrifice of Africa*, 120.

197. Katongole, *Sacrifice of Africa*, 77.

198. Cavanaugh, "Discerning," 204.

Nigerian Brethren in the name of national interest.[199] This does not, however, dismiss the seeming division between the church and the world. If, as stated in Ephesians, there is unity in Christ, what of those who are intentionally not part of Christ's body? Hauerwas would answer that although there is not yet full unity, the Christian's relation to those outside of Christ is one of hospitality and love.[200] Additionally, these divisions are not imposed by Christ, but exist already and are already overcome in the resurrection of Christ. A parallel qualification of what might be taken as an imperialistic church exists in which Hauerwas asserts that the Peaceable kingdom of God is witnessed to by the church but not contained by the church.

In another attempt to wrench the notion of politics from its conventional and limited understanding, Cavanaugh gives an example of speaking at a church on issues of global economic injustice. Toward the end of the session, the group discussed what actions to take, and someone suggested that they write to Congress. Cavanaugh says they ended up taking a "more interesting approach" (using the same phrase as Katongole), getting to know local farmers and buying directly each week.[201]

I maintain that while this approach may be "more interesting" it is not necessarily better or any more effective than the first option.[202] In this he follows Hunter (and others) seeming to make a fetish of allegedly non-Washington DC politics as better at the exclusion of the work on policy.[203] While I fully support stretching our understanding of politics outside the Washington DC Beltway, these reactions overcompensate for a Washington-centric view. Perhaps, rather than expanding the mindset

---

199. This was an example I used while teaching peacebuilding theology and practice in northeastern Nigeria at Ekklesiyar Yan'uwa a Nigeria's Kulp Bible College (now Kulp Theological Seminary), the seminary of the Church of the Brethren in Nigeria.

200. Hauerwas, "Beyond the Boundaries," 167, and Hauerwas, *Peaceable Kingdom*, 91.

201. Cavanaugh, "Discerning," 196–208.

202. While resolving the problem may not appear to be closely linked to Christian discipleship, presumably though formation of the disciple is important, Jesus's healing or challenging exclusion was not solely aimed at forming the disciple but *actually concerned with* the suffering person.

203. A more positive approach is at times indicated by Cavanaugh when he writes, "'The role of the church is not merely to make policy recommendations to the state, but to embody a different sort of politics, so that the world may be able to see a truthful politics and be transformed. The church does not thereby withdraw from the world but serve it, both by being the sign of God's salvation of the world and by reminding the world of what the world still is not." Cavanaugh, "Discerning," 404.

of the public, this approach might abandon the political (in the Washington sense) to elites or corporations or big money. To say that Washington is not the only form of politics does not change the reality that policy made in Washington under a wide range of influences from a range of special interests dramatically affects not only the marginalized in the United States, but countries and populations around the globe. The non-national experience of the church is a resource for challenging narrow nationalistic trade and foreign policy.

Hauerwas claims that "the tension of the kingdom is not that caused by unrealized ideals; it is a tension between faithfulness and unfaithfulness."[204] He is critical when concepts like love and justice are referred to, as if when these words are stated, all that needs to be said has been said. When these words become ideals abstracted from the narrative and person of Jesus they become less than they could be.[205] They become abstractions that are thought to be commonly understood markers, but are, in reality, unlikely to contain as much heft as assumed. Into this space Hauerwas often asserts the need to provide a so-called "thick" description of ecclesial practices. Hauerwas notes that his eschatological claims about Jesus do have "immediate ethical implications" that are not in favoring one type of political system over another, but in having become "part of a peaceable kingdom that has been made possible by the life and death of Jesus Christ." This "peaceable kingdom" is an *actual* thing, not an idea, but is not located solely in the church, or in this or that institution or practice. He asserts, "It is not our task to make the 'world' the kingdom; but it is our task to be a people who can witness to the world what it means to be so confident of the Lord of this world that we wish for no more than our daily bread."[206] It is non-coercive witness rather than control through power or violence that defines the vocation of the church:

---

204. Hauerwas, "Reality of the Kingdom," 117.

205. He writes early in his career, "Yet it must be questioned if any discriminating social judgments by the Christian can be made without buying in at some point to the language of justice. But this does not necessarily mean that the Christian's use of the language of justice is limited to the form as he receives it from the world. Rather the Christian must realize that it is exactly his task to transform the language of justice by refusing to accept it as given and by insisting that justice is only properly understood under the norm of Christ." Hauerwas, *Vision and Virtue*, 219–20.

206. Hauerwas, *Against the Nations*, 117.

> Thus, within a world of violence and injustice Christians can take the risk of being forgiven and forgiving. They are able to break the circle of violence as they refuse to become part of those institutions of fear that promise safety by the destruction of others. As a result, some space, both psychological and physical, is created where we can be at rest from a world that knows not who is the king. Such rest, however, is not accomplished by a withdrawal from the world, nor is it a rest in which there is no movement. For to be a part of God's kingdom means that we have found ourselves in the ongoing story of God with his people. That story provides us rest exactly because it trains us with the skills to face the dangers and threats of this existence with courage and patience.[207]

Though Hauerwas challenges the church's full buy-in to the "domination system,"[208] or violent state politics, he does not preclude limited engagement.[209] Asserting this in a continuous manner in an aggressive, some would say, even belligerent tone has contributed to the feeling by some that Hauerwas is sectarian. Hauerwas has regularly challenged such labeling. Cavanaugh also questions this usage of "sect" terminology, noting that, "The most common objection to the suggestion that the church itself embodies a politics is that such a politics is sectarian." He continues, "Such an objection depends on a relatively novel sociological use of the term 'sect.'" Whereas traditionally this term would apply to those groups that have separated themselves from the main body of the church, or "outside the authority of the church . . . In the twentieth century . . . [it] came to indicate a group whose practices put it at odds with the dominant culture and political elites of the nation-state. The underlying assumption is that it is not the church but the nation-state that is 'catholic.'"[210] That is,

---

207. Hauerwas, *Against the Nations*, 117.

208. Wink, *Engaging the Powers*.

209. "They are able to break the circle of violence as they refuse to become part of those institutions of fear that promise safety by the destruction of others." Hauerwas and Sherwindt, "Kingdom of God," 135.

210. Cavanaugh, "Church," 404. Cavanaugh also notes in the same entry (397), "What is lumped together under the term 'Christendom' is in fact a very complex series of attempts to take seriously the inherently political nature of the church and its instrumental role in the integral salvation of the world in Jesus Christ." He seeks to parse the development of the church's shifts in embodiment or disembodiment of its political nature. As Cavanaugh notes, this is much broader than a Weberian defined politics, which he summarizes as "the idea that politics is defined as having to do with attaining and maintaining power over the apparatus of the state." He will assert with

the referent point for normality or at least the starting point from which groups' engagement is measured (at least with the sect language) shifts from having its locus in the church to the state. This is, in part, the shift that Charles Taylor documents in *A Secular Age*.

Though Hauerwas does not aim for church withdrawal or disengagement with the world, he *does* primarily focus on the church as a distinct community. This community is formed and shaped as a people who worship God and embody particular practices in relation to the world.

A Nonviolent Church

For Hauerwas, nonviolence, peace, and peacemaking stand as a core experience and identity of the church. However, since chapter 4 will consist of a deeper engagement with Hauerwas on peacemaking and related ideas, this treatment will be minimal. This section is included here, however, since omitting it would unbalance this chapter's account of Hauerwas's work in ecclesiology. Hauerwas asserts in a characteristically blunt fashion that as a body constituted by Christ the church *is* nonviolent:

> We believe that Christians, when they are thinking like Christians, will discover that they cannot underwrite the assumption that war is one of the necessities of life. For as Christians we believe war is but a name for the powers defeated by the death and resurrection of Jesus. So let us no longer serve such "elemental spirits," but rather be what we are: the church of Jesus Christ. We are bold to call for the abolition of war because we believe war has been abolished through the triumph of the resurrection of Jesus Christ.[211]

The tactic of making this statement in such a matter-of-fact way is a noteworthy rhetorical approach. In it, Hauerwas appears to be doing two things. First, he is making a declarative statement rather than a sociological observation. He is also continuing to stake a claim for theology. Secondly, he is shifting nonviolence, peace, and peacemaking into the realm of "theology proper" rather than relegating it to a position that is secondary to more basic theological content.[212] Hauerwas asserts that the church

---

Hauerwas, who also clearly states that not all politics include violence, that "politics" cannot be reduced to the politics of the nation-state.

211. Hauerwas, *War and the American Difference*, 46.

212. Hauerwas asserts in *Community of Character* (37): "The separation between

(or the Christian) is nonviolent rather than that non-violence is an effect of a theological ethical framework. In his continued effort to dissolve the distinction between theology and ethics he seeks to move nonviolence and peacemaking from being a potential byproduct of theology to being a normative characteristic of what makes the church the church.[213]

A Peacemaking Community

The nonviolent community does not turn from conflict but sustains a politics and virtue of peacemaking. Though chapter 4 will explore this in depth, the more ecclesiological components of peacemaking will be introduced here.

Hauerwas avers, "Therefore, claims for the distinctiveness of the church, and thus Christian ethics, are not attempts to underwrite assumptions of superiority or Christian dominance. Rather they are meant to remind Christians of the radicalness of the gospel. For the gospel cannot be adequately summed up by appeals that we should love our neighbor as ourselves but is meant to transform us by teaching us to be God's peaceable people."[214] The *church is a peacemaking community* is a descriptive statement of what the church *is* as much as it is a statement of where the church ought to be headed and what it should be doing. For Hauerwas, peace cannot be added or subtracted at will from the witness and life of the church. Peace is rather bound into the fabric of this body. It is an essential element of the church, but it does not remain simply in definitional space. It is necessarily lived out in the practical and mundane, both in activities such as baseball and in addressing sin in the church

---

Jesus and social ethics is exhibited by the very way we have learned to formulate the problem—i.e., 'What is the relation between Christology and social ethics?' . . . In contrast I will argue that what it means for Jesus to be worthy of our worship is explicable only in terms of his social significance."

213. Though Hunter allows a version of this he asserts that rather than peace, it is in fact violence that is the central focus of Anabaptists, of whom Hauerwas is the examined representative. Hunter writes, "Yet war is not the central problematic [for Anabaptists] but violence itself—broadly defined. This is why the state figures so prominently within the Anabaptist imagination. The state is the locus of self-legitimating violence and its very existence is defined by the exercise (or threat of exercise) of coercion. Its power is always manifestly or latently coercive. As such it has the authority to compel citizens against their will and to wage war on other nations." Hunter, *To Change the World*, 159.

214. Hauerwas, *Peaceable Kingdom*, 60.

community.²¹⁵ Additionally, peacemaking in many arenas emerges directly out of nonviolence and a commitment not to kill. Hauerwas writes,

> From this perspective the search for Christian unity is not only an imperative demanded by the gospel but an essential exercise of practical reason. If we are a church in diaspora, it is all the more important that local churches refuse to be isolated from one another. Our refusal to be isolated from one another, our willingness to share what we have learned from our attempts to faithfully worship God, is crucial if we are to exemplify for the world the peace that is essential for the discovery of the goods in common. The Christian refusal to kill surely is imperative if we are to sustain the conflicts necessary to learn from one another.²¹⁶

This refusal to kill extends the possibility of a sustained conflict in so much as there is not a quick "out." In relation to foreign policy and the supposed use of just war principles to determine and govern the use of force, this assertion is notable. Additionally, on first read such a statement has a poetic hook. However, in most of the conflicts in most of our lives the option to kill is not an open option. In a typical church conflict over which contractor to use for a repair or which pastor to hire, the possibility of ending the conflict through murder is rarely on the table.²¹⁷ I doubt Hauerwas would object to this counter. I imagine, based on other responses, that his response would be: The community practices and the discernment that allow it to come to such a commitment to nonviolence are a form of training in peace that results in better equipping for conflict than if they had not been so trained. Certainly the "being together" to find goods held in common as a description of congregational life or practical ecumenism is an accurate description of the processes to find peace. Does *the church as peacemaking community* reflect a particular practice (such as a sacrament) or is it a broader, hopefully concrete, descriptor of practice? Hauerwas tends toward a broader, almost philosophical, description of the church that defies many typical discussions and debates over ecclesiology.

---

215. See Hauerwas, "Taking Time for Peace" and "Peacemaking."

216. Hauerwas, *War and the American Difference*, 146.

217. There have been, of course, many instances historically when Christians have killed for things that, to the outsider, appear minor. Conflict which escalates rarely emerges out of the blue but is in response to layers of accumulated actual or perceived wrongdoing or some other impetus.

Conclusion

In this chapter, I have sought to lay out Hauerwas's ecclesiology as part of his larger project and as the foundation of his work on peacemaking. By challenging the distinctions between theology and ethics, theology and the gathered worshiping community, between Christology and ecclesiology, and between peacemaking and nonviolence, Hauerwas seeks to challenge the consideration or practice of these which are detached from the others. Additionally, his challenge to abstraction in theological reflection seeks to root thought and action in the community gathered for common purpose. In the next chapter, the topic of peacemaking will be explored at length. Even when the connection to ecclesiology is not in the foreground it is nonetheless the context of such action. In this section, I have asserted that Hauerwas defines the church by its action and material existence described by its worship, witness, having a history, as distinct or peculiar community, as nonviolent, and as a peacemaking community. In the next chapter these final sections will be extensively expanded.

Chapter 4

HAUERWAS ON PEACE AND PEACEMAKING

I will challenge the oft-made presumption that Christianity is a technology designed to aid those who are Christians to escape our temporality.

—STANLEY HAUERWAS, *WORK OF THEOLOGY*, 90

HAUERWAS IS A THEOLOGIAN of peace. He became convinced of the centrality of peace through the work of John Howard Yoder.[1] For Hauerwas, peace is not an optional addition to being a Christian but is intimately bound up in core practices and beliefs of the church, such as Christology, worship, and reading Scripture. Due to this deep integration, it is impossible to state his peace position abstracted from his broader work.[2] Whereas in chapter 3 I sought to map the contours of his writing on

1. Hauerwas, *With the Grain of the Universe*, 218–25.

2. I assume that Hauerwas would hate the term *peace position*. In *With the Grain of the Universe* (215), Hauerwas notes that Barth resisted the notion that his theology was a "position" since that implies merely a set of beliefs. In *Hannah's Child* he writes, "It is so tempting to think that you need to have a 'position' if you are going to be a 'thinker.' . . . I realize that it may seem odd for me to speak of not having a 'position,' given the fact that many of my theological and ethical colleagues would characterize me as someone with a strong position. This characteristic is not entirely unfair; nonetheless, it is wrong. It is true that I am a pacifist, but that does not mean pacifism is a 'position.' Positions too easily tempt us to think that we Christians need a theory. I am not a pacifist because of a theory. I am a pacifist because John Howard Yoder convinced me that nonviolence and Christianity are inseparable." Hauerwas, *Hannah's Child*, 60.

the church, in this chapter I will demonstrate how peace and peacemaking emerge as a main thread within his writing. I will also observe that, in contrast to common convention, he does not separate nonviolence, peace, and peacemaking into discrete topics. This chapter will be divided into three sections: 1) the formation of the peaceable body; 2) consideration of several key texts; and 3) peacemaking in public. These divisions aim to demonstrate how Hauerwas grounds peacemaking in the church (the gathered body), how he asserts and develops peacemaking through certain key texts, and how this peacemaking is necessarily oriented outside the church as a function of the church's vocation of mission.

In the first section, I will consider the formation of bodies (Christians) in the body (the church). For Hauerwas, this formation is a concrete, historically contingent process through which Christians and the visible gathered community of the church become simultaneously shaped by Jesus, worship, and the common reading of Scripture. This process is not limited to the space within the church walls nor is it for the narrow purpose of spiritual betterment. Here, the body is formed into an alternative politics, a peaceable community. This section will form a link from ecclesiology discussed in chapter 3 to more explicit engagement on peacemaking in later sections of this chapter. Although peacemaking is less explicit in this first section, Hauerwas assumes that it is peacemaking nonetheless.

The second section will consider several of Hauerwas's key texts on peace and peacemaking: "Jesus: The Presence of the Peaceable Kingdom," from *The Peaceable Kingdom*, and two essays from *Christian Existence Today*, "Peacemaking: The Virtue of the Church" and "Taking Time for Peace: The Ethical Significance of the Trivial." These two essays receive greater focus because they provide detailed examples of important moves relating to peacemaking. *Peaceable Kingdom*, Hauerwas's most extended work, explicitly features peace as a prominent topic or framework and demonstrates critical connections between ethics and theology, imitation of Jesus as an ethical source, the centrality of peace in understanding Jesus, and the necessity of peacemaking. "Peacemaking: The Virtue of the Church" is, significantly, one of the few texts in which Hauerwas uses the language of peacemaking. In other places, he consistently asserts the need to perform or practice the faith—which is substantially tied up with his understanding of Jesus and peace—but he does not regularly use language of peacemaking. Though this essay is largely concerned with

Christians' addressing conflict within the church, even here, he indicates how this is should be lived out in public.[3]

The necessity of living out peacemaking in public will be addressed in the final section with a focus on two texts: "Which Church? What Unity? Or, An Attempt to Say What I May Think about the Future of Christian Unity" (in *Approaching the End*), and *War and the American Difference*. Here, Hauerwas offers examples of peacemaking in particular contexts. "Which Church?" deals with ecumenism, an example of peacemaking that addresses divisions in the wider church. Since Hauerwas attaches great significance to the church's public action through witness embodied in the practices of the church, inter-church peace and unity carries substantial weight. The second text, *War and the American Difference*, demonstrates peacemaking as a witness against war. Again, Hauerwas closely ties this to the formation of the peaceable body and the public challenge of this body to the habits of war.

Overall, in this chapter I will provide a picture of Hauerwas's vision of peacemaking by examining several key texts. Though Hauerwas does not always explicitly name *peacemaking*, its components are present in many parts of his writing on peace, nonviolence, and politics. Hauerwas provides a rich store of resources for peacemaking by challenging the divisions between theology, ethics, and politics, as well as through his reflection on the embodied nature of the life of the church as defined by Jesus's social ethic and abolition of war.

Formation of the Peaceable Body

The formation of peaceable bodies (Christians) and the peaceable body (the church) are, for Hauerwas, central to the ministry of the church (a politics). In order for the church to enact its ministry of peacemaking, it must itself be formed into a peaceable body. One cannot know or talk about peace abstracted from theology or detached from the bodies of the church and Christians. Hauerwas resists the assumption that peace, particularly the acceptance of war, can be added or subtracted from the theology and life of the church.[4] This is also the case for ethics. He has often

---

3. "First, I think we must say that it is the task of the church to confront and challenge the false peace of the world which is too often built more on power than truth." Hauerwas, "Peacemaking," 95.

4. "I have written often on the ethics of war and peace, but this is the first book that has those motifs as its primary focus. I have avoided focusing on war and peace

said that the *and* in ethics and theology represents a fundamental error when considering how Christians should live in the world as discussed in earlier chapters. In fact, this is the stated purpose of *The Blackwell Companion to Christian Ethics*, which Hauerwas coedited with Samuel Wells:

> Once, there was no "Christian ethics." And yet the Church was able to form and sustain disciples. To ears used to hearing the confident assertions of modernity, this may seem a curious, almost unintelligible claim. It seems curious because Christians and non-Christians alike assume that insofar as Christianity is credible in modernity it is so because of the 'morality' represented by the description 'Christian.' It seems unintelligible because Christian ethics names a compromise that theology made in modernity in which Christian convictions would still have a hearing in contemporary debates so long as they were detached from the Church's practices.[5]

A similar conviction animates Hauerwas's thoughts on peace. Peace, rightly understood, cannot be abstracted from Christian theology. Peace is intrinsic to core theological commitments of the Trinity and the work and ministry of Jesus the Christ.[6] Much of the rest of this chapter will explore these claims in greater depth. This first portion, however, will develop the ecclesiological focus of chapter 3 in the direction of peace. As such, this claim on the centrality of peace and the inseparability of ethics and theology forces me not only to demonstrate a connection but, as Hauerwas's thought would have it, show that peace, ethics, and theology for Christians are part of a whole that if extracted from each other become unintelligible. This makes my task of explication dangerous since

---

because to do so might give some the impression that nonviolence is all that Christianity is about. If nonviolence becomes an abstraction, an ideal Christians pursue that can be separated from our convictions about the cross and resurrection, nonviolence threatens to become another manipulative form of human behavior. I hope, therefore, that my attempt to (re)describe war as an alternative to the sacrifice of the cross at once illumines why war is so morally compelling and why the church is an alternative to war." Hauerwas, *War and the American Difference*, xvii.

5. Hauerwas and Wells, "Why Christian Ethics Was Invented," 28.

6. These are highly contested areas of theology as well. It also raises the question of what constitutes the defining of the borders of "Christian" thought. That is, what is needed for thought to be Christian or not Christian, acceptable or not acceptable for Christian thought, or whether or not these question of orthodoxy, heresy, incoherence, or defensibility of a particular theology. I take Hauerwas, in general, as attempting to move beyond such distinctions but also to remain solidly with the "traditional" parameters of theology.

linguistic and literary convention makes the isolation and definition of terms seem unavoidable.[7]

Hauerwas's assertion of the centrality of Christian nonviolence or pacifism[8] is rejected by many theologians and ethicists. Because Hauerwas defines peace as integral to Christian life, there are fragments of peace language woven through many essays which do not explicitly address peace.[9] The nature of this approach means that a concise summary of his "position" on peace is virtually impossible. This is particularly evident in *The Peaceable Kingdom*, which is ostensibly about peace but is also a primer on ethics. Since chapter 3 dealt with Hauerwas's ecclesiology in detail and since the alternative peaceable body in his work is the church, this section will build on these arguments by teasing out specific implications for peace and peacemaking.

---

7. This need to categorize and define may be a mark of scholasticism that Jennings asserts is "a complex process of disassociation and dislocation that was connected to the prescribed habits of mind for those who would do scholarly theological work. . . . The social vision that holds court in the theological academy imagines its intellectual world from the commanding heights of various social economics: cultural, political, and scholastic . . . I mean that the regulative character of their intellectual posture created through the cultivated capacities to clarify, categorize, define, explain, interpret, and so forth eclipses its fluid, adaptable, even morph-able character. The eclipse is not due to the emergence of a new intellectual style but points to a history in which the Christian theological imagination was woven into processes of colonial dominance." Jennings, *Christian Imagination*, 8. That this appears "unavoidable" buttresses the claim of the pervasive and formative nature of this structure of control.

8. Convention calls this position pacifism. I do not prefer this term: for one thing, as an "ism," it sounds like a political ideology. For another, misunderstanding and linguistic similarity often assumes pacifism to be related to being passive. This is particularly evident in US foreign-policy discussions about military interventions in which the suggestion that armed intervention is opposed is automatically assumed to be advocating passivity.

9. Favorably summarizing Yoder's work, Hauerwas says, "His more basic objection to this form of pacifism is theological rather than pragmatic since it assumes a Constantinian view of the world as it attempts to conform states and statesmen to the demands of the gospel. Such an assumption confuses the church with the world . . . Christian pacifism stated in its simplest form is that Christians cannot see how war can be an imperative of the Christian life. . . . To understand Yoder's defense of pacifism we must look at his basic theological commitments. For Yoder, the fundamental fact from which the Christian faith springs is God's action in Jesus." Hauerwas goes on to lay out more fundamental theological positions, and then notes that "Christian life is therefore nothing less than an imitation of the way of Jesus." Hauerwas, *Vision and Virtue*, 200–201. As such, peace and peacemaking are not add-ons but are integrally woven throughout the heart of the gospel.

Virtue, Character, and Narrative in Formation

Hauerwas argues that there is a priority of ethical formation within the church which allows for the right reading of Scripture and, in particular, the understanding of peace.[10] He also asserts that without peace as a hermeneutic, one cannot rightly understand the central teachings of Jesus in the Sermon on the Mount.[11] While this is a provocative declaration, it also seems to be blatantly circular, perhaps intentionally so.[12] Given Hauerwas's insistence that the church's conceptual resources be kept in-house rather than importing alien theoretical or political frameworks, one must ask where this peace hermeneutic comes from other than from Scripture. Even if the "in-house" concepts come from general church tradition, one cannot say that peace—particularly strict nonviolence—is a generally held assumption in church tradition.[13] How, then, does Hauerwas sustain a non-foundational, "in-house" claim to peace?[14]

MacIntyre builds on the idea of philosophy and theology as a craft akin to a trade, which one learns through hands-on practice.[15] He confronts the challenge of being both a reader and interpreter of a text in which the reading requires the training that is gained through the reading.[16] He writes, "The person in this predicament requires two things: a

---

10. See Huebner's discussion of Yoder's epistemology in relation to narrative theology in *Precarious Peace*, 49–68.

11. Hauerwas, *Unleashing the Scripture*, 64.

12. "Though the position I hold involves a certain kind of relativism, as I have tried to suggest elsewhere it is not a vicious relativism; there is no conceptual reason that prevents me from making judgments or from seeking to change the mind of those from other traditions." Hauerwas, *Community of Character*, 101. See also Stout, *Ethics after Babel*, 52.

13. There have, of course, been strands that run through church history, even when the "ideal" practice of peace was sustained only by monks or priests. See Cahill, *Love Your Enemies*, for an extended examination of this history.

14. In *Ethics after Babel* (180), Stout writes, "When Gustafson speaks of religious experience, he is not appealing to a kind of prelinguistic or nonpropositional awareness of god. Experience may be prior to reflection, but It is not prior to 'the context of a religious community, with its first-order religious language, its liturgies and symbols, and its procedures for transmitting a heritage.'"

15. MacIntyre, *Three Rival Versions of Moral Enquiry*.

16. Attacking this division also means that the right action must be done rightly. According to Hauerwas in *Performing the Faith* (158), "This means that someone may 'copy' the actions of a just person, but the action quite literally is not the same action if the habits that make the agent just are absent. That is why attempts to understand the relation between liturgy and motivation for action, as cause to effect, are so disastrous

teacher and an obedient trust that what the teacher, interpreting the text, declares to be good reasons for transforming oneself into a different kind of person—and thus a different kind of reader—will turn out to be genuinely good reasons in the light afforded by that understanding of the texts which becomes available only to the transformed self."[17] Perhaps this makes most sense for those newly entering into the community. That is, there may be some element of belief, but participation is not contingent on full comprehension of all nuances of doctrine. Hauerwas has often challenged the assumption that responsibility can only be assumed if one knows what one is doing at the time of doing and freely chooses the act. For him, one can never fully know what one is getting into, whether it is in pledging faithfulness in marriage or in making a career choice. The new Christian gains greater understanding during and through participation in the worshiping community, liturgy, and ministry of the church. As such, the primary focus is on the experience of the community *rather* than from an established theoretical or dogmatic foundation. Hauerwas has on many occasions asserted a non-foundational approach.[18] For an

---

for an account of the moral life as the life of virtue. If what we are and do morally as Christians is intelligible abstracted from liturgical action, then we have, perhaps with the best intentions, reproduced the modern assumption that action descriptions can be divorced from agents." Just actions require just agents—though presumably a just action done for the wrong reason is still better for the community or the person than an unjust act. By focusing so intently on the agent of the action rather than the effects of those actions on the community, Hauerwas tips his hand to his privileged social position. This does not mean that the manner of the action is unimportant, it might be better to say, just actions are *always* preferable (with the obvious need to define justice) and it is best when the just action is done with the proper intent and character. I doubt Hauerwas would disagree with this. He would likely assert, however, that too much focus on the end result and the efforts to regulate that with the legal system is symptomatic of a degraded society that lacks an account of common history and morality. Hauerwas goes on to discuss his suggestion that parents who wish to teach their children to be "moral" should introduce them to baseball. While this makes some sense in an abstract way, it still seems like a stretch to recommend baseball (or any other team sport) as a means of moral formation. There are certainly values of cooperation and discipline to be derived from sports, but participation for boys is just as likely to instill misogynistic assumptions about being tough and "manly." As an analogy, however, this example may be instructive. Stout uses baseball in a way that seems like a more accurate analogue. Stout, *Ethics after Babel*, 276.

17. MacIntyre, *Three Rival Versions of Moral Enquiry*, 82.

18. In *Church as Polis* (33), Arne Rasmussen provides a simple and useful definition of non-foundational theology: "This means that instead of starting the argument with some universal principles or criteria that every rational person should accept, one starts from shared conviction."

example of this, see "The Church's One Foundation is Jesus Christ Her Lord, or In a World without Foundations All we have is the Church," in *Good Company*. To rightly be formed into a peaceable body requires not simply a rule against violence but a peaceable community of reading, action, prayer, and discernment.

Hauerwas attempts to get away from a universal principle.[19] Rather than a universal principle that exists separate from the experience of a particular community, Hauerwas seeks to bring these "foundations" closer to the surface of human experience. He attempts to show this foundation within the church. This includes locating peacemaking within the church.[20] Discussing Hauerwas, Kallenberg writes, "For early Christian writers, theology is identical to ethics because the gospel embodied in the text was none other than the gospel embodied in the community that preserved *this* text as its cannon."[21] This, of course, is not so much a substitution of the foundation with a non-foundation floating free in the middle of our experience. Rather, the foundation is embedded in a community with particular practices and traditions of reasoning through specific questions. Even though this does not extend "the whole way down" to a universal foundation, it is nonetheless rooted in some manner.[22]

For Hauerwas, theology starts with a particular community rather than universal principles. This approach in part comes out of Hauerwas's reading of Wittgenstein and Yoder. Many post-liberals claim Wittgenstein as a major influence on their work, but (Hauerwas included) do not engage Wittgenstein in any sustained way. Kallenberg, however, notes that despite little overt engagement, Hauerwas's work has been shaped by Wittgenstein—a subtle taking on of Wittgenstein's project to teach the reader to think rightly. As such, the struggle and not the conclusion is the point of the work of theology.

19. After noting Cavanaugh's observation that "globalization is but the extension of capitalist markets that give the illusion of diversity," Hauerwas comments, "As a result, if MacIntyre is right that the discovery of the good through practical reason is a local affair, the particular practices necessary for the discovery of the common good are undermined by the processes associated with globalization." Hauerwas, *War and the American Difference*, 137.

20. Such rootedness of peacemaking in a community makes possible sustained engagement, which is critical for sustaining the difficult work of peacemaking.

21. Kallenberg, *Ethics as Grammar*, 158.

22. Stout provides a useful discussion of the practical process that sustains moral discourse without going the whole way down to a basic philosophical principle. In particular, he shows that Bellah and Swindler's attempt at Socratic methodology in interviewing points to the pragmatic (and not philosophical) way that people understand and enact right and wrong as well as *telos* in their lives. Stout, *Ethics after Babel*, 191–219.

Peacemaking emerges from the virtue of peace and the confrontations necessary as part of living as truthful people.[23] Forgiveness emerges out of being forgiven and accepting this forgiveness. God's action is the starting and ending, which forms the people in part through the Scripture but then also informs how the community reads Scripture. The "word of God" is not delivered as a whole, nor is a foundation possible outside the dynamic relationships of the community and God through history.[24]

The hermeneutic of peace requires a peaceable body. Nicholas Healy challenges this tack, noting that Hauerwas's argument seems to tie the truthfulness of his position to the presence of such a church.[25] Since there are few such peaceable churches, then the argument may not hold. In this case, theology may be a form of sociology, which simply describes what is in fact the case. The work of Hauerwas is not, however, sociology. While he asserts the presence of such communities and community practices, his approach is more akin to providing illustrations in a sermon than to demonstrating a general rule by compiling specific examples. In a sociological approach, the absence of such examples would demonstrate the inadequacy of the theological work. One might then ask the further question: Is Hauerwas theologically describing an actual community, or

23. "It is a unity that profoundly acknowledges our differences because we have learned that those differences are not accidental to our being truthful people—even when they require us to confront one another as those who have wronged us." Hauerwas, "Peacemaking," 95.

24. The approach of not having a foundation appears to be, in part, a repudiation of particular epistemological assumptions of modernity, but also a tactical way to retrieve and re-embed the locus of theological speech within the church. Hauerwas refers to this as "confident" theological speech: "Not only are Yoder and the pope the kind of witnesses that Barth's theology requires—they are the kind of witnesses who must exist if Christians are to recover the confident use of theological speech that Barth exemplifies so well. Moreover, because confident Christian speech has been compromised by the disunity of the church, it is important, as I hope to show, that John Howard Yoder and John Paul II are one in their witness to the One who moves the sun and the stars and is to be found in the manger." Hauerwas, *With the Grain of the Universe*, 217. Palestinian theologian Mitri Raheb demonstrates this when he writes, "People begin with geo-political realities and conclude with theologies. My thesis is that God came to defeat geo-politics and he succeeded. Because without God, Palestine would have continued as a land at the periphery. Yet because God chose to reveal himself in this land, it became central to history, which is why it is found at the center of ancient maps. Because of God. The moment God identified himself with this land, everything changed." Raheb, *Faith in the Face of Empire*, 89.

25. Healy, *Hauerwas*. See in particular chapter 4, "The Empirical Church and Christian Identity," 73–99. In *Work of Theology* (267), Hauerwas dismisses Healy on this point with little comment, noting that this is a worn-out argument.

is he providing examples as a way to change the rest of the church? In the introduction to the collection of sermons in *A Cross-Shattered Church,* he writes that he is "convinced that the recovery of the sermon as the context for theological reflection is crucial if Christians are to negotiate the world in which we find ourselves."[26] That the sermon is a central theological act points to the centrality of the gathered community. The sermon is not simply a literary product, but part of the action of the church.

Peter Dula, himself a Mennonite, asks a question similar Healy's concerning the Mennonite communities that Hauerwas so frequently lauds and from which Hauerwas discovered peace.[27] Dula is uncertain that the communities Hauerwas refers to in general actually exist in the particular. This concern carries more weight because these communities would seemingly fit Hauerwas's ideal of an identified ecclesial community shaped by common worship, shared practices, peacemaking, and history. If so, is the approach of Hauerwas another variation of the problem of universal principle by discussing a more generalized account from the specific witness? Without distilling rules or accounts that include multiple examples, it may be that we are left with infinitely long descriptions of infinitely particular cases. For example, the life of a congregation is determined by many things. These details could be described to the granular detail in every part of the community. If our heroic theologian cum sociologist/historian/genealogist/philosopher/etcetera was to describe the life of the congregation at all possible levels, there would be a potentially complete understanding.[28] This would not, however, provide a prescription for future action nor give a picture of closed causation; it would only recount how the situation happened to end up. Nassim Nicolas Taleb challenges the tendency to "narrative fallacy" and to ascribe

---

26. Hauerwas, *Cross-Shattered Church,* 12.

27. Dula, "Wittgenstein among the Theologians," 22.

28. Randy Woodley discusses the difference between Euroamerican and Native American assumptions on educational process and expertise. Woodley, *Shalom and the Community of Creation,* 96–100. Mastery and control of the subject matter are noted as relevant topics to consider. Having examples that are described in detail and "prove" the possibility of a particular form of community seems to be commonly desired but also rather out of sync with Hauerwas's approach, which often challenges Enlightenment epistemic principles. Some of these issues were raised in a conversation with Canadian First Nations Christian theologian Reverend Dr. Terry LeBlanc at the Sojourners Summit Conference in Washington, DC, in 2015. He discussed his efforts to establish First Nations theological education programs; I discussed my work on Hauerwas.

causation with the assumption that professionals in the field in question will be able to propose a solution the next time this particular situation arises.[29] Taleb, at least, asserts that such back narrating tends to lead not toward wisdom but to the delusion of expertise. The picture and causal links could, as is seen in all these disciplines represented in our heroic theologian, be challenged on any number of accounts. Such a challenge undermines confidence that if I do X then Y is *necessarily* the result. So, while there is value in systematic study, the level of confidence in descriptions of causation as discovered through anecdotes should be minimal.

Taleb attempts to give tools for acting in the face of uncertainty in his *Antifragile: Things that Gain from Disorder*. In biblical and theological parlance, this is often designated as wisdom, or biblical wisdom literature. Such wisdom is the ability to act well in the face of uncertainty and ambiguity.[30] The acting in the face of uncertainty is not built on the assumption that the contingency can be engineered away but aims to establish skillful action through practice. This practice, rightly oriented, is located in the community of the church. Michael Baxter challenges whether practical engagement with trying to live the church in the world can really be as theologically substantial as Hauerwas asserts. In particular he describes a Catholic Worker house's struggle with zoning laws, which came out of a very particular theological commitment. This struggle, though based on theological commitment, was done by making a legal argument and engaging the zoning laws of their city.[31]

The question of the direction of reasoning as theology→reality or reality→theology can be problematized at length. In practice, Hauerwas's approach is perhaps most analogous to a sermon in which there is a simultaneous exploration of an idea and a Scripture text and demonstration that a particular action or characteristic is possible for Christians and the church. As such, it is both descriptive and exhortatory. As noted above, Hauerwas asserts that sermons help Christians negotiate the world. He believes that "sermons are crucial if we are to recover the stories that make it possible to recover Christian practical reason. Put differently, I try to use sermons to develop the imaginative skills to help us see the world as judged and redeemed by Christ."[32] For Hauerwas,

29. Taleb, *Black Swan*, 62–84.

30. See Lederach, *Moral Imagination*, 113–29, for an approach to peacemaking that amounts to this relatively fluid process,

31. Baxter, "Church as *Polis*?," 132.

32. Hauerwas, *Cross-Shattered Church*, 16.

sermons are a performance in the church's struggle to rightly worship God. They are neither pre- nor post-work: they *are* the work—though not the entirety of the church's work. This process, in the context of the centrality of peace, brings about the imaginative skills needed to both resist violence and make peace without resorting to violence or coercion.

Kallenberg also asserts that Hauerwas's position is to some extent contingent on exemplary communities. He writes, "Hauerwas's failure to accommodate liberals by translating the gospel into terms that they can already understand is not an instance of fideism because the gospel can be more powerfully and clearly displayed in the actual life of the church, enculturation into which constitutes the whole of salvation. Of course, the absence of such a church would severely weaken Hauerwas's position."[33] Kallenberg goes on to note that such a claim would shift the center of Hauerwas's work to his sermons and other "less scholarly" work that is more explicitly derived from within the church. While Kallenberg asserts that contingency on an actual community is required, his account is slightly different. In this, Hauerwas's engagement through sermons is in fact part of the church such that these are performances in a church context and are then part of the *church as demonstration*. As a result, sermons are not somehow separate from the life of the church; they do, in fact, constitute the very life of the church. While sermons are certainly part of imagining and exhorting toward a possibility for the life of the church, they are not something external to that church. Theological engagement with the Bible through the context of the celebration of liturgy

---

33. Kallenberg, *Ethics as Grammar*, 159. See also the introduction to Hauerwas, *Cross-Shattered Church*, 19.

is, then, the real performance of the church.³⁴ This still leaves many questions, not the least of which being how Hauerwas can move forward in this space.

I will try to resolve some of these questions by following the flow of Hauerwas's thought regarding virtue, ethics, narrative, and liturgy. In essence, Hauerwas believes that people are formed in virtue and character within a community that is formed by its participation in a particular peaceable narrative. Additionally, though Hauerwas does not always take the reader there, much of this work and the above remarks on his approach are extremely pertinent for the ambiguities of practice of peacemaking (as will be demonstrated in chapter 5). The following will lay out an alternative foundation built on the church's resources found in its body, liturgy, narrative, and practices.

In "Character, Narrative, and Growth in Christian Life," Hauerwas connects moral life—particularly the discussion between moral development and seemingly related Christian concepts—and narrative formation. While he explores some work on moral development in this essay, he also notes that the related language of Christian thought is not simply a more "colorful ways to talk about moral development." This is the case because "the language of spiritual growth, holiness, and perfection directs attention to the development of the moral self in a manner quite different from the contemporary concern with moral development . . . The translation of the language of perfection into the language of development, however, involves a transformation that robs the language of its religious import."³⁵ To maintain the theological significance this description must be part of the ongoing narrative:

---

34. Of this type of on-site reflection, Jeffrey Stout writes, "Moral philosophy is not practiced from the vantage point of omniscience, above history. It begins, for any of us, at some particular site, where some moral languages are in use . . . Let us say that moral philosophy thus conceived, is a kind of reflexive ethnography. It begins at home, with languages in use, and then reaches out to other possibilities, accessible from its particular historical position. Its first method is participant-observation, its initial aim the understanding of all-too-familiar uses of words and related goings-on. It benefits from thick description, from dredging up old documents, from long visits to strange places, from flights of artistic imagination—from all the ways in which new possibilities of moral observation, inference, and action can be brought into view. We must begin in a particular place, but that need not and should not condemn us to stay at our starting point. Breadth of vision remains a good to be pursued, even if our perspective can never be eternity." Stout, *Ethics after Babel*, 72–73.

35. Hauerwas, "Character, Narrative, and Growth in Christian Life," 130.

> What we need is not a principle or end but a narrative that charts a way for us to live coherently amid the diversity and conflicts that circumscribe and shape our moral existence ... I am suggesting that descriptively the self is best understood as a narrative, and normatively we require a narrative that will provide the skills appropriate to the conflicting loyalties and roles we necessarily confront in our existence. The unity of the self is therefore more like the unity that is exhibited in a good novel—namely with many subplots and characters that we at times do not closely relate to the primary dramatic action of the novel. But ironically without such subplots we cannot achieve the kind of unity necessary to claim our actions as our own.[36]

While this theme is crucial for understanding Hauerwas generally, it is also key when observing links in his work between Christology, nonviolence, embodied ethics, and peacemaking. If the Christian's overriding story is that of being a peacemaker, then making peace is what Christians do when acting out their own stories. Peacemaking, then, is not simply a set of technical skills like mediation and conflict analysis, but is woven into our lives. Peacemaking is a "skill of seeing our present and future in the hands of God [that] frees us from the necessity of wielding violence to control history."[37] *Skills* are not referred to here in the technical sense of mastering formal processes.[38] They are, rather, skills to discern what is needed in the particular moment and also to correctly apply a theory to a given relationship.

To demonstrate this, Hauerwas tells a story showing that something more than an elaborate theory is needed for moral formation and discernment. He tells of his father's care in crafting a rifle and his rejection of this gift with a comment on gun policy. He writes, "I am struck by how little I would have been helped by becoming more sophisticated in ethical theory or even by conforming my life more completely to the best

36. Hauerwas, "Character, Narrative, and Growth in Christian Life," 144.

37. Hauerwas further states, "Pacifists have no corner on knowing how to live peaceably. Indeed I suspect that most of us who call ourselves 'pacifist' have little idea what is entailed in such a description. To say that I am a pacifist in fact is an attempt to make a commitment in public in hopes that others will force me to explore what such a commitment entails—i.e., it is a challenge to the imagination." Hauerwas, *Against the Nations*, 60n7.

38. In "Peacemaking: The Virtue of the Church" (96), it almost appears, however, that Hauerwas *is* using the word in a technical sense. The difference is that rather than skills learned as *skills* or *techniques*, these are habits learned through following the teaching of Matthew 18 within the church community over time.

ethical theory of the day. My problem was not that I lacked skill in moral argument and justification, but that I lacked character sufficient to acknowledge all that I owed my parents while seeing that I am independent of them."[39] He goes on to say that stories help us located ourselves in relation to others and that freedom is "not no story but a true story."[40] He addresses some of these challenges by focusing on formation of virtue, character, and narrative.

Formation of Virtue through Narrative

Given the relatively extensive groundwork I developed in the introductory portion of this section and the intention to spend a majority of the chapter specifically on Hauerwas's work which more explicitly addresses peace and peacemaking, this section on virtue and character as well as those below on ethics/theology, narrative, and liturgy will be kept relatively brief. While these areas are critical to framing and sustaining his work on peace and peacemaking they are also more regularly commented on and as such need less treatment.

For Hauerwas, right action must be based on right, or virtuous being: "An ethic of virtue centers on the claim that an agent's being is prior to doing."[41] In the essay, "Peacemaking: The Virtue of the Church," Hauerwas explicitly links his thinking on virtue to Aristotle on virtue, but does not elaborate extensively. In this he sets an example of *virtue* as a more substantially formed person beyond simply learnings a set of skills used to deduce the proper decision in the face of a moral dilemma. Such a formulation does not preclude rational inquiry, technical skill,[42] or defense of one's action but asserts that this is *not* a non-historical or individualistic practice.[43] Though he shifts in emphasis, he does not completely reject character in favor of narrative and community as defining places of virtue. These locations and practices of virtue do, however, tend to displace character as Hauerwas's thought develops.[44] He then shifts

---

39. Hauerwas, "Character, Narrative, and Growth in Christian Life," 147.
40. Hauerwas, "Character, Narrative, and Growth in Christian Life," 148–49.
41. Hauerwas, "Character, Narrative, and Growth in Christian Life," 113.
42. Hauerwas, *War and the American Difference*, 137.
43. For a consideration of Hauerwas's work on craft and formation, see Shuman, "Discipleship as Craft," 315–31.
44. See Wells, *Transforming Fate into Destiny*, 38.

toward church practices as both forming and political as a reoccurring or organizing framework. Though the shifts occur and indicate important developments, they do not indicate any significant rejection or about face in concern. These all are variations on formation of Christians and the church, which has often been called discipleship. Hauerwas writes in *Community of Character*, "The Christian life requires the development of certain kinds of habits, but those very habits require us to face ambiguities and conflicts through which our virtues are refined."[45] Within peacemaking it is this engaging of both conflict and ambiguities that define the church's vocation of peacemaking.

MacIntyre's work challenged Hauerwas's early writing on character. Hauerwas notes that though he had felt that he needed an account of agency to sustain character, he later realized that "character is not the qualification of our agency, but our character constitutes our agency."[46] MacIntyre's *After Virtue* helped him realize that "the mistake was to try to defend an account of agency to sustain what it means for us to take ownership of what we do on grounds that first-person avowals of action cannot be described in third-person language. I was, in short, trying to defend action qua action as a logically primitive notion."[47] What was particularly influential for Hauerwas was the way that this connected him to narrative, which in turn, more closely tied him to the story of Scripture and of the church. This was a move toward concreteness. He writes of these realizations: "I knew actions begged for narrative display, but I did not realize that action qua action cannot be made intelligible unless we acknowledge the narrative that renders the action intelligible."[48] Though narrative may not determine action, action must be understood within the narrative.

An example that links to peacemaking illustrates this point. In 2014, a group of North Americans proposed offering themselves as hostages in exchange for the schoolgirls abducted by Boko Haram from a school in northeast Nigeria.[49] The context is what makes this action intelligible. The Americans were from the Church of the Brethren, which started what is now called Ekklesiyar Yan'uwa a Nigeria (Church of the Brethren

---

45. Hauerwas, *Community of Character*, 150.
46. Hauerwas, "How to Be an Agent," 74.
47. Hauerwas, "How to Be an Agent," 74.
48. Hauerwas, "How to Be an Agent," 74.
49. Miller, "Resolution Supports Nigerian Brethren."

in Nigeria) in the 1920s and built the school in Chibok in the 1930s. The connection has maintained over time. As a historic peace church, the Church of the Brethren has from its beginnings rejected participation in war. This *nonresistance* gradually grew into *peacemaking*, accompanied by a deep commitment to service. Additionally, a number of those who made this offer were from the Christian Peacemaker Teams, a group that actively gets in the way of violence; these individuals, thus, were formed in the practices of dangerous peacemaking. One can see, then, how this narrative makes the action intelligible.

Hauerwas does not fully elaborate on the connection between virtue enacted in practical reason to address and adapt in the complex and ambiguous situations of conflict. This is a natural connection and extension of Hauerwas's thought that can be seen in John Paul Lederach's book, *The Moral Imagination*. Hauerwas's work on virtue provides both a foundation for his work as well as a useful structure to support a form of peacemaking for the church. Lederach describes the purpose of this work as follows:

> Transcending violence is forged by the capacity to generate, mobilize, and build the moral imagination. The kind of imagination to which I refer is mobilized when four disciplines and capacities are held together and practiced by those who find their way to rise above violence. Stated simply, the moral imagination requires the capacity to imagine ourselves in a web of relationship that includes our enemies: the ability to sustaining a paradoxical curiosity that embraces complexity without reliance on dualistic polarity; the fundamental belief in and pursuit of the creative act; and the acceptance of the inherent risk of stepping into the mystery of the unknown that lies beyond the far too familiar landscape of violence.[50]

In Hauerwas's view, the formation of virtue and character as part of the peacemaking community then manifests the capacity for the moral imagination described by Lederach.[51] The formation of virtue is a necessary condition for peacemaking in the face of conflict and violence.

50. Lederach, *Moral Imagination*, 5. The relationship between Lederach in *The Moral Imagination* and Hauerwas on peacemaking will be explored in chapter 5.

51. Hauerwas refers to the importance of imagination when he states, "Pacifists, have no corner on knowing how to live peaceably. Indeed I suspect that most of us who call ourselves 'pacifist' have little idea what is entailed in such a description. To say that I am a pacifist in fact is an attempt to make a commitment in public in hopes that others will force me to explore what such a commitment entails—i.e., it is a challenge

One may then ask, if virtue is formed by narrative, who controls or defines the narrative? Hauerwas works to remake ethics as integral to theology while at the same time reclaiming theology as the language of the church. In this he posits theology as a legitimate form of knowledge that is not owned by any sort of universal person; nor can it be detached and knowable apart from the practices and life of the church. This is less parochial than it may sound. Hauerwas does not believe that the church is synonymous with the kingdom of God; neither does it have an exclusive grasp on the kingdom of God. Non-Christians, in his view, often do a better job of living the kingdom than Christians.[52] Though this presence is not contained within the church, the shape of the life of the church that is formed by a particular narrative is the means by which Hauerwas understands the kingdom of God. This then raises the question of ownership again, which takes us beyond his qualification above. Further, depending on how you modify the preceding sentence, if the kingdom presence is understood only when narrated through the story of the life of the church, then even the presence of the kingdom outside the confines of the church is, to some extent, under the control of the church.[53] Whether this is a form of coercion or violence that belies Christian peacemaking remains an open question.

Hauerwas posits that narrative gives shape to convictions but goes further, saying that we only know what our convictions are by the stories we tell. In "A Story-Formed Community: Reflections on *Watership Down*" (in *A Community of Character*), he resists the idea that the story may simply illustrate what might be said more simply. This is, perhaps, related to modes such as aesthetics, as described in Kallenberg's *Ethics as*

---

to the imagination." Hauerwas, *Against the Nations*, 60n7.

52. Hauerwas also writes, "To be sure, the church is not the kingdom, but neither is the life Christians share together something less than the kingdom's inbreaking." Hauerwas and Sherwendt, "Reality of the Kingdom," 119.

53. This narrative control is a form of possession. While this may desirable within the life of the church, when it relates the kingdom beyond the walls of the church it begins to feel possessive, as if the presence of God and the kingdom is thing to be lost or maintained coercively. Those of an Anabaptist stream have certainly been in a minority ecclesial status in relation to the broader church. Despite this numerical minority situation many have gained ecumenical space and respect despite historical persecution. Additionally, in the United States, Christianity is the largest religious population though it has generally been experiencing a loss of cultural influence.

Grammar, addressed above. As such, it would be a form of knowledge that lies outside generally accepted "scientific" modes of rationality.[54]

Hauerwas similarly seeks to reattach ethics both to the person and to the community, particularly as this relates to the story and enacted story (liturgy) of the church. He also asserts the ongoing and open-ended nature of theology. He posits that one cannot take a final position, since theology is an ongoing conversation about God. Since the discussion emerges out of a narrative, and history and is part of the its ongoing development, then theology, even when not narratively construed, is still narrative based. Since there are no universal principles detached from any particular history, and the end goal of theology is not to derive any such principles, then even apparently abstract theology is narrative contingent and embedded. Hauerwas challenges such attempts at abstraction. He notes that much writing on ethics has been based on substantive claims about Christology and the incarnation rather than being modeled after the life and teaching of Jesus. He states that the early church's Christology "did not consist first in claims about Jesus' ontological status" but relied on telling his story.[55] In this, the teaching and example found in the life of Jesus are often lost or downplayed. From this framing, ethicists have made broad assertions and then sought to apply them in particular cases. Hauerwas argues that this approach loses a nuance particular to Christians.[56] How this narrative is enacted and formed within the community must now be addressed.

---

54. In this vein, Taylor writes, "Science by its very nature involves our taking an objective, and in this sense universal perspective on things. To see human life in the view from nowhere, or to use a term of the epoch, from the standpoint of the 'impartial spectator', is to think in universal, and no longer parochial terms. But this rise is now coded as exclusively in the register of the understanding; the will remains constant. Within this framework, it is clear why the quality of the will is irrelevant to ethics. What is needed is to work out what we ought to do is purely disengaged reason." Taylor, *Secular Age*, 254.

55. Hauerwas, *Peaceable Kingdom*, 73–74.

56. "A nuance particular to Christians" doesn't seem to do it. It may be that the "big" theological concept of incarnation is too abstract and so aims too far toward universality or universal claims. Would critical theorists and theologians agree with this challenge to liberal universal presumptions? I imagine Hauerwas would assert that this effort towards universality is an aspect of modernity and, as such, shows up in both conservative and liberal projects in modernity.

Liturgy as Forming and as Practice of Narrative

Formation into the peaceable body takes place, in part, through liturgy. By practicing the narrative of the peaceable kingdom and Jesus, the church and Christians themselves become peaceable and capable of peacemaking. To describe and assess this, I return to "Suffering Beauty: The Liturgical Formation of Christ's Body," which is found in *Performing the Faith*. I am focusing on this essay, which was originally written for the annual meeting of the Society for Catholic Liturgy in 2001, because it pulls together several strands of thinking addressed in the first section of this chapter. In this essay, he posits prayer as the work of justice, while challenging the division between theology and ethics. He then asserts that one must be formed by the beauty of liturgy to challenge evil.

Hauerwas states, "Worship is not what we do to motivate the passion for justice. Worship, which from beginning to end is prayer, is justice."[57] Here, he begins breaking down the distinctions that govern assumptions of causation (and priority given to particular actions). He seeks not only to break down the divisions between actions and worship but to do so between forms of prayer, and the very existence of the church in the world as well. He notes, "For Christians prayer is sacrifice, because we pray in the name of Christ. Just as Jesus is the Father's prayer for the world, so God's church, through the miracle of the Spirit's work, makes us God's continuing prayer for the world. This means quite literally that there is nothing more important for Christians to do than to pray, in particular, for our enemies."[58] Prayer, then, is the form of life of the church.

In the inability of many Christians to articulate the value of worship there is an impulse to describe the strange practice of worship by the "community good" it produces. These benefits are typically the creation of community or the motivation for justice. Of this tendency Hauerwas asserts, "When liturgy becomes a motivation for action that does not require the liturgy for the intelligibility of the description of what we have done, then we lose the means as Christians to make our lives our own."[59] He goes on a few pages later with a similar statement, concluding

---

57. Hauerwas, "Suffering Beauty," 152.

58. Hauerwas, "Suffering Beauty," 153.

59. Hauerwas, "Suffering Beauty," 153. Following a substantial quotation from Saint Gregory, Calivas writes, "These words of St. Gregory are not the words of a moralist—a set of aphorisms that appear removed and unrelated to the harsh realities of practical or real life. The Fathers of the Church, like the prophets before them,

that if the separation is maintained, then "we have, perhaps with the best intentions, reproduced the modern assumption that action descriptions can be divorced from agents."[60] Hauerwas reiterates this theme in many forms, as he seeks to claim worship as well as peacemaking and justice as central to the church's life—without allowing a causation or prioritization or a displacement of theology by ethics.

Central to Hauerwas's argument is that beauty is an integral facet to consider in liturgy and worship. There is a relationship between the minimalism of the assumption that the only important work is that which "gets things done for justice" and the *and* in theology *and* ethics or worship *and* ethics. This is the assumption that liturgy and worship can be useful but are not essential for ethics. He asserts, "Fragmentation is the social condition that creates the politics that makes intelligible the question: 'What is the relation between liturgy and ethics?'"[61] This emphasis on worship does not, however, pull the church back into itself to disengage from the world. Though people have expressed fears that Hauerwas contributes to the separation of the church from the world, his work is not the negation of the practical but the push to ensure that *all* is worship, practical, public, and political.[62] He writes,

> The beauty, the goodness, and the truth of our liturgy is tested by our being sent forth. If we are not jarred by the world to which we return, then something has gone wrong. The feeling of being out of place need not last long or even occur after every Eucharist, but the beauty we have beheld in the gift of God's Son leaves its mark. Formed by such beauty we no longer desire to live by the lies that would have us call lies true, evil good, and ugliness beautiful. Through prayers, prayers that often we know

are neither moralists nor politicians. Their function is to teach people the truths of God, the world and human life, so that these teachings may be translated into godly action, whether in personal or public life." Calivas, "Experiencing the Justice of God in Liturgy," 296.

Though Calivas provides an Orthodox read on liturgy that is in line with several themes of Hauerwas, such as the relationship between liturgy and ethics, the remaining division between practice and liturgy in his articulation would likely provoke a response from Hauerwas. Though substantively very close, the linguistic constraints in description remain. Hauerwas's insistence that the liturgy *is* the political/public witness, however, persists in giving an air of insularity that Calivas might overcome while remaining liturgically robust.

60. Hauerwas, "Suffering Beauty," 158.
61. Hauerwas, "Suffering Beauty," 153.
62. For example, see "Church is Mission."

not what we pray, we become incorporated into God's prayer for the world.[63]

The necessity of "jarring" and reengagement protects Hauerwas from the risk of fleeing the world. It is not that life, or more specifically peacemaking, happen only in the streets rather than in the church, but that church as gathered community is necessarily in mission—outwardly focused though liturgically formed. For the church to enact its ministry of peacemaking it must itself be formed into a peaceable body.

From Peace to Peacemaking

Hauerwas attempts to move the conversation about peace beyond what is often an impasse between traditionally framed just war theory and pacifism. He seeks to problematize assumptions about pacifism and to move the conversation beyond deliberations of participation or nonparticipation in war.[64] My goal in this section is to analyze Hauerwas's effort to place peace at the center of Christian theology and ethics by grounding peacemaking in the community. This peacemaking is a core practice that requires both action and patience, recognizing that efforts for peace, while foundational, must not overdetermine Christian life. I begin by examining *The Peaceable Kingdom* as an early and extended example of Hauerwas's ethical/theological work and the interwoven nature of peace.

The Peaceable Kingdom *(1983) as Foundation for Peace*

Hauerwas opens chapter 5 of *The Peaceable Kingdom*, entitled "Jesus: The Presence of the Peaceable Kingdom," with the assertion that all the chapters to this point build toward this one.[65] The chapter is comprised of several subsections: 1) "The Ethical Significance of Jesus"; 2) "Jesus, Israel, and the Imitation of God"; 3) "Jesus and the Kingdom of God"; 4) "The Resurrection: The Establishment of a Kingdom of Forgiveness

---

63. Hauerwas, "Suffering Beauty," 164–65

64. Though this view is seemingly in the same stream as the World Council of Churches' work on Just Peace as found in the *Ecumenical Call to Just Peace* and the *Just Peace Companion*, Hauerwas's approach is markedly different. This is at least in part because he often challenges and examines the more basic assumptions, practices, and theological/philosophical underpinnings of peace.

65. Hauerwas, *Peaceable Kingdom*, 72.

and Peace"; and 5) "The Ethics of Salvation and Faith." I will proceed by looking more closely at the chapter along these divisions. Here again, we see the close intertwining of Hauerwas's thinking on Christology, ethics, and peace. Although this is the key chapter in a work with the word *peaceable* in the title, it is as much or more about Jesus as it is focused on peace per se.

In the earlier chapters, Hauerwas develops several themes that build a broad foundation for the centrality of Jesus in the ethics of the kingdom of God. He begins this chapter with the section titled "The Ethical Significance of Jesus." Hauerwas notes that the extensive scholarship on the life of Jesus has led to the generally accepted conclusions that the Gospels are not an objective, that is, uninterpreted account.[66] This does not undermine the centrality of the life and teachings of Jesus, as found in the Gospels, in terms of ethical considerations.[67] This is not a problem "since the very demands of Jesus placed on his followers means that he cannot be known abstracted from his disciples' response."[68] This makes it clear that Hauerwas intends to place theology as a discipline of the church within the church.[69] He further asserts that Jesus's followers used stories to express Jesus's significance rather than ontological claims around Christology.[70]

If, however, the Epistles were written before the Gospels, is Hauerwas's claim challenged? Whether or not the written form of the Gospels existed prior to that of the Epistles, an oral tradition of the Gospel stories was certainly present. It is out of particular happenings or actions that those around Jesus begin to say, "Surely, he is the Son of God"—whether or not these were the soldier's words or the disciples' additions. Rather than focus on whether or not a particular statement would have been made by a person in that time and place, this form of reading allows simply that this statement was part of the early community.[71] In this,

66. Hauerwas, *Peaceable Kingdom*, 73.

67. Willard Swartley engages the ethical significance of Jesus, imitation, and peacemaking in *Covenant of Peace*.

68. Hauerwas, *Peaceable Kingdom*, 73.

69. Hauerwas asserts, "One of the most important questions you can ask theologians is where they go to church." Hauerwas, *Sanctify Them in Truth*, 157.

70. Hauerwas, *Peaceable Kingdom*, 73.

71. In *Hannah's Child* (49), Hauerwas gives a glimpse into his approach to the Bible. He writes, "For interpretation of Old Testament texts we were expected to take seriously questions concerning how the history of Israel was to be reconstructed. I

Hauerwas shows his major concerns: his desire to "get around to doing theology" rather than linger in methodology; his insistence that theology must relate to discipleship in the church; and his effort to move the ethical question away from the point of decision.

While certain traditions, such as the Church of the Brethren, hold the notion of the centrality of Jesus in ethical reflection, Hauerwas notes that Christian ethics has typically been based on Christology rather than Jesus.[72] Rather than ethics expanding from substantive claims of the incarnation or another theological concept, Hauerwas asserts that the community's reading of the texts forms the context for the church's life. As such, the "Gospels as stories of life are meant not only to display that life but to train us to situate our lives in relation to that life."[73]

Hauerwas also examines the role of imitation in "Jesus, Israel, and the Imitation of God."[74] He notes that imitation should not be understood in individualist terms, but as relating to Christianity's social nature. Additionally, he notes that mimicking the actions of a virtuous person does not necessarily make one virtuous. For example, in the context of Jesus's temptation, Hauerwas asserts,

> God's kingdom, it seems, will not have peace through coercion. Peace will come only through the worship of the one God who chooses to rule the world through the power of love, which the world can only perceive as weakness. Jesus thus decisively rejects Israel's temptation to an idolatry that necessarily results in violence between peoples and nations. For our violence is correlative to the falseness of the objects we worship, and the more false they are, the greater our stake in maintaining loyalty to them and protecting them through coercion. Only the one

---

remember one of our seminars turned on the question of whether Abraham, who may or may not have existed, was a camel or ass nomad. Mr. Childs thought it quite amusing when I suggested that, being unable to keep up with the debate, I might just as well read the text without the presumption that the meaning of the text depended on historical reconstruction."

72. Hauerwas, *Peaceable Kingdom*, 72. Additionally, it is often said that Yoder's book, *The Politics of Jesus*, played a central role in bringing this mode of ethical reflection (back) into dominant streams of theology.

73. Hauerwas, *Peaceable Kingdom*, 74.

74. "It is not surprising that the early Christians assume that by imitating the 'Way' of Jesus they were imitating the 'Way' of God himself. For the content of the kingdom, the means of citizenship, turns out to be nothing more or less than learning to imitate Jesus' life through the task of being his disciple." Hauerwas, *Peaceable Kingdom*, 80.

true God can take the risk of ruling by relying entirely on the power of humility and love.[75]

God will not have peace through coercion: God will rule only through love. Violence is related to falseness of the objects being worshiped. In this, right action is formed through imitation rather than by coercion. It is notable that God risks something in this noncoercive approach. This is theologically significant and, given the role of imitation in ethical formation, it becomes a challenge to those who seek to follow God. This is particularly poignant for those whose identity and narrative is shaped by America, with its history of violence.[76] For those schooled in the assumption of the efficacy of violence, conforming to God's risky noncoercion will be disruptive. In this disruption, a peacemaking facet of the community becomes visible. This ethic of imitation and conflict creation as part of peacemaking form the foundation on which peacemaking stands at the core of Christian life.[77]

If God's noncoercive action is what Christians are to imitate, then the notion of imitation is much more sophisticated than it initially sounds. Though Hauerwas's suggestion is useful and interesting, it introduces questions similar to those he raises concerning ethical systems based more on substantive claims of Christology than on the life and teachings of Jesus. Obviously, Hauerwas writes as an academic theologian and ethicist, so it his job to explore nuances. One could compare his work in this regard to George Lindbeck's *Nature of Doctrine*, which ostensibly seeks to move Christians to a world subsumed by the biblical witness and yet is based almost exclusively in theory. This is not necessarily a problem, but is important to observe.

Perhaps it is for this reason—the desire to ground his assertions in practice as well as theory—that Hauerwas moved later in his career towards including sermons in his books or publishing books of sermons. It also relates to his comments that modern theologians spend so much of their time working out a methodology or saying why it is hard to do theology in modernity that they rarely get around to actually doing any. The inclusion of sermons is Hauerwas's attempt at "getting around to doing theology." Though Hauerwas does not make the connection, when his approach of "getting around to doing theology," peacemaking as a core

---

75. Hauerwas, *Peaceable Kingdom*, 79.
76. Woodley, *Shalom and the Community of Creation*, 133–35.
77. See Hauerwas, "Peacemaking."

practice, and his comments on imagination are considered at the same time, their relationship strengthens the possibility of dynamic peacemaking. Such an assertion would be, rather than extensive theorizing, the church should live its core commitment to peace in provisional and fragmentary but nonetheless community-sustained efforts of peacemaking.

Hauerwas continues with "Jesus and the Kingdom of God." This imitation is not an end in itself but part of being a part of the kingdom.[78] Imitation, or following the way of Jesus, is an entering into the larger story, which has a future and an end: "We must learn to see the world as Israel had learned to understand it—that is, eschatologically. Though it sounds powerful and intimidating, in fact it is quite simple, for to view the world eschatologically is to see it in terms of story, with a beginning, a continuing drama, and an end."[79] He describes this training and entering into the eschatological story as discipleship: "Discipleship is quite simply extended training in being dispossessed. To become followers of Jesus means that we must, like him, be dispossessed of all that we think gives us power over our own lives and the lives of others. Unless we learn to relinquish our presumption that we can ensure the significance of our lives, we are not capable of the peace of God's kingdom."[80] This dispossession is not based on a general principle but on joining Jesus in specific dispossession on the cross. Hauerwas writes, "The cross is Jesus' ultimate dispossession through which God has conquered the powers of this world. The cross is not just a symbol of God's kingdom: it is that kingdom come."[81] So the kingdom is in fact Jesus and the cross of Jesus rather than something solely future or ethereal. The kingdom is the concrete and difficult reality of the cross, which is then the site of the manifestation of the power of God.[82] Though a number of liberation theologians have chal-

---

78. Hauerwas, *Peaceable Kingdom*, 82.

79. Hauerwas, *Peaceable Kingdom*, 82.

80. Hauerwas, *Peaceable Kingdom*, 86.

81. Hauerwas, *Peaceable Kingdom*, 87.

82. How does the "taking up the Cross" and dispossession relate to persons or communities who have been forced into such positions by racism or some other form of exploitation? Cannon, in *Black Womanist Ethics* (3), writes, "Dominant ethics also assumes that a moral agent is to a considerable degree free and self-directing. Each person possesses self-determining power. For instance, one is free to choose whether or not she/he wants to suffer and make sacrifices as a principle of action or as a voluntary vocational pledge to crossbearing. In dominant ethics a person is free to make suffering a desirable moral norm. This is not so for Blacks. For the masses of Black people, suffering is the normal state of affairs."

lenged the exhortation to voluntarily embrace suffering, the practice of peacemaking will take some form of dispossession or sacrifice. This is not necessarily an embrace of suffering in general, but a specific disciplined effort in a difficult task as a vocation of the church. Suffering is not itself intrinsically valuable, but is part of the peacemaking vocation, which is, almost by definition, difficult.

Continuing through chapter 5, in the section "The Resurrection: The Establishment of a Kingdom of Forgiveness and Peace," Hauerwas builds on the statements of discipleship as dispossession established in the cross of Jesus and the power of God made manifest in the resurrection. He describes "the Kingdom of forgiveness and peace," beginning by claiming the possibility of rest. Sabbath is no longer a specific day but is the shape of the possibility of rest for the people of God. In this we see a deepening of the notions of peace, but also a prioritization even in the face of the highly urgent. Rather than simply an absence of violence, it is the presence of the fullness of life.[83] This life is made possible by Christians' confidence that their lives are in God's hands.[84] This is not acquiescence to the *status quo* but an invitation to confident, nonviolent action that allows us to act hopefully.[85] Hauerwas writes, "Jesus' death was not a mistake but what was to be expected of a violent world which does not believe that this is God's world. In effect Jesus is nothing less than the embodiment of God's Sabbath as a reality for all people. Jesus

83. Woodley (*Shalom and the Community of Creation*, 19) discusses *shalom* with the *harmony way*, which he (a Keetoowah Cherokee) posits as a common understanding: "In my own relationships with other indigenes, I have heard similar testimonies of a type of harmony way of living and understanding life—from Zulu, Inca, Maasai, Sami, Maori, Inuit, Australian Aboriginal, and Hawaiian peoples. I don't think it is an understatement to say that the ancient Semitic shalom construct, or what we broadly refer to as the Harmony Way, is the Creator's original instruction for the way in which all societies should be ordered, and for how life on this planet should be lived."

84. Such rest and confidence makes possible living in the present. Former Ekklesiyar Yan'uwa a Nigeria (Church of the Brethren in Nigeria) President Rev. Dr. Samuel Dali stated that since many of EYN's members are refugees in Cameroon, they will plant churches there. The EYN people can, in the face of tremendous suffering, continue to act as agents. Maintaining confidence in God is not a passive acceptance of the status quo, but an agency maintained even while being victimized. This is critical when we think of confidence in the work of God. Sometimes people have maintained, or been accused of maintaining, the status quo by saying, "Trust in God." This may, indeed, often be the case. Dr. Dali, however, is motivated by simultaneous trust and opportunity for action.

85. Though Hauerwas does not frame this in broader terms of struggles for justice, it is in this space that such action resides.

proclaims peace as a real alternative, because he has made it possible to rest—to have confidence that our lives are in God's hands."[86] Free from the presumption that we must control history we are free to rest in God, free from the assumptions of Constantinianism.

A variation of this theme returns in chapter 8, "Tragedy and Joy: The Spirituality of Peaceableness." An interesting and somewhat open question is, How does one live non-anxiously and joyfully in the face of actual threat? This is a critical insight for my work in Washington, DC, policy advocacy on peacebuilding and in response to violent conflict, although I am, for the most part, not in harm's way. Indeed, Washington, while a high-profile target, is also heavily guarded. The question, then, is whether this focus on rest holds up theologically and practically. To reverse this question, one might ask, What is gained by not trusting God? Since trusting in God does not preclude the possibility of action, there is arguably no practical reason why one would not trust in God. However, Hauerwas's exhortation to trusting and rest is posited as a part of non-reliance on violence as a possible action. Elsewhere he asserts that Christians' unwillingness to resort to violence makes peace possible. As such, this will disrupt the acceptance of violence by many Christians as occasionally necessary.

In the final section of chapter 5, "The Ethics of Salvation and Faith," Hauerwas asserts that Christians learn peace, and what peace means, in the context of imitation and the community. The community is not a training ground for peace otherwise derived (say, from a political or ideological commitment), but through the community's training in peace, it also learns what this peace is: "It is not that we have a prior definition of peace and then think of Christ as the great exemplar of that peace. Rather what Jesus has done enables us to know and embody God's peace in our lives by finding peace with God, with ourselves, and with one another."[87] Though Hauerwas insists on practices and concrete embodiment, he is decidedly not referring to techniques or skills of negotiation, mediation, or any other type of mechanism. While not opposed to such work, he resists reducing this churchly skill to a step-by-step manual.

> Though it is often tried, such skills can never be reduced to techniques. For example, learning to live in such a way that I need not fear death means coming to a real understanding that Jesus

---

86. Hauerwas, *Peaceable Kingdom*, 87.
87. Hauerwas, *Peaceable Kingdom*, 93.

> has for all times defeated death. The skill does not come easily, yet it is the truth. The challenge is in making it true by myself. But the Good news is I cannot learn it by myself. We learn such truth only by being initiated into it by others. That is why the question of the nature and form of the church is the center of any attempt to develop a Christian ethics.[88]

Though such "skills" cannot be reduced to mere techniques, Hauerwas does not wholly dismiss the need for learning peacemaking. What he aims to avoid is the notion that one can forgo the formation of virtue and skill, which is acquired through repeated practice under the tutelage of a master practitioner. Although given Hauerwas's commitment to a theology, this master practitioner would presumably be in the church, he asserts on several occasions that the church does not exclusively possess this skill or commitment.[89]

With this he moves to chapter 6, "The Servant Community: Christian Social Ethics," where he argues that the form of the church is more important than techniques for establishing peace. This turn is precisely what I find critical and helpful with Hauerwas's work. When peace and nonviolence are debated in Christian theology and ethics, it is easy to fixate on questions of whether or not the Christian or the church can support the use of force against this or that threat or in general. While keeping the conversation broad, Hauerwas moves beyond questions of participation in military actions to the basis for peacemaking.

To remain at this level, however, risks getting stuck in abstraction or theory. In chapter 2 of this work, I minimized questions of just war and pacifism, but observed turns toward greater social engagement of Christians in the early twentieth century—or at least greater articulation of social engagement as a Christian duty at that time. That Hauerwas causes Christians to withdraw from such endeavors is a reoccurring critique. While I cannot disprove such a claim empirically, Hauerwas's work, with *The Peaceable Kingdom* as a strong example, clearly does not support withdrawal—unless one reads only the titles some of his essays

---

88. Hauerwas, *Peaceable Kingdom*, 95. "Reducing" may be problematic since it seems to imply that one is greater than the other. Presumably developers of such techniques might consider such techniques higher than theology. Given the difference of disciplines and the desire to embody nonviolence even in such discussions, avoiding hierarchy is advised.

89. See, for example, Hauerwas, "Keeping Theological Ethics Imaginative," 60.

and books.⁹⁰ His work seeks simply to articulate a stronger and more theological basis for such engagement. For example, he notes that the use of both female and male pronouns over and against the Greek use of only the male does not indicate early Christian egalitarianism; rather, it "reminds us that the telos of the Christian community was one in which the male and female alike were included."⁹¹ When out of this recognition come actions commonly associated with egalitarianism, one is acting *theologically* in a very practical manner. This theological character will presumably not be of highest importance for the one benefiting from the "egalitarian-like" action, but in practical terms for the Christian, such a theological commitment may be more closely woven into the fabric of life. While the division between theologically derived and ordinary egalitarianism is likely neither sharp nor particularly relevant, for Hauerwas this is part of an attempt at theological re-narration for the strengthening of the church's life and witness. Such strengthening matters because God matters.

In chapter 8, on the spirituality of peaceableness, Hauerwas begins by looking at an exchange between the Niebuhr brothers in *The Christian Century* during the First World War. He writes, "The joy that characterizes the Christian life is not so much the fulfillment of any desire, but the discovery that we are capable of being people who not only desire peace but are peaceable. Joy thus comes to us as a gift that ironically provides us with the confidence in ourselves which makes possible our living in God's peace a present reality."⁹² Statements like this provide a key for understanding Hauerwas's claims for the presence of peace or the need to *be*, such that while cautioning against the assumption that activism for peace is a central goal for Christians, he is not counseling inaction, apathy, or quietism but rather building the possibility for substantive peacemaking.⁹³ The sabbath rest Hauerwas advocates is a replacement

---

90. Huebner (*Precarious Peace*, 69) raises Hauerwas's concern that particular words get identified with particular churches, such that the word says at once too much and too little. This happens in political discourse as well with certain phrases or words acting as markers of a particular political or religious leaning. *Justice, Social Justice*, and *Peace and Justice* often act as such markers in political and theological discourse. I do not consider Hauerwas's attack on such political and theological jargon to be a wholesale rejection, but it may have been the cause of some of the critiques leveled against him.

91. Hauerwas and Pinches, *Christians among the Virtues*, 64.

92. Hauerwas, *Peaceable Kingdom*, 147.

93. Hauerwas would object to the notion of doing something *for the purpose of*

for the anxiety that forces the issue through coercion or violence. He does not, however, assume that there is a necessary progression from non-joy to violence but rather that spirituality and assumptions about the possibility of the use of violence may short-circuit the imagination toward nonviolent solutions.[94] It is not simply a sense of tragedy but a recognition that despite our inability to assure peace we can trust that peace is present. As he states,

> The Christian sense of tragedy that accompanies our commitment to God's peace is not the last word about the world. For if the peace we believe God has made present is unsettling it is equally the basis for joy and thanksgiving. We discover that the patient hope that requires us wait in the face of violence is not some means to a greater good, but the good itself. Such a patience is less something we do or accomplish than it is our recognition of what God has made possible in our lives. Thus it is bad faith for Christians to let their patience be turned into resignation in the face of violence, for we know that we are not by nature a violent people.[95]

Though such statements do not give technical advice on peacebuilding, they do open critical space for imaginative engagement.[96] Further, by challenging the potential for resignation, he works to establish sustained peacemaking and presence.[97]

---

building a foundation for peace.

94. In *The Moral Imagination* (19), Lederach begins by telling four stories of peacebuilding. He then says, "What made these changes possible? Though working their hardest and very skilled at their trade, at the moment of the initial meetings it was not the techniques used by the mediators nor the nature and design of the process . . . not the local or national political power, exigencies, the fears of a broader war, nor the influence and pressure from the international community that created the shift. It was not a particular religious tradition: the stories in fact cut across religions. It was not political, economic, or military power in any of the cases. What then created the moment, a turning point, of such significance that it shifted whole aspects of a violent, protracted setting of conflict? I believe it was the serendipitous appearance of the *moral imagination* in human affairs.

95. Hauerwas, *Peaceable Kingdom*, 146.

96. I address this theme in my final chapter when I consider Hauerwas's work alongside peacebuilding literature, focusing particularly on Lederach's *Moral Imagination*.

97. How do we consider patience versus restlessness in the face of injustice or violence? At times, oppressed communities have been exhorted to be "patient," as if a little more time will mean that the wrong will be made right. While I do not believe this is what Hauerwas intends, clarification on these lines is needed. Indeed, this may be related to a criticism I mount in the final chapter: Hauerwas would benefit from

Continuing in chapter 5, Hauerwas states that as forgiven people, Christians have indeed lost control of their lives. To forgive can be a form of power but to be forgiven is to lose control.[98] This is part of living nonviolently: "But because we have learned to live as a forgiven people, as a people no longer in control, we also find we can become a whole people. Indeed, the demand that we be holy is possible only because we find that we can rest within ourselves."[99] Though Hauerwas doesn't make this claim, this sort of mental, emotional, and spiritual rest can be related to ideas and practices of trauma healing. For example, in *Sites of Violence, Sites of Grace*, Cynthia Hess explores the potential connection between Yoder's work and trauma. Trauma is also linked to society's need to secure security and to the things society is willing to do while living in fear of insecurity. Both the persistent fear of terrorism and other insecurities, such as sickness, accident, and broken relationships, rob the fearful of both joy and rest.

The Peaceable Kingdom begins to develop many themes to which Hauerwas returns throughout his career. In this work, he develops a framework that entwines peace and its relations into the fabric of his larger theological ethical project. These are so closely integrated that to remove one from the other would greatly distort the direction of his writing. In his work, peace and peacemaking, ethics as imitation of Jesus, and the community are of one piece. This then embeds peace and peacemaking in the heart of being Christian. Though he does not delve deeply into how this plays out in practice, he insists that it be enacted.

"Peacemaking: The Virtue of the Church"

I turn now to the essay in which Hauerwas most directly addresses *peacemaking*. The essay "Peacemaking: The Virtue of the Church" is one of the only instances in which Hauerwas explicitly uses the language of peacemaking.[100] Though, he works on related ideas he does not regularly use

greater engagement with communities struggling against injustice. Cone (*Black Theology of Liberation*, 4) asserts, "Theology can never be neutral or fail to take sides on issues related to the plight of the oppressed. For this reason it can never engage in a conversation about the nature of God without confronting those elements of human existence which threaten anyone's existence as a person."

98. Hauerwas, *Peaceable Kingdom*, 89.
99. Hauerwas, *Peaceable Kingdom*, 89.
100. Hauerwas, "Peacemaking," 89–100.

this particular biblical term. Here, I will assess Hauerwas's explicit moves from peace to peacemaking as a practice of the church, both within the church and from the church into the broader community. In short, I find that this essay exemplifies peace and peacemaking as a dynamic practice that is characteristic of communities and should be more broadly defined than as the absence of conflict or violence. I will note, however, that though Hauerwas's argument holds together, he introduces a degree of ambiguity by his inclusion and use of Aristotle at a key juncture.

Hauerwas begins the essay by quoting Matthew 18:15–2: "Confront your brother or sister who sins against you." He then asks, if we are a people of peace, how do we account for this command to intentionally stir up conflict? "Yet," he continues, "I want to suggest that we will understand peacemaking as a virtue of the church only when we see that such confrontation is at the heart of what it means to be a peacemaker."[101] As such, peace found in the gathered body is not simply theological but entails action and imagination. At times peacemakers must intentionally provoke conflict.

Much of this essay, in fact, rests, first, on the assertion that peacemaking requires confrontation and that for Christians this is not optional; and second, on his claim that peacemaking is a virtue. In fact, the mandatory nature of peacemaking and virtue characteristics are intrinsically linked: "I want to suggest that we will understand peacemaking as a virtue only when we see that such a confrontation is at the heart of what it means to be a peacemaker."[102] Though he does not say it at this point, such confrontation is often closely related to seeking justice.

Virtue is a theme for which Hauerwas is well known, and was discussed in greater detail earlier in this chapter. In this section, I will explore the role of virtue in Hauerwas's account of peacemaking. Virtues are characteristics that define us. Typically, they are thought of as positive characteristics within an individual. Hauerwas asserts that some virtues can exist only in relation to others. Hauerwas refers to Aristotle, who argues that "some virtues such as justice and friendship, are correlative to certain kinds of relations and cannot exist without those relations being valued by a community. Peacemaking is that sort of virtue insofar as the church believes that peace (and a very particular kind of peace at that) is

---

101. Hauerwas, "Peacemaking," 90.
102. Hauerwas, "Peacemaking," 90.

an essential characteristic of its nature."[103] Because the church is a body made up of many bodies, the virtues of the church must be relational. Hauerwas notes that peacemaking is not an action typically associated with a virtue, but that certain virtues can only exist in relationships. Peacemaking is one such virtue. I will return to this point later.[104]

Hauerwas continues, noting that rather than peacemaking being about the resolution of conflict, it may often first cause conflict or at least confrontation.[105] He claims that the text in Matthew shows peacemaking as confrontation which is not boring, noting that while many may be interested in working toward peace, the actual prospect of a state of peace does not appeal to many people. Hauerwas hopes that this example will save us from assuming that peace is boring. He also notes that many of us think that our conflicts, or another's sin against us, do not warrant a confrontation but that we should rather wait it out. Jesus, however, seems to assume differently "about what is necessary to be a community of peace and peacemaking. It seems that peace is not the name of the absence of conflict, but rather peacemaking is a quality of life and practices engendered by a community that knows it lives as a forgiven people. Such a community cannot afford to 'overlook' one another's sins because they have learned that such sins are a threat to being a community of peace."[106] Critical to this is the understanding that "our lives are not our own," such that an affront to me is not so much against me but against the community.[107] The integral connection between this focus on peacemaking and chapter 3's work on ecclesiology also becomes evident in this. Hauerwas asserts that peace is more than the absence of violence or conflict, but

---

103. Hauerwas, "Peacemaking," 90.

104. It should be noted that in this essay, Hauerwas uses *peace, peacemaking,* and *peacekeeping* seemingly interchangeably. The equivocal use of peacemaking and peacekeeping is perplexing, given that peacekeeping is a specific term for a particular process or effort within international relations and conflict.

105. "Rather, as Christians we will best serve God and our neighbor by seeking to form common life in the world as we find it. That may well mean we must attempt to develop institutions, such as the university, that make it possible to engage in the kind of exchanges MacIntyre thinks necessary for the development of practical reason. What we cannot fear or repress in the name of peace is conflict. Christians, particularly Christians in diaspora, owe one another as well as their neighbor truthful judgments that come only by have our convictions exposed to those who do not share them." Hauerwas, *War and the American Difference,* 146.

106. Hauerwas, "Peacemaking," 91.

107. This would also seem to provide some structure or backing for justice seeking in the community.

does not go very far in defining this nor does he draw on existing work on peace to elaborate.[108]

Hauerwas asserts that the Matthew passage shows that the peace of Jesus is the peace of truth rather than the peace of rest.[109] Because this peace is based on truth, sins cannot be left unchallenged. If we don't challenge sinners, we leave them abandoned in their sin. This does not become a confrontation of power over others because we are also forgiven sinners. "Our ability to be truthful peacemakers depends on our learning that we owe our lives to God's unrelenting forgiveness."[110] As such, truthfulness is a matter of allowing ourselves to be in a position of weakness and to develop the ability to name this. "To be sinned against or to know we have sinned requires that we have a language and correlative habit that makes it possible to know what it is to be a sinner."[111] This habit and practice of confrontation and forgiveness is or will become a common history, which allows such confrontation to be a process of peace rather than a stoking of conflict.[112]

Being a church at peace in a world at war means that the church "cannot help but be a community that confronts the world in uncompromising manner."[113] Unable to ignore past or present, the church challenges the forgetfulness on which the world's peace is often built. So even in this essay, which focuses on peacemaking as an internal practice of the church, there is an outward movement toward the world. In Ephesians, Jews and Gentiles are brought together in "one body through the cross." Hauerwas writes, "Peacemaking among Christians therefore, is not simply one activity among others but rather is the very form of the one who 'is our peace.'"[114] This builds on the work of *The Peaceable Kingdom* described above. Imitation is not just for individuals but also for the gathered community, the Body of Christ.

---

108. Other than Yoder's writing, Hauerwas generally has not engaged in depth with literature on biblical, theological, or peacebuilding practice or theory. Though Hauerwas reads widely, on certain central themes his reading attention seems rather erratic.

109. Hauerwas, "Peacemaking," 92.

110. Hauerwas, "Peacemaking," 93.

111. Hauerwas, "Peacemaking," 93.

112. Hauerwas, "Peacemaking," 94.

113. Hauerwas, "Peacemaking," 94.

114. Hauerwas, "Peacemaking," 95.

There are two immediate outcomes of this stance. First, the church must challenge the "false peace of the world which is too often built more on power than on truth."[115] Secondly, Christians are "prohibited from ever despairing of the peace possible in the world."[116] While focusing on the internal life of the church, they have an outward movement as well—described earlier as mission. The manner in which the church conducts itself internally and the patterns of its life as a body prepare it for a particular way of life in the world. This is the case both in liturgical practices and with peacemaking. Hauerwas writes, "Peacemaking as a virtue is an act of imagination built on the long habits of the resolution of differences."[117] He goes on to say that though peacemaking as he describes it is community specific, it is not community limited. Though the "brother" in Matthew 18 is a Christian, the overall focus of Matthew is ongoing out beyond the church. Processes and habits such as these push the church into the public space to make peace. This peacemaking must not be narrowly defined as interpersonal conflict resolution, but broadly, based in biblical concepts of justice, wholeness, and transformed relationships and systems.

I now turn to a closer look at Hauerwas's use of Aristotle's conception of virtue as it relates to peace and peacemaking in the church. While there seems to be a key pivot in this essay from peace as a characteristic of the church to peacemaking as a virtue of the church through the work of Aristotle, I do not believe that this move is as contingent on Aristotle as it initially seems. There is only one minor assertion based on the work of Aristotle, and it is on the nature of what can be included in a list of virtues. Since in "The Renewal of Virtue and the Peace of Christ," Hauerwas asserts that there is no particular reason why Christians have a stake in the renovation of virtue as a framework, then it is not clear what he achieves by stretching the definition of virtue to include peacemaking. The critical part is his assertion that peacemaking is central to the Christian life. While peacemaking may turn out to be a virtue, its centrality for the Christian is not contingent on this. There are a number of ways to get from peace as a characteristic and peacemaking as a necessary practice of the church. An extended quotation from this essay gives a view of his line of argument:

---

115. Hauerwas, "Peacemaking," 95.

116. Hauerwas, "Peacemaking," 95.

117. Hauerwas, "Peacemaking," 95. The theme of imagination will be picked up later in the discussion of Lederach's *Moral Imagination*.

I want to suggest that we will understand peacemaking as a virtue only when we see that such confrontation is at the heart of what it means to be a peacemaker. Even more important, however, I think that by attending to this passage we will be able to see how peacemaking, as well as any virtue, is correlative to a community's practices. This is a crucial issue if we are to appreciate peacemaking as a virtue. Courage, temperance, and even humility are usually acknowledged as virtues much more readily than is peacemaking. For many, peacemaking may sound like a "good thing," but they would be hesitant to call it a virtue. Peacemaking is usually seen more as a matter of political strategy than a disposition to forming the self. Some people may even be peaceful, but that hardly seems a virtue.[118]

Why are we reticent to think of peacemaking as a virtue? I suspect it is because we think of virtues as personal characteristics that everyone should possess irrespective of their membership in any specific community. But, as I hope to show, such an understanding of virtue is far too limited. For as Aristotle argues, some virtues, such as justice and friendship, are correlative to certain kinds of relations and cannot exist without those relationships being valued by the community. Peacemaking is that sort of virtue insofar as the church believes that peace (and a very particular kind of peace at that) is an essential characteristic of its nature.[119]

It seems less that the church is reticent to call peacemaking a virtue because the category of virtue is in itself problematic than there is ambivalence about Hauerwas's claims of the centrality of peace and nonviolence for the church.[120] Many Christians, historically, would balk at the assertion that "peace . . . is an essential characteristic of its [the church's] nature." Additionally, as Swartley notes, there is a paucity of direct engagement with peace within New Testament theology and ethics.[121] While in this essay this basic argument for peace and peacemaking

---

118. Hauerwas, "Peacemaking," 90.

119. Hauerwas, "Peacemaking," 90.

120. Indeed, it may be that *virtue*, as a pre-Christian term, may be too quickly taken up even though the Greek and Christian forms of virtues are not necessarily compatible. See "Renewal of Virtue and the Peace of Christ" in Hauerwas and Pinches, *Christians among the Virtues*, 55–69.

121. Swartley, *Covenant of Peace*, 5.

is minimal, in a number of other cases (most significantly in *Peaceable Kingdom*), Hauerwas in fact makes the case for the centrality of peace.

Hauerwas only addresses peace and peacemaking as a virtue of the church on two occasions. Related topics such as witness, activism, or politics come up more frequently, along with a significant focus on virtue. In his later essay, "Explaining Christian Nonviolence: Notes for a Conversation with John Milbank and John Howard Yoder," Hauerwas briefly revisits "Peacemaking: the virtue of the church."[122] There is a shift, however. He references Aquinas more than Aristotle, and the language of virtue is connected to peace rather than peacemaking. In "Peacemaking: The Virtue of the Church," he asserts that peacemaking is the virtue of a community characterized by peace; in "Explaining Christian Nonviolence," he names peace as the virtue. Peace is a virtue as opposed to it being the eschatological goal. He writes, "Peace is not a virtue only in the sense that it is encompassed in charity—which is at once a virtue and an activity—through which we love God and our neighbor." He seems to equivocate on the terminology of peace and peacemaking.[123] This rela-

---

122. Hauerwas, *Performing the Faith*, 182.

123. Hauerwas also confusingly substitutes *peacekeeping* for *peacemaking* for a short section of "Peacemaking: The Virtue of the Church." In this instance, it seems as though this is an accidental rather than an intentional distinction. A colleague noted that *peacekeeping* as a specific term may not have been in common use at the time Hauerwas wrote this essay. After this conversation, I reread *The Work of Theology* (2015), and noticed that Hauerwas used *peacemaking* and *peacekeeping* together but still with no reference in indication that he was thinking of peacekeeping as a particular action of a military or the United Nations. He writes, "We can trust the church because the church is the sort of community that it is. It is a community of active peacemaking and peacekeeping in which no one exists in isolation or grows up in isolation." Hauerwas, *Work of Theology*, 39.

In his discussion of Yoder in *With the Grain of the Universe*, he also uses "nonresistance" and "nonviolence" interchangeably, without commenting on the fluidity of his terminology: for example, "Yoder's case for Christian nonviolence is compelling because his understanding and justification of nonviolence cannot be separated from the Christian conviction that God is our creator and redeemer. In other words, Yoder forces us to see that the doctrines of God and nonviolence are constitutive of one another . . . Nonresistance but names the way God has chosen to redeem us . . . That Christians are committed to nonviolence does not entail, as often assumed, that Christians must withdraw from the world." Hauerwas, *With the Grain of the Universe*, 220.

Carl Bowman (*Brethren Society*, 349–53) discusses the transformation from the language of "nonresistance" (based on Jesus teaching "do not resist the evil doer" in Matthew 5:39) to a more activist peace position in the first half of the twentieth century. Though Bowman tracks this change of language within a particular historic peace church, Hauerwas does not indicate these nuances in *With the Grain of the*

tionship is similar to the tension between faith and works in the books of Romans and James. This analogy may not formally illuminate this relationship, or provide a biblical foundation for the relationship between peace and peacemaking, but it suggests a possibility.

After asserting that peacemaking is a virtue of the church based on the need for particular virtues requiring relationship, and that peace is a necessary characteristic of the church, Hauerwas explores further the implications of conflict and confrontation as part of peacemaking. Such confrontation of sin requires a truthfulness that is far from comforting.[124] In order for the church to be a "community of truthful peace," it must also be a community of the forgiven. For this confrontation to work it must be in the context of forgiveness. The recognition that the confronter and the one confronted are both sinners and forgiven means that forgiveness cannot be extended self-righteously.[125] Sharing this "common history" which includes forgiveness as well as repentance is what makes this commitment to confrontation a practice of peacemaking rather than "another way to continue conflict."[126] He notes, "From this perspective, we should not be surprised if peacemakers and peacemaking appear anything but peaceful. Moreover, if the church is to be a community of peace in a world at war, it cannot help but be a community that confronts the world in an uncompromising manner."[127] Peacemaking is then based both on confrontation and on being a community that bears witness in the face of war. Peacemaking is also central to the church's identity: "Peacemaking among Christians, therefore, is not simply one activity among others but rather is the very form of the church insofar as the church is the form of the one who 'is our peace.'"[128]

Christians must be willing to confront the false peace that is "built more on power than on truth" and are "prohibited from ever despairing of the peace possible in the world."[129] Since peacemaking is a central

---

Universe. It is possible that he picks up this language from earlier Yoder works, which would have reflected similar linguistic conventions within Mennonite circles. See, for example, Stutzman's *From Nonresistance to Justice*, and Hershberger, *War, Peace and Nonresistance*.

124. Hauerwas, "Peacemaking," 92.
125. Hauerwas, "Peacemaking," 93.
126. Hauerwas, "Peacemaking," 94.
127. Hauerwas, "Peacemaking," 94.
128. Hauerwas, "Peacemaking," 95.
129. Hauerwas, "Peacemaking," 95.

identifier, it can be both resilient and honed over time. As Hauerwas states, "Peacemaking as a virtue is an act of imagination built on the long habits of the resolution of differences."[130] The Matthew 18 passage is directly related to going to the fellow Christian, but since that community understood itself as going into the nations to witness to God's peace, this confrontation also applies to those outside the community.[131] Hauerwas continues, "Therefore the habits of peacekeeping acquired by the church are no less relevant when the church confronts those not part of our community and who may even threaten or wrong our community. For it is our belief that God is no less present in our enemy calling us to find the means of reconciliation."[132] Though peacemaking cannot be reduced to a series of techniques and is itself a theological act, it nonetheless provides the training and resolve to work for peace outside the walls of the church. Hauerwas writes (with a curious temporary switch to "peacekeeper"):

> Contrary to usual stereotypes, this means that peacekeepers, rather than withdraw from politics, must be the most political of animals. Peacekeeping requires the development of the processes and institutions that make possible the confrontation and resolution of differences so that violence can be avoided. The problem with politics, at least as politics is currently understood, is not that it involves compromises but that is it so little believes in truth. As a result, it becomes but a form of coercion without due acknowledgement that it is so. In such a situation the church can be a peacemaker by being the most political of institutions.[133]

Such peacemaking work is not done by heroic individuals but must be sustained by the community. As such, peacemaking is a virtue of the community.

Hauerwas's use of the Aristotelian concept of virtue raises several unnecessary difficulties. Are there other more biblical or Christian theological ways that Hauerwas supports this turn? In *War and the American Difference*, Hauerwas observes that Daniel Bell's account of justice is more scriptural than Nicholas Wolterstorff's.[134] Since this is a value that

---

130. Hauerwas, "Peacemaking," 95.
131. Hauerwas, "Peacemaking," 96.
132. Hauerwas, "Peacemaking," 96.
133. Hauerwas, "Peacemaking," 96.
134. Hauerwas, "Jesus, the Justice of God," 107.

is held generally by Hauerwas, his own work would benefit from such a scriptural development.

A second concern relates to his flexible use of the words peace, peacemaking, and nonviolence. Hauerwas emphasizes the relatedness of being and doing, and he challenges the distinction between theology and ethics. In light of this, when Hauerwas asserts the centrality of nonviolence and peace (which he tends to use interchangeably), he is asserting the centrality of the practicing of peace—or peacemaking. Given the conceptual vagueness of peace for many people this tendency to assume the relation risks misunderstanding. Particularly given the ready assumption that peace is primarily an absence of conflict and violence, the defining of these terms and their relationship is essential for clarity.

This section has explored Hauerwas's connection between virtue and peacemaking. I have raised questions about the value of stretching the concept of virtue as described by Aristotle to include peacemaking, suggesting that there are other scriptural ways to arrive at this conclusion. Additionally, I have suggested that Hauerwas introduces a degree of conceptual vagueness by his interchangeable use of the words *peace, nonviolence,* and *peacemaking.* In "Peacemaking: The Virtue of the Church," he focuses primarily on conflict within the church community. In the next section, I will explore some ways in which he takes this outside the church community. These directions are closely related to chapter 3's consideration of ecclesiology and Hauerwas's work on mission and witness.

"Taking Time for Peace: The Ethical Significance of the Trivial"

My aim for the broader section "From Peace to Peacemaking" is to describe and assess Hauerwas's effort to place peace at the center of Christian theology and ethics by grounding peacemaking in the church. Peacemaking is a core practice that requires both action and patience, recognizing that efforts for peace while foundational must not overdetermine Christian life. In this subsection, I focus on how Hauerwas maintains that, even though peace is foundational to the church's theology and practice, urgent social action for peace must not tyrannize the Christian life. In the essay "Taking Time for Peace," in *Christian Existence Today,* Hauerwas addresses the overwhelming threat of the nuclear bomb and how this is often either ignored or thought to radically override all other concerns and fundamentally reshape human existence. Here I describe Hauerwas's argument, including his exhortation to value "the trivial" and sabbath rest, while raising a concern about how this message may be heard in differing contexts of social awareness, concern, or apathy. In the end, I affirm this approach as being adequately concerned for peacemaking while acknowledging human finitude.

As a counterpoint to certain urgent approaches to peacemaking, particularly those actions which resist violence and are often associated with anti-war activism, Hauerwas explores the theology and spiritual practices of rest and engaging in the "trivial":

> In effect Jesus is nothing less than the embodiment of God's sabbath as a reality for all people. Jesus proclaims a peace as a real alternative, because he has made it possible to rest—to have confidence that our lives are in God's hands. No longer is the sabbath one day, but the form of life of a people on the move. God's kingdom, God's peace, is a movement of those who have found the confidence through the life of Jesus to make their lives a constant worship of God. We can rest in God because we are no longer driven by the assumption that we must be in control of history, that it is up to us to make things come out right.[135]

It is important to note that the emphasis on rest does not preclude action.[136] Hauerwas's primary concern is that the Christian's world be oriented around God rather than a particular injustice or threat. Such orientation does not exclude work for justice, peace, or the common good but is the lens, paradigm, or structure in which this is framed. It is

---

135. Hauerwas, *Peaceable Kingdom*, 87.

136. "Thus, within a world of violence and injustice Christians can take the risk of being forgiven and forgiving. They are able to break the cycle of violence as they refuse to become part of those institutions of fear that promise safety by the destruction of others. As a result, some space, both psychological and physical, is created where we can be at rest from a world that knows not who is its king. Such rest, however, is not accomplished by withdrawal from the world, nor is it a rest in which there is no movement. For to be a part of God's kingdom means that we have found ourselves in the ongoing story of God with his people. That story provides us rest exactly because it trains us with the skills to face the dangers and threats of this existence with courage and patience. Rest is possible because we find that the kingdom is not a static place or a way of being, but a journey that we have been graciously offered the opportunity to undertake. To be part of that journey means that we must be a particular kind of people formed by a particular set of virtues." Hauerwas, *Against the Nations*, 118. In this, the links between correctly imagined action and rest (which is not remotely passive) are quite clear.

a giving up of the presumption that we must make things come out right, which, according to Hauerwas, opens the possibility of using coercion and violence when things begin heading the wrong direction. A similar theme emerges in his writing on sickness and medicine, such as in "Doing Nothing Gallantly" in *Approaching the End,* and in his reflections on the work of Jean Vanier with the L'Arche communities in, among other places, his essay on "The Politics of Gentleness."[137] By accepting limitation and weakness as well as refusing to put what Sider calls "handles on history" to make it turn out correctly,[138] Hauerwas acknowledges finitude while staying connected to the work of bearing witness, peacemaking, and charity as part of a theologically robust justice.

In "Taking Time for Peace," Hauerwas responds to the urgency of the threat the nuclear bomb. Though it is not footnoted and he does not indicate location, his opening lines give the impression that this essay was initially an address at an event focusing on the Christian ethical imperative to oppose the nuclear arms race. In the face of the bomb, Hauerwas writes on rest and "the trivial." When threatened with potential annihilation, people have a tendency to either disassociate and live numbly ignoring the looming apocalypse or to allow the threat to become an all-consuming concern that fundamentally changes reality.[139] The rest he urges does not, however, mean coming to terms with the bomb. This, he states, "is not only nonsensical, it also seems nothing less than absurd and immoral. For it asks us to learn to live essentially as people who cannot face or acknowledge our responsibility in creating such a world; it asks us to abandon our own moral agency to a technological imperative."[140] The solution is to acknowledge the presence of this menace, recognize our complicity in its creation,[141] trust in God (rest), and work with proper zeal and humility to address this absence of peace.

Though Hauerwas seeks to hold the above set of parameters in balance, his primary focus is on those who insist on the reality-altering nature of the bomb. Against the belief that one is either for or against the

---

137. Hauerwas, "Politics of Gentleness," 77–99.

138. Sider, *To See History Doxologically,* 153.

139. Hauerwas, "Taking Time for Peace," 253–54.

140. Hauerwas, "Taking Time for Peace," 254.

141. While certainly a generic humanity is responsible, it is not the case that everyone is. Is Hauerwas's "we" Christians, Americans, Americans with the educational, economic, and privilege to be actively complicit in the system? Is this a marker of his (unacknowledged) social location?

problem with no in-between, Hauerwas asserts that while this is "quite admirable," it is also "totalitarian."[142] He asserts that we "will be making a mistake if we allow the bomb to determine our lives spiritually. Put simply, we will not be working for a peace worth having if we assume that peace means only the elimination of the bomb from our lives."[143] To reclaim our lives from such domination we need to embrace the trivial. He asserts, "By refusing to let them [totalitarians] claim every aspect of our life as politically significant, we create the space and time that makes politics humane."[144] While the bomb is significant, it does not alter God.

> For us to have the means to live in the face of the bomb, God can be no mere symbol. For us to have the means to live in the face of the bomb, we need the mighty and frightening presence we find in the giving of the law and the cross of Jesus. God is not powerful because we need a God of power, but rather God's power is manifest in those who continue to be drawn to a people trained in the trust made possible by God's presence. God's power is not the coercive power of the totalitarian but the power that attracts and claims because of its sheer goodness. God's power is manifest in his patience, through which he creates the time for us to learn that our lives are distorted as long as we think we, rather than God, rule this world. God has given us the time to learn that and, as his followers, we would be false witnesses if

---

142. I wonder if Hauerwas is actually against this alleged totalitarianism. There are many other instances where he seems to adopt such all-encompassing assertions. As many have noted, he is certainly not opposed to rhetorical and hyperbolic flourishes that challenge his readers' commitments. See, for example, Hauerwas, "Taking Time for Peace," 255.

143. Hauerwas, "Taking Time for Peace," 256. This, however, raises the question of whether the phrases "the bomb determining our spiritual lives" and "peace being simply equated with the elimination of the bomb" are actually synonymous. It would seem that one could say that the bomb in some way fundamentally alters reality since there is now a human-derived possibility of absolute destruction looming and yet not believe that the removal of this threat is the fullness of peace. One could also say that there is a fundamental shift in reality due to the bomb and that God is still bigger and thus more determinative. One could also say that imminent destruction is the peacemaking task of present primary importance but not think that its removal solves all problems.

144. Hauerwas, "Taking Time for Peace," 256. It should be noted that later in his career, he claims that more, or perhaps nearly all, of church life is "political." Though he does not articulate it here, I believe that his usage of political in this essay is not the same as his later usage. The usage in "Taking Time for Peace" is more in line with conventional uses of the term in the United States, that is, politics as Washington, DC, or some other facet of governance.

we acted as if such time were not available. That is why we can and should take the time, even in the face of the bomb, to be at rest—to observe the Sabbath.[145]

As noted earlier, Hauerwas appears to be writing to those who feel a great deal of responsibility and apocalyptic urgency for resisting the bomb and who assert that a radical reordering of life is necessary. It should also be noted that he perceives that those he addresses might assume that they rule the world[146]—forgetting that God remains powerful and "God's power is manifest in [God's] patience." In this passage, the imitation of God as ethics is visible along with right ordering of relation to God in worship and nonviolence. This nonviolence of God is articulated as "noncoercive," attracting and claiming, and "sheer goodness." Living virtuously, toward holiness, is to live in a non-distorted manner.

Though this is part of "rest," it is not against active engagement for peace. Hauerwas writes,

> Let us continue to try to find ways to help our political leaders to discover the means to end the constant spiral of nuclear build up. . . . More important, however, we need to know that our efforts to eliminate or reduce the number of nuclear weapons cannot help but be hollow if they do not participate in the peace that comes from worshiping a God who has given us the time to enjoy the trivial.[147]

Against the rush of the urgency of eradicating the bomb, Hauerwas reminds the reader, "Peace takes time. Put even more strongly, peace

---

145. Hauerwas, "Taking Time for Peace," 257.

146. Ruling the world as an assumption would seem to be a rather narrow segment of humanity. Identifying that this is directed at a particular segment of humanity would be one instance where Hauerwas would benefit from more closely attending to his and his audience's social location. In saying this, it does not mean that this essay has no value for those who do not "assume rule." Certainly, those who do not rule may also have their worlds wrongly ordered but likely in a much different way with different theologies to challenge. Elsewhere, Hauerwas challenges liberation theologians who would too closely associate poverty with a virtue. In his commentary (*Matthew*, 64), he writes in connection to the Sermon on the Mount: "Paul does not assume that our poverty of spirit is the same as Jesus' self-emptying, but rather that Jesus' poverty has made it possible for people to exist who can live dispossessed of possessions. To be poor does not in itself make one a follower of Jesus, but it can put you in the vicinity of what it might mean to discover the kind of poverty that frees those who follow Jesus from enslavement to the world."

147. Hauerwas, "Taking Time for Peace," 257.

creates time by its steadfast refusal to force the other to submit in the name of order. Peace is not a static state but an activity which requires constant attention and care."[148] In order to learn how to take the necessary time, Christians must rest and recognize that the slow work of caring for lemurs, or watching the unfolding of a baseball game, is also valuable. Though we live in a society that seems filled with violence, much of our lives is in fact "constituted by peaceful and peacemaking activities . . . Such activities may appear trivial or uninteresting precisely because they are so common, but they are no less morally significant for that. For the willingness to take time to care for the trivial is exactly the disposition that provides the basis for our learning to be peaceful people capable of finding peace as a community."[149] Hauerwas reminds the reader to notice common and peaceful actions. In this, he is narrating and theologizing common experience as peaceful experience, so that the truly significant can be noticed and appreciated: "Put differently, without the trivial life would have no duration, as we keep time by giving the trivial significance through memory. Ultimately, nothing has ultimate significance, not even the survival of the world, but we can be significant to one another by taking the time to learn to be at peace."[150]

On many occasions Hauerwas has challenged the notion that we can live without history. This is an exhortation to attend to one's location. Though a sermon or lecture may be understood outside its context,[151] it is in some way shaped for that particular context. Noting the context or commenting on how this has shaped the context would be useful in this particular piece. Commenting on Yoder's work on doxology, Sider writes, "Interpreting history as praise risks generating tremendous complacency in the face of injustice, violence, suffering, and death. Christian ethics in America, from Walter Rauschenbusch to Stanley Hauerwas,

---

148. Hauerwas, "Taking Time for Peace," 258.

149. Hauerwas, "Taking Time for Peace," 259.

150. Hauerwas, "Taking Time for Peace," 263.

151. In the opening chapter in a collection of sermons, *Cross-Shattered Church* (22), Hauerwas writes, "I have not revised these sermons to free them from the circumstance in which they were written. That they were written for a specific time and occasion does not, in my estimation, present any obstacle to understanding them." Perhaps this is both an affirmation of his commitment to leave Christian speech untranslated as well as a challenge to those who assert Hauerwas assumes that particular speech is for particular people and therefore sectarian or walled off from the broader community.

could be depicted as the history of Christians confronting just such complacency."¹⁵² This "tremendous complacency," especially in the face of unrelenting news that disproportionately covers the tragic and horrendous, is what concerns me about "Taking Time for Peace." While I have no objection to the framework of Hauerwas's argument, my impression is that many more Christians are at risk of the "tremendous complacency" than are at risk having their lives overdetermined by the struggle for peace.

Hauerwas might object by saying that a large part of his argument is for the purpose of narrating Christians' lives so that they see the predominance of peaceful activities. Again, I would agree but remain concerned by our ability to justify our own narcissism. So, for example, travel to experience another culture may be taking time for peace as well as building connections and appreciation across borders. It could, however, equally be a large expenditure of monetary resources on myself rather than on my congregation's program to address hunger, an environmentally devastating use of fossil fuels for travel, part of the global capitalist corporate system which has commoditized cultural artifacts of marginalized groups for consumption by those privileged enough to travel, and an over-scheduled "vacation" that distracts me from spiritual practices and lacks much resemblance to a sabbath or rest. As with many of Hauerwas's essays this piece was presented at a particular forum for a particular audience. Though location is not indicated I conjectured earlier that it seems to be a presentation in a context of great urgency regarding nuclear weapons. Since this would be a very particular audience that is not reflective of every person's degree of urgency a statement of the initial context of this presentation or qualifying the rhetorical intent would potentially be of great value for directing the theological challenge to Christians which is the intent of the essay. Though Hauerwas gets at the concern that most of us go on living as if nothing is wrong and that one response is to "voluntarily tyrannize" ourselves,¹⁵³ he does not address the rhetorical positioning of this particular essay. If the audience is complacent and not overcome by the urge to organize politically, the rhetorical intent of this essay may be misappropriated.

My goal in this section, "From Peace to Peacemaking," was to describe and assess Hauerwas's effort to place peace at the center of Christian

---

152. Sider, *To See History Doxologically*, 138.
153. Hauerwas, "Taking Time for Peace," 255.

theology and ethics by grounding peacemaking in the church community. This is a core practice that requires both action and patience, recognizing that efforts for peace, while foundational, must not overdetermine Christian life. I showed how Hauerwas attempts to move the conversation about peace beyond what often appears to be an impasse between traditionally framed just war theory and pacifism. I demonstrated how he seeks to both problematize assumptions about pacifism and move the conversation beyond deliberations of participation or nonparticipation in war. To this end, I assessed *The Peaceable Kingdom*, "Peacemaking: the Virtue of the Church," and "Taking Time for Peace: The Ethical Significance of the Trivial" as examples of Hauerwas's thought on the central nature of peace and how this is inseparable from peacemaking.

Peacemaking: Peace Lived in Public

After this consideration of the formation of the peaceable body, I turn now to consider peace lived in public. The point of much of Hauerwas's work is that what is thought to be private should be considered public. We cannot, however, wholly break from the convention of referring to private and public spaces (as even Hauerwas might allow). In "Peacemaking: The Virtue of the Church," this is even nominally visible when he avers that the peacemaking practices of the church as exhorted by Matthew 18 train the church in the skills to make peace outside the church community. We have already seen that much of Hauerwas's work is linked in some manner to peace. For the purposes of this section, I will focus on two specific areas: ecumenism and witness as resistance to war.

I will assess two works showing Hauerwas's thoughts on how peace and peacemaking are necessarily embodied and lived. The first is "Which Church? What Unity? Or, An Attempt to Say What I May Think about the Future of Christian Unity" in *Approaching the End*. In this essay, Hauerwas gives an account of his views and work on ecumenism and church unity. The second example is Hauerwas's book *War and the American Difference: Theological Reflections on Violence and Nationalism*, which I will consider as an act of peacemaking witness in resistance to war. In these works, Hauerwas successfully demonstrates peacemaking in public through his theological ethical writing.

I will first address some preliminary questions that Hauerwas raises. In "The Nonresistant Church: The Theological Ethics of John Howard

Yoder" in *Vision and Virtue,* Hauerwas walks through Yoder's understanding of the ethical theological basis for pacifism. He observes the typical critiques of Yoder's position and shows how Yoder responded to these. Most of these arguments have been already addressed, so I will not reiterate them here. I do want to highlight several claims that are useful for this part of my study. One is the recognition of the role of the pacifist in larger Christian ethical discourse. Hauerwas is very aware of the role that a pacifist position can play in expanding the conversation.[154]

Hauerwas outlines the typical challenges to the "responsibility" of Yoder-type pacifism. He then notes that this has "become a kind of 'conventional wisdom'" rarely discussed explicitly, and asserts, "Such a discussion is long overdue for when such significant assumptions are accepted as true in themselves the original qualifications and nuances surrounding them become lost."[155] Hauerwas then reviews some of the challenges of translating Christian pacifism into a "moralistic" program or policy objectives. What I am most interested in is his turn to a more positive statement of how Christians can engage with the world. By positive, I don't mean in line with the world, but rather attending to what Christians *should* do rather than simply why it is difficult to do anything well.[156]

---

154. In my work in policy advocacy for the Church of the Brethren in Washington, DC, I have often thought of this as well. A question that I will raise but not fully address here is; if a position is consciously pushing the edge of the spectrum of conversation would this person hold the same position if they were somehow isolated and not speaking in conscious relation to other positions? That is, if I argue that US military force should not be used to rescue an ethnic and religious minority stranded on a mountain in the midst of devastating invasion by a group that seems to have no restraint, do I think this is the correct thing to do or do I argue this because I recognize that there is a consistent strong tendency and pressure for largely military "solutions" to US foreign-policy objectives and that my position may help moderate this tendency? In such a strategy or tactic there is an ethical commitment to not use force but there could also be a strategic hesitancy or unwillingness to bend on this absolute out of recognition of dominant countervailing discursive forces. Such discursive forces might include both the lobbyists from military contractors (recognizing that lobbying by these contractors may not be as direct as this—such as a former politician who had strong contacts with those who have strong contacts with the industry engaging in "persuasion" of former political colleagues), the entertainment industry which is filled with the assumption of the effectiveness of violence and the "necessity" of force or justice of retaliation, or broader political assumptions of the priority of the United States whose absolute invulnerability must be protected at all cost.

155. Hauerwas, *Vision and Virtue,* 198.

156. Considering Hauerwas, Ryan writes, "Christian community does not simply

Based on Christ's Lordship over the state, Hauerwas asserts that Christians have no "theory of the state" derived from the gospel; instead, they meet the state with specific criticisms. Rather than basing their critique and practice on natural law or some other more universal position, the Christian should engage out of the particularity of the Christ: the "Christian witness to the state will always express itself in terms of specific criticisms to concrete injustices."[157] Christians are to engage in specific *particular* critiques rather than attempt to develop a comprehensive theory to which to bend the state. This particularity comes up in many places in Hauerwas's work, both methodologically and epistemologically, and in theological engagement.[158] Continuing his commentary on Yoder, Hauerwas writes, "Christian criticism of the state must operate without universal moral principles presupposed by natural law theories or social ethics based on general anthropological assumptions. Christian social criticism is based only in Christ and such concrete principles of social criticism can be known only mediately."[159]

This idea of specificity in critique as part of method raises an interesting question around peacebuilding theory, and in particular around the use of case studies as a theoretical method in peacebuilding theory. What is gained in working on conflict X by reading a case study of conflict Y?[160] I take it that case studies are typically used to illustrate possible methods of peacebuilding practice, which are then transferable to another

---

happen; it must be built. Part of that building is the work of Christian ethics. The specific role of Christian ethics is to help the church in the present day to make the stories of Jesus and the people of Israel its own—that is, to practice their re-telling. Thereby, the communal nature of narrative knowing is carried out in the church's self-constituting practice." Ryan, *Politics of Practical Reasoning*, 134.

157. Hauerwas, *Vision and Virtue*, 209. This theme will be picked up in the final chapter addressing religion in US foreign policy.

158. Often work on peacebuilding provides case studies as part of its literature. My master's thesis in international relations focusing religion and peacebuilding was an analysis of case studies on religious actors in peacebuilding. This use can, however, go two ways. It can be assumed to be able to develop universal prescriptions from these or can be instances of hyper-particularity. The latter can, of course, be linked to a sort of cynicism, which states that we cannot in fact learn anything about peacebuilding from these cases, or a sort of detached sociological observation abstracted from the task of building peace.

159. Hauerwas, *Vision and Virtue*, 209.

160. Jennings's work on the development of whiteness and race, particularly assumptions of universality and transferability may be relevant, though this may stretch his applicability of his intention slightly.

context of conflict.¹⁶¹ As such, if we see religious leaders engaged in interfaith dialogue in Nigeria, perhaps this method should also be used in the Central African Republic, Jakarta, or New York. I would not fully disagree with this approach, but there are limitations and risks associated with the assumption of transferability. Probably the most useful aspect of case studies—which parallels Hauerwas's use of stories—is the training of the reader in reading reality.¹⁶² By continued reading of analysis and examples in peacemaking, the reader is formed in the habits of reading and action. This relates closely to Hauerwas's work in virtue and formation, addressed earlier in this chapter and to be further elaborated in the discussion of future directions in chapter 5.

Returning to the conversation more directly related to the challenge of "responsibility," Hauerwas via Yoder asks what it means for the church to act responsibly in the world. Here, he tries to break up the monopoly on who is presumed to define *responsible*. He claims, "The crucial question is not whether the church should or should not be responsible for society, but rather what that responsibility is." He continues, "It is surely being irresponsible if it attempts to change the world through the shortcut of using means unfitting to its ends."¹⁶³ Regarding the church's relation to the poor and disadvantaged, Hauerwas argues (in opposition to James Cone¹⁶⁴) that "Christian social ethics is not determined solely in terms of

---

161. My thesis for my master's degree in international relations was a study of case studies on religious actors in peacebuilding. Upon graduation, I immediately went to work peacebuilding in northeast Nigeria. As such, a substantial amount of my training in peacebuilding was related to analysis of case studies.

162. Consider Hauerwas's work on reading as formation as well as Jennings on translation but also reading the world theologically. Jennings (*Christian Imagination*, 195) writes, "Equiano did more than simply read his life in the light of Scripture. He, like many who would follow him, read the entire world into the broad scriptural narrative." Jennings asserts that the world is ordered in part through literacy and reading, and that this is controlled by forms of whiteness. In case studies it is relevant to consider under whose gaze the assessment and telling of the case of peacebuilding is written. The context from which and into which the case study is taken is also relevant. Even across allegedly similar contexts (say within Nigeria—or better yet, within northeastern Nigeria), cases are not automatically transferable given the multitude of cultures even within a relatively small geographic area. In Nigeria, however, though there are more than 500 languages, the colonial language of English is the official common language. In this case the common language is foreign and as such then creates less internal dominance by a particular local language—of course mastery of the colonial language and habits then becomes a potential step towards dominance.

163. Hauerwas, *Vision and Virtue*, 211.

164. "Theology can never be neutral or fail to take sides on issues related to the

the interest of the poor and disadvantaged."[165] To do so would be to "fail to bring the healing word of the gospel to the poor by drawing back from the judgment that the political tactics used by the poor, while perhaps achieving greater justice according to the world, only makes them as men more subject to the powers of this world."[166] He rightly notes that it is hard to say this without being misunderstood, since the church has often been much more concerned about critiquing the actions of the poor than condemning those who have oppressed the poor.[167]

In this, I doubt that Hauerwas's position is actually as far from that of liberation theologians as it might seem. He is, instead, proposing a different line of thought. He posits Jesus as definitive, with justice so defined and enacted through the life of the church, that it (justice) is a necessary result. Liberation theology posits justice for the oppressed as its starting point.[168] In *The Church as Polis*, Rasmusson discusses Jürgen Moltmann's work as a political theology that fastens the church's work to the political movements that are thought to exemplify the church's values. Hauerwas affirms Yoder in challenging this position.[169] In this, he does not, however, pull back from the "political" but seeks rather to redefine it in explicitly theological terms and embed it within the life of the church. What he challenges is a narrowly defined political space that is reducible to electoral or legislative politics.

One of the most interesting and constructive (in terms of engaging society) ways in which Hauerwas goes beyond Yoder is in his challenge to Yoder's claim that violence is inherent in the essence of the state.

---

plight of the oppressed." Cone, *Black Theology*, 4.

165. Hauerwas, *Vision and Virtue*, 214. On a related note, Copeland, while still arguing strongly for liberation, writes in *Enfleshing Freedom* (102): "With the expression *mystical body of Christ*, I want to reaffirm salvation in human liberation as an opaque work, that is, a work that resists both the reduction of human praxis to social transformation and the identification of the gospel with even the most just ordering of society."

166. Hauerwas, *Vision and Virtue*, 215.

167. Jennings (*Christian Imagination*, 238–39) offers a related comment on the catechizing of slaves.

168. Dorrien (*Economy, Difference, Empire*, 64) notes that Reinhold Niebuhr challenged the inclusion of a love ethic into social ethics, but that Niebuhr's thinking assumed love as foundational for doing ethics and political action in the first place: "But something nagged at him. Something was missing from his stark dichotomizing between love and justice. The later Niebuhr realized what it was: that the love ethic kept him and others in the struggle, whether or not they succeeded. *That* was its relevance."

169. Hauerwas, *Vision and Virtue*, 216.

Hauerwas agrees with Hannah Arendt in saying that violence is only basic to the state when it "is no longer sustained by the common wills of those that make it up."[170] Power, not violence, is the essence of the state; and "power is not necessary because men are inherently deficient in some way, but because men have sufficient resources to see part of the good."[171] When the state is no longer most basically defined by violence, there is a greater space for engagement by the Christian who refuses the use of violence on common challenges in society and the community. It is interesting to note that this early work of Hauerwas (1974) feels much more constructive in terms of the relationship between Christians and the state than works twenty years later, and more in line with his thinking after 2000.[172] These moves take Hauerwas's broad work on peace and his narrow work on peacemaking, specifically between Christians, into the public sphere. There are two parts to this section. The first will look at his work on ecumenism while the second will more directly take the church into the public sphere.

"Which Church? What Unity?"

Hauerwas asserts that peace is at the center of the church and that *being* the church is the *mission* of the church.[173] In light of these assertions, the unity of the church becomes of utmost importance. In "Which

---

170. Hauerwas, *Vision and Virtue*, 218.

171. Hauerwas, *Vision and Virtue*, 219.

172. Since I am not a scholar of recent religious and political history, I will not attempt to suggest whether this reflects his engagement with the political and religious space of the times of his writings. He has on a number of occasions stated that the theologian's task is not atemporal but relates to present pastoral concerns. This being the case, if my observations of the tone of his work are accurate, then it seems reasonable to investigate the feel of the era as it relates to his approach to his work. One conjecture is that his more negative-sounding titles, which occur in the late 1980s and early to mid 1990s, are in some way responding to the assumptions surrounding the Cold War (and "End of History) and the assumed unipolarity of the United States as a liberal democracy.

173. In a sermon, "Sent" (*Working with Words*, 168), Hauerwas writes, "God is whittling us down. We are a church that is quickly losing its power and status in the world as we know it. Those losses may well mean that whatever witness we are capable of making will be a witness without protection. The witness of those who have come before us must serve as a reminder that to be without protection is the condition necessary to learn to live at peace with one another. For if we fail to live peacefully with one another the witness we bring will not be a witness to the gospel of Jesus Christ."

Church? What Unity? Or, An Attempt to Say What I May Think about the Future of Christian Unity," found in *Approaching the End: Eschatological Reflections on Church, Politics, and Life* (2013), Hauerwas begins by noting George Lindbeck's questioning why he has not taken part in the ecumenical project, particularly in official ecumenical deliberations. By way of a narrative response, Hauerwas describes his early encounters with ecumenism—he was in graduate school during Vatican II—and his eclectic ecclesial experiences and commitments, as well as his disinterest in ecumenical projects that seek bureaucratic unity without addressing divisions of nationalism and poverty. He then recounts and largely affirms Yoder's thinking on ecumenism. He begins by noting, "Where Christians are not united, according to Yoder, quite simply the gospel is not true in that place. An extraordinary claim, but one I think true about the kind of truth the gospel is. What I find particularly compelling about this claim is that the truth is determined by 'place.' This is not vulgar relativism, but rather an implication that the gospel by its very nature requires a witness of a community."[174] Truthfulness is linked to a particular action: witness. Though some wonder if he has reduced all theology to ethics, Hauerwas responds that this merely demonstrates that theology cannot be abstract or detached from the worshipping community.

> The search for Christian unity is not only an imperative demanded by the gospel but an essential exercise in practical reason. If we are a church in diaspora, it is all the more important that local churches refuse to be isolated from one another. Our refusal to be isolated from one another, our willingness to share what we have learned from our attempts to faithfully worship God, is crucial if we are to exemplify for the world the peace that is essential for the discover of the goods in common.[175]

Here, Hauerwas draws connections between worship, Christian unity, and public life, connecting politics with what Hauerwas calls goods in common. Ecumenical work is not only a theological imperative but a practical necessity for living the vocation of the church.

It is not only the locality of actual churches that matters. Hauerwas attempts to change "the ecumenical subject" by challenging the movement's tendency to divide faith and order from works.[176] Additionally, the

---

174. Hauerwas, "Which Church?," 110.
175. Hauerwas, *War and the American Difference*, 146.
176. Hauerwas, "Which Church?," 112.

types of issues thought to divide, such as church polity, are not the most significant. He writes, "Yoder makes the extraordinary claim that where Christians are divided—and by divided Yoder means at the very least that they have commitments that could lead them to kill one another—the gospel cannot be true."[177] This turn again indicates Hauerwas's concern with the habits associated with the relationship to the nation-state as well as church relations across national borders. He continues, "For if God is killing us, as Lindbeck suggests, I suspect our death is due to the habits of Christendom. The future may well be a church that has the disciplines of mutual accountability necessary for the unity constituted by the body and blood of Jesus."[178] But certainly at least *some* of the questions of polity mirror Hauerwas's questions. For Anabaptists, historically, that has quite clearly been the case. Even now denominational polity and policy guides whether the denomination will act punitively or restoratively. Attempts to establish automatic retributive mechanisms appear to be closely related to the retributive, law-based, and power-based politics of the nation-state. So while unity in polity is not the entirety of Christian unity, it would seem to be relevant to the questions Hauerwas is more concerned about.

Interchurch unity is linked to familiar themes within Hauerwas's thinking. It is critical but not defined by institutional mergers or formal statements.[179] In this respect, Hauerwas escapes the more typical grooves of ecumenical discussion. It may be the case that the issues of polity and institution are of little interest, but that Hauerwas believes these discussions function according to a set pattern. A variation of this approach can be seen in the work of his former student, Chris Huebner. Huebner notes that Hauerwas is concerned about particular words being used by particular churches because they function as a kind of "self-confirming shorthand that inhibits genuine theological inquiry and meaningful dialogue more generally. . . . As a result, they fail to communicate matters of rich and substantive detail that genuine communication involves. . . . If there is a kind of speech present, it is that of monologue, not a dialogue that is vulnerable to correction from another."[180] Huebner asserts that in

---

177. Hauerwas, "Which Church?," 114.

178. Hauerwas, "Which Church?," 118.

179. It should be noted, however, that Hauerwas speaks positively of formal statements in regards to Geoffrey Wainwright's work on ministry and Eucharist. See Hauerwas, "Which Church?," 99.

180. Huebner, *Precarious Peace*, 70.

ecumenical discussions, there is a tendency to divide up topics in a way that seems to assume no connection between the particular topics. Mennonites, for example, are often expected to talk about peace and baptism in a way that "implies that they [peace and baptism] are somehow prior to other theological commitments without which they are unintelligible."[181] This occurs in discussion of ethics or political matters when they are assumed to be secondary to more basic theological questions. In this it is implied "that ecclesiology is not itself somehow involved in questions of identity, that the church does not name a way of life that is different than that of nations and ethnicities."[182] Huebner proposes a "radical ecumenism" that seeks to embrace vulnerability and embrace the "monster within" rather than seeking to win the other over or manage tolerance. In this he seeks to get beyond ecumenism as negotiated middle ground or a general acceptance of peculiarity that mimics global capitalism (what he calls "non-interruptive tolerance").[183]

In the work of church unity, Hauerwas challenges the assumption that we know what we mean when we say *ecumenism*. He also seeks to upset established patterns of communication that leave those engaged less than vulnerable or able to discuss the church as if it is detached from questions of nation-state loyalty and war.[184] Though these questions are important, Hauerwas does not indicate where or how they should be raised if Christians remain comfortably isolated. Huebner allows that the "radical ecumenism" he outlines can in fact happen at official ecumenical consultations, though undoubtedly such engagements are not limited to these structures and events. For Hauerwas, the fundamental failure of Christian unity lies in the ability through church history for Christians to kill other Christians—most recently made possible by dominant allegiance to the nation-state.[185] (In fact, I take this to be the primary aim

---

181. Huebner, *Precarious Peace*, 73.

182. Huebner, *Precarious Peace*, 74.

183. Huebner, *Precarious Peace*, 79.

184. Van der Borght describes the process of the World Council of Churches Faith and Order Commission in addressing issues of national and ethnic identity following the Bosnian conflict. In this struggle, religious identity was violently pitted against national and ethnic identity. He notes after a drawn-out process that left some churches feeling uncomfortable about raising questions around nationality, the project shifted: "The question of the unity of the church is no longer central. Instead, the issue now is how churches can be assisted in reconciliation work in situations of conflict. The focus shifted from the ecclesiological dilemma to an ethical challenge." Van der Borght, "Just Peace and the Unity of the Church," 44.

185. Though killing one another sounds rather dramatic on most occasions

of *War and the American Difference,* which will be examined as a whole in the following section.)

It is the possibility of Christians killing one another that Katongole and Wilson-Hartgrove address in *Mirror to the Church: Resurrecting Faith after Genocide in Rwanda* and Katongole addresses in parts of *The Sacrifice of Africa.* Katongole, never formally a student of Hauerwas but having written his Ph.D. dissertation on his epistemology, develops key directions of Hauerwas's work in an extraordinary way. After telling of a visit to Nyange where the priest suggested killing those seeking refuge in the church building by bulldozing it, Katongole writes, "At Nyange it became clear to me that the resurrection of the church begins with lament. If the church is the body of Christ, we have to confess that it was betrayed and crucified by its very members in Rwanda. The tragedy in Rwanda, however, was but a mirror reflecting the deep brokenness of the church worldwide."[186] This brokenness, demonstrated through willingness to kill, is rooted in an identity that prioritizes nation-state, racial, or ethnic group identity over that of Christ. This connection puts Christian unity at the center of Hauerwas's work.

War and the American Difference: *Exemplifying Witness*

War and the American Difference will be assessed here as a form of resistance to war as a mode of peacemaking in public. While some of Hauerwas's many other works on war will be brought into this section, the structure and approach will follow that of the book. Before commencing, it should be noted again that the focus of my project is peace and peacemaking and not pacifism versus just war theory. While these discussions

---

Hauerwas asserts that the commitment not to kill opens greater possibility and necessity to make peace. I discuss this at greater length in chapter 5. Regardless, the work of peace is certainly undercut—especially if one is committed to an embodied theology and life in the manner Hauerwas urges—when there is an absence of unity and peace. Such disunity is, of course, cultivated in many ways: some bureaucratic and institutional; others relating to a host of other divisions. For example, "Different denominations in Korea were introduced by American missionaries. Korean churches were under heavy influence of denominationalism from the beginning. Missionaries from different denominations planted their own denominations in Korea. This means that Korean churches began not as one big church but as divided churches. Korean churches therefore needed an ecumenical movement from the beginning." Heekuk, *Christianity in Korea,* 115.

186. Katongole and Wilson-Hartgrove, *Mirror to the Church,* 163.

are in the background, this section is not a reconsideration of these important areas. Certainly, Hauerwas works from an allegedly pacifist position, but such labels largely undercut the possibility of a discussion that is helpful in shaping the church into a body that builds peace.[187] While *War and the American Difference* is ostensibly about war, the concluding section proposes ways in which the church may live peace. I consider the entirety of the book an act of witness, and as such it functions as an act of peacemaking, by Hauerwas. Resisting war is, in fact, one facet of peacemaking and peacebuilding. Earlier chapters of the book critique assumptions of American Christianity regarding the church and the state, the middle and final sections provide resources for constructively moving beyond these critiques.

War and the American Difference is divided into three sections: "War and America," "The Liturgy of War," and "The Ecclesial Difference." Hauerwas's purpose is "to convince Christians that war has been abolished,"[188] and that at the "heart of this book is [the] attempt to imagine what it means for the church to be an alternative to war."[189] While in other contexts, Hauerwas takes "witness" as a topic, in this book he directly engages the reality of war and the church, which is an act of witness. He does this by first attempting to disrupt our assumptions about Christianity in America and about the reality of war. He then moves on to examine what he calls the "liturgy of war," and the way that this liturgy is used religiously. Finally, in "The Ecclesial Difference," he plumbs the existence and life of the church for resources to provide both resistance and a thicker alternative to the practice of war.

In considering the book as a whole, the framing of Hauerwas's purpose is important. As he states, "This is a modest book with an immodest purpose: to convince Christians that war has been abolished. The grammar of that sentence is important: the past tense is deliberate. I do not want to convince Christians to work for the abolition of war, but rather I want us to live recognizing that in the cross of Christ war has already been abolished. . . . Christians can and should live in a world of war as a people who believe war has been abolished."[190] The action of God is

187. I recognize that this statement may be disproportionately shaped by an American context in which a hyper-partisan political scene has infiltrated many areas of public discourse.

188. Hauerwas, *War and the American Difference*, xi.

189. Hauerwas, *War and the American Difference*, xiii.

190. Hauerwas, *War and the American Difference*, xi.

prior to our action. Living in this way may allow Christians to get beyond feeling guilty or assigning blame, and also provide freedom to live peacefully. Hauerwas asserts, "The moral challenge of war is too important for us to play the game of who is and who is not guilty for past or future wars. We are all, pacifist and nonpacifist alike, guilty. Guilt, however, is not helpful. What can be helpful is a cooperative effort to make war less likely."[191] Not only is apportioning blame unhelpful, but by getting past guilt, joint effort becomes possible.[192] The church as an alternative community, as a politics, is still in view: "Because Christians believe we are what the world can be, we can act in the hope that the world can and will positively respond to the witness of peace. That witness begins with Christians refusing to kill one another in the name of lesser loyalties and goods."[193] He expands in the vein of Huebner in *A Precarious Peace* on the problem of associating a single focus for the church.

> I have written often on the ethics of war and peace, but this is the first book that has those motifs as its primary focus. I have avoided focusing on war and peace because to do so might give some the impression that nonviolence is all that Christianity is about. If nonviolence becomes an abstraction, an ideal Christians pursue that can be separated from our convictions about the cross and resurrection, nonviolence threatens to become another manipulative form of human behavior. I hope, therefore, that my attempt to (re)describe war as an alternative to the sacrifice of the cross at once illumines why war is so morally compelling and why the church is an alternative to war.[194]

The first section, "America and War," consists of three essays: "War and the American Difference: A Theological Assessment," "America's God," and "Why War is a Moral Necessity in America: Or, How Realistic is Realism?" While this book has a greater topical focus than some of Hauerwas's other books, these chapters are a collection of essays, and as such are thematically related but do not necessarily build on each other. In the first, Hauerwas compares assumptions about the differences

---

191. Hauerwas, *War and the American Difference*, xiv.

192. Taking this statement seriously addresses, at least in part, two main criticisms of Hauerwas: that collaboration is unwelcome (perhaps because of an apparent sharp distinction between the church and the world) and that he encourages withdrawing from public life and action.

193. Hauerwas, *War and the American Difference*, xiii.

194. Hauerwas, *War and the American Difference*, xvii.

between religion and the state in Europe and America. He refers to the work of Charles Taylor, noting that "war is a moral necessity for America because it provides the 'unum' that makes the 'pluribus' possible."[195] Here, Hauerwas begins to set the stage for a deeper challenge to the place of war in the church in America. He first asserts that given the Protestant church's increasingly tenuous existence in America, it can now be free to live without pretension to power.[196] He writes, "If I am right that we are now facing the end of Protestantism, hopefully that will leave the church in America in a position with nothing to lose. When you have nothing to lose, all you have left is truth. God may yet make the church faithful—even in America."[197] The church that "has nothing to lose" can then live freely following the Spirit.[198]

In these first three chapters, Hauerwas sets out to undermine American assumptions about America, the church, and war. For example, he questions the possibility of using just war principles (let alone nonviolence or pacifism) to guide US military policy. He asks,

> For example, what would an American foreign policy determined by just war principles look like? What would a just war Pentagon look like? What kind of virtues would the people of America have to have to sustain a just war foreign policy and

---

195. Hauerwas, *War and the American Difference*, 4.

196. Whether or not Anabaptist groups in the United States may properly be called mainline Protestant can be debated. Institutionally, however, groups such as the Church of the Brethren and Mennonites are facing these same difficulties even though historically they have been somewhat different. This difference seems to have affected at least certain thought. On Yoder, Dula and Huebner write, "Those post-colonialists and post-structuralists taught us that the formation of Western politics and identity came at the expense of its colonial others. Yoder taught us to include the Anabaptists as one of the original colonial others. So Yoder's anti-foundationalism comes not from a close reading of Quine or Wittgenstein, but rather, as with postcolonialists, from a marginalized, persecuted minority's recognition that the establishment's categories themselves worked to defend against any possible destabilization from its others. Whereas George Lindbeck and Stanley Hauerwas had to learn how to occupy the space of minority and unlearn the habits of establishment, as a Mennonite Yoder was already there and so betrayed none of post-liberalism's anxiety about the need to secure the church's ongoing survival in an increasingly secular world. In a similar way, it might be suggested that for Yoder, 'exile' was not a regrettable fait accompli of late modernity. It was a fact of Anabaptist history." Dula and Huebner, *New Yoder*, xvii.

197. Hauerwas, *War and the American Difference*, 20.

198. Having nothing to lose and thus living freely is one possible option. While having "nothing to lose" may be a necessary condition it does not seem to be a sufficient cause. One could as easily live wracked by anxiety in the face of such vulnerability.

Pentagon? What kind of training do those in the military have to undergo in order to be willing to take casualties rather than conduct a war unjustly? How would those with the patience necessary to ensure that war be the last resort be elected to office? Those are the kind of questions that advocates of just war must address before they accuse pacifists of being "unrealistic."[199]

In this, Hauerwas seeks to engage with just war theory enough to demonstrate that as an actual restraining practice on US military policy, it is largely irrelevant.[200] War and just war theory are obviously related to discussions of peace and peacemaking, but they are not oriented to the same literature. Whereas just war theory is theoretically used by and in relation to nation-states, peace and peacemaking are much more far reaching in the actors involved. Peace and peacemaking in Christian theological ethics corresponds to the growing and developing academic field of peacebuilding. These chapters move toward providing resources for resisting the assumptions of war in America, but my interest lies mainly in the later chapters.

In Part 3, "The Ecclesial Difference," Hauerwas engages in what might be considered more constructive moves relating to peace.[201] The first in this section is chapter 8, "Jesus, the Justice of God." For those concerned with his attacks on conceptions of justice—for example when he calls justice "a bad idea"[202]—this chapter provides a way forward. He notes at the start that these rhetorical flourishes are meant to "call into question abstract accounts of justice often associated with liberal political theory, which assumes a just social order is possible without people who constitute that order being just."[203] As such, his critique, even though

---

199. Hauerwas, *War and the American Difference*, 26.

200. Daniel Bell critiques such an approach in *Just War as Christian Discipleship* (91). He calls this "Just war with too many teeth" writing, "This form of abuse [of just war theory] is the mirror image of just war without teeth. Whereas just war without teeth effectively erases the moral force of the tradition, just war with too many teeth exaggerates the bite, or moral force, of the criteria by strengthening them in a manner that renders them all but impossible to meet. If the first abuse effectively abolished the bar, this abuse raises the moral bar too high."

201. *Constructive* as opposed to critical or *deconstructive* does not mean that this latter are not useful, but that in constructive work he is proposing an approach rather than commenting on the shortcomings of another approach, action, or theoretical framework.

202. Hauerwas, *After Christendom?*

203. Hauerwas, *War and the American Difference*, 100.

it does not propose an alternative, is important work in the ongoing conversation that is theology. For Hauerwas, this theology is part of the church and the work of the church, rather than a purely academic discussion abstracted from the life of the church. Additionally, he is concerned that accounts of justice by Christians often proceed as if Scripture and theology are primarily motivators to get Christians out of the pews to do justice, which is assumed to be an external standard. In these instances, it is assumed "that justice can be understood apart from Christian theological convictions and practices."[204] This approach, probably unintentionally, "displaces the church" which "results in a subtle displacement of Jesus. Jesus is relegated to being a motivator to encourage Christians to get involved in justice. Even if Jesus is thought to have practiced justice in his ministry, he is appealed to as a symbol or example to follow. For what really matters is not Jesus, but justice."[205] As an alternative to this alleged displacement he asserts,

> For Christians, the work of justice first and foremost begins with their participation in Christ's work. The liturgy, particularly baptism and Eucharist, becomes the form justice takes because through those rites we are incorporated into Christ, becoming God's justice for the world. In Bell's language, Jesus does "not justify individuals who then go do justice on their own; rather, Jesus justifies persons in communion. Jesus justifies his body, the church. Being made just and doing justice are a matter of being immersed in the life of the ecclesial community; to do justice is part of the community whose life is centered in and ordered by Jesus, God's justice."[206]

This is justice that is known through Jesus and while engaged in "the system" for justice does not neglect the particularity of people.[207]

---

204. Hauerwas, *War and the American Difference*, 101.

205. Hauerwas, *War and the American Difference*, 102.

206. Hauerwas, *War and the American Difference*, 104, discussing Bell, "Jesus, the Jews, and the Politics of God's Justice," 87–111.

207. Hauerwas (*War and the American Difference*, 116) writes, "Bell acknowledges that view through the lens of modernity's politics, such a view of justice—justice shaped by the works of mercy—will be dismissed as 'philanthropy.' But that is exactly the perspective that must be rejected if the justice that is the church is not to be identified with the justice of the nation-state. Wolterstorff worries that if justice is identified by Bell's 'Spirit-blown mobile community,' we will lack the universality necessary to sustain appeals to justice as such. But no theory of justice will be sufficient to do that work. Rather than a theory, God has called into the world a people capable

The sustaining of conflicts and working toward resolution is something to be embodied in the church and lived before the world.[208] This is similar to James Davison Hunter's "faithful presence."[209] Hunter proposes what he sees as a different way of action from the typical ways that Christians seek to change the world. In this, he may sustain a false sense of division between faithful local witness and broader national level witness when he does not include anything on Christians engaging in national or international policy level work (Hauerwas has this tendency as well). Such an omission may be symptomatic of the continued tendency to maintain divisions between private and public or political and apolitical. If this is a parallel exclusion then one must ask on what basis does Hunter (and to an extent Hauerwas) hold the sphere of a particular faithful witness as *de facto* more appropriate for the church?

In chapter 10, "A Worldly Church: Politics, Theology, and the Common Good," Hauerwas works toward a vision of the church that adequately accounts for its situation of diaspora in the globalized world which seeks to flatten differences by limiting diversity to matters of choice in consumption. This builds on his challenge to abstract accounts of justice to affirming "the alternative church in its concrete localities."[210] He suggests, "That the churches now find ourselves in diaspora may well be a gift God has given us to help us rediscover the slow hard work of Christian unity. That work, the work Rahner characterizes as 'little local offenses,' may not result in demonstrable statistical successes, but such successes are not the purpose of the church."[211] Hauerwas began the book by challenging assumptions about America and war and ends with focus on the formation of community that can do the "hard work." This hard

---

of transgressing borders of the nation-state to seek the welfare of the downtrodden."

208. "Our refusal to be isolated from one another, our willingness to share what we have learned from our attempts to faithfully worship God, is crucial if we are exemplify for the world the peace that is essential for the discovery of goods in common. The Christian refusal to kill surely is imperative if we are to sustain the conflicts necessary to learn from one another." Hauerwas, *War and the American Difference*, 146.

209. "A theology of faithful presence is a theology of engagement in and with the world around us. It is a theology of commitment, a theology of promise. It is disarmingly simple in concept yet in its implications it provides a challenge, at points, to all of the dominant paradigms of cultural engagement of the church." Hunter, *To Change the World*, 243.

210. Hauerwas, *War and the American Difference*, 137.

211. Hauerwas, *War and the American Difference*, 139.

work is not separate from the resistance to war but necessary for sustained and substantive resist and the building of peace.

In spite of having war-related themes as a focus, *War and the American Difference* is a Hauerwasian example of peacemaking through resisting violence. Though some may object that peacemaking needs to be more than words, this work of practical political, theological, and critical reasoning contributes to the undoing of American and American Christians' assumptions about their place in the world and the "necessity" of war. Such an act is an act of peacemaking. Hauerwas not only challenges underlying assumptions, but he suggests ecclesial alternative practices.

Conclusion

In this chapter, I considered several key texts providing a picture of Hauerwas's vision of peacemaking. Though "peacemaking" is not always explicitly named, its components are present in many parts of his writing on peace, nonviolence, and politics. With his challenge to the divisions between theology, ethics, and politics, as well as the embodied nature of the life of the church defined by Jesus, Hauerwas provides useful resources for peacemaking. It will be my contention in the next chapter that Hauerwas's work can and should be extended to particular peacebuilding practices and that it should be expanded to include other theological dialogue partners, particularly in the area of racism.

Chapter 5

WHERE HAUERWAS DOESN'T TAKE US

HAUERWAS'S WORK IN ECCLESIOLOGY and peace creates the space in which he could move more substantially into peacemaking. His work on concrete practices and his assertion of the centrality of nonviolence to the Christian understanding of Jesus, as well as his direct writing on peacemaking, make substantial considerations of peacemaking in practice a natural step in the progression of his work. My thesis is that the work of Stanley Hauerwas, particularly on ecclesiology, nonviolence, peace, and peacemaking, can be usefully extended into more specific engagement on peacebuilding. In this chapter I will also propose several ways in which such extension can happen. Since peacebuilding is broad and incorporates many disciplines, both theoretically and practically, I address two specific areas where Hauerwas's work can fruitfully be employed or should be critiqued: religion in US foreign-policy considerations and racial justice. I will posit trajectories that his work suggests but which he does not fully explore. Though these areas correspond with the streams of thought I highlighted in chapter 2, this selection was not deliberately imposed on Hauerwas's work but on what emerged as important lines of argument that his work suggested. By suggested, I mean that given his work, commitments, and repeated themes, these are areas that one would expect him to make more extensive constructive contributions or that one can develop beyond Hauerwas's thinking while remaining in line with his commitments.

In the following sections, I will demonstrate how these areas are natural next steps for Hauerwas. The question then remains: If I am correct in my assertions, why has Hauerwas not made these moves? This question becomes even more salient considering the volume of Hauerwas's writing. I will seek to answer this question, albeit in a speculative and tentative way, highlighting particular commitments as well as weaknesses that are critical for understanding Hauerwas.

On several occasions Hauerwas has said that though more should be said, if the teacher waits long enough the students will eventually write it.[1] Though I have not studied with Hauerwas himself, perhaps I can claim him as a teacher after having spent so much time with his work.[2] In that role, he might very well respond in this manner to my suggestions of what he should say on peacemaking.[3]

Lederach's *The Moral Imagination* might be the book Hauerwas have written if he were an international peacebuilding practitioner rather than a theologian.[4] While there are certainly areas of overlap between the literature of theological ethics and peacemaking, I will not attempt to mount a comprehensive cross-disciplinary exchange. To facilitate a manageable but fruitful endeavor, I will focus on a narrower range of peacebuilding with particular focus on *The Moral Imagination*. I will then consider Hauerwas's work in relation to the increasing recognition of the role of religion in international relations and US foreign policy. Hauerwas's writing contains resources and commitments to address racial justice, but he has largely not addressed this topic.

Hauerwas's Peacemaking and Lederach's Moral Imagination

Though not a specifically theological work, *The Moral Imagination* emerges out of Mennonite practice. It is based on values which can be

---

1. One such instance is on Dan Bell's work on justice, discussed in "Jesus: The Justice of God" in Hauerwas, *War and the American Difference*, 99. Additionally, in *The Work of Theology* (120), Hauerwas responds to a suggestion that he should make his work more material, "What are you waiting for? If you think Christian people should have a problem with war you need to think about how to preach that. If you think the church needs to be distinct, what does that mean for your budget?"

2. Charles Pinches observes some distinctions between those who wrote a dissertation under Hauerwas's direction and those who in engage in some other manner. He notes that his distinction is arbitrary but helpful for limiting the scope of this particular article. Pinches, "Hauerwas and Political Theology," 513–42.

3. This, of course, assumes that he is at least in partial agreement with my assessment. Though I cannot be sure that he would be in agreement with my assessment, I believe that my suggested trajectories are generally consonant with his work.

4. My hope and belief is that these vocations are by no means mutually exclusive.

shown to emerge from Mennonite life.[5] In this first section, I will seek to demonstrate that Lederach proposes a framework of peacebuilding practice that Hauerwas *would* propose if he were a peacebuilding practitioner. The implication is that *The Moral Imagination* is a vital resource for Christians seeking to live Hauerwas's vision of peace, nonviolence, and peacemaking.[6] Hauerwas regularly critiques the notion that a particular practice can be abstracted from the community and retain coherence.[7] Variations of this conundrum have been addressed elsewhere in this project so for now it will suffice to say that this dilemma is most acute when considering (so called) pacifism in which an absolute, or near absolute ruling on the possibility of violence, seems to be made in an inflexible manner. This is perhaps most notable when engaging foreign-policy questions of war as a person or community committed to pacifism. Since neither Lederach nor this project is narrowly focused on this question, the concern is less significant here.

Though *The Moral Imagination* focuses on peacebuilding *practice*, it is not overly procedural, technical, or embedded in an academic discipline or professional skill set, such as mediation. Though not driven by technique, it is nonetheless practical in that it provides guidance to the practice of peacebuilding. In this, it is similar to Hauerwas's writing on ecclesiology and peacemaking. Hauerwas is extremely practical, even while he eschews all variations of how-to as well as systematic analysis

---

5. Marshall observes that when the Christian conflict transformation practitioners she interviewed began to speak in more explicitly theological terms they tended to shift from language of "transformation" to "reconciliation." Marshall, "Conflict, God, and Constructive Change," 2.

6. As I wrote, I began to wonder if this is why I was drawn to both these writers. I discovered a calling to peacemaking as an Anabaptist who discovered I was an Anabaptist among American evangelicals. The discovery that I was Anabaptist coincided with a call to peacemaking, steps to study for such work in graduate school (somewhat ironically in international relations at a Catholic university), and finding Hauerwas's *Performing the Faith: Bonhoeffer and the Practice of Nonviolence* in a bargain book bin in the bookstore at Moody Bible Institute.

7. Baxter challenges Hauerwas on how "theological" politics plays out in practice. Additionally, though Lederach's work is not necessarily always done *on behalf* of Mennonites or within Mennonite structures it may be a stretch to say that it is "abstracted from" this community. Presumably though important, denominational or related structures do not fully encompass the life of that church. While I will not seek to resolve this here I simply note that though Lederach does not call his work in *Moral Imagination* "Mennonite peacebuilding," a relevant relationship remains.

and recommendation. Lederach, too, specifically expresses concern with technique-oriented approaches to peacebuilding:

> I am uneasy with the growing technique-oriented view of change in settings of violence that seems to dominate much of professional conflict resolution approaches. . . . The gnawing sensation emerges from what I increasingly hear and feel as I work with people who are from these settings, more often than not, in my case, at the level of local communities. What I find are three prevalent feelings: suspicion, indifference, and distance.[8]

Lederach's uneasiness with this approach to social change mirrors Hauerwas's dislike of over emphasis on theological ethical method that Hauerwas asserts plagues modern theology.[9] Hauerwas challenges such divisions of academic disciplines; Lederach notes in his introduction that his book is not embedded in any one particular academic discipline. This cross-border work provides a guide that is simultaneously practical and theoretical.[10] Not only does this approach mark a similarity in working style, but it serves as a bridge from Hauerwas's theological ethics to peacebuilding-related literature.

As noted, this section will not seek a comprehensive comparison of Hauerwas on peacemaking and Lederach in the *Moral Imagination*, but I will consider several common themes and approaches. Though parts will relate to my third chapter, on Hauerwas's ecclesiology, most of my attention will be on chapter 4's description and assessment of Hauerwas's peacemaking.

Hauerwas is known for his work on virtues. Though he avoids addressing virtues as such, I have an even narrower interest within his work. In chapter 4, I asserted that virtues are part of the formation of the peaceable body (of the church) and bodies (of Christians). Hauerwas asserts that people gathered around and through a narrative of peace are formed into peaceable people and thus are given a vocation of peacemaking in the world. Hauerwas does not comment extensively on this. His focus tends toward the formation of the church and its right worship of God, with

---

8. Lederach, *Moral Imagination*, 52.

9. For Hauerwas's consideration of his approach to theology see his "How I Think I Learned to Think Theologically," 11–31.

10. In *Moral Imagination* (33), Lederach does say, "And there is nothing more practical than a good theory." Though it's hard to imagine Hauerwas saying such a thing, I do not think they are far off in practice. Hauerwas does this with his consistent challenge to persistent errors in theology and church practice.

caveats appended, to the effect of "and, of course, this means Christians will participate and collaborate to work for peace in the world." With this approach, Hauerwas resists turning "the Christian virtue of peacemaking" into a technique or formula to be applied. At times, this undercuts the applicability of his work on peacemaking; however, it may leave open a greater possibility for creative engagement.[11] Though not synonymous, Hauerwas's work on the virtue of peacemaking is not unlike Lederach's "essences." Lederach states,

> Rather than seek the "rules" of simplicity, I became curious about what constitutes the core "essences" of peacebuilding. These I came to see as a small set of disciplines, practices, out of which the complexity of peacebuilding emerges in all its beauty. Put in a slightly different way, I asked myself about essence in this way: What disciplines, *if they were not present,* would make peacebuilding impossible? On exploration I discovered that when held together and practiced, these disciplines for the moral imagination that make peacebuilding possible.[12]

For Hauerwas, the ability to make peace in the world derives from the habits and skills formed by addressing sin via confrontation and peacemaking within the church in the mode of Matthew 18.[13] This willingness to confront, make peace, and forgive emerges from a commitment to truth honed through the worship of God. Through worshiping God (an apparently simple act that according to Hauerwas takes a lifetime to learn), the community is formed peaceably and thus is trained in the skills to work for peace. The "simple" disciplines Lederach proposes are "the centrality of relationships," "the practice of paradoxical curiosity," "space for the creative act," and "willingness to risk."[14] This is less split-second intuition than it is skills honed as a master craftsperson. Of course, the latter includes many intuitive decisions about the feel of the situation that happen without conscious effort. Though such intuition may not be easily

---

11. On the very opposite end would be a formulaic manual with step-by-step instructions. For example, parts of a Victim Offender Reconciliation Program training that I took followed this format because of its interaction with juvenile criminal justice structures. In that aspect of the training, legal and procedural necessity mandated such an approach, while other parts of the training focused on more flexible parts such as listening and building trust.

12. Lederach, *Moral Imagination*, 34.

13. Hauerwas, "Peacemaking: The Virtue of the Church," 89–94.

14. Lederach, *Moral Imagination*, 34–39.

articulated, it may, perhaps, be better described as a slow rather than instantaneous process. In this vein, Lederach describes his work with the Maryknoll Center for Research, which produced *Artisans of Peace*.[15] Lederach's task was to describe the peacemaking process theologically, despite his stated lack of theological qualifications, and discern themes within these discussions. Though the peacebuilders were involved deeply in the work of peacebuilding in their communities, they were often unable to describe their work or the theory behind it. Lederach called this a "theology of mystery."[16]

Hauerwas has challenged large abstract democracy and pushed for local politics and practical reasoning. This "practical reasoning" also appears in his theological "method" when he asserts that theology starts in the middle, is located within a tradition, and is never complete. Hauerwas writes, "I want to show that the proper way to construe human knowledge of God is neither from 'the bottom up' nor from 'the top down' (insofar as this strategy merely reproduces the epistemological dualisms upon which modernity founders) but is according to the mutual interpenetration of grace and nature as exhibited in the inescapably analogical and historically ordered uses of language by which God's relation to God's creation is articulated."[17] In this it is an ongoing discussion with struggles not unlike his approach to politics. He writes, "The very fact that doctrines are hewn from bitter controversy and tested through time is sufficient reason to make them the focus of theology.[18] In his trust that orthodoxy emerges and should be trusted by the history of struggles, Hauerwas seems to not adequately account for power and manipulation in this vision. Though I still think that he should better account for this, he trusts that the Holy Spirit is actively involved and thus makes the church more than it would seem to otherwise be.[19] Such trust may be adequately theologically robust but allows uncertainty particularly in light of the proliferation of varieties of theological visions embodied in countless denominations as well as the diversity within those denominations and even local congregations. Though he does not reject political engagement and collaboration with the world, he does assert that the

---

15. Cjka and Bamat, *Artisans for Peace*.
16. Lederach, *Moral Imagination*, 164.
17. Hauerwas, "Truth about God," 88.
18. Hauerwas, *Work of Theology*, 33.
19. Hauerwas, "How the Holy Spirit Works."

local politics of being the church is central.[20] He asserts that the first task of the church is to be the church and challenges the tendency to discount the local politics of practical reasoning in the church and community as irrelevant for "real" politics in the capital city. In his view it is at the local level of politics that truthful and peaceable people may be formed and participate. It is not, however, that the *purpose* is to participate in the *real* politics, but that to bear peaceable noncoercive witness, a peaceable people must be formed. Lederach asserts a variation, which is, as one would expect, more oriented toward practice. Lederach writes, "People in settings of great violence astutely recognize that distance and apathy go hand in hand.[21] When the change processes are molded and shaped without engagement, in other words, without voice or accessible conversation, then the process is held at a distance, and a sense of apathy and manipulated change emerges and grows."[22] Also related to Hauerwas are comments on peace accords, assumptions of where power lies, and linear conception of causation, conflict, and peacebuilding process. Both value community level practical reasoning, politics, and peacebuilding, but also recognize the practical need for the local to complement high-level efforts or hold them accountable.[23]

---

20. See Cavanaugh, "Politics of Vulnerability," 104–5, for a helpful discussion of localness and complex space.

21. In the 2013 policy position adopted by the Church of the Brethren's Annual Conference we made a similar point about drone warfare and the incarnation. "All killing mocks the God who creates and gives life. Jesus, as the Word incarnate, came to dwell among us (John 1:14) in order to reconcile humanity to God and bring about peace and healing. In contrast, our government's expanding use of armed drones distances the decisions to use lethal force from the communities in which these deadly strikes take place. We find the efforts of the United States to distance the act of killing from the site of violence to be in direct conflict to the witness of Christ Jesus." See "Church of the Brethren," 52–57.

22. Lederach, *Moral Imagination*, 57.

23. Though Hauerwas chafes at the possibility that such efforts are for the purpose of making democracy work, I believe that this is an accurate reading of his assertions. Perhaps an analogous situation is his view of the relationship of theology and ethics. In *The Work of Theology* (23), he makes a succinct statement of this relationship that is helpful for the discussion here. He writes, "That I have written much and have written broadly I should like to think reflects my conviction that theology must be the ongoing effort to construe the world as God's good work. That I understand the work of theology in this way is one of the reasons that I have grudgingly been willing to be identified as an 'ethicist.' Ethics at least suggests that theology is a practical science, but the very distinction between theology and ethics can reproduce the deleterious distinction between theory and practice. I certainly do not deny that theology properly

For Hauerwas, "the trivial" and "rest" are facets of patience, which is needed for making peace. In "Taking Time for Peace," he asserts that in the face of great urgency and seemingly imminent destruction caused by the possibility of nuclear weaponry, Christians must resist having their lives over-determined by the bomb. To counteract this self-tyranny, Christians should take time for trivial (although not insignificant) actions such as baseball and raising lemurs.[24] This does not mean Christians should not participate in attempts to change politicians' actions,[25] but it does mean that survival is not the ultimate good. This patience is in part learned by the rejection of violence. Lederach describes such patience in the work of web watching, noting as well that "one of the Lakota's core values that accompanies the healing process is patience."[26] Additionally, Lederach describes the moral imagination being present in the seemingly trivial and foolish action of a well-known cellist playing publicly during shelling:

> On one occasion, during a lull in the shelling, a TV news reporter approached the cellist seated in the square [who was playing in public for twenty-two days following the Bread Massacre in which twenty-two people were killed by snipers and mortars while waiting for bread] and asked, "Aren't you crazy for playing music while they are shelling Sarajevo?" Smailovic responded, "Playing music is not crazy. Why don't you go ask those people if they are not crazy shelling Sarajevo while I sit here and play my cello." The moral imagination that gave hope and the strength to resist, a creative act that transcended the madness of violence, was found in the hands of a cellist who sat fast in the midst of the geography of hate.[27]

---

understood has speculative, or I would prefer contemplative, moments, but I have tried to show that fundamental theological convictions about the Father, the Son, and the Holy Spirit are inseparable from the work they do for the formation of a people set loose in and for the world. Accordingly, if you think Christians have 'beliefs' that need to be applied, I assume that something has gone wrong in your understanding of the grammar of theology." The phrase "inseparable from the work they do for the formation" is a helpful, concise attempt of Hauerwas to describe what is commonly said to be the connection between theology and ethics.

24. Hauerwas, "Taking Time for Peace," 259–63.

25. "Let us continue to try to find ways to help our political leaders discover the means to end the constant spiral of nuclear buildup." Hauerwas, *Christian Existence Today*, 257.

26. Lederach, *Moral Imagination*, 104.

27. Lederach, *Moral Imagination*, 156–57.

In "Taking Time for Peace," Hauerwas links both rest and the trivial with Christian peacemaking.[28] Lederach develops variation of this in stillness. In this attentiveness and patience is critical even in the face of urgent problems. To be still then allows watchfulness, which is needed for peacebuilding. Hauerwas would say that this rest is needed not only for effectiveness, but in order to have one's life rightly ordered towards God. Lederach writes,

> The fundamental nature of stillness flies in the face of common notions of getting something to change. Change, we believe, is about promoting, nudging, and even pushing. Activism argues with the world: "Don't just stand there, do something!" Stillness says in response: "Don't just do something, stand there!" The paradox is this: Stillness is not inactivity. It is the presence of disciplined activity without movement. Stillness is activism with a twist. It is the platform that generates authenticity of engagement, for it is the stage that makes true listening and seeing possible. What makes stillness possible? Stillness requires a commitment to patience and watchfulness. Its guideposts are these: Slow down. Stop. Watch what moves around you. Feel what moves in you.[29]

Uses of narrative are also present in both writers. Specifically referencing Hauerwas, as well as narrative in other disciplines, Lederach writes, "In other words, beyond a particular methodology of scientific inquiry or the practice of personal therapy, the use of narrative that we wish to explore is one which involves the formative stories of genesis and place (Hauerwas and Jones, 1997). If we take such a long view of identity and group formation seriously, we shall come to recognize that the formation of group identity arising from the past, the construction of its future, and its very survival are about finding place, voice, and story."[30] Lederach asserts that to understand a conflict and contribute to a sustaining peace, the peacebuilder must attend to the narrative of the communities and conflict. This is a different take on narrative than Hauerwas typically uses. For Hauerwas, narrative is useful because it is the way of Scripture,

---

28. "The character of the rest of the Spirit makes possible has the character of the time given in Sabbath. Sabbath time is the time of perfect activity, a time of prayer and contemplation, made possible by the gift of the Spirit." Hauerwas, *Work of Theology*, 42–43.

29. Lederach, *Moral Imagination*, 104.

30. Lederach, *Moral Imagination*, 142.

theology, and the people of God.[31] As such, narrative counteracts American Christians' tendency to buy into the "liberal" story of having no story. Narrative is not simply a tool but an integral element of truth. However, Hauerwas also not only claims to be part of the Christian story, but recognizes that he is also shaped by stories of being Texan. In this, he is more obviously closer to Lederach.[32] Lederach writes,

> So how do people living in geographies of violence remember and change? As was so clearly stated in the psalmist's reflections, it is not by creating a land of forgetfulness. Social amnesia may be useful for political pragmatism, but it is a recipe for weak communities incapable of true identity and correspondingly genuine relationships. The land of forgetfulness creates communities without vocation. The challenge of linking memory and vision lies primarily with the vocation of the moral imagination, which can only be exercised in that place that lies between the local and the public, between personal biography and the shaping of responsive social structures.[33]

Hauerwas has asserted the need for narrative as well as strongly critiqued the notion that we get to choose our own story—or the story about not having a story. Lederach's final chapter on vocation is also a useful point of contact with Hauerwas on narrative. Lederach writes, "When we approach the mystery of risk as part of peacebuilding in settings of violence, I believe we are exploring life purpose more than professional effectiveness."[34] In the vocation of the peacebuilder, the connection, work, and risk goes deeper than a job or even career.[35]

---

31. After years of working with "story" and "narrative," Hauerwas expresses concern in "The Narrative Turn" (139) that narrative has become a defining narrative *as such*. He notes that the last time he "wrote" on narrative (the writing was mostly by the co-author Greg Jones) was in 1989, a work that was reprinted in 1997 as *Why Narrative: Readings In Narrative Theology*.

32. I write that in this Lederach and Hauerwas are "more obviously closer" meaning *not* that in this they are obviously closer but that at least on the surface this particular use of "narrative" seems to be closer. In this moment I cannot attempt to sort out or conjecture Lederach's underlying epistemology in relation to revelation and his theology in relation to a version of natural theology.

33. Lederach, *Moral Imagination*, 62.

34. Lederach, *Moral Imagination*, 165.

35. Lederach, *Moral Imagination*, 169.

Imagination and a wide-ranging approach shape both Lederach and Hauerwas.[36] Hauerwas utilizes a wide range of sources across academic disciplines, addresses particular needs in his writing rather than being more "systematic," and aims to integrate rather than separate and categorize the church's life (theology, liturgy, ethics, worship, common meals, mission, preaching, etcetera). His effort to embrace the whole means that his responses and literary engagements are not necessarily within his expertise as an ethicist. Hauerwas, as well as Lederach, *intentionally go further* than the prescribed boundaries of their academic disciplines. This intentional act disrupts the often-felt need to control, manage, and engineer a solution or argument. This allows for surprise—what Lederach calls serendipity—to appear. Lederach asserts that peacebuilding is more like an art than a formula or technique. He writes,

> The aesthetics of social change proposes a simple idea: Building adaptive and responsive processes requires a creative act, which at its core is more art than technique. The creative act brings into existence processes that have not existed before. To sustain themselves over time, processes that have not existed before . . . Professional excellence increasingly has emphasized the technology, the technique and the skills of process management as tools that legitimate and make possible training, replication, and dissemination. . . . In the process of professionalization [of peacebuilding] we too often have lost a sense of art, the creative act that underpins the birth and growth of personal and social change. I fear we see ourselves to be—and have therefore become—more technicians than artists. By virtue of this shift of perception our approaches have become too cookie-cutter-like, too reliant on what proper technique suggests as a frame of reference, and as a result our processes are too rigid and fragile.[37]

The Lederach-style peacebuilder interested in exploring theology and Christian ethics may gain from Hauerwas; and the Hauerwasian seeking to embody peacemaking would benefit from *The Moral Imagination*.

36. Joel Lehenbauer describes Hauerwas in "The Theology of Stanley Hauerwas," 168. "To do ethics from the perspective of those "out of control" means Christians must find the means to make clear to both the oppressed and the oppressor that the cross determines the meaning of history. Christians should thus provide imaginative alternatives for social policy as they are released from the "necessities" of those that would control the world in the name of security. For to be out of control means Christians can risk trusting in gifts so they have no reason to deny the contingent character of our existence."

37. Lederach, *Moral Imagination*, 73.

This is not to say that one necessarily leads to the other or vice versa but that each is suggestive of the other. In this I am not suggesting that Lederach is subject to the same critique as Hauerwas or that Lederach's peacebuilding requires the "peculiar" Christian theology of Hauerwas.[38] Additionally, by suggesting that *Moral Imagination* is a natural step for Hauerwas's students set on peacemaking does not mean that Hauerwas would not find this a tiresome attempt at "applying" his work.

Hauerwas's Peacemaking and Racial Justice

Racial injustice in the United States is a long-standing cause of the absence of peace, which must always be defined in the fullest sense and not simply in relation to particular conflict or violence.[39] The work of Hauerwas, particularly on ecclesiology and narrative, nonviolence, peace, and peacemaking, should be extended to connect to literature on issues of racial justice. I will argue that Hauerwas should interact more extensively with a wider range of writers (not just academic disciplines) and should attempt to deal with issues of racial justice.[40] I will posit trajectories that Hauerwas's work suggests but does not fully explore.[41] Though as a white man, Hauerwas cannot fully comprehend or respond to racism and racial injustice, given his prominence, privilege, and previous areas of work, it is incumbent for him to attempt this with honesty and humility. James Logan, a black Mennonite theologian writes,

---

38. Since my denomination, the Church of the Brethren, has historically referred to itself as a peculiar people based on nonconformity, I do not intend this in a derogatory way, but use it to designate particularity and a intentionally contentious approach.

39. See, for example, Woodley, *Shalom and the Community of Creation*. Woodard-Lehman ("Body Politics and the Politics of Bodies," 297) writes on this form of violence in relation to the work of Hauerwas: "It remains for Hauerwas to specify how his radical ecclesiology is a politically significant form of resistance to dominative power. This remainder can be brought into relief with respect to a specific form of dominative power: racism and racialization as expressed in subtle, passive forms of violence. In order for Hauerwas's radical ecclesiology to be true to its pacifistic and Eucharistic center, this politics must resist all forms of violence—even, and perhaps especially, those masked in seemingly nonviolent forms.

40. Though Huebner ("Work of Reading," 285–86) accurately describes Hauerwas as widely read, there is a strange racial limitation to this breadth. That he is "more than willing to be drawn into unfamiliar territory" further highlights this gap.

41. For example, Hauerwas considers Dr. King's nonviolence in "Martin Luther King Jr. and Christian Nonviolence," 83–95.

> Hauerwas has consistently failed to muster the courage to seriously engage what has long been a salient problem deeply rooted *within* the Christian narrative, the very same narrative that calls Christians to truthfulness on Hauerwas's account. This problem is the problem of race, in particular the problem of Black people as pariah people in church and society . . . And it is irrefutable that even "peaceable" and "nonviolent" Anabaptist families of Christians have played their part in, and benefited from, the racism that is embedded in American custom and common practice. Given the collusion of peace churches with the crying shame of racism, it is surprising that Hauerwas has yet to seriously confront the racism of the peace churches as a towering breach in Christian truthfulness. Hauerwas has generally failed to confront racism as a distortion of the grammar of the Christian faith. One has to be stunned by the utter dearth of writings and active *public* concern by Hauerwas (and the overwhelming majority of White theologians).[42]

Theological, ethical, historical, and social analytic writings interrogating racism, its structures, and its theological ethical manifestations are increasingly available.[43] Not only are these necessary texts for white theologians, but they are requisite for community reflection as well. James Cone writes, "To reflect on this failure is to address a defect in the consciousness of white Christians and to suggest why African Americans have needed to trust and cultivate their own theological imaginations."[44] Kelly Brown Douglas opens *Stand Your Ground* with a telling of the formation of racial injustice.[45] J. Kameron Carter tells of the formation of race through Enlightenment academic developments,[46] while Willie James Jennings discovers critical developments in European missionary and colonial actions.[47] Delores Williams and Katie Cannon demonstrate theological, spiritual, and ethical reasoning in the black literary tradition.[48] In the *Cross and the Lynching Tree*, Cone more narrowly focuses on comparisons of Christ's cross and the lynching tree in the work of

---

42. Logan, "Liberalism, Race, and Stanley Hauerwas," 524–25.

43. James Cone's memoir provides a vivid account of his early work developing a black liberation theology. Cone, *Said I Wasn't Gonna Tell Nobody*.

44. Cone, *Cross and the Lynching Tree*, 32.

45. Douglas, *Stand Your Ground*, 3–44.

46. Carter, *Race*.

47. Jennings, *Christian Imagination*.

48. Williams, *Sisters in the Wilderness*; Cannon, *Black Womanist Ethics*.

black artists. These accounts demonstrate injustice and continued agency within this injustice, as well as robust narrative engagement with the black Christian experience that stretches the boundaries of "normative theological and ethical writing."[49]

One of the few instances in which Hauerwas writes specifically on race is in "Race: The 'More' It is About: Will D. Campbell Lecture University of Mississippi, 2006."[50] In this essay honoring the work of a white man, Hauerwas's argument largely follows his typical trajectory of noting that though the church attempts to make changes politically by adopting political frameworks and assumptions from sources outside itself, it should focus rather on *being* and the deeper theological issue. He writes, "Yet the church, in an effort to still show her relevance, imitates the governmental authority by adopting a largely humanitarian approach: by advocating law and order, democracy, the rights of man, human dignity, constitutional process, and public schools."[51] He then quotes Will Campbell himself, saying, "these things are good but are they the most basic, most distinctive, concern of the church?"[52] While these are genuine areas of concern, and Hauerwas is right to note that they are rooted in a theological problem,[53] it begins to feel like an excuse not to do more difficult work. James Logan, for example, affirms Hauerwas's critique but notes, "Yet sometimes liberal dimensions of justice in the context of 'inalienable rights' and 'equal dignity and justice for all' help place limits on the degree to which Black folk will get our social-political asses kicked; this while we all continue to struggle toward interrelated beloved communities that might render justice unnecessary."[54] If Hauerwas had gained this from an African American theologian who had to bear the struggles, this would be much less concerning. He continues by noting, correctly, that many people mistakenly think Americans no longer have a race problem

---

49. Jennings (*Christian Imagination*, 7) notes his dismay at the formation of the "scholastic disposition." "Normative" means the generally accepted and "canonical" (as determined by predominately white male guild members) sources for theological and ethical reflection.

50. In Hauerwas and Coles, *Christianity, Democracy, and the Radical Ordinary*, 87–102.

51. Hauerwas, "Race," 89.

52. Campbell, *Race and the Renewal of the Church*, 3–4, quoted in Hauerwas, "Race," 89.

53. Hauerwas, "Race," 90.

54. Logan, "Liberalism, Race, and Stanley Hauerwas," 527–28.

because some black families have had economic success and moved to the suburbs.⁵⁵ Similarly to Campbell, he notes that integration often means African Americans joining and needing to fit in with white communities, and that that the subsuming of particularity into a universal is a form of genocide.⁵⁶ Since Christians should think theologically, they are challenged in "humanistic" categories by the more theologically robust oneness that is found in Christ.

> How then did Christians begin to think of race as a natural category? According to Campbell, they did so when the emphasis in Christian theology began to be on humans rather than God. Nothing is more indicative of such an emphasis than the presumption of modern liberal Christians that the race problem can be solved politically. Such a presumption serves to legitimate the modern nation-state, which, ironically, has been the primary agent for the categorization of people by race.⁵⁷

From this engagement with Campbell, we see several of Hauerwas's common themes reappear, as well as a strange silence on the topic of racial justice and a lack of interaction with writers from within the African-American community.

Hauerwas's writings on mission and peacemaking are helpful resources in thinking about racial justice. The church has helped to perpetuate racial injustice and disunity within its body even as it has sought to make peace and seek justice. Hauerwas's writing on the non-sectarian church and mission (in opposition to the sectarian nature of the nation-state) can challenge the segregated nature of US churches.⁵⁸ Though theologians of color and the black church do not "need" Hauerwas or any other white solution, the white church needs him and other white theologians to publicly struggle and repent for these injustices.⁵⁹ Additionally, the obvious should be stated: it is not as though there is one white and one black experience, or that these are the only two categories, or even that

---

55. Hauerwas, "Race," 94–95.
56. Hauerwas, "Race," 97.
57. Hauerwas, "Race," 99.
58. Hauerwas expresses ambivalence about missions, which seems to largely relate to race and colonialism ("Sent: The Church is Mission," 165).
59. Logan ("Liberalism, Race, and Stanley Hauerwas," 530–31) asserts that though the experience of the narrative is different, there is in fact a shared story. Additionally, even largely Euro-American peace churches are closely connected to the genocide of Amerindians because of the benefit derived from stolen lands.

these categories stand as coherent descriptors of experience. Similarly, Americans must remember that the realities of the United States are not the only realities and that there are other churches and other communities from which they can learn. Limited vision, in part a result of limited interaction, results in what Jennings calls a "disfigured" imagination:

> I anticipate some resistance to the fundamental claim of this work, that Christian social imagination is diseased and disfigured. In making this claim I am not saying that the church is lost, moribund, or impotent. Rather, I want my readers to capture sight of a loss, almost imperceptible, yet articulated powerfully in the remaining slender testimonies of Native American peoples and other aboriginal peoples. This loss points out not only to deep psychic cuts and gashes in the social imaginary of western peoples, but also to an abiding mutilation of a Christian vision of creation and our own creatureliness. I want Christians to recognize the grotesque nature of a social performance of Christianity that imagines Christian identity floating above land, landscape, animals, place, and space, leaving such realities to the machinations of capitalistic calculations and the commodity chains of private property. Such Christian identity can only inevitably lodge itself in the materiality of racial existence.[60]

Jennings also sees a contribution that theology can make to the examination of colonial realities.

> Theology, however, needs a different narration ... What is needed ... is not primarily a historical account of the phenomenon of theology at the *arche* of colonialism, for example, the medieval theological character of colonialist imagination: rather, theological reflection itself can aid in our analysis of the world that has come upon us. It can also reveal the redemptive elements buried inside the colonialist operation, elements that truly can open up possibilities of a new world beyond the tragedy of the remade one. Theology in this regard is indeed filled with hope but also analytical, enabling a clearer grasp of the machinations of death and the demonic at work in the world. Theological reflection also opens up the possibility of a conversation that has yet to happen: a Christianity born of the colonialist wound speaking to itself in its global reality, pressing deeply inside the miracle of its existence, battered, bruised, marginalized, yet believing,

---

60. Jennings, *Christian Imagination*, 293. It is interesting to note that even though Jennings and Hauerwas both taught at Duke and both work on imagination, Hauerwas is not included in Jennings's index and I am unaware of Hauerwas citing Jennings.

loving, Christian. For better or worse, many of those whom Fanon called the wretched of the earth became and are in fact Christians.[61]

This proposed role for theology is similar to Hauerwas's suggestions and practices. As part of Hauerwas's commitment to peacemaking, however, his work must pay more attention to racial justice and the work of a broader range of writers. In an essay entitled "Taking Time for Hauerwas's Racism," Jonathan Tran considers the challenge of Hauerwas's relative silence on the problem of racism in America.[62] Neither fully defending or accusing Hauerwas, Tran's approach is to frame his relative silence as a form of patience.[63] I will argue that, even accepting the general premise of Tran's essay, there are ways that Hauerwas can live his peacemaking without inappropriately presuming to understand or speak.

On theological issues, Hauerwas asserts the need for confident speech. In *With the Grain of the Universe*, he writes,

> Not only are Yoder and the pope the kind of witnesses that Barth's theology requires—they are the kind of witnesses who must exist if Christians are to recover the confident use of theological speech that Barth exemplifies so well. Moreover, because confident Christian speech has been compromised by the disunity of the church, it is important, as I hope to show, that John Howard Yoder and John Paul II are one in their witness to the One who moves the sun and the stars and is to be found in the manger.[64]

61. Jennings, *Christian Imagination*, 290–91.

62. Tran, "Taking Time for Hauerwas's Racism," 246–64. James Logan heavily uses Hauerwas's work on punishment in *Good Punishment?*, 219, but expresses astonishment at Hauerwas's relative silence on racism: "I was surprised by his general omission of a discussion of the relationship between punishment, White racism (especially its anti-Black dimension), and imprisonment." He adds, "I have been stunned by the utter dearth of writings and active concern by Stanley Hauerwas (and the overwhelming majority of White theologians) regarding the American democratic and Christian church struggle with the sin (and crime) of anti-Black racism." Logan, *Good Punishment?*, 221.

63. Certainly, racial justice as a response to racial injustice is not limited to Americans of African descent who arrived in North America through slavery. This has been experienced by many groups. Additionally, not all injustice is perpetrated by "white" Americans of European descent. While grouping the entire population as "white" and "of color" has certain descriptive value, this also continues to create not only binaries that may or may not be helpful but seems to essentialize all experience in a way that disallows diversity of experience of both dominance and oppression.

64. Hauerwas, *With the Grain of the Universe*, 217

Though such theological speech is made problematic by modern theology, Hauerwas seeks to develop the confidence to speak. Analogously, while the history of race in America and Hauerwas's place within this makes speech about race problematic, it does not preclude the need to attempt such speech. Additionally, since Hauerwas has learned much from Yoder, and Yoder is part of a church tradition that was formed in marginalization and violence, his work should be more conducive to such reflection, even if he is a few steps removed.[65]

Tran opens his essay noting that a number of readers who are generally sympathetic to Hauerwas's work have expressed frustration and confusion over why Hauerwas has maintained relative silence on issues of racial justice. Considering a particular challenge to Hauerwas, Tran asserts,

> By Hauerwas's racism, I mean a feature of what existence that makes it intensely difficult for him to see the very things Woodard-Lehman ["Body Politics and the Politics of Bodies"] presses him so hard to protest. The disciplinary apparatus of racism has been uniquely created *for* minorities in a way the remains largely imperceptible to white people; its clandestine ploys allow white participation critical for its production and continuation.[66]

That is, *not seeing* is part of the structure and privilege. It is this relative blindness that makes it difficult for Hauerwas to see. But Hauerwas *does* see something. He writes, for example,

> Our great problem, I suspect, with the integration of black Americans into the story of America is that they carry a story that cannot easily be accommodated within the story of white

---

65. Huebner and Dula comment on the shape of Yoder's work in *The New Yoder* (xvii): "Those post-colonialists and post-structuralists taught us that the formation of Western politics and identity came at the expense of its colonial others. Yoder taught us to include the Anabaptists as one of the original colonial others. So Yoder's antifoundationalism comes not from a close reading of Quine or Wittgenstein, but rather, as with postcolonialists, from a marginalized, persecuted minority's recognition that the establishment's categories themselves worked to defend against any possible destabilization from its others. Whereas George Lindbeck and Stanley Hauerwas had to learn how to occupy the space of minority and unlearn the habits of establishment, as a Mennonite Yoder was already there and so betrayed none of post-liberalism's anxiety about the need to secure the church's ongoing survival in an increasingly secular world. In a similar way, it might be suggested that for Yoder, 'exile' was not a regrettable fait accompli of late modernity. It was a fact of Anabaptist history."

66. Tran, "Taking Time for Hauerwas's Racism," 254.

Americans. I am not referring to the story of slavery itself, which simply reminds us that we have been less than decent people. Rather, I am referring to the story of pointless suffering that the black man carries which simply is not part of our story as Texans or Americans. The only way to finally deal with such a challenge is violence—namely refuse to recognize such people until they have become like us.[67]

---

67. Hauerwas, *Christian Existence Today*, 38. He also comments in *Matthew* (79), "The forgiveness of debts signals that nothing is quite so political as the prayer that Jesus teaches us. To have debts forgiven certainly challenges our normal economic and political assumption. But the forgiveness of debts is also at the heart of truthful memory. No people are free from the past or present that is not constituted by injustices so horrific nothing can make them right. There is, for example, nothing that can be done to 'redeem' the slavery that defined early America. Faced with the tragedy of slavery, the temptation is simply to forget that America is a country of slavery or to assume that the wound of slavery has been healed by African Americans being given the opportunity to become as well-off as white Americans. But the forgetfulness that money names cannot forever suppress the wound of slavery." Additionally, he writes, "But history tells us people experience repressive politics for challenging such "oneness." It is difficult to imagine those who have faced slavery and genocide can be in solidarity with those who believe we can let bygones be bygones." Hauerwas, "Christians, Don't Be Fooled." Werntz, considering the contribution of Hauerwas on suffering in Philippians, writes, "In other words, in the attempt to refuse a Deuteronomic understanding of suffering—that our physical suffering is intricately related to the sins we have committed—we run the risk of saying that suffering is a-moral and without sense; what begins as a good intention ends with us denying moral reasoning any capacity to rehabilitate or transform suffering." Werntz, "Fellowship of Suffering," 148. Though Werntz is considering Hauerwas's work on medical ethics there would seem to be certain parallels with suffering under systemic oppressions. Though in the latter case the causes are human induced and thus more closely related to ethical critique of humans or human community/structures the challenge of considering suffering in relation to God remains significant. Hauerwas's work on medical ethics, in particular his tying this to ecclesiology, may help with resisting "neutrality" but also not moving to trying to attribute "sense" to what otherwise seems senseless. The participation *with* suffering and Werntz's discussion of suffering as an example for the community but not in some way beneficial for the suffering example may be expanded by M. Shawn Copeland. She writes, "This shouldering of responsibility obliges us in the here-and-now to stand between poor women of color and the powers of oppression in society, to do all that we can to end their marginalization, exploitation, abuse, and murder. In memory of the cross of Jesus, we accept this obligation, even if it means we must endure rejection and loss. Moreover, this 'shouldering' summons us to take intentional, intelligent, practical steps against 'the socially or technically avoidable sufferings of others.' For, Christian solidarity repudiates every form of masochism and any assent to suffering for its own sake. Solidarity affirms life—even in the face of sin and death." Copeland, *Enfleshing Freedom*, 101.

This relative blindness is the challenge of whiteness and its dominance. So, if Hauerwas is unable to see clearly, and recognizes this at least in part, then what is the way forward? A relatively simple step would be to read the stories and the ethical and theological reflection from within the community. Given Hauerwas's breadth of reading, it would be surprising if he has not read extensively of these experiences. Since he tends to write about what he reads one would expect to find more notation, comment, or footnoting from such sources. However, though he *tends* to write about what he reads this is not always the case. For example, he notes in *Performing the Faith*, that although he has often read works by and about Bonhoeffer, this particular work published near the end of this career was the first time *he* wrote about Bonhoeffer in any extended way.[68] This being the case it may be that Hauerwas has read the works, but does not feel adequate to respond.

On this note, Tran challenges the notion that Hauerwas should completely understand racism. He writes,

> While he struggles against that which he sees as racist, he also misses a lot and in turn benefits from that relative blindness. Much to his credit, Hauerwas doesn't pretend to get it, doesn't play that game in its personal or professional versions. Only white people expect white people to get race, and the presumption that white people *should* get race only underscores yet another instance of the supremacy of whiteness.[69]

This is a valuable point. It is, however, much different to assume (as a white person) that Hauerwas should *get* race than to say he should *attempt to* understand. His struggle may be part of his personal experience, but as someone whose work is essentially public through words, this aspect of his personal life needs to be expressed publicly. Though Hauerwas often makes bold statements in his writing, he also spends much of his time struggling to makes sense or problematize a particular issue. In this space of public vulnerability that he could attempt to engage the topic of racism.

Additionally, it should be noted that Hauerwas is not averse to strongly critiquing himself or the (usually American) church. He has done so with some regularity in regard to Christian anti-Semitism. Tran notes this, commenting,

---

68. Hauerwas, *Performing the Faith*, 35.
69. Tran, "Time for Hauerwas's Racism," 255.

None of this is to deny the stances Hauerwas has taken on behalf of minorities throughout his long career. Indeed, I would venture to say his good work on behalf of some of us serves as a kind of penance for a racism Hauerwas has never denied. If this makes him less of a racist than those who refuse to come to terms with their racialized heritage, this only means that those of us minorities who have come to love this white man would rather hang out with him and his unapologetic provinciality than those who hide under the guise of a colonizing political correctness.[70]

As Tran is a former student and personal friend of Hauerwas and *not* African American, his mild absolution of Hauerwas's racism would seem at least somewhat problematic. This is, however, not mine to judge. Though Tran is certainly not proclaiming or granting this penance strongly, this seems like a problematic statement. It may be the case though that this is merely taking the edge off Hauerwas's "being a racist." Whether he is or is not, as if there is simple either/or, may not be the question. Rather, I posit that as a prolific and prominent white male American theological ethicist, Hauerwas is obliged to *attempt* a response that helps the church (particularly white-dominated churches) to face racial injustice. Hauerwas's work on peacemaking, particularly in "Peacemaking: The Virtue of the Church," bases Christian peacemaking primarily on the Matthew 18 search for truth and confrontation in the face of sin. Though Tran's piece adds valuable nuance to what could easily be a general condemnation, the confrontation needed for peacemaking seems to be lacking. Tran too quickly explains for Hauerwas.[71] If Tran were to follow Hauerwas's clear

70. Tran, "Time for Hauerwas's Racism," 255.

71. Though I hesitate to conjecture as to why Tran does not provide a stronger critique, there may be two reasons. The first is that this is an instance of Healy's comment that those who have written (and in Healy's view inadequately challenged Hauerwas) on Hauerwas are mostly people who are his friends. He writes, in *A (Very) Critical Introduction* (3): "This book is a very critical introduction solely to what he has written, to his texts . . . Although this may seem an obvious point, consider the fact that most books on Hauerwas are written by people who know him. I have found that some of those who know him well seem to see in his work things I cannot find, and vice versa." Even though such friends may be up for a fight, Healy asserts that, based on what they know about him, they are too quick to read more into Hauerwas's texts than is actually there. On a related point, it could be that Tran recognizes that Hauerwas's approach is much more subtle than a more blunt denouncing of racism. There have been times when Hauerwas has engaged in an attack on racism. In *Hannah's Child* (224), however, Hauerwas notes giving a speech "castigating segregationists" with enough vigor for someone to comment that he was so self-righteous he "had been tempted to become

admonition to confrontation based on Matthew 18, then he would likely have applied a sharper critique. In the face of ongoing racial injustice seen in police violence against unarmed black people, mass incarceration, and the divided response to unrest, such a subtle approach is inadequate.

Hauerwas Should Broaden His Dialogue Partners

While it may not be necessary to respond to every social issue (think Yoder—the church should speak but not necessarily on issues in which it lacks authority or investment; or Hauerwas—political movements and language should not drive the mission of the church), becoming friends creates a greater possibility for empathy. As we become friends and become part of the stories of those who are suffering, we will as a matter of justice, charity, and peacemaking seek to address this suffering. Additionally, given the church's implication in both implicit, explicit, intentional, unintentional actions, or cases of inaction, such action is imperative of the body generally as well as the leadership.

In chapter 3, I dealt briefly with Hauerwas's assertion of the church as mission. I noted several of Willie James Jennings's assertions concerning missionary endeavor, the formation of the Christian theological social imagination, and the development of race. These are relevant to my recommendation that Hauerwas expand his circle of dialogue partners. Such dialogic engagement is quite dissimilar from fifteenth- or seventeenth-century European missions to Latin America or Africa; however, Jennings asks that such formative encounters be part of theologians' consideration of the racialization of theology. Given the present intensity of discussions and actions concerning racism in the US, these concerns remain urgent.[72]

Cone's critique of Reinhold Niebuhr's lack of engagement with Harlem in contrast to Williams's findings about Dietrich Bonhoeffer's engagement and relationships in Harlem provide a parallel critique and example of the necessity and value of friendship and engagement leading to forceful speech.[73] Whereas Williams documents the significance of Bonhoeffer's time in the African American community for shaping

---

a segregationist." However, patience, even if eschatological, may not be Hauerwas's to practice in this instance.

72. Douglas, *Stand Your Ground*.

73. Cone, *Cross and the Lynching Tree*, 30–64; Williams, *Bonhoeffer's Black Jesus*.

his concrete and radical theology, Cone asserts that Niebuhr lacked both urgency and deep concern, which was either caused by or contributed to his very limited interaction with the black community and its literature. Though I am not assessing Niebuhr or Cone's portrayal of him on racism, an overview of Cone's chapter on this topic in *The Cross and the Lynching Tree* is not only illustrative but raises a number of concerns similar to those I have of Hauerwas's writing. Though Hauerwas has asserted that he does not engage extensively in issues of race (for example, he does not want to "use" Martin Luther King Jr.), at a very minimum he should engage with a more diverse set of writers.[74] This diversity would reflect the breadth of God's creation, the "breaking down of barriers" in Christ (Ephesians 2:14), the expanding nature of the Gospel seen at Pentecost, and the biblical vision of Revelations 7:9. This diversity is an expression of God's creation and inclusion of all. Particularity remains, but commonality is discovered through friendship. Such friendship affords greater possibility for speaking with truth and urgency.[75]

Urgency requires empathy. Empathy requires a window or experience into the life of the other.[76] As Cone notes, "It was easy for Niebuhr to walk around in his own shoes, as a white man, and view he world

---

74. Sara Morice Brubaker asserts this in a review of Hauerwas's *The Work of Theology* in *The Christian Century* (Brubaker, "Work of Theology"). This engagement, given Hauerwas's practice, will likely be generative. Though Hauerwas is often seen as quite critical of those he engages, he is also often very enthusiasticly bent on engagement. Boersma writes, "What I do know is that his book review was a remarkable display of generosity that somewhat puzzled me but that, more importantly, also made me sit up and take note of Hauerwas's remarkable ability not to lose sight of points of significance that may lie hidden behind obvious points of disagreement." Boersma, "Realizing Pleasant Grove," 312.

75. For example, Hauerwas wrote the foreword to *Can War Be Just in the 21st Century?* He notes (xi) that the reason he is contributing to a book working primarily from the just war tradition is because Tobias Winright, his friend, asked him to.

76. "A healthy particularizing of consciousness—which I contend is a significant effect of interracial friendships that endure over time—is a key step in moving away from a positivist, and therefore false, conception of objectivity. As such, it is the first step toward a fallible and nondogmatic conception of how we can (collectively) better understand the world we live in. In the case of interracial friendships, a friend who understands that her way of interpreting a racial situation is only *one* way (and maybe not the best way) is well on her way toward achieving a more objective understanding of the complicated and ever-changings meanings attendant on the racial formation in the United States. Thus, a friendship between two people associated with different racial groups in a society like our own that is organized by race always holds at least the potential for expanding each friend's epistemic and emotional horizons." Moya, "Racism Is Not Intellectual," 182.

from that vantage point, but it takes a whole lot of empathic effort to step into those of black people and see the world through the eyes of African Americans."[77] Of course even with the greatest degree of empathy and "walking in the other's shoes," the experience is not shared but may be in some way proximate.[78] Cone is more optimistic about this possibility than I would expect. He writes,

> It has always been difficult for white people to empathize fully with black people. But it has never been impossible. In contrast to Niebuhr and other professors at Union Seminary, the German theologian Dietrich Bonhoeffer, during his year of study at Union (1930–1931), showed an existential interest in blacks, befriending a black student named Franklin Fisher, attending and teaching Bible study and Sunday School, and even preaching at Abyssinian Baptist Church in Harlem. Bonhoeffer also read widely in African American history and literature . . . and expressed outrage over the 'infamous Scottsboro trial.' . . . Niebuhr in contrast, showed little or no interest in engaging in dialogue with blacks about racial justice, even though he lived in Detroit during the great migration of blacks from the South and in New York near Harlem, the largest concentration of blacks in America.[79]

Not only did Bonhoeffer show "an existential interest" but "to empathize fully with black people" has "never been impossible." It was, at least in part, the lack of extended contact and interaction with the African American community that made this empathy and urgency so difficult for Niebuhr. Cone also notes that while Niebuhr attended some leftist meetings where black writers and artists were present, he never cited

77. Cone, *Cross and the Lynching Tree*, 40.

78. Of Hauerwas, Logan observes in "Liberalism, Race, and Stanley Hauerwas" (525–26) that he "goes on to contend that, 'I have written about the South, which obviously involves race, but I have not written about 'the struggle.' He also notes that, 'I am . . . a white southerner from the lower-middle class who grew up in the practices of segregation.'" Logan continues, "Since Hauerwas does in fact appear to know that the habits of racism have been deeply written into the narrative of his own life, he ought to also know, then, that the story of 'the struggle' is as much *his* story as it was King's story."

79. Cone, *Cross and the Lynching Tree*, 42. Palestinian theologian Yohanna Katanacho writes of the need for and possibility of empathy in the Israeli-Palestinian conflict, "If John's Jesus preached today, he would claim that no Israeli Jews can be children of Abraham until they act like Abraham and stand with oppressed Palestinian refugees. Similarly, John's Jesus would challenge that no Palestinians can be true followers of Jesus unless they identify and empathize with the survivors and victims of the Holocaust." Katanacho, "Reading the Gospel of John through Palestinian Eyes," 115.

black intellectuals in his writing.[80] So while not strictly isolated, there was a thinness to his direct relationships with people, communities, and the literature they produced. Cone continues, "Despite all Niebuhr's writing and speaking about racism, he expresses no 'madness of the soul,' no prophetic outrage against lynching."[81] Cone questions Niebuhr's "limited perspective, as a white man, on the race crisis in America. His theology and ethics needed to be informed by a critical reading and dialogue with radical black perspectives."[82] Cone challenges gradualism and observations of progress, noting that these are often "merely tokenism." He writes, "There is very little justice in any educational institution where black presence is less than 20 percent of the faculty, students, and board members. There is no justice without power; there is no power with one, two, or three tokens."[83] Such concern about power should have been of great interest for Niebuhr given the focus of his work.

In addition to his work in theology and ethics, Niebuhr wrote history, but consistently omitted or minimized the African American experience:

> Niebuhr did not mention [the situation of African Americans], finding it apparently not a substantial concern. This was a serious failure by an American religious leader often called this nation's greatest theologian. How could anyone be a great theologian and not engage America's greatest moral issue? Unfortunately, white theologians, then and since, have typically ignored the problem of race or written and spoken about it without urgency, not regarding it as critical to theology or ethics.[84]

In Cone's observations about Niebuhr, there are many parallels to Hauerwas. In both cases, the work done is both theological and ethical while being intentionally rooted in narrative and/or historic experience. Both Niebuhr and Hauerwas are highly regarded and influential theologians and ethicists. Both are white American men teaching in prominent theological institutions near major concentrations of the African American communities and intellectual life. Both write extensively on social issues and ethics, but fail to address racial justice with urgency, though their writing would easily connect to this. Both lack

80. Cone, *Cross and the Lynching Tree*, 42.
81. Cone, *Cross and the Lynching Tree*, 56.
82. Cone, *Cross and the Lynching Tree*, 60.
83. Cone, *Cross and the Lynching Tree*, 61.
84. Cone, *Cross and the Lynching Tree*, 52.

substantial engagement with African Americans either interpersonally or through literature. While there are many substantive differences between Niebuhr and Hauerwas, these similarities are notable. Fortunately, the relatively simple step of friendship and exposure to the writing and other cultural production of this community would go far in addressing this shortfall.[85]

In order to build on his assertions of the non-national or the nation-state defying nature of the church, Hauerwas should engage theologians and church from the majority world. Though his writing challenges the assumptions of the United States as normative or as an assumed hegemony, he to a degree mimics this in US-centric theological exchange.[86] In cases where he has included chapters based on international lectures, they were in the UK and Australia—predominantly white English-speaking countries.[87] It is not just the content of the public speech that is

---

85. Hauerwas is obviously aware of the significance of friendship. See his essay, "Friendship and Fragility," 70–88; also Sider, "Friendship, Alienation, Love," 61–86.

86. "This work also joins the growing conversation regarding the possibilities of a truly cosmopolitan citizenship. Such a world citizenship imagines cultural transactions that signal the emergence of people whose sense of agency and belonging breaks open not only geopolitical and nationalist confines but also the strictures of ethnic and racial identities. This is indeed a noble dream even if it is a moving target given the conceptual confusions and political struggles around multicultural discourse. Yet I hope to intervene helpfully in this conversation by returning precisely to the question of the constitution of such a people and such a citizenship. However, rather than building the hope of cosmopolitanism from the soil of an imagined democratic spirit, I seek a deeper soil. That deeper soil is not easily unearthed. It is surely not resident at the surface levels of Christianity and ecclesial existence today. Yet Christianity marks the spot where, if noble dream joins hands with God-inspired hope and presses with great impatience against the insularities of life, for example, national, cultural, ethnic, economic, sexual, racial, seeking the deeper ground upon which to seed a new way of belonging and living together, then we will find together not simply new ground, not simply new seed, but a life already prepared and offered to us." Jennings, *Christian Imagination*, 10–11.

87. "But [Acosta's] experiences, like those of so many others did not challenge Old World textual authorities; it extracted from the geographic authority and laid supposed authority to the side. But what is the effect of a geographic extraction from the performance of ancient textual authorities, Christian and non-Christian? How does that removal of true speech, true sight regarding the materiality of the world affect the doctrine of creation? A Christian doctrine of creation is not dependent on geographic precision; however, it is not wholly independent of geographic accuracy. Belief in creation has to refer to current real-world places or it refers to nothing. Acosta understood this and made adjustments to Old World theories, both philosophical and theological. It is with exactly these conceptual adjustments that Acosta opened up a new performance of the doctrine of creation and paved the way for the enfolding of theology inside racialized existence, inside whiteness." Jennings, *Christian Imagination*, 85.

important; also significant is the manner in which theological language is construed and the reflective processes are learned and managed. Jennings comments,

> The social vision that holds court in the theological academy imagines its intellectual world from the commanding heights of various social economies: cultural, political, and scholastic. I don't mean that scholars in the theological academy think they are in charge of the academic or political worlds. I mean that the regulative character of their intellectual posture created through the cultivated capacities to clarify, categorize, define, explain, interpret, and so forth eclipses its fluid, adaptable, even morph-able character. This eclipse is not due to the emergence of a new intellectual style but points to a history in which the Christian theological imagination was woven into processes of colonial dominance. Other peoples and their ways of life had to adapt, become fluid, even morph into the colonial order of things, and such a situation drew Christianity and it theologians inside habits of mind and life that internalized and normalized that order of things.[88]

It is not only the topics that are deemed worthwhile for theological consideration, but also the very processes of doing the work which take a colonially formed shape. Again, it is not so much that Hauerwas needs to have mastered either the topic or regional and cultural specifics, but that through friendship and the church, which is not bound by the nation-state, he is free to work across the divisions that typically divide.

Religion in Foreign Policy Formation and Analysis

As an avowed theologian,[89] can Hauerwas contribute to US foreign-policy formation? Can those who follow him do so?[90] In Hauerwas's allegiance to Yoder, his answer to "can?" would be a qualified yes.[91] Hauerwas would

88. Jennings, *Christian Imagination*, 8.

89. Though Hauerwas's work is usually classified as theological ethics, he has claimed that he is simply doing theology. He has also resisted the possibility that, for the Christian, ethics can be abstracted from or done separately from theology.

90. See Miller, *Wise as Serpents, Innocent as Doves*, 161 for a discussion of Mennonite Central Committee in Washington and learning multiple languages.

91. There is a persistent notion that Hauerwas, because he is so consistently critical, opposes participation in political or public matters. (Though admittedly in an April 17, 2017 podcast with the National Council of Churches Hauerwas notes, "I'm not going to do ethics for the State Department" (Martin, "Holy Week, Syria, and

say there is nothing that precludes Christians *in general* from this kind of interaction with the nation-state.⁹² This interaction must also be concrete

---

Chrsitian Ethics"). Though he notes this, it seems that his purpose would allow for a nuance between "doing for" and engaging with on the matter.) Neill, for example, states, "I will take Stanley Hauerwas as my interlocuter because it is Hauerwas more than anyone else who has argued that the faithful ought not cooperate with liberal justice." Neill, "Political Involvement and Religious Compromises," 33.

Though as Neill engages with Hauerwas and Cole's *The Radical Ordinary* and as such focuses on ways that Hauerwas allows engagement in politics, his initial overstating of this opposition discounts Hauerwas's regular assertions that despite his criticism he has a presumption of engagement. The critique is to reorder primacy of language and practice. Neill then distinguishes between levels of political participation. He writes, "By political participation in this context I do not mean voting, opinion-formation, news tracking, and other everyday activities that are expected of responsible citizens. I mean rather the specialized political activities—call them second-level activities—that are pursued by citizens who are much more civically minded than the majority of the population" (Neill, 34). He then goes on, seemingly to imply that in general Christians have not participated in the political process and are increasingly doing so. However, politicians consistently not only discuss religious faith but invoke this language, if only in banal "God bless America" endings to public speeches.

Throughout the article it seems that Neill is speaking in a register that is incongruent with Hauerwas. It may be that when Hauerwas critiques "liberalism" it is more broadly construed than Neill. Hauerwas's critique of liberalism is less partisan than nation-state system. As Hauerwas writes, "Religion is the designation created to privatize strong convictions in order to render them harmless so that alleged democracies can continue to flourish on difference [might it not be that this is necessary to control Christian hegemony?]. Indeed, if there is anything new about the current situation, it is that we are coming to the end of Protestant hegemony in America. This is a strange claim, to be sure, given the rise of the so-called religious right represented by the Bush Administration. Indeed I suspect that some may associate my robust theological perspective with the aggressive Christianity associated with the religious right. As far as I know, however, no representative of the religious right has claimed me for an ally. That they have not so claimed me is certainly appropriate because I regard the religious right as representatives of a truncated, if not idolatrous, form of Christianity. Indeed I think the religious right is a desperate attempt of Protestantism to make sense of itself as a form of civil religion for America. That is why the Christianity represented by the religious right is at once so strident and pathetic." Hauerwas, "End of Religious Pluralism," 284–85.

Critique then can be aimed at a several different levels and in ways that does not preclude participation but challenges particular ideologies and idolatries. Gossai writes, "In the United States, patriotism is narrowly construed and understood as lending support for state-sanctioned positions, so voices that challenge the state are deemed unpatriotic, often silenced, and frequently demonized. Micaiah's pronouncement establishes with unencumbered clarity that state ideology, as powerful as it may be and as widely as it is embraced by state operatives, must not be confused with divine affirmation." Gossai, "Challenging the Empire," 107.

92. Certain organizations intentionally do not receive US government funds so

and not simply a general affirmation. Though Hauerwas has often been critical of modes of American Christian engagement in politics or their framing and engagement in social issues, his intentionally *theological* ethics and politics can fill a particular role in US foreign-policy formation.[93] This fits with emerging trends in international relations theory and humanitarian practice in which enforced secularized discourse is being challenged.[94]

Not only can Hauerwas's work play a role in theoretical work in international relations generally, but it can contribute to specific US foreign-policy debate and implementation.[95] Whereas it is often assumed that the broader topic (in this case, international relations) is more easily engaged than the specific (in this case, religion in US foreign policy), Hauerwas's writings challenge the primacy of the general or theoretical over specific and practical work. For example, Hauerwas states that Christians do not require a theory of politics, but he would surely assert that a church worker who has spent years working internationally,

---

as to remain free of the need to temper criticism, but continue to advocate in relation to programmatic work on the ground. This is an example of degrees of engagement rather than wholesale engagement or disengagement. Of course, Hauerwas's assertions on the political nature of the church would mean that even when not directly engaged in a limited way through advocacy the Christian's witness remains political.

93. Hauerwas writes of his politics, "I am a pacifist because I think nonviolence is the necessary condition for a politics not based on death. A politics that is not determined by the fear of death means that no strong distinction can be drawn between politics and military force." Hauerwas, "September 11, 2001," 121. The use of the word "can" with reference to the role of theological ethics should play in foreign-policy formation may feel insignificant, but to assert "must" or "should" would be too strong for Yoder or Hauerwas. The latter, they would claim, would reassert Constantinian assumptions that the church must rule. The use of theology or reading foreign policy theologically is required for Christians, but theology is not the *only* relevant discourse.

94. See Ager and Ager, "Challenging the Discourse on Religion, Secularism and Displacement." In this essay (43), Ager and Ager note that "the professionalization and technocratic discourse of faith-based organizations required for them to access state funding and global policy for a results in programming and reports that are indistinguishable from those produced by secular organizations."

95. Perhaps a distinction needs to be made between Hauerwas's work being *directly* useful and practices he urges ending up being useful. These are certainly different. Of course, if we take what we learn from Hauerwas into foreign-policy work then he is still in some way directly connected even if the Secretary of State is not exhorted to read Hauerwas's *With the Grain of the Universe*. I take Emmanuel Katongole's *Sacrifice of Africa* to be one such work. Additionally, Shaun Casey's work in the US State Department's Office of Religion and Global Affairs is an example of a seminary professor's participation. See Willard, "Shaun Casey Talks."

gaining substantial cultural and historical knowledge, could provide important advice to policy makers. The challenge in this is the framing of "important." Important for challenging or refining or is it important for building political cover for an already determined decision? In this, I think of Episcopalian and Presbyterian work in South Sudan and Church of the Brethren work in Nigeria. Because of their long-term institutional and individual engagement in these regions, their depth of knowledge and relationship far outstrips that of shorter-term NGO and Foreign Service staff.[96] Though the connection of Hauerwas's work *via* the formation of Christians who then participate in foreign policy is the most obvious, this contribution can be more directly useful. Though this sounds tentative, it simply means that theological ethics and discourse is a legitimate and useful discipline for use in US foreign-policy formation, not that it should be the dominant discipline. The church needs to exercise humility in terms of the possibilities and limits for its control.[97] According to Brandon Morgan,

> It may be that he [Hauerwas] sees the humility of the church as a vital lesson of his theology as a whole, possibly because he has accused the church of pridefully attempting to control the reins of history as a way of bringing salvation to the world. Depending on whom he is writing against, his emphasis on the church's humility may remain implicit in, or almost tertiary to, his concerns. So it is a lesson often left for his interpreters to develop more clearly. From my perspective, these paths of Hauerwasian argument are all of a piece, making the church outspoken about its commitments and informing it of its status as specially graced, that is, gathered and directed by a Christological lordship which is not always recognizable and whose direction cannot always be known in advance.[98]

---

96. See America's Dream Palace for a historical account of the intentional development of Middle East Policy expertise within the DC policy world. The relationship and involvement of former missionaries is both fascinating and concerning. Khalil, *America's Dream Palace*.

97. On the connection in Hauerwas of control and being forgiven: "To be a forgiven people means that we live by trust and not by control." Huebner, "Ethic of Character," 191.

98. Morgan, "Lordship of Christ," 67.

Additionally, such theological ethics would not be limited to Christian theology but would necessarily include a variety of streams from multiple religions.[99]

In this section I am particularly interested in examining analysis of religion in international relations and conflicts but also the role of either religious actors or theology in the work of analysis and policy formation through the lens of Hauerwas's work. My thesis is that theological ethics[100] can inform, but not dominate, analysis and policy formation. As a subset of this, I will seek to demonstrate that while theological ethics/ethicists/church workers can and should engage in this work in a multilingual manner, they need not fully translate in "common parlance." A risk of this assertion in the US is that Christians have historically dominated and so the inclusion of theologically specific language has been a tool of dominance. A key is allowing for the particularity and value of this speech without oppressing groups outside of this.

Since this is not topic that Hauerwas has specifically written on (other than a few related side comments), this section will base the consideration on the approaches seen developed in Hauerwas. Since his non-focus on this may also be illustrative, not only will I seek understand what he has said but also what he has left unsaid. It should be noted, however, that whereas the earlier chapters were primarily concerned with examining and assessing his views, this chapter will be more constructive *beyond* what he has said. Though there are areas that Hauerwas has not addressed extensively, I do not intend to contribute to the misconception or misrepresentation that Hauerwas's critique of modes of social and political engagement entails a rejection of engagement.[101] In this section

---

99. One of the challenges then is that there is no single "*the* Christian" view. There is not even a single view within the Catholic church or even dramatically smaller subsets of small Protestant groups such as the progressive stream of Church of the Brethren theology. There is a strong possibility that inter or intra communion theological arguments end up playing out in unexpected locations. One minor example of this is varying views on the Just War Theory and Just Peace between Catholic groups in the Interfaith Working Group on Drone Warfare I convene in Washington, DC.

100. Theological ethics rather than theology, social ethics, Christian ethics, or religious studies because while not "purely theological" in the manner of systematic theology on the Trinity, nor necessarily narrowly Christian, nor detached from substantive theological claims; theological ethics remains connected across these fields while remaining linguistically closer to the speech of congregational life.

101. As discussed earlier, Hauerwas repeatedly rejects the notion that he encourages disengagement and consistently asserts this after nearly every extended criticism.

I will aim to expand beyond analysis of Hauerwas to suggest and show ways that this engagement can happen.

Inclusion of Theology in the Policy Formation Process

It is my task in this section to demonstrate how Hauerwas can be useful in the sphere of foreign-policy formation and international relations, but also consider his shortcomings. Hauerwas makes this difficult as a result of either inattention, disinterest, or obstinacy (for example by challenging the notion that theological ethicists have particular responsibilities in relation to the nation-state or must demonstrate their usefulness non-theologically).[102] Until relatively recently, there has been little or no attention paid to religion in international relations and other social sciences.[103] Though the September 11, 2001, attacks as well as the rise of

---

102. In his January 27, 2017, *Washington Post* opinion piece ("Christians, Don't Be Fooled: Trump Has Deep Religious Convictions") written shortly after Donald Trump's inauguration as President of the United States, Hauerwas mounted a rebuke of Trump, and a theological challenge to him, but primarily addressed American Christians. Trump could be corrected by this, but on high-level views rather than specific policy or strategic decisions. One could deduce policy directions from this critique, but concrete recommendations are at least one step removed. See Hauerwas, "Christians, Don't Be Fooled."

103. Douglas Johnston, founder of the International Center for Religion and Diplomacy, has been instrumental in bringing attention to religion. The collection *Religion and Foreign Affairs* brings together many useful essays. In one of these, Rosalind I. J. Hackett notes, "Prior to the early 1990s, literature had been lacking in the area of religion in the public sphere, notably at the international level. This lack of recognition of religion caused scholars and observers to downplay the significance of religion in domestic and global affairs. The early 1990s marked an upsurge in literature recognizing the role of religion in the public sphere" (54). While academic attention as well as bureaucratic structures (such as the US Department of State's Office of Religion and Global Affairs) are becoming more interested in engaging religious actors, it is my experience in the Church of the Brethren's Office of Peacebuilding and Policy that engaging as a religious actor remains somewhat challenging. This may, however, be as much that the proliferation of non-governmental actors simply makes getting a hearing difficult.

On the logistical end, this may in part be a matter of capacity since the US government tends to give its grants to large development agencies or contractors. The Church of the Brethren has been assisting Ekklesiyar Yan'uwa a Nigeria (EYN) and the region of northeastern Nigeria in responding to the Boko Haram insurgency. The US denomination has substantial and long-term relationships there (the relationship has existed since the 1920s and EYN has nearly a million members)—an unprecedented connection for the region. As of the time of writing, however, the Church of the Brethren Crisis Response has received no federal grant money.

various forms of violence perpetrated by groups asserting religious affiliation have increased attention to the potential role of religion in war, peace, and international affairs, in much analysis, religion remains a peripheral concern.[104] When religion is included, it is often mentioned in a cursory way that oversimplifies or essentializes religion and violence. On responding to the refugee crisis, Erin K. Wilson and Lulca Mavelli write, "To simply understand 'religion' in terms of either 'good' or 'bad' maintains religions subordination to the secular in contemporary public discourses. In order to develop a more nuanced analysis and responses to the contemporary crisis, we need to broaden our understanding of what 'religion' is, noting its infinite variation across different cultural and political contexts and levels, and the politics that sit behind how 'religion' is defined and used in relation to the contemporary refugee crisis."[105] Conflict analysis is both very complicated (we do not often even fully understand our own motivations) and incredibly location and context specific. In commenting on causation, I do not intend to provide a model for the "right" way of doing this, nor do I think that economics and politics are not pivotal. It is more the case that these factors are unable to be separated into distinct categories. In many cases the national myth of origins is profoundly theological (if not necessarily tied to a particular religious tradition). Such a national religion may or may not live in a comfortable relation to various non-state religious institutions.[106] Hauerwas and theological ethics provide skills of reading to develop greater appreciation for substantive religious claims.

Though I will not propose a wholly new analytic framework for the assessment of religion in conflict,[107] I will consider the way

104. There is a question of whether this has in fact been an increase in religiously motivated attacks or whether there is simply greater awareness or great articulation of religious issues. Andrew J. Bacevich's note that the United States contributed $4–5 billion to the Taliban in the 1980s to work against the Soviet Union contributes to putting the assertion of "rise" in question. Bacevich, *America's War for the Greater Middle East*, 54.

Toft et al., *God's Century*. This has also been my observation working in policy and analysis in Washington, DC. In this context, however, there is also the anxiety of religion playing a politically and religiously partisan role. Also, the fact that certain actors (usually conservative) use or are perceived to use concern for religious freedom to support Christians and oppose others contributes to the omission of religion from analysis.

105. Wilson and Mavelli, "Refugee Crisis and Religion," 5.

106. Cavanaugh explores this in *Migrations of the Holy*.

107. It may turn out that this is in fact a new analytic framework. In saying this I

Hauerwas-style theological ethics may play a unique role in such assessment. In this, the model is in part an anti-theory in that we must go forward without providing a theory in advance (which is, of course, a specific tactic that may in fact be a type of theory or at least a methodology). The need is often felt for either an organizing principle, a hierarchy of causal factors, or a broad comprehensive statement of detail. The former risks artificially pruning critical aspects while the latter, if done with substantial energy, will be a theoretically ever-expanding set of policy guidance and briefing materials.[108] Though religion is increasingly seen as a relevant factor in foreign-policy formation, this has not led to the inclusion in theology in the process. In what follows, I will consider ways in which the discipline of theology and theological ethics in the vein of Hauerwas can contribute to this formation process.

Hauerwas on Challenging Christians—Shaping Christians for Action

Hauerwas is often seen as critical.[109] More specifically, Hauerwas is regarded as "difficult" for American Christians. Though he has at times been relentlessly critical, he does this because he cares deeply. He also feels implicated in the critiques, and so is not being critical from a distance or presuming to stand in judgment unscathed, While I do not intend to say Hauerwas says X but he really means Y, it is relevant that Hauerwas's famously sharp criticism is largely aimed at those with whom he feels associated such as mainline Protestants and elites within teaching institutions and church structures.[110]

---

mean that I will not propose a comprehensive framework which approaches an algorithmic status.

108. This seems to have been a contributing piece of President Obama's approach. Along with his interest in maintaining greater control, it may account for why he so vastly increased the size of the National Security Council. See DeYoung, "How the Obama White House Runs Foreign Policy." See also Taleb, *Antifragile*.

109. Ahn uses Hauerwas's critique of Constantinianism to challenge the US churches' deferring to the state on issues of legality of types of immigration and thus abandoning its vocation of hospitality. He rightly does not assume that this is relevant only for issues of war. Ahn, "U.S. Immigration Crisis," 322.

110. A colleague (who was not very familiar with Hauerwas's work) noted that Hauerwas sounds rather brash and aggressive in a way similar to particular politics that were very visible at the time. However, since Hauerwas also is quite self-critical, this is very much unlike the typical politician.

The difficulty Hauerwas poses may be useful for challenging assumptions about how the world works, the Christian's relationship to the United States of America, and the role of the US in international relations.[111] Hauerwas would say he is not giving instruction in general terms, but writes largely for Christians,[112] though, even Hauerwas would allow, no sharp division[113] exists between "the church" and "the world." Despite interest of engaging outside the church, he primarily aims to shape Christians specifically rather than the world generally.

The "the world" language appears in the New Testament and is picked up perhaps most enthusiastically by Anabaptist groups which began life persecuted by "the world," which was in fact those who were said to be Christians and often in good standing with the church structures. The felt hypocrisy of Christians who allegedly had the right beliefs and doctrine, killing and persecuting Christians with different beliefs pushed some Anabaptists to seek more visible practices. This is the Constantinian reversal that writers like Yoder have often discussed. Previously it was not socially beneficial to join the church so those who joined did so out of conviction. Post Constantine it was socially beneficial to be part of the church and the "true" church was invisible. While many have challenged the historical simplicity of such an account the relationship of the Christian to the world and church, surely is affected by the social standing of the church and the risk or benefit of joining.

---

111. US dominance and maintaining this is one such area in need of critique. "Few foreign policy issues have attracted more attention in recent years than the problem of sustaining the U.S.-led liberal international order." Mazarr, "Once and Future Order," 25. Such a statement may indicate the fundamentally conflicted nature of certain types of Christians being involved in international relations and foreign policy, The fact that this is not evenly problematic across the board for American Christians indicates sharp divisions within that group and between them and the rest of the world. Hauerwas's sharp critiques have resulted in him being labeled a prophet. He rightly observes that such a label is more complicated than it may seem.

112. Ahn demonstrates a use of Hauerwas in this manner. Hauerwas challenges the church, which is a political actor. Theologian ethicist Hauerwas is then held alongside social philosopher Habermas to a useful end. Ahn, "U.S. Immigration Crisis," 319–45.

113. Cavanaugh writes, "Hauerwas has long been concerned with local forms of church that resist the dominant myths of America. What he has sometimes struggled to articulate is how those forms of church can be seen as doing more than resisting or participating in the dominant society, and how they can be seen as participating in other networks of connectivity that leave the imagination of a dominant society behind." Cavanaugh, "Politics of Vulnerability," 106.

That Hauerwas has taken some of Anabaptism as his ecclesial identity while also at times seeming to allow that orthodoxy can be enforced or closely aligning with the tradition while pulling from marginalized ecclesial life causes some difficulty. While he rightly notes that in the land of individualism following one's conscience is much different than under ecclesial hegemony, those of us in traditions influenced by radical pietism may wonder at his seeming trust in the authoritative church structure. Siggelkow's observation that though Hauerwas started off from Yoder's peace church pacifism his development along the lines of Macintyre and Milbank on tradition and practice may introduce elements that may be out of joint with a more thoroughly *peace* church (which may be different than a rigid adherence to Historic Peace Churches) theology.[114]

What originally drew me to Hauerwas was his strongly stated Christological peace embedded within a robust church and discipleship. At times when Anabaptist peace churches became more ecumenical, they seem to assume a progressive/liberal political framework as similarly basic. While some variation of this would be indeed where most people would categorize me politically, Hauerwas seemed to provide an articulation that made theology more basic in a way I found useful. Though, of course, one's relation to politics is largely at the core of the question of how the Christian engages in policy/political sphere/social action the "difficulty with Hauerwas" is that relatively empowered American Christians are challenged in assumptions of this work. One criticism of Hauerwas is that he would likely say "we" in this sentence without fully acknowledging that these assumptions are not across the board for Christians or even American Christians. Gloria Albrecht asserts this strongly about Hauerwas[115] and womanist theologians such as Katie Cannon would raise such issues generally, if not specifically of Hauerwas. Cannon writes, "For example, dominant ethics makes a virtue of qualities that lead to economic success—self-reliance, frugality, and industry . . . Racism does not allow Black women and Black men to labor habitually in beneficial work with the hope of saving expenses by avoiding waste so that they can develop a standard of living congruent with the American ideal."[116] Similarly, Patrick Cheng in *Rainbow Theology* challenges numerous theologies of liberation and from marginalized groups have perpetuating their own

---

114. Siggelkow, "Toward an Apocalyptic Peace Church."
115. Albrecht, *Character of Our Communities*, 103–10.
116. Cannon, *Black Womanist Ethics*, 2.

narrowness and exclusion. To counter this, he proposes a "queer of color" theology that embraces multiplicity. This disruption may also prove generative for non-theological analysis in International Relations.

Is Hauerwas's self-limited focus on shaping Christians problematic? Does he need to write for *everyone*? One might say that the ethicist and theologian's task should be more universal since everyone should live ethically or that the Gospel is for all.[117] Hauerwas frequently states that though he is primarily concerned that the church be the church, this in no way means that the church should generally withdraw and not participate.[118] Given this assertion there seems to be no reason that an intentional conscious limiting of scope should *necessarily* be problematic. I have, however, in the section on racial justice asserted that in this case the limited constructive engagement *is* a problem for several reasons. Hauerwas seeks to dislodge assumptions about how Christianity relates to America and how Christians should understand themselves. Hauerwas's consideration of the formation of Christians and the church will be addressed below.

International Relations and the Process of Foreign-Policy Formation—Hauerwas Slows It Down

Hauerwas's slow work of theology challenges the fast work of policy to hesitate before assuming understanding or passing over details that do not conform to standard analysis.[119] Much analysis and foreign-policy formation happens as events unfold;[120] that is, it often happens quickly

---

117. Cavanaugh discusses the tensions between Hauerwas's and Romand Coles's engagement on radical democracy and Christianity. Though in basic agreement, Cavanaugh ("Politics of Vulnerability," 109) writes, "Worship perhaps marks the most significant difference between Hauerwas and Coles." Philip Kenneson also explores the connection in "Gathering: Worship, Imagination, and Formation."

118. In this, he is similar to Yoder. Richard Bourne calls this the church as "embodiment of an alternate sociology. It displays the quality of non-conformed involvement in society." Bourne, *Seek the Peace of the City*, 135.

119. For a theoretical consideration of speed see Virilio, *Speed and Politics*.

120. Toole writes, summing up his project of *Waiting for Godot in Sarajevo*, "Nothing is certain, yet we must act. Hence it has been my work in these pages to map the terrain of that uncertainty, a vast terrain, to be sure, but one full of possibilities—possibilities that stand out in the glow of that new light that comes to be just at the point where Foucault and Jesus meet" (270). It is one thing for a professor writing in critical theory to say such things; it is, however, quite another thing for foreign-policy

by people who also work on a myriad of other issues. The need for in-depth analysis is then filled by a range of academics, think tanks, and often conveyed by lobbyist or advocates who seek to provide guidance and move opinion. Beattie notes, "Only the factors that strike the respective analysts as being most significant are taken seriously; the rest of the information will be ignored. Extremely importantly, only those organizations or interests having established a large measure of name recognition, credibility, and significance are likely to have their materials or messages read . . . [the] informational overload is heaped on individuals who, for the most part, have a very slim knowledge base in this issue area. This state of affairs flings the door wide open to powerful single actor constituents and highly skilled lobbyists."[121] Even organizations whose work it is to do such research, are often moving rapidly either to keep up with events or because it is their institutional practice (for example, so they can cover more geographic areas and maintain a high level of fundable work). At times, a researcher or advocate works extensively on a particular theme or issue, but even so, they often "fly in" to do the report. In this context, they may be inclined to import a category, framework, or experience from another location to interpret the present case. Without adequate reflection, categories and biases are easily incorporated.

I experienced this on several occasions when discussing the crisis in northeast Nigeria and the role of religion. Often, I hear responses, which can be paraphrased as "I have seen this in many other places." This is, of course, true up to a point. While such cataloguing or importation of an analytic framework is helpful for quickly understanding a situation, it also can lead to shearing off relevant detail.[122]

---

formulators to project any uncertainty. The public, at least in the United States, seems to need a leader that projects little to no uncertainty. Of course, there are many layers of government and not all are nearly so much in the public eye as top-ranking spokespeople. Nonetheless, their bosses require rapid and extensive analysis and recommendation. The meeting of the "terrain of the uncertain" and the projection of certainty despite certainty is fruitfully considered. The question, then, arises, Is the certainty merely a projection or are the people who excel (or at least remain) in these jobs prone to greater (perhaps unwarranted) certainty? Nearing the end of Barack Obama's tenure as President, there were countless assessments of his foreign policy. Much attention was given to his seeming relative tentativeness, deliberation, and hesitancy to act. See, for example, Stephens, "What Obama Gets Wrong," 13–16.

121. For more on think tanks, see McGann, *Fifth Estate*. Concerning the work of lobbyists and advocates, Beattie, *Congress and the Shaping of the Middle East*, 109–10.

122. In *Precarious Peace*, Chris Huebner mounts a parallel critique of ecumenical dialogue processes. In both, mechanisms of efficiency allow for the deletion of

Since all analysis entails a taking in of extra details and then reducing them to a usable size and shape, judgments are *necessarily* made about what is relevant or not. If necessary, it will be done well or poorly, but will nonetheless happen. This occurs both in relation to which events are considered relevant but also concerning cultures, characteristics, and dynamics of particular people and communities. Mayra Rivera explains, "Seeing someone as African American or Latino reveals the effects of social histories. We have become habituated to see quickly, without thinking about it, those traits considered relevant for classifying people according to those racial categories as constructed in the United States."[123] Judgments of relevant data are not only made but often made unconsciously.[124] David Spurr writes similarly when he closely examines how framing and racialized colonial observation shapes journalism.[125]

Hauerwas's work is an effort to challenge this habit of seeing quickly in theology.[126] For David Toole, seeing *quickly* is related to seeing all as *the same* or with a homogenizing affect. In *Waiting for Godot in Sarajevo*, he comments on Yoder's work, asserting, "The more our stories

---

particular detail. While all detail cannot be included, the embrace of processes that mechanize and formalize this decision in bureaucratic protocol allows for systems of control to remain intact. This means that certain disciplines, institutions, or those who can master these disciplines and institutions (systems of power) maintain control. In this arrangement, certain peoples are given easier entry or experience. Others, due to exclusion, need to play the system in order to have the chance (certainly not guarantee) of becoming the "decider."

123. Rivera, *Poetics of the Flesh*, 139.

124. About ethical reasoning, Stout writes, "Debate often functions as a centrifuge. The force it exerts rapidly transforms an untidy mixture of appreciations and misgivings into distinct and determinate theoretical possibilities, each of uniform density and purity, waiting only for the familiar labels. We then ask—all to confidently, as if our political options had to be described in this way—whether a given contribution to the debate is really a variety of optimism or pessimism, liberalism or communitarianism, a call for conservation of the established order or a call to replace it. That established, we rapidly send it to its appointed position on the shelf, grouped with others of its kind. Any contribution that resists the process of separation seems essentially impure, so we either discard it or label it an imperfect instance of its kind." Stout, *Ethics after Babel*, 276–77. Though Stout is not talking about foreign-policy analysis and formation such analysis almost always occurs with debate over the appropriate action. Though this is often framed in terms of strategic, for national interest, or allies, it is rarely completely separated from ethical considerations or argumentation that mirrors such considerations.

125. Spurr, *Rhetoric of Empire*.

126. Bourne raises the use and limitation of analogy in theology in *Seek the Peace of the City*, 122–24.

are homogenized, the more our memory is programmed, the more our mind is evacuated, and the more we come to live in the uncluttered clean space of the Panopticon."[127] Such seeing imposes a structure upon observation, that tends to universalize majority opinion and bias.[128] Michelle Alexander cites examples of the racialized assumptions that emerge when witnesses to a crime do not actually see the perpetrator: "In fact, for nearly three decades, news stories regarding virtually *all* street crime have disproportionately featured African American offenders. One study suggests that the standard crime news 'script' is so prevalent and so thoroughly racialized that viewers imagine a black perpetrator even when none exists. In that study, 60 percent of viewers who saw a story with no image falsely recalled seeing one, and 70 percent of those views believed the perpetrator to be African American."[129]

Charles Pinches writes, "This is why vocabulary is so important. Words, descriptions, do not occupy a sort of neutral space that hovers over lives and actions, as if we might be able to describe the world in a disinterested fashion, later adding in judgments about how we will act in it."[130] This represents a limitation and a racialized view. There is also the aspiration of all-seeing, and the myth of this possibility through the use of drone surveillance by the military. On this ideal, Grégoire Chamayou writes,

> The eye of God, with its overhanging gaze, embraces the entire world. Its vision is more than just sight: beneath the skin of phenomena it can search hearts and minds. Nothing is opaque

---

127. Toole, *Waiting for Godot in Sarajevo*, 242.

128. Hauerwas writes of an instance when a professor challenged him because he had no theory "that would enable Christians to talk with Buddhists." He writes, "By 'theory' people often mean the necessity of a third language to mediate between two traditions. Such a language is often said to be necessary in pluralist societies in order to mediate differences in the public square. Calls for a third language fail to consider, however, that such languages are anything but neutral. Moreover, the assumption that traditions are airtight closed systems is a gross oversimplification. Significant traditions are amalgams of many influences that provide often surprising connection with other traditions. Before assuming the inability to communicate, you have to listen and look . . . I, however, apologized for being deficient in such a theory, but asked, 'How many Buddhists do you have here in Conway? Moreover if you want to talk with them, what good will a theory do you? I assume that if you want to talk with Buddhists, you would just go to talk with them. You might begin by asking, for example, 'What in the world are you guys doing in Conway?'" Hauerwas, "End of Religious Pluralism," 293.

129. Alexander, *New Jim Crow*, 106.

130. Pinches, "Proclaiming: Naming and Describing," 171.

to it. Because it is eternity, it embraces the whole of time, the past as well as the future. And its knowledge is not just knowledge. Omniscience implies omnipotence. In many respects, the drone dreams of achieving through technology a miniature equivalence to that fictional eye of God. As one soldier writes, 'Using the all-seeing eye, you will find out who is important in a network, where they live, where they get their support from, where their friends are.' . . . The press informs us that in the course of 2009 alone, American drones generated the equivalent of twenty-four years' worth of video recording.[131]

The presumption of omniscience due to a theoretically comprehensive gaze may be a variation of the assumed superior knowledge (regarding race in the US) due to the historic presumption and policy of control through genocide of indigenous peoples and the enslavement of Africans. Kelly Brown Douglas links methods and myths of control and superiority through present laws in *Stand Your Ground: Black Bodies and the Justice of God*.

Hauerwas's challenge to this is termed "making strange." For Hauerwas, the sermon is the primary location of theological reflection.[132] The preacher's task is to "make the Word strange."[133] As such, a primary task of theology is challenging habituated thought.[134] Additionally, for

131. Chamayou, *Theory of the Drone*, 37–40.

132. In *Cross-Shattered Church* (12), Hauerwas writes, "I am convinced that the recovery of the sermon as the context for theological reflection is crucial if Christians are to navigate the world in which we find ourselves."

133. Does Hauerwas get this phrase from John Milbank? The latter writes, "Today, theology is tragically too important. For all the current talk of theology that would reflect on practice, the truth is that we remain uncertain as to where today to locate true Christian practice. This would be, as it has always been, a repetition differently, but authentically, of what has always been done. In his or her uncertainty as to where to find this, the theologian feels almost the entire ecclesial task falls on his own head: in the meager mode of reflective words he must seek to imagine what a true practical repetition would be like. Or at least he must hope that his merely theoretical continuation of the tradition will open up a space for wider transformation. In the past, practice already 'made strange,' already felt again the authentic shock of the divine word by performing it anew, with variation. The theologian could articulate this and add her own further twists that might contribute to renewed vision. Yet today it can feel as if it is the theologian alone (as in another cultural sphere the artist, or the poet) who must perform this task of redeeming estrangement; the theologian alone who must perpetuate that original making strange from which was the divine assumption of human flesh, not to confirm it as it was, but to show it again as it surprisingly is." Milbank, *Word Made Strange*, 1.

134. "Theologians engage in a distinct ascetic practices by attending to this

Hauerwas, theology is an ongoing process which requires continuous reassessment and critique of assumptions (particularly around issues of nation-state loyalty). John B. Thomson writes, "For Hauerwas, liberation starts not with the liberation of humankind, or with the cosmos, but with the liberation of the church, since . . . it is only as the church recovers her distinctive identity and freedom that she can truthfully display the freedom of the Gospel."[135] These observations, however, seem to get us to the same spot as many other critical writers across numerous disciplines. Critique of journalistic writing and literature seeks to spot and shake free particular biases embedded in observation (racialized, Western centric, etc.).

Hauerwas's work not only engages some of these assumptions (focusing, for example, on liberalism, modernity, and American exceptionalism), but seeks to train readers in the language of Christianity. Though such training is not comprehensive in the particularities of a given subject, it is valuable on several fronts. In the context of the US and the relative Christian hegemony, religious discourse is more than adequately present. In this space, Hauerwas specifically challenges nearly every assumption of such religiosity that had newly elected President Donald Trump say "God Bless America" and Lady Gaga urge unity over the Super Bowl while singing God Bless America, both within early 2017.

However, although Hauerwas challenges these broad assumptions, his work often remains abstract. In an essay considering Stout and Hauerwas's exchange on concreteness, Pinches mentions Wendell Berry as an example of someone who gets beyond the abstract. He states, "Herein lies the deepest problem with Stanley Hauerwas—and perhaps the main reason Stout's criticisms are directed principally at him. He is not summoning his will."[136] Such summoning is for the formation of communities. Stout asserts that Hauerwas remains caught in the abstract in criticism rather than taking adequate account of his relationship to communities and neighbors.

---

deferral [multiple tellings in the Gospels] and to the way each narrative renounces its own closure, surrendering and transforming itself in the reader's understanding and raising questions about its own life experiences, and in the context of the experiences of a community, by reflecting on the way one has thought in the past about God, love, evil, theologians make interpretive decisions about which stories are primary and, within each story, which meanings are dominant." Roberts, "Theology and the Ascetic Imperative," 194.

135. Thomson, *Ecclesiology of Stanley Hauerwas*, 180.

136. Pinches, "Stout, Hauerwas, and the Body of America," 13.

While such comparison may be illustrative for foreign-policy analysis, it could still be merely a parallel example of intellectual work. Even so, it remains useful and provides a unique contribution. For Hauerwas, theology is process, which will not end.[137] Kallenberg compares this with Wittgenstein's therapeutic approach to philosophy, in which the process is at least as important as the product that is necessarily never final. But then how does this approach directly influence policy formation? Is it that Hauerwas should be read by foreign-policy practitioners, or that because of what Hauerwas reads, or the way he that he approaches reading is helpful to the task? It may be that his approach to reading is helpful, and so, through reading Hauerwas, we are taught to read in his style. In *Wilderness Wanderings*, Hauerwas lifts up McClendon as a teacher of such reading.[138] The process of reading rather than a final "product" is the point, it is not merely a necessary but undesirable tool. Huebner discusses Hauerwas on the work of reading in "The Work of Reading: Hauerwas, MacIntyre, and the Questions of Liberalism" in *Unsettling Arguments*. The practice of learning the craft of reading is shaped through the reading of Hauerwas. Additionally, the notion that ethics can precede theology (in some manner) is also useful for framing an approach to analysis which prioritizes the concrete and descriptions over theory. While theory is still present, this may break analysis free from its overbearing control, which has a tendency to overpower and reshape according to its image.[139]

137. According to Hauerwas and Coles, seeking a "final word" may in fact be a form of violence. Hauerwas and Coles, "Long Live the Weeds and the Wilderness Yet," 355.

138. "So McClendon must persuade us, if we are to become good readers, to give up our need to control the world. We must instead believe that truthfulness, not war and violence, is the way the world acquires a history befitting its ordering to God's kingdom." Hauerwas, "Reading James McClendon Takes Practice," 171.

139. Not only is mode of observation relevant, but how analysis is controlled and the terms defined has enormous bearing on how a situation is understood. I wrote the following paragraph while revising policy positions for Churches for Middle East Peace: "Since most CMEP member organizations allow that there are times when the use of lethal force is legitimate (when done within particular frameworks which prioritize nation state sanctioned violence) any condemnation of violence from within a generally accepted just war theory or JWT influenced framework will almost necessarily be toward violence by security force and against non-centralized or minimally centralized violent resistance. If we say the IDF can use violence at times then the possibility of legitimate use of violence to resist oppression should be acknowledged (which I know we won't do). This is obviously a potentially enormous conversation which probably wouldn't help finish the policy paper. I imagine various critical, political, and racial theorists would observe that there is a seemingly built in preference/

Hauerwas challenges the assumption that we can see rightly. He says to new students, I don't want you to make up your mind; you don't have a mind to make up until I form it. Additionally, one of his overriding purposes in *War and the American Difference* is to challenge the assumption that we know what we are talking about when we talk about war. This also extends to broader foreign policy.

Reading (like) Hauerwas—Hauerwas Trains the Reader

Huebner writes, "Stanley Hauerwas is a reader. In fact, it might be argued that he is first and foremost a reader."[140] Hauerwas discusses the importance of *how* one reads when he states, "Much of the work of theology involves helping us to develop and remember the reading skills necessary to avoid isolating one part of Scripture from the rest." [141] In this section I assert that Hauerwas's practice of reading as an integral part of his theological ethics provides a useful tool for the process of foreign-policy formation and analysis. There is not one method of engagement that is universally ideal. For example, it may not be that *in general* Christians should engage the state on these issues or that Christians should engage all parts of the state in the same way (either in mode of engagement or across the board rejection or approval of the state's agenda). Additionally, it is not that political analysts *in general* should read theology as a whole (always need to read a little Barth before *Politico*). Rather, for all these there are instances where such a person should engage in such a task or text, and this should be an acknowledged useful practice. Such an acknowledgement of usefulness would not, of course, mean universally accepting the conclusions of those engaged in this policy formation and analysis with this lens or reading and theology. Readers must join in the non-controlled (Hauerwas might say non-policed) discursive space of argumentation. One of Hauerwas's complaints is that the "liberal political order" and Christians within it police such interactions.[142] While theoreti-

---

trust (by some) of the military institutions, institutions in general, and the nation-state." Hauerwas raises some similar questions in "Nonviolent Terrorist," 91.

140. Huebner, "Work of Reading," 284.

141. Hauerwas, *Cross-Shattered Church*, 17.

142. Hauerwas, *Dispatches from the Front*, 105. While "policing" has a coercive sound this may also be able to be framed as "attending to speech." A colleague recently discussed a family member's general grasp of social issues but not having the "proper" way to discuss this. While helping to shape language is important, the need to support

cal work on international relations would likely be included in Hauerwas's rejection of a theory of politics for the church, particular engagement with particular communities,[143] even if via the State Department, clearly falls within his interests and affirmed work.[144] It is not entirely clear, however, what Hauerwas means by a "theory of politics." Whereas a theory of politics would seem to indicate a more elaborate system, he at times seems to equate "having a theory" with being committed to democracy. For Hauerwas, a commitment to democracy by Christians is likely an instance of politics taking primacy over Christian practices and theology. In his view, "theory," rather than an elaborate philosophical system, is a pre-theological or non-theologically derived or ecclesially-based practice. Certainly, democracy entails a great deal of theory, but for most of the population, it remains quite simple—perhaps the right to vote, a system of checks and balances, and a general adherence to a rule of law. Hauerwas appears not to draw a sharp line between positions on policies or politics and a theory. In a response to 9/11, he writes, "American imperialism, often celebrated as the new globalism, is a frightening power. It is frightening not only because of the harm such power inflicts on the innocent but because it is difficult to imagine alternatives. For example, pacifists are often challenged after an event like September 11 with the question: Well, what alternative do you have to bombing Afghanistan?" Such questions assume that pacifists must have an alternative foreign

---

such concern for social issues and also caring for the relationship remain in some degree of tension. Particularly for white American Christians, the good impulse to care for others often gets tangled in many racialized assumptions and patterns of thought.

143. Majawa develops a theory and theological support for a "genuine" democracy in Africa. To describe a "genuine" version is a theoretical task, but he engages this from the community of Africa (which is of course many communities but shares certain distinctives from other parts of the globe) and from specific texts of the church. See Majawa, "Church's Role in Defining Genuine Democracy in Africa," 99–119.

144. "To be sure, Bell and Cavanaugh are concerned with finding concrete practices Christians can live by in our present troubled time—in fact, this is true of virtually every Hauerwas student now writing. Hauerwas has convinced (or trained) us all that for Christianity to matter politically, it cannot be another theory of statecraft but rather must become embodied in the practices of a people, especially the people called Church. However, for this to be well and honestly done, 'embodiment' needs to spread out. That is, we need to be able to name and envision a wide variety of ways in which Christians—or even others not called by that name but whose lives reflect true grace—daily trace out in their lives the patterns of faith, hope, and love." Pinches, "Hauerwas and Political Theology," 527.

policy. I have something better—a church constituted by people who would rather die than kill."[145]

While working to revise the policy positions of Churches for Middle East Peace (CMEP), a version of this became relevant. CMEP has historically been committed to a "two-state" political arrangement in regard to the relationship between Palestine and Israel. Many analysts, politicians, and activists now say that the possibility of two states is either closed or rapidly closing. Additionally, two-states was never a simple policy formulation, but a name for a complex and wide-ranging set of political commitments, processes, and policies. For many groups, the commitment to a two-state solution is not a theory but a practical arrangement that would create the possibility of greater justice, security, and peace in the region. This is complicated by layers of theological, historical, and strategic commitments and experiences. So, for Hauerwas, would CMEP's choice to advocate either a two-state solution or not be an example of the church holding a political theory? The fact that this rises not out of an abstract political theory, but out of theological commitments for justice and peacemaking along with historic relationships with other Christians and interfaith engagement in the region, would certainly be relevant. Such a political arrangement and the process of getting to it or abandoning it are hardly abstract or detached from the well-being of individuals, communities, institutions, and people groups. While I support Hauerwas's assertion that a political theory is not the most basic commitment for a Christian, it must also be allowed that the implications of political arrangements and actions, which are in part based on something that may resemble a "theory," have implications for people which clearly fall within the concerns of loving one's neighbor and working for their wellbeing.

The practice of reading (as well as practices of the community and theology) are more basic than theory.[146] Hauerwas challenges disciplinary boundaries and seeks to provoke a scrappier, less refined argument. Not only is this argument less polished, but theology necessarily must keep going without a conclusion or arriving at a completed system. Such an approach challenges the need for closure and completeness. For Hauerwas, the desire for completeness or control may lay at the root of our willingness to use violence to make history turn out right. Christians

---

145. Hauerwas, "September 11, 2001," 127.

146. Hauerwas has said in *Cross-Shattered Church* (144) that if one needs a theory to worship, then one should worship the theory rather than Christ. In this he seeks de-prioritize method and theory.

may mistakenly believe that their power, or potential power, comes from politics or control; Hauerwas, however, asserts, "The threat comes not in a swarm of military might, nor, for that matter, in a barrage of innovative political ideas. It comes rather as theology."[147] This theology is expressed in the form of witness rather than control. Morgan writes on Hauerwas and Barth,

> Acknowledging the mystery of the church's future requires a willingness to forgo control of history and instead to hand it over to the lordship of Christ. This handing over implies ecclesial humility about the church's role within that history, which invites the church community to see its witness to Christ's redemption as authorized by Christ's work yet perpetually inexplicable as to where God's mission might reach and what difficulties may need to be borne. In this sense, one could read Hauerwas's strong ecclesial turn as sustaining a Barthian distinction between Christ's lordship and the church insofar as he admits a future that remains, as Barth says, 'in the hands of God.'[148]

While there may be challenges with Hauerwas's turn to ecclesiology, the church is more concrete than a more purely Christological focus. In this Hauerwas may maintain a theological primacy similar to Barth while sustaining more physical connections to the world. If Morgan is right that, despite its bold claims, Hauerwas's church has humility, then Hauerwas may help to get beyond the need for anxious control but also beyond assertions of the need to act "responsibly." Both of these alleged necessities begin to flatten the theological dynamism of the church's work. Bearing witness without seeking to control then seems to build space for church-based policy advocacy.[149] If a Christian is directly hired by the state to do this work, does this necessarily constitute an attempt to gain control? While it certainly *could* be so, it is more likely intended as a modest contribution to the work. Though positions in government include varying degrees of power, in a democracy with various forms

---

147. Hauerwas, "Witness," 53.

148. Morgan, "Lordship of Christ," 69.

149. For Hauerwas, witness is not merely a public speaking in which Christians talk but bears at least certain components of dialogue: "It is important to observe that witness in no way is meant to avoid the importance of argument. Yet to have an argument requires that Christians first listen to what the other has to say. Such listening, moreover, may well cause us to learn better what we have to say. Such listening may even create epistemological crises with Christian self-understanding." Hauerwas, "Nonviolent Terrorist," 99.

of checks and balances, even the highest office does not hold absolute control. At a church retreat where I was speaking on refugees and immigration, a pastor recognized that policy advocacy was valid but felt that under the Trump Administration it was a waste of time. This person seemed to think that if the "correct" person were in then all would be in order. This, however, fails to realize that once in office there is a pull towards the conventional path by a range of factors, including legal mechanisms to restrain and check power, bureaucratic slowness, professional staff who remain, alliances, and other branches of government. While leadership has notable impact, it is not the only factor that matters. It may, then be a form of humility to serve within such a system. It also may be a form of humility to engage the system on issues of policy from the outside through ministries of the church. Is, however, this ceding the conversation? Some would argue that the system is such that real change or real justice cannot be worked at from within. Additionally, in the US where Christianity is the dominant religion it is quite likely that the Christian is serving under another Christian who is of differing view. As such, working "in humility" in relation to this arrangement may as much be a form or affirmation to the particular theology, which could then make it a church issue. Additionally, the state, as defined by separation of Church and state, typically (at least officially) strips out religious reference. Working within such a context then may be ceding the argument to a particular theology of the state.

For Hauerwas, the pretension of seeking completeness is idolatry. There is a difference, however, between a system of theology and systematic engagement. Nancy Murphy provides an example of this in her description of Yoder's systematic approach in which he is not seeking to build a system of theology: "The task . . . then, will be to show that Yoder's theology fits the form of a scientific research program. This means that we must be able to isolate a core theory—a central thesis from which all the rest of the theoretical structure (the network of auxiliary hypotheses) follows."[150] Though Murphy does not include Hauerwas in her investigation, Hauerwas regularly asserts that he has picked up many approaches from Yoder, but he has not commented on Murphy's assessment. Whether or not his coherence and systematic approach compares to Yoder's is, however, a much bigger and far ranging question. This is in large part

---

150. Murphy, "John Howard Yoder's Systematic Defense," 44.

because even in the case of Yoder, the systematic approach is observed by a commenter but not stated by Yoder.[151]

Hauerwas consistently emphasizes particularity and urges a thick description along with embodied witness rather than mere belief or doctrine. Though Stout is a vigorous critic of Hauerwas, they agree at least on the need for a close description. Stout writes, "Immanent criticism can take full advantage of all conceptual resources available to any kind of criticism. It can burrow deep into its own culture's past in search of forgotten truths, learn enough about an alien culture to put our practices and institutions in fresh perspective, and imagine ways of life that have never been. It is immanent only in claiming no privileged vantage point above the fray."[152] Such a description is often called *fine grained* or *granular*. In lauding this approach, Hauerwas may simply believe that if one looks very closely, then one is more likely to see the truth. Seeing the truth through the practice paying attention to small details may be true insofar as close looking challenges what are said to be universal descriptions. However, even this close looking requires judgments that are based on particular, even if unstated, assumptions. Additionally, while looking closely, which usually happens over a long period of time, one may accumulate biases that become further entrenched over time. This may be the case in the analysis of violent conflict and close identification with parts of the community. For example, in my policy and peacebuilding work on northeast Nigeria in Washington, DC, the Church of the Brethren and my (relatively) long term engagement are used as credentials for shaping opinion. Not only is the engagement long-term but very specific. The experience is not with the "whole" of Nigeria but with a limited location. Within the whole community this experience is limited in geographic scope but deep in terms of duration and level of interaction. This depth,

---

151. Though not specifically commenting on Yoder's work as systematic, Heidebrecht does not specifically address any systematic quality to Yoder's work, he observes that though Yoder speaks negatively about the impulse toward engineering history, he functions systematically. Heidebrecht writes, "Throughout his work Yoder sounds like an engineer when he shifts his focus from the relationship of the church to the world, to the life of the church. For as much as he downplays the priority of mechanisms, causality, and probabilities when it comes to social history writ large, a case can be made that he is very interested in mechanisms, causality, and probabilities when it comes to church history. Indeed, it would appear there is a significant point of tension between Yoder's providential perspective on the history of the world and his interventionist perspective on the history of the church." Heidebrecht, "Not Engineering, But Doxology?," 121.

152. Stout, *Ethics after Babel*, 282.

for example, is evident in the preface of a grammar of the Margi language published in 1963 the author notes basing this work in part on "Grammar Notes" by the Church of the Brethren Mission.[153] Such institutional depth of engagement does not guarantee good analysis but certainly may contribute in a number of ways. Commenting on Hauerwas's reading of particularity, Huebner writes,

> This is why Stanley so often speaks out against abstraction, and in particular the sort of abstraction associated with applied ethics. To describe cases in the factual, impersonal terms of applied ethics, he claims cannot but distort the 'realities' with which they are purportedly concerned by obscuring the rich and complex texture of ordinary life. In particular, it gives the impression that such descriptions are neutral when, in fact, they presume a number of normative commitments that are, if nothing else, open to debate... This gives the impression that certain things, such as the unavoidability of violence, are natural and necessary, that they can somehow be read off the surface of the world.[154]

Huebner asserts that though Hauerwas does not extensively reflect on the role of reading in his work, it plays an important role. He writes, "It is through reading, among other practices, that we 'learn how to say' the world. The world is constituted by descriptions, and the negotiation of descriptions require careful attention to the intricacies of language and grammar."[155] For Hauerwas, reading is a wide-ranging exploration of the world, and offers training in describing and seeing as well. After considering critiques of Hauerwas's reading by Stout and Milbank, both of whom focus on his theoretical writings and claim Hauerwas is too simplistic of a reader, Huebner asserts that when Hauerwas engages "ordinary" topics, his work becomes more adequately nuanced and theological. This supports my claim that Hauerwas's style of work may be useful for engaging the particulars of foreign policy and religion.[156]

---

153. Hoffmann, *Grammar of the Margi Language*, v.

154. Huebner, "Work of Reading," 286.

155. Huebner, "Work of Reading," 286.

156. Hauerwas quotes Yoder, writing, "Yoder makes clear his admiration for King, noting that 'there is no such thing as a nonviolent strategy to be used for liberation anywhere and everywhere. The essence of nonviolent action includes charismatic creativity. It needs prophetic insight into timing and symbolism which is more like the artist than the strategist. It demands precise analysis of social systems that is more like the sociologist than the ideologue. Nonetheless it is possible to say that in the labors of King we have seen the maturity or the roundness of an understanding of nonviolent

Though Hauerwas would resist a theory of foreign policy, his work is useful in the task of close description, particularly in relation to religion and war, as well as for challenging the assumption that certain descriptions are normative and neutral.

Urging close observation and using eclectic sources are hallmarks of Hauerwas's style. Ranging outside typical disciplinary boundaries, while generating a degree of unevenness and uncertainty, is critical for the practitioner of analysis and policy formation. Referring to Stout's description of *bricolage*, Kallenberg writes, "However, the fact that Hauerwas's work can be described in terms of *bricolage* does not imply a rampant arbitrariness in his method. The *bricoleur* is as skillful in the selection of resources as in the effecting of a repair. Similarly, there is a method to Hauerwas's madness."[157] This approach uses whatever materials happen to be on hand. Such an approach is instructive for foreign-policy formation, which must work not only with a variety of sources but is assessing issues that are not limited to a single discipline. Additionally, given the nonlinear and uncertain nature of causality, even if one could fully comprehend a situation in advance through the lens of a particular discipline, an effective response requires diverse approaches to formulate and effective response. A limitation of view is quite clear, for example, when analysts insist that a group claiming to be a religious movement is "actually" economic or political. Additionally, given relational dynamics and the need for building trust even at the highest levels of government, the question of who the actors are and what they represent is significant. Though such movements are rarely "purely religious" as defined in Western post-enlightenment terms,[158] claims of religiosity cannot be written off so quickly.

Kallenberg, writing on Hauerwas and Wittgenstein, focuses on the process and role of theology and philosophy. Particularly, he considers the way these descriptions challenge common descriptions and assumptions

---

liberation which could illuminate and give direction to other cultures for ways to work in favor of other causes." Hauerwas, *War and the American Difference*, 84, quoting John Howard Yoder, *Nonviolence: A Brief History*, 46. Similarly, Richard Bourne notes Yoder's insistence that the church does not need a theory of government to critique the government. See "Governmentality, Witness, and the State," 101.

157. Kallenberg, *Ethics as Grammar*, 55.

158. The meaning of what constitutes "purely religious" is unclear, but is likely shaped by Western notions of religion having to do with spirit and having nothing to do with the material, political, or cultural stuff of the world.

of causation.¹⁵⁹ If, however, one shifts from the "theoretical" to the "practical," how do we avoid getting boxed in by the so-called "necessities" with their nearly predetermined response and outcome? Does this not also undercut the role of theology? The perceived need for immediate responses arguably drive much of the assumptions in Washington that "We need to do something," which is almost always a military action. Incorporating theology, particularly in the form of theological ethics, as part of close description challenges those alleged necessities. However, the likelihood of including theology in a helpful and nuanced way, and not merely as a tool for justifying a predetermined decision, appears uncertain.¹⁶⁰

Particular observations may be best made from within the community or at least sustained by communities of discourse that remain linked to the broader communities. Kallenberg notes, "The impasse that resulted from modernity's assumption that ethics *must* be done either from 'the bottom up' or from 'the top down' was surmounted by Wittgenstein, who labored to show that language and world were internally related; one cannot begin from either the top or the bottom. One must begin in the middle of a particular, concrete community whose identity-constituting form of life is determinative for the proper application of the means by which ethics and theology take place at all, namely, their common language."¹⁶¹ This *within*, of course, has many potential variations. For example, if one were engaged in assessment and observation of conflict and peacebuilding in northeast Nigeria, such observation could be made by a member of Ekklesiyar Yan'uwa a Nigeria from Kwarhi next to Mararaba-Mubi in northern Adamawa state, a member of that community living in another part of Nigeria, a Nigerian generally, or a Church of the Brethren worker from the US. These would-be observers are more from middle of this community than a detached observer, but likely vary in their attentiveness to detail and awareness of their biases. Additionally, all may hold

---

159. "By means of his grammatical mischief, Wittgenstein sought to dismantle the totalizing claims of mathematics, psychology, history, and theology. But above all, he strove to offer alternatives to the scientific picture of mechanical causality that had been so thoroughly ingested by twentieth-century western culture." Kallenberg, *Ethics as Grammar*, 200.

160. An American Christian's inability to allow criticism of Israeli policies would be one such example. Even this, though, has taken many turns historically. See Mae Elise Cannon's description of the history of engagement by American Christian churches in Israel and Palestine in "Mischief Making in Palestine," 49–66.

161. Kallenberg, *Ethics as Grammar*, 147.

various preconceptions which radically skew their analysis. On a flight from Abuja, I once spoke with Nigerian lawyer from the south working in Abuja and London. Though Nigerian, he had never been to the north or northeast part of the country and though highly educated and informed, had views of the northeast that were wildly problematic from my point of view. For example, he suggested that the Christians from this area (who speak Hausa, Margi, Kibaku, and other languages and are indigenous to those areas) could be helped by being moved wholesale to the southern, "Christian," part of the country. While this observation may seem to undermine my comments on proximity, it illustrate that proximity is at least partially relative, and that a discursive process in which theological ethics are included is needed to formulate policy that appropriately accounts for religion. Proximity, then, is a necessary but not sufficient aspect of analysis.

Theological language is at times a necessary part of describing particularity. Preaching describes but also "makes strange." Kallenberg writes, "Preaching then, for Hauerwas, is not a matter of apologetics but evangelization. Preaching confronts the preacher and hearers alike with the reality of the Lord who rules from the cross and graciously summons all to bring every aspect of their lives under the dominion of his life-giving reign. Preaching at its most fundamental level has to do with truth."[162] In this, it both disrupts patterns of thought and to trains in a particular language.

If Hauerwas is interested in truth and political analysis is interested in truth, does Hauerwas add any value? Can Hauerwas's work on truth in theological speech be useful for political analysis? Since practitioners need to come to a conclusion quickly, it is likely that rather than taking a neutral stance, they will portray the facts in a particular way. Some of this will be simply part of their seeing, but often it is intentional. Through the inculcation of the language of faith, Christians are empowered to see the world truly and discover the goods they hold in common. Reflecting the influence of Wittgenstein, Hauerwas continually emphasizes, "You can only act in a world you can see, and you can only see by learning to say. Words make our world; which should not be surprising to a people who confess that both words and the world are created by the Word."[163] As such, words are not value free, but contingent and created.

162. Kallenberg, *Ethics as Grammar*, 141.

163. Kallenberg, *Ethics as Grammar*, 147. Mitri Raheb (*Faith in the Face of Empire*, 89) offers a relevant comment: "People begin with geo-political realities and conclude

Simultaneously, words are used to create and shape people's perceptions, which then also shape reality. When one seeks to describe and change reality through policy it happens through language which is embedded in linguistic and value-contingent realities, not through neutrality.[164] The world is not observed and then described in neutral language but is embedded in linguistic and value-full realities.

Hauerwas suggests that in a world of inelegant speech and distorted vision, well-formed sermons "may turn out to be the most important contribution Christians can make to a politics that has some ambition to be truthful."[165] The question then arises: How does the preacher ascertain truth? While the answer, through "the Spirit in the discerning body" or "the Spirit in the authoritative ecclesial body" carries theological weight, it is hard to sustain this at the level of the individual preacher. History is full of examples of Spirit-led preaching, but also many examples of contradictory views preached at the same time on the same issues. One might also ask: What is it in the vocation of the preacher that gets closer to the truth? Hauerwas would likely assert that as one who regularly works with the tradition, the preacher is trained to speak truthfully.[166] However, in the case of theological ethics and policy analysis, the correlation between seeking the truth about matters of policy and that of theological may differ.

At a minimum, it requires careful observation. Stout writes helpfully, albeit not in connection to foreign policy, "How can we discover the first moral language of America? Only, I think, by participant-observation in the middle-class home, in the classroom, on the playground, on ghetto

---

with theologies. My thesis is that God came to defeat geo-politics and he succeeded. Because without God, Palestine would have continued as a land at the periphery. Yet because God chose to reveal himself in this land, it became central to history, which is why it is found at the center of ancient maps. Because of God. The moment God identified himself with this land, everything changed."

164. This is why US Supreme Court and political appointments are so contentious and typically extremely partisan.

165. Kallenberg, *Ethics as Grammar*, 148.

166. "By calling this knowledge practical, I wanted to remind us that we do not even know what it means to call God good except from learning what it means to be a creature and redeemed through the cross and resurrection of Jesus of Nazareth. Therefore 'practical' names the necessity of transformation of the self by inclusion in a truthful community so that we can even gain the skills capable of speaking of God as trinity." Hauerwas, "On God: Ethics and the Power to Act in History," 205.

streets and so forth."¹⁶⁷ Stout even allows that description can have power enough to teach skill: "I would say that the requisite experience can, in some instances, come at second-hand, through a skillful reporter's thick descriptions, although MacIntyre seems skeptical of this."¹⁶⁸

Reading theological ethics for the purpose of training for observation and analysis of religion in foreign policy may be possible. Such reading is part of a wide-ranging deliberation that brings an array of disciplines and discourses into a discursive space. Such space is for the purpose of discovering truth and acting rightly on this truth. Such an uncontrolled process, intent on truth, may not fit well within either the divisions of disciplines in academia or the general public space. Robert Dean asserts, with regard to Hauerwas's preaching: "Modern liberal societies with their conflation of the exercise of authority with authoritarianism and their endless deferral on the question of truth, lack the resources for genuine political deliberation concerning the common good. In this context, the very act of preaching is a prophetic activity and an integral part of the church's political witness because it exemplifies the exercise of truthful political authority that the world could not otherwise imagine."¹⁶⁹ Stout notes that this deliberation and social criticism is something like a crucible.¹⁷⁰ Reading (like) Hauerwas then is a *process* bent on truth, which challenges and problematizes generalized and pre-set descriptions. This habit of reading is useful for helping foreign-policy formation break free from so-called necessities.

---

167. Stout, *Ethics after Babel*, 270.

168. Stout, *Ethics after Babel*, 267.

169. Dean, "Unapologetically (A)Political," 139.

170. "At its best, social criticism is more crucible than centrifuge. It holds together all the appreciations and misgivings that reasonable people in our society feel . . . The familiar labels reflect a failure of imagination. They also frustrate the effort to build consensus for specific projects of political experimentation and social amelioration. Yet we go pinning them on one another or ourselves, in part because it is easier to strike moral poses than to come up with moral balanced descriptions and concrete political proposals, and in part because the moral poses of our opponents seem to call out so urgently for censure or satire (just as ours do to them)." Stout, *Ethics after Babel*, 277.

Hauerwas and Practical Reasoning

For Hauerwas, theology is a form of practical reasoning.[171] Such reasoning is based in a community that contains internal connections as a community as well as to its tradition. The foreign-policy practice of the US is a community with traditions.[172] This is evident in a common history of the nation,[173]—but also in texts read during training and other catechetical methods of bringing on new staff. Such training must equip staff to address a plethora of situations and cultures, while also transmitting a sense of shared identity, common purpose, and vision of work. Hauerwas would not, however, be content to have a general lesson drawn from his theological method and applied to foreign policy. Hauerwas has strongly criticized this type of preaching (which draws what Hauerwas considers general lessons that can be learned anywhere) and this style would not, presumably, be particularly compelling for foreign-policy practitioners either. Nonetheless, though the analogue is limited, and a general lesson may be inadequate, this is a starting place.

Though Hauerwas does not rigidly identify with a particular denomination, he locates himself squarely within the church rather than a more amorphous "faith community" or religion in general. For Hauerwas, the assumption of unity and close similarities between faith traditions is imposed by those committed to an abstract ideal of universal experience. He has said that we cannot assume (or impose) unity in the abstract, but must discover commonality through getting to know one another.[174] Canadian Mennonite theologian A. James Reimer speaks to this point out of his own experience:

---

171. "Sermons are crucial if we are to recover the stories that make it possible to recover Christian practical reason." Hauerwas, *Cross-Shattered Church*, 16.

172. As we neared the inauguration of President Elect Donald Trump there was a great deal of uncertainty how much he would break from these traditions. By appointing heads of foreign policy with little to no formal foreign-policy experience and extreme or narrow views he has indicated a desire to break with traditions. Since the entirety of the foreign service related staff is not appointed or able to be changed it remains to be seen how much the whole apparatus can be moved. See Michaels, "Trump and the 'Deep State,'" 52–56.

173. Anderson, *Imagined Communities*, 4.

174. He also comments on listening: "However, I do not want the way I argue to belie the significance of gentleness. I hope I will prove to be an adequate listener, because learning to listen is basic to the gentle character of life in L'Arche . . . To learn to listen well, it turns out, may require learning to be a gentle person." Hauerwas, "Politics of Gentleness," 79.

My involvement in Christian-Muslim dialogue over the past decade with Iranian doctoral students studying in Toronto and in a series of four academic conferences (2002 in Toronto, Ontario: 2004 in Qom, Iran; 2007 in Waterloo, Ontario; and 2008 in Qom Iran) have convinced me that agreement on universal moral and religious principles cannot be arrived at in abstraction but emerges through particular encounters between different communities of belief. In other words, *one gets to the universal through the particular.* The success of our Mennonite Christian and Shi'a Muslim exchange is based on the dialogue between members of two believing communities, out of which emerged some commonalities and differences, not by first establishing abstractly some universal norms upon which we could agree and then basing our dialogue on these. Any global ethic, if such a thing exists, will have to evolve through the authentic and open encounter between particular religious and cultural traditions.[175]

Such discovery of commonality while living in particularity then disarms the hegemonic impulses that Hauerwas sees as violent. Speed,[176] impatience,[177] control of causation and outcomes are part of domination that undergirds, and in fact *is*, violence). Huebner gets at several variations of this in *A Precarious Peace* when he seeks to interrogate notions of ecumenism and patience.[178] In these, a predetermined framework makes the action more efficient and predictable. For Huebner, channeling Yoder, such an approach does violence to the possibility of witnessing God's grace and seeks to take hold of history and control the outcome. Bourne, however, suggests that Huebner makes too definite Yoder's skepticism about such efforts to control.[179]

---

175. Reimer, "Anabaptist-Mennonite Political Theology," 82.

176. See Huebner on Virilio in *Precarious Peace*, 115-32. Additionally, Hauerwas and Coles state, "Radical democracy is the politics of small achievements. Such, politics takes time, which suggests that there may be some deep connections between Christianity and radical democracy. This is surely the case given the death-determined politics of our time, the politics of compulsory speed, which assumes that we do not have the time to take the time to listen to one another or to remember the dead." Hauerwas and Coles, *Christianity, Democracy, and the Radical Ordinary*, 4.

177. See Kreider, *Patient Ferment of the Early Church*, 245-96.

178. See chapter 4, "Radical Ecumenism, or Receiving One Another in Kuala Lumpur," in Huebner, *Precarious Peace*, 69-82.

179. Bourne (*Seek the Peace of the City*, 248-49) questions Huebner's reading of Yoder: "Huebner's point seems to me to conflate Yoder's cautionary skepticism in to regard to the Constantinian danger of 'putting handles on history,' as he put it, with

To adequately insert Hauerwas on Hauerwas's terms into such conversations, they must go deeper than *theology as motivation* for peacebuilding or *as a religious studies approach to conflict analysis*. This is not meant to undervalue or devalue these two approaches; it is just that they are not Hauerwas's approach.[180] Such a reading may be analogous to critical theorists using Yoder. Though he lies somewhat outside their typical scope, he is seen as a useful and creatively enriching dialogue partner.[181] Such discursive practices can generate new space for possibility through speaking. Such speaking is not unlike dialogue but is broader in scope and less formal in process and structures.[182] This may take place as theological or ethical reflection "on the ground," but perhaps more importantly in this situation as building friendships and participant listening, observation, and reflection. In this, the above consideration of Hauerwas and John Paul Lederach can inform action.

Formation

Rather than contributing solely to a theoretical framework, a natural way for Hauerwas to advance the formation of foreign-policy considerations is through the formation of the people, particularly Christians, who work in this field. The sections below will consider formation through theology in the training of practitioners generally, of Christians, and of the church as a whole. While such formation may be seen by some as too focused on the individual, changing the system requires, at least in part a convincing of individuals or particular groups to address a particular set of legal, institutional, cultural, or political parameters. Such work is certainly complex and lodged in many places, even permeating throughout the entirety of society. However, such changes are made by particular

---

a total rejection of transformative agendas. That may even be to imbibe precisely the sort of (Reinhold) Niebuhrian dichotomy between effectiveness and fidelity that Yoder deconstructs."

180. Hauerwas may be too narrow in his stated appreciation for various approaches. In challenging particular habits that he observes in American Christians, Hauerwas at times speaks in ways that undercut his peaceable witness. I believe this is in part because, although he is in a position of power, he sees himself as an outsider.

181. Martens asks if the widely divergent uses of Yoder are really "rooted in Yoder's corpus." Martens, "Universal History and a Not-Particularly Christian Particularity," 131.

182. See Huebner, *Precarious Peace*, 109–10.

individuals. Part of the work of advocacy and/or internal policy or systems change is both identifying and engaging at strategic points as well as building one's or one's organization's capacity to change gain power at those points. Because of this, formation and particular skills are needed for the policy actors to respond in a particular way. For my purpose here, this means in analysis and response in the case of religious dynamics in foreign policy.

Theology in Training—Implications for Training Policy Workers

Could theology then act as training material for Foreign Service officers or international relations practitioners and theorists? Such individuals are increasingly receiving training in religions and cultures.[183] Hauerwas has consistently considered that the role of theology and liturgy in shaping the Christian is to teach the person to "speak Christian." To properly speak, one must struggle to learn, enact, and inhabit the particular language world. To learn about another religion or tradition within Christianity, one must discuss particulars with the other, rather than assume a universal experience or commonalities beforehand. Given his assertion that it takes a lifetime to learn to speak thusly, Hauerwas would doubt that a course in the theology of multiple religions would take the student very far. However, beginning to learn to inhabit the theological language is, nonetheless, important. In an essay that was originally an address to a graduating seminary class, Hauerwas writes, "For what you have learned to do in seminary is read. By learning to read you have learned to speak Christian."[184] Hauerwas's notions of witness and mission alongside Yoder

---

183. Though such training is taking place more frequently now, in 2005, Thomas Farr could write, "Often part of a secular elite that earnestly desires the privatization of religion, our diplomats are further handicapped by the absence of systematic training or any strategic context for discussing religion." Farr, "Public Religion, Democracy Promotion, and U.S. Foreign Policy," 469–70.

184. "That you have learned to read and speak means you have been formed in a manner to avoid the pitfalls I have associated with contemporary ministry. For I want to suggest to you that one of the essential tasks of those called to the ministry in our day is to be a teacher. I hope to convince you if you so understand your task you will discover that you have your work cut out for you. But this is very good news because now you clearly have something to do . . . To learn to be a Christian, to learn the discipline of the faith, is not just similar to learning another language. It *is* learning another language." Hauerwas, *Working With Words*, 86, 87.

on exile and ecumenical and interfaith interaction may help us take a critical step. On Yoder, Bourne writes,

> The life of diaspora citizenship, says Yoder, is one of "cosmopolitan homelessness." In many ways this correlates with the arguments for the prophetic nature of immanent criticism we encountered at the outset of our discussion. Yet the "cosmopolitan" focus of Yoder's view, I suggest, highlights a level of constructive involvement and diverse levels of engagement that is missing from philosophical invocations of the exilic nature of criticism, which often correlate "exile" solely with detachment or postmodern flux. The recounting of missionary encounters . . . can now be placed within the wider context of continuing exilic presence. The missionary challenge to sing the song of the Lord in a foreign land led the Jews to become polyglots—to maintain loyalty to their own culture while learning the languages of Babylon and participating creatively within the city of exile.[185]

Much of humanity regularly understands events theologically or religiously (or at least heavily infuses their interpretation of events in this manner).[186] Despite this immense influence, religion seems to be often excluded from consideration as an "actual" factor that needs to be taken into account by many US foreign-policy practitioners and analysts or in grossly simplistic ways usually to the effect that being Muslim equals being a terrorist. To learn to read events theologically, while *theoretically* useful, seems to be *practically* implausible. In the US Congress, for example, staff members often cover multiple topic and regional areas. In *Congress and the Shaping of the Middle East*, it is noted that of the

---

185. Bourne, *Seek the Peace of the City*, 235. "That David Burrell has been drawn into the lives of Jews and Muslims is not because he is cosmopolitan. Rather he has been drawn into the lives of Jews and Muslims because he is a Catholic. He exemplifies Yoder's contention that the closer we are drawn to Jesus the closer we must be drawn to those who do not pray as Christians do to the Father, Son, and Holy Spirit. But Burrell has learned that Jews and Muslims recognize in Christians who pray something of their own lives. In that recognition, moreover, is any hope that we are not doomed to reject one another from fear." Hauerwas, "End of Religious Pluralism," 293.

186. One of the challenges with this assertion is that it appears that many groups blatantly use religious language and framing to justify the actions that they want to do for other reasons. This is often claimed for Boko Haram in northeastern Nigeria. Less significantly but still notable is that within the first five hours in Nigeria in November 2016, two different government workers hinted that they were giving me preferential treatment because I was Christian.

staff covering the Middle East and/or Israel-Palestine, few had even a single university course in these areas.[187] Additionally, many of these staff members are relatively recent university graduates. In this space, the proposal that these people gain a theologically nuanced understanding of the populations' understanding of the political process, policy, and situation seems farfetched. Likewise, to simply and crudely add a "religious component" to analysis may be either unhelpful or, in fact, negatively influence both accuracy and policy guidance. Because of this speed of events, formation through theology *prior* to the point of decision is necessary. Here, Hauerwas's assertion that theology is both a credible and necessary discipline within the university is particularly important.[188] It is not that theology should be the *dominant* discipline but that it stands as an important sphere of knowledge and argumentation beyond those training to be clergy or theologians. Additionally, Hauerwas's belief, shared with John Milbank, that the sharp division between disciplines undermines knowledge is pertinent.[189] Reading only politics, or US politics, or *only* any other disciplines reduces the ability to work creatively. Additionally, since our ability to read and comprehend is limited, we must build networks across academic and professional disciplines as well as across the range of other communities. This is in part a critique of those (such as myself) inside the Washington belt-way. Insular communities are easily limited in their ability to think beyond themselves.

Formation of Christian Foreign Policy Practitioners

In chapter 3, I considered the role of formation within Hauerwas's writing. There are many Christians or others with a church connection in foreign-policy positions. As such, if the church were to become more formative in Christians' lives, then theology could play a more significant role in foreign policy.[190] Of course, these individuals function within a system

---

187. "Only an extremely small number had a background in the arcane politics of the Middle East. I asked all of my interviewees if they had studied the Middle East, and a strong majority—64 percent—had never taken a single course in Mideast politics. Those who had studied the Middle East had usually only taken just one course." Beattie, *Congress and the Shaping of the Middle East*, 110.

188. See especially Hauerwas, "Theological Knowledge and the Knowledges of the University," 12–32.

189. Milbank, "Conflict of the Faculties," 39–57.

190. Of course, many politicians and varieties of government workers would

and as such the greater formation will not *necessarily* quickly or radically shift outcomes. The formation of Christian lives in the church is one of Hauerwas's main concerns; but stated in this manner it sounds more parochial or self-righteous than Hauerwas intends it to. A variation of the role of faith is often said to be in play when political leaders assert the formative role of spirituality or faith formation in their impulse toward civil service and concern for the problems of the world. At least in the US, this is a common refrain of those seeking election or reflecting on their motivation for the work. Kelly Brown Douglas describes how African American leaders have taken on the religious assumptions of Christianity and American piety. She demonstrates how speakers such as Frederick Douglas and Martin Luther King Jr. turned American exceptionalism back on itself to challenge injustice.[191] Using American exceptionalism carries certain risks. It can be used as a genuine belief or can simply be a tactic. To fight for belonging is understandable but the militarism and imperialism of US foreign policy is not a neutral phenomenon. Hauerwas focuses on the common assumptions of American exceptionalism. The qualification of loyalty to the nation-state is a common refrain in Hauerwas. While to some this sounds sectarian, Hauerwas rightly asserts that the nation-state with its limited boundaries and concerns is the truly sectarian entity.

Formation of Churches Which Then Engage and Resist

Hauerwas's work can help churches build a critique of war and strengthen efforts to resist it, as well as learn how to resist retaliation and participation in armed struggle in communities caught in violence. Such community or intranational violent conflict is not strictly an issue of foreign policy (unless it is deemed to need a response from the international

---

already claim this to be the case. Despite this, Hauerwas challenges the American church, saying things like "If your church celebrates Thanksgiving your salvation is in question." In seeking to challenge the acquiescence of the church to the state, Hauerwas becomes overly committed to a particular assessment of the condition of the church (as if there is a unified experience). His point is often to challenge our notion that there is a significant difference between liberal and conservative churches in America. While it may be true that both streams (as if there were only two) are determined by the assumptions of modernity, such a blanket critique by Hauerwas puts into question his affirmation of particularity.

191. Douglas, *Stand Your Ground*, 210–20.

community).[192] However, drawing a sharp division between intranational or international violent conflict is relatively arbitrary and does not fit with the present focus on church engagement with such conflicts. In *War and Conflict in Africa*, Paul Williams describes part of this challenge of definition: "First, the problem of *definition*: What, exactly, should analysts be counting—wars, major/minor armed conflicts, battles, massacres, banditry, riots, demonstrations, or all of these things? In sum, what types of events should be taken as indicators of armed conflict, as opposed to, say, criminal acts and individual homicides?"[193] Though communities are less involved in foreign-policy discussions in the capital,[194] decisions in capitals certainly have implications for them. Additionally, many relevant areas of definition remain ambiguous. For example, how does one define "international" and "foreign," the implications and spillover effects of intrastate conflicts, or the suspect distinction between conflicts of the nation-state and other conflicts, communities, and the relationship to peacebuilding and violence. All of these are, at a minimum, relevant for such a conversation.

In communities living with violence, peacemaking must be articulated as an integral facet of faith and practice. In this, I am thinking particularly of my work with Ekklesiyar Yan'uwa a Nigeria (Church of the Brethren) in northeast Nigeria, but also of newly forming Church of the Brethren congregations in the Democratic Republic of the Congo. I have also experienced this in evangelical Church of the Brethren congregations in the US where for cultural and political reasons, "peace" is sometimes viewed with suspicion, even though the Church of the Brethren is a historic peace church. If peace is seen as a side project (in contrast to

---

192. For a consideration of protection and global governance, see Ferris, *Politics of Protection*, 126–73.

193. Williams, *War and Conflict in Africa*, 15. Such an issue arose in 2016 in the Nigeria Working Group I convene. There was disagreement about how to discuss the steep rise in violent deaths in the Middle Belt of Nigeria between Fulani herders and farmers. Both groups acknowledged reasonably substantiated external support for violent conflict, stealing cattle, and conflict over grazing and farming rights. One group called this activity militancy (which would imply intent beyond monetary) and the other asserted it was simply banditry and only (or at least primarily) about resources. Incidentally, both groups asserted that religion was a component in this escalation.

194 With the rise of various actors in civil society there are more ways that communities can be directly engaged. At the same time there are more questions being raised about the professionalization of bureaucracies and "activist" fields (such as peacebuilding) such that "normal" citizens are isolated from genuine participation.

Hauerwas's view[195]) or an external political program, it will be more likely to be set aside or abandoned when funding is cut or conflict gets too hot. In a conversation with a colleague who works with international NGOs he asked if the escalation of violence in northeast Nigeria was frustrating given my work in that context. In his experience, much peace-related work is shorter term rather than an integral piece of a large community's identity. In this shorter-term project engagement, violence is a failure of a program, whereas for my work and the church it is distressing because of the relationship rather than frustrating. Obviously having peace as part of an identity is not universal even within a specific group, and the efforts for peace remain quite difficult, but the resiliency of the commitment is arguably greater in such groups.

While I imagine Hauerwas would have little interest in engaging the theoretical debate about the analysis of religion in social science generally or the study of conflict in particular,[196] he has consistently urged Christians to act in public *as Christians*.[197] Arguing for this explicit inclusion does not necessarily mean that he seeks to aggressively dominate public discursive space but that he seeks to resist forms of nation-state hegemony.

Much of the deciding/discerning process that has been described above happens in the context of churches or government. Since this is a relatively flexible process and it is situation specific, to give a general example of this is difficult. This also happens introspectively for an

---

195. Hauerwas writes, "I am a Christian. I am a pacifist. Being Christian and pacifist are not two things for me." Hauerwas, "September 11, 2001," 121.

196. In *Theology and Social Theory*, Milbank asserts that theology is a legitimate knowledge. Hauerwas also works within a variation of this assumption. This is not however, the analysis of religion within social science. Often such analysis is conducted out of detached curiosity or a desire to harness the impulse of religion for a particular end. The consistent attempt to force an outcome, which Hauerwas says is at the root of our tendency to resort to violence, also plays out in the manner of speaking. He writes, "But then the ministry, like a commitment to nonviolence, does not promise success. For as Yoder reminds us, "Jesus did not promise his followers they would conquer within time if they did things right. Rather the love that refuses to achieve the good through the disavowal of violence, the refusal to use mechanical models of cause and effect to force history to move in what is assumed to be the right direction, means the promise of victory can only be found in the resurrection. Victory, moreover, means for those in ministry the willingness to do the same thing over and over again in the hope that by doing so the Christian people can speak truthfully to one another and the world." Yoder, *Working with Words*, 92.

197. Hauerwas, "Nonviolent Terrorist," 177–90.

organization or individual and at times a strategic compromise is embraced. For example, the Church of the Brethren in the US decided to apply for grants from the US government in order to support our humanitarian relief work with the Church of the Brethren in Nigeria during the height of the Boko Haram insurgency. This was a conscience decision to break with standard practice which kept a distance between the church and such government funds. The need to resist the militarism of the nation-state and the potential that receiving funds would compromise this ability as well as a historic distancing from the government lay behind this policy.

Emmanuel Katongole's *The Sacrifice of Africa: A Political Theology for Africa* is an important text for considering the ability of the church to resist violence. In this work, as well as in *Mirror to the Church: Resurrecting Faith after Genocide in Rwanda*, Katongole does an exemplary job of articulating social ethics in the vein of Hauerwas in particular contexts. Hauerwas has asserted that reading such descriptions trains individuals to rightly discern or read the world. He typically frames this as a theological task but it also applies to the practical theological task of religious peacemaking, and to the broader practice of peacebuilding as well. Since Hauerwas remains removed from analysis directly applicable to international relations and foreign-policy deliberations, and Katongole has been a student of Hauerwas, I will take a closer look at Katongole's work as a practical example of what Hauerwas's work suggests. I take Katongole to be carrying on and extending Hauerwas's work; as such, I use it to examine the potential implications of Hauerwas's work as well as to illustrate the potential of Hauerwas's work.

Katongole starts by asking why it is that though Christianity is thriving in Africa and there is a renewed interest in social ethics, these ethics do not explain why war, tribalism, poverty, corruption, and violence have been endemic in Africa's social history.[198] From here he launches in a very Hauerwasian way into challenging the primacy of the nation-state and the assumption that if Christianity is to prove useful it must contribute to making it the state work better.[199] He goes so far as to say, "These recom-

---

198. Katongole, *Sacrifice of Africa*, 1.

199. In my community of faith-based organizations working to change policy in DC, the desire "to make the state work better" is, at least for the most part, based in the desire to care for communities that suffer from bad policy. The effort to make better policy is then not necessarily tied to a hope for a better state in the abstract but for a state that better servers all, particularly those typically marginalized. I recognize that

mendations do not pay sufficient attention to the possibility that politics in Africa, and the nation-state in particular, have not been a failure, but have worked very well."[200] In this, he asserts that what is seen as dysfunction in the nation-state in Africa is in fact exactly what such a political system requires.

He further explores the use of narrative in such a project, which again is in line with Hauerwas. As he states, "Stories not only shape our values, aims, and goals; they define the range of what is desirable and what is possible. Stories, therefore, are not simply fictional narratives meant for our entertainment; stories are part of our social ecology."[201] He goes on to assert that the name of Africa, then, names a set of narratives and stories. This description is not simply a neutral and value-free. He asserts that Christian ethics must "shift its exclusive focus on strategies for fixing the structures of democracy and development and get into the business of stories."[202] Politics is the performance of stories.[203] On a high (perhaps abstract) level this makes sense. The system may be so bent on maintaining the status quo that it must fundamentally be challenged in order to get somewhere better. However, in the meantime small and often rather mundane policy decisions can wreak havoc or make marginal (sometimes substantial) improvements. These policy decisions may fit within the larger or overarching story of a particular nation-state or region but are also part of stories of institutions or individual policy makers or implementers. As a church worker tasked with shifting policy, I continually use stories or parts of stories to change the understanding of the impacts of the policy, action, or lack of action. This is both where I agree and disagree with Katongole. The strategies for change are a series of arguments and stories, embodied and spoken which move government action. By way of example: If I meet someone from the State Department that I do not already know, but who I think it would be important to know, I will tell as series of stories or allude to stories which will hopefully make this connection of interest to them. I will describe our church's engagement in their issue or region of focus, tell about my personal work in relation to this, reference one of their colleagues whom I have met with, and/or tell

---

this does not disprove Katongole's point but I highlight it because this type of perception arises regularly from those observing from outside policy engagement.

200. Katongole, *Sacrifice of Africa*, 2.
201. Katongole, *Sacrifice of Africa*, 2.
202. Katongole, *Sacrifice of Africa*, 3.
203. Katongole, *Sacrifice of Africa*, 3.

about my office's engagement with a particular ecumenical, interfaith, or NGO coalition. All of this will be to both gain credibility (for the purpose of influencing an action) as well has make an argument why a particular policy or mode of engagement should or should not be pursued. Even so called "abstract" principles or values that may be referenced are in someway story contingent. According to Katongole, "The challenge is not so much one of being 'saved from' the realities of nation-state politics in Africa, but having resources and skills to engage that politics from a more determinative account of reality."[204] Such an account is most obviously relevant for those who identify as Christians or are otherwise moved in some way by the claims of Christian social ethics or a political theology. One might then argue that Katongole or Hauerwas still would be limited to seeking to shape the lives of Christians even if these Christians are engaged in public issues or working in the public sphere. While this would not be incorrect *per se*, it assumes that various spheres of ethics, Christian social ethics, for example, or Muslim social ethics, or, simply, social ethics, are isolated discourses. In this view, the social ethics of the nation-state is theologically neutral. However, as many critiques have shown, such neutrality is an illusion. So, if it is an illusion and all ethics are indeed theological, and the theological social ethics of national religion do not have unquestioned prominence, then Christian social ethics (as well as many others) may join the fray of foreign-policy formation and politics. Of course, this assertion is complicated in the US and many other countries by the broad assumption that the national religion that formed its social ethic is in fact Christian. In this, the conflation of Christianity with a national civil religion is a notable danger.

Both Katongole and Hauerwas seek to help the church be more capable of both resisting violence and challenging the narrative of the nation-state. Katongole writes, "I kept wondering whether Christianity in Africa had become so interwoven into the story of violence that it no longer had a vantage point from which to resist violence."[205] This parallels Hauerwas's attempt to challenge the militarism and assumptions of the American exceptionalism of American Christianity.[206] Katongole calls this an "imaginative landscape" and "script" which institutions and the

204. Katongole, *Sacrifice of Africa*, 4.
205. Katongole, *Sacrifice of Africa*, 9.
206. "Since violence is reflected in the very way that we think about thinking, it follows that peace must name a simultaneous counter-politics and counter-epistemology that radically shifts the terms of the debate." Huebner, *Precarious Peace*, 116.

church perform unwittingly.²⁰⁷ In this he seeks to challenge the assumptions of the narrative categories we assume and the ways these assumptions dictate channels of policy recommendations. Additionally, they both seek primarily to shape the way that Christians or the church engage in social ethics or theology rather than in a broader arena of policy formation.

Though I will not reiterate chapter 3's discussion of formation in Hauerwas, I will note that it challenges deeply engrained habits, and that these habits are often displayed in speech. In "Speaking Christian" in *Working with Words*, he challenges the omission of the name of Jesus during a prayer for the more ambiguous "god." He cites examples of this occurring with a military chaplain who was teaching ethics and a Methodist clergyperson who spoke of Jesus as a "way to God" rather than as the second person in the Trinity. In his framing, peace, for the Christian, is always linked with or qualified by Jesus. Does this necessity undermine the possibility to engage outside the church? Though Hauerwas's aim at reforming the church and its speech may be particular with a tendency toward exclusivity,²⁰⁸ he consistently challenges the possibility of a clean division between religion and politics.²⁰⁹

Given his effort to re-theologize the church in public life and the centrality of nonviolence in his work, Hauerwas's writing is a valuable resource for the church resisting war but could also be more constructively engaged in religion and peacebuilding in relation to US foreign policy.

---

207. Katongole, *Sacrifice of Africa*, 9.

208. Hauerwas challenges words of critique or praise such as exclusivity as politically ideological words that are not adequately theological for Christians.

209. In *Migrations of the Holy*, Cavanaugh asserts that religious meaning still exists; it has simply migrated to the state. If, like Cavanaugh and Taylor, we do not assume a division between the secular and religious, then these are not separate spheres. Davis asserts that theology is forcefully returning: "If the theological was marginalized in the age of Western secular modernity, it has now returned with a vengeance. Theology is reconfiguring the very makeup of the humanities in general, with disciplines like philosophy, political science, literature, history, psychoanalysis, and critical theory, in particular, feeling the impact of this return." Davis, "Introduction," 3.

Douglas Johnston of the International Center for Religion and Diplomacy writes, "The divisive influence of religion has long been recognized. Its more helpful aspects have not. In the West, this is largely the result of over two hundred years of post-Enlightenment prejudice." Johnston, "Religion and Foreign Policy." Challenging this division could, however, mean an attempt for a particular religion or subset of a religion to rule as a theocracy. It could also raise some issues in line with Yoder's nonviolent epistemology. See Barber, "Epistemological Violence, Christianity, and the Secular."

His work can develop the skills for resistance and also describe in a theologically substantive way how churches, and perhaps other religious groups, may think about a particular conflict.[210] For those outside religious communities, these descriptions of actions derived from theology and religion are often not evident. This has been my experience working in advocacy, policy, analysis, and peacebuilding regarding the Boko Haram insurgency and the resultant crisis of internally displaced persons and refugees. Though I will not assess presently how this situation should be viewed, I note that analysts often seem to question that a group may actually be acting on religious conviction (even if they misunderstand the tenets of that particular religion).[211]

As I discussed at the end of chapter 4, witness and critique can be a form of resistance, which can be a form of peacemaking. It has often been noted that peace is more than the absence of violence, war, or conflict. If people want a lasting peace, they must not simply seek a cessation of the bad, but work to build the good. This focus of peacebuilding, while correct, may distract from the "no" to war or violence. Given the prevalence of war and violence, the massive investment by US military contractors to convince policy makers to use military means, the ubiquity of violence in media, and national militaristic liturgies that shape public consciousness, it is not enough to build capacity for peacebuilding. There must be an active resistance against the use of force. This realization is particularly poignant in the face of the "global war on terror" and open-ended US legislation such as the 2001 Authorization of Use of Military Force (AUMF) which grants enormous leeway for use of lethal force. In this space, dominating voices shape the discourse about what is deemed possible. To stake a claim outside the dominant narrative may open greater space or isolate the alleged radical. As such, principles must stand in tension with tactics, though the process of setting aside theological ethical commitments for the sake of strategy is fraught with peril.

One challenge is to consider what such engagement entails. If the purpose is to analyze religious actors so that the state may advance its objectives militarily, then assistance will likely prove problematic. Such a

---

210. This is still at some remove from US foreign policy.

211. There is a strong stream of Christian activism in the United States that advocates rather one-sidedly for Christians at the exclusion of others in the international sphere. This, along with US military adventures and the myth of the United States as a Christian nation, lead many (including at times myself) to feel queasy about the inclusion of religion or religious actors.

process may, however, help a church receive funds from the state or from another nongovernmental agency. A risk would be, this could mean or not mean that the state could control or manipulate criticism of its policies by this particular church. Many of these questions, at least in part, relate not to the state being "the" state but a bureaucracy engaged through an enormous conglomeration of not fully agreeing nor fully dissenting bureaucrats, policy advisors, and programmatic staff. So, while "the state" as a concept is useful at some level, pragmatically, even official staff and elected officials are much more diverse and diffuse. Even within the relatively limited (given the entirety of the government structures) realm of the US Department of State, the coordination and alignment of views is relatively limited on certain issues or regions.

This may point to the need to "just get on with it." Christians (and those of other faiths) have always worked in foreign-policy institutions. These Christians, however, have generally not worked in these capacities *because* they were theologians or ministers, but because they possessed useful knowledge, skill, or experience. On the topic of American foreign-policy understanding of the Middle East in the early 1980s, Bacevich notes, "But among those paid to think about strategy, soldiers and civilians alike, history and religion counted for little. In the wake of World War II, in large part due to the primacy assigned to nuclear issues, economists, mathematicians, political scientists, and specialists in game theory had come to exercise an outsized influence in framing the debate over basic national security policy. On matters where so little history existed, historians seemingly had little to offer and could therefore be safely ignored. As for theologians, with rare exceptions, they were excluded altogether. National security was a thoroughly secular enterprise." He then footnotes the following, "Reinhold Niebuhr was the obvious exception, but the impact of his views in policymaking circles did not extend much beyond providing moral justifications for actions policymakers were already inclined to make."[212] Policy formation that draws on strategic, analytic, public relations, and ethical considerations, even when not explicit, would seem, in Bacevich's view, to benefit from the inclusion of theologians *as theologians*. Additionally, these employees were able to hold their jobs because they could keep their theology private or their department was adequately "colonized" by one strain of religion so as to maintain a particular hegemony.

---

212. Bacevich, *America's War for the Greater Middle East*, 48–49.

Such "getting on with it" is a variation of the "critical pragmatism" that I briefly laid out in my master's thesis.[213] Though foreign-policy practitioners, advocates, and peacebuilders need not become professional theologians, an engagement with texts allows at least a brief immersion into worlds of thought and questions that stretch perceptions. Hauerwas's method of practical reasoning, rather than a grand strategy, allows for criticism and dialogic engagement without fully buying into the assumption that this is the main work of the church, the state's mythology and totalizing tendencies, or abstract theories of justice. Instead, Hauerwas states,

> As Christians we will best serve God and our neighbor by seeking to form common life in the world as we find it. That may well mean we must attempt to develop institutions, such as the university, that make it possible to engage in the kind of exchanges MacIntyre thinks necessary for the development of practical reason. What we cannot fear or repress in the name of peace is conflict. Christians, particularly Christians in diaspora, owe one another as well as their neighbor truthful judgments that come only by have our convictions exposed to those who do not share them.[214]

Christians, then, enter the conflict (which in this case is foreign-policy formation) through the church's work or through direct participation. This space, though fragmented, is the location of evolving work, which is not free of ambiguity but remains open as a space of necessary peacemaking. By "evolving" and "ambiguity" I indicate that the risks and possibilities are ever-present and changing. The risks require a community posture of discernment. This is not simply a hand-wringing anxiety or detachment to maintain theological and ethical purity, but it also is not an easy dismissal of the ways that Christian ethics challenge the nation-state. Church, as an institution, takes up political, rhetorical, and geographic space.

Conclusion

In this chapter, I explored ways in which Hauerwas's work in ecclesiology and peace creates the space in which he could move more substantially

---

213. Hosler, "Blessed Are the Peacemakers," 17–20.
214. Hauerwas, *War and the American Difference*, 146.

into particular practices of realms of peacemaking but does not. His work on concrete practices and the strong assertion on the centrality of nonviolence to the Christian understanding of Jesus make peacemaking in these settings a natural step. I argued that the work of Stanley Hauerwas, particularly on ecclesiology, nonviolence, peace, and peacemaking, can be usefully extended to connect literature on peacebuilding, religion in US foreign-policy considerations, and issues of racial justice.

Bibliography

Ager, Alastair, and Joey Ager. "Challenging the Discourse on Religion, Secularism and Displacement." In *The Refugee Crisis and Religion: Secularism, Security and Hospitality in Question*, edited by Luca Mavelli and Erin Wilson, 37–51. London: Rowman and Littlefield, 2017.

Ahn, Ilsup. "The U.S. Immigration Crisis and a Call for the Church's Lifeworld Politics: Why Should Hauerwas Collaborate with Habermas on the U.S. Immigration Crisis?" *Crosscurrents* (September 2014) 319–45.

Albrecht, Gloria. *The Character of Our Communities: Toward an Ethic of Liberation for the Church*. Nashville: Abingdon, 1995.

Alexander, Michelle. *The New Jim Crow: Mass Incarceration in the Age of Colorblindness*. New York: New Press, 2012.

Alexis-Baker, Nekeisha. "Freedom of the Cross: John Howard Yoder and Womanist Theologies." In *Power and Practices: Engaging the Work of John Howard Yoder*, edited by Jeremy M. Bergen and Anthony G. Siegrist, 83–97. Waterloo, ON: Herald, 2009.

Anderson, Benedict. *Imagined Communities: Reflections on the Origin and Spread of Nationalism*. Rev. ed. London: Verso, 2006.

Baan, Ariaan. "Stanley Hauerwas and the Necessity of Witness." *Zeitschrift fur Dialektische Theologie* 29.59 (2013) 34–49.

Bacevich, Andrew J. *America's War for the Greater Middle East: A Military History*. New York: Random House, 2016.

"Baptism, Eucharist and Ministry (Faith and Order Paper no. 111, the "Lima Text)." https://www.oikoumene.org/en/resources/documents/commissions/faith-and-order/i-unity-the-church-and-its-mission/baptism-eucharist-and-ministry-faith-and-order-paper-no-111-the-lima-text.

Barber, Daniel Colucciello. "Epistemological Violence, Christianity, and the Secular." In *The New Yoder*, edited by Peter Dula and Chris K. Huebner, 271–93. Eugene, OR: Cascade, 2010.

Baxter, Michael. "The Church as *Polis*? Second Thoughts on Theological Politics." In *Unsettling Arguments: A Festschrift on the Occasion of Stanley Hauerwas's 70th Birthday*, edited by Charles R. Pinches et al., 132–50. Eugene, OR: Cascade, 2010.

Beattie, Kirk J. *Congress and the Shaping of the Middle East*. New York: Seven Stories, 2015.

Bell, Daniel. "Jesus, the Jews, and the Politics of God's Justice." *Ex Auditu* 22 (2006) 87–111.

———. *Just War as Christian Discipleship: Recentering the Tradition in the Church Rather than the State*. Grand Rapids: Brazos, 2009.

Bender, Harold S. *The Anabaptist Vision*. Scottdale: Herald, 1960.

Bennett, Jana Marguerite. "Being 'Stuck' between Stanley and the Feminists: The Proverbial Rock and a Hard Place." In *Unsettling Arguments: A Festschrift on the Occasion of Stanley Hauerwas's 70th Birthday*, edited by Charles R. Pinches et al., 229–45. Eugene, OR: Cascade, 2010.

Biesecker-Mast, Gerald. *Separation and the Sword in Anabaptist Persuasion: Radical Confessional Rhetoric from Schleitheim to Dordrecht*. Telford, PA: Cascadia, 2006.

Biggar, Nigel. "Is Stanley Hauerwas Sectarian?" In *Faithfulness and Fortitude: In Conversation with the Theological Ethics of Stanley Hauerwas*, edited by Mark Thiessen Nation and Samuel Wells, 141–60. Edinburgh: T. & T. Clark, 2000.

Boersma, Hans. "Realizing Pleasant Grove: The Real Presence of the Eschaton in the Life of Stanley Hauerwas." *Modern Theology* 28.2 (April 2012) 308–14.

Bonhoeffer, Dietrich. *Ethics*. New York: Simon & Schuster, 1995.

Bourne, Richard. "Governmentality, Witness, and the State: Christian Social Criticism with and Beyond Yoder and Foucault." In *Power and Practices: Engaging the Work of John Howard Yoder*, edited by Jeremy M. Bergen and Anthony G. Siegrist, 99–115. Waterloo, Ontario: Herald, 2009.

———. *Seek the Peace of the City: Christian Political Criticism as Public, Realist, and Transformative*. Eugene, OR: Cascade, 2009.

Bowman, Carl F. *Brethren Society: The Cultural Transformation of a "Peculiar People."* Baltimore: Johns Hopkins University Press, 1995.

Boyd, Gregory A. *Crucifixion of the Warrior God: Interpreting the Old Testament's Violent Portraits of God in Light of the Cross*. 2 vols. Minneapolis: Fortress, 2017.

———. "The Cruciform Hermeneutic." In *Crucifixion of the Warrior God: Interpreting the Old Testament's Violent Portraits of God in Light of the Cross*, 1:417–552. Minneapolis: Fortress, 2017.

The Brethren Encyclopedia. 3 vols. Philadelphia: Brethren Encyclopedia, 1983–84.

Brubaker, Sarah Morice. "*The Work of Theology*, by Stanley Hauerwas." *The Christian Century*, September 30, 2015. https://www.christiancentury.org/reviews/2015-09/work-theology-stanley-hauerwas.

Budde, Michael. "Collecting Praise: Global Cultural Industries." In *The Blackwell Companion to Christian Ethics*, edited by Stanley Hauerwas and Samuel Wells, 123–38. Malden: Blackwell, 2004.

Cahill, Lisa Sowle. *Love Your Enemies: Discipleship, Pacifism, and Just War Theory*. Minneapolis: Fortress, 1994.

Calivas, Alkiviadis C. "Experiencing the Justice of God in Liturgy." In *Violence and Christian Spirituality: An Ecumenical Conversation*, edited by Emmanuel Clapsis, 287–98. Geneva: WCC, 2007.

Cannon, Katie G. *Black Womanist Ethics*. Atlanta: Scholars, 1988.

Cannon, Mae Elise. "Mischief Making in Palestine: American Protestant Christian Attitudes Toward the Holy Land, 1917–1949." *Cultural Encounters* 7.1 (2011) 49–66.

Carter, Craig A. *Politics of the Cross: The Theology of the Social Ethics of John Howard Yoder*. Grand Rapids: Brazos, 2001.

Carter, J. Kameron. *Race: A Theological Account*. Oxford: Oxford University, 2008.

Cavanaugh, William T. "Church." In *The Blackwell Companion to Political Theology*, edited by Peter Scott and William T. Cavanaugh, 393–406. Malden: Blackwell, 2004.

———. "Discerning: Politics and Reconciliation." In *The Blackwell Companion to Christian Ethics*, edited by Stanley Hauerwas and Samuel Wells, 196–208. Malden: Blackwell, 2004.

———. *Migrations of the Holy: God, State, and the Political Meaning of the Church*. Grand Rapids: Eerdmans, 2011.

———. *The Myth of Religious Violence: Secular Ideology and the Roots of Modern Conflict*. Oxford: Oxford University Press, 2009.

———. "A Politics of Vulnerability: Hauerwas and Democracy." In *Unsettling Arguments: A Festschrift on the Occasion of Stanley Hauerwas's 70th Birthday*, edited by Charles R. Pinches et al., 89–111. Eugene, OR: Cascade, 2010.

———. *Theopolitical Imagination: Discovering the Liturgy as a Political Act in an Age of Global Consumerism*. London: T. & T. Clark, 2011.

Chamayou, Grégoire. *A Theory of the Drone*. Translated by Janet Lloyd. New York: New Press, 2013.

Charles, Mark. "Transcript of Homily at Call to Action 2016—Lamenting the Mythology of a Christian Empire." *Wirelesshogan* (blog), November 13, 2016. http://wirelesshogan.blogspot.com/2016/.

Cheng, Patrick S. *Rainbow Theology: Bridging Race, Sexuality, and Spirit*. New York: Seabury, 2013.

"Church of the Brethren." http://www.brethren.org/about/statements/2013-resolution-against-drones.pdf.

Cjka, Mary Ann, and Thomas Bamat, eds. *Artisans for Peace: Grassroots Peacemaking Among Christian Communities*. Maryknoll: Orbis, 2003.

Coleman, Monica A. *Making a Way Out of No Way: A Womanist Theology*. Minneapolis: Fortress, 2008.

Collier, Charles M., ed. *The Difference Christ Makes: Celebrating the Life, Work, and Friendship of Stanley Hauerwas*. Eugene, OR: Cascade, 2015.

Cone, James H. *A Black Theology of Liberation*. 20th anniversary ed. Maryknoll: Orbis, 1986.

———. *The Cross and the Lynching Tree*. New York: Orbis, 2011.

———. *Said I Wasn't Gonna Tell Nobody*. New York: Orbis, 2018.

Conley, Aaron D. "Loosening the Grip of Certainty: A Case-Study Critique of Tertullian, Stanley Hauerwas, and Christian Identity." *Journal of the Society of Christian Ethics* 33.1 (2013) 21–44.

Copeland, M. Shawn. *Enfleshing Freedom: Body, Race, and Being*. Minneapolis: Fortress, 2010.

Davis, Creston. "Introduction: Holy Saturday or Resurrection Sunday? Staging an Unlikely Debate." In *The Monstrosity of Christ: Paradox or Dialectic?*, edited by Creston Davis, 2–23. Cambridge: MIT Press, 2009.

Dean, Robert. "Unapologetically (A)Political: Stanley Hauerwas and the Practice of Preaching." *Didaskalia* (September 1, 2015) 131–38.

Deane, Herber A. "Augustine and the State: The Return of Order Upon Disorder." In *The City of God: A Collection of Critical Essays*, edited by Dorothy F. Donnelly, 51–73. New York: Lang, 1995.

De Gruchy, John W. "Democracy." In *The Blackwell Companion to Political Theology*, edited by Peter Scott and William T. Cavanaugh, 439–54. Malden: Blackwell, 2004.

DeJonge, Michael P. "Bonhoeffer's Non-Commitment to Nonviolence: A Response to Stanley Hauerwas." *Journal of Religious Ethics* 44.2 (2016) 378–94.

De La Torre, Miguel A. *Doing Christian Ethics from the Margins*. New York: Orbis, 2004.

DeYoung, Karen. "How the Obama White House Runs Foreign Policy." *The Washington Post*, August 4, 2015. https://www.washingtonpost.com/world/national-security/how-the-obama-white-house-runs-foreign-policy/2015/08/04/2befb960-2fd7-11e5-8353-1215475949f4_story.html?tid=sm_tw&utm_term=.e773480ff3d0.

DeYoung, Karen, and Craig Whitlock. "Rescue Mission for Yazidis on Iraq's Mount Sinjar Appears Unnecessary, Pentagon Says." *The Washington Post*, August 14, 2017. https://www.washingtonpost.com/world/national-security/2014/08/13/5fdd3358-2301-11e4-86ca-6f03cbd15c1a_story.html .

Doerksen, Paul G. "Share the House: Yoder and Hauerwas Among the Nations." In *A Mind Patient and Untamed: Assessing John Howard Yoder's Contributions to Theology, Ethics, and Peacemaking*, edited by Ben C. Ollenburger and Gayle Gerber Koontz, 187–204. Eugene, OR: Cascade, 2004.

Doerksen, Paul G., and Karl Koop. *The Church Made Strange for the Nations: Essays in Ecclesiology and Political Theology*. Eugene, OR: Pickwick, 2011.

Dorrien, Gary. *Economy, Difference, Empire: Social Ethics for Social Justice*. New York: Columbia University Press, 2010.

———. "Social Ethics in the Making." In *Economy, Difference, Empire: Social Ethics for Social Justice*, 393–409. New York: Columbia University Press, 2010.

Douglas, Kelly Brown. *Stand Your Ground: Black Bodies and the Justice of God*. New York: Orbis, 2015.

Dula, Peter. "Response." In *The Difference Christ Makes: Celebrating the Life, Work, and Friendship of Stanley Hauerwas*, edited by Charlie M. Collier, 71–76. Eugene, OR: Cascade, 2015.

———. "Wittgenstein among the Theologians." In *Unsettling Arguments: A Festschrift on the Occasion of Stanley Hauerwas's 70th Birthday*, edited by Charles R. Pinches et al., 3–24. Eugene, OR: Cascade, 2010.

Dula, Peter, and Chris K. Huebner, eds. *The New Yoder*. Eugene, OR: Cascade, 2010.

Durnbaugh, Donald F. *Fruit of the Vine: A History of the Brethren: 1708–1995*. Elgin, IL: Brethren, 1997.

Enns, Fernando, and Annette Mosher, eds. *Just Peace: Ecumenical, Intercultural, and Interdisciplinary Perspective*. Eugene, OR: Pickwick, 2013.

Estep, William R. *The Anabaptist Story: An Introduction to Sixteenth-Century Anabaptism*. 3rd ed. Grand Rapids: Eerdmans, 1996.

Farr, Thomas F. "Public Religion, Democracy Promotion, and U.S. Foreign Policy." In *Religion and Foreign Affairs: Essential Readings*, edited by Dennis R. Hoover and Douglas M. Johnston, 469–70. Waco: Baylor University Press, 2012.

Ferris, Elizabeth G. *The Politics of Protection: The Limits of Humanitarian Action*. Washington, DC: The Brookings Institute, 2011.

Finger, Thomas M. *A Contemporary Anabaptist Theology: Biblical, Historical, Constructive*. Downers Grove: InterVarsity, 2004.

———. "Did Yoder Reduce Theology to Ethics?" In *A Mind Patient and Untamed: Assessing John Howard Yoder's Contributions to Theology, Ethics, and Peacemaking*, edited by Ben C. Ollenburger and Gayle Gerber Koontz, 318–39. Eugene, OR: Cascade, 2004.

Fisher, Simon, et al., eds. *Working With Conflict: Skills and Strategies For Action.* London: Zed, 2000.

Fitzkee, Donald R. *Moving Toward the Mainstream: 20th Century Change Among the Brethren in Eastern Pennsylvania.* Intercourse: Good, 1995.

Fulkerson, Mary McClintock. "'They Will Know We Are Christian by Our Regulated Improvisation': Ecclesial Hybridity and the Unity of the Church." In *Blackwell Companion to Postmodern Theology*, edited by Graham Ward, 265–79. Oxford: Blackwell, 2001.

Gay, Douglas C. "A Practical Theology of Church and World: Ecclesiology and Social Vision in 20th Century Scotland." Unpublished PhD diss., University of Edinburgh, 2006.

Gener, Timoteo. "Christologies in Asia." In *Jesus Without Borders: Christology in the Majority World*, edited by Gene L. Green et al., 59–79. Grand Rapids: Eerdmans, 2014.

Gingerich, Mark. "The Church as Kingdom: The Kingdom of God in the Writings of Stanley Hauerwas and John Howard Yoder." *Didaskalia* (Winter 2008) 129–43.

Goossen, Rachel Waltner. "The Failure to Bind and Loose: Responses to Yoder's Sexual Abuse." *The Mennonite*, January 2, 2015. https://themennonite.org/feature/failure-bind-loose-responses-john-howard-yoders-sexual-abuse/.

Gossai, Hemchand. "Challenging the Empire: The Conscience of the Prophet and Prophetic Dissent from a Post-Colonial Perspective." In *Post-Colonial Interventions: Essays in Honor of R.S. Sugirtharajah*, edited by Tat-siong Benny Liew, 98–108. Sheffield: Sheffield Phoenix, 2009.

Granberg-Michaelson, Wesley. *From Times Square to Timbuktu: The Post-Christian West Meets the Non-Western Church.* Grand Rapids: Eerdmans, 2013.

Green, Gene L., et al., eds. *Jesus Without Borders: Christology in the Majority World.* Grand Rapids: Eerdmans, 2014.

Gutierrez, Gustavo. *A Theology of Liberation: History, Politics, and Salvation (15th Anniversary Edition).* New York: Orbis, 1988.

Hackett, Rosalind I. J. "Rethinking the Role of Religion in Changing Public Spheres: Some Comparative Perspectives." In *Religion and Foreign Affairs: Essential Readings*, edited by Dennis R. Hoover and Douglas M. Johnston, 53–64. Waco: Baylor University Press, 2012.

Hauerwas, Stanley. *After Christendom? How the Church is to Behave if Freedom, Justice, and a Christian Nation Are Bad Ideas.* Nashville: Abingdon, 1991.

———. *Against the Nations: War and Survival in a Liberal Society.* Minneapolis: Winston, 1985.

———. *Approaching the End: Eschatological Reflections on Church, Politics, and Life.* Grand Rapids: Eerdmans, 2013.

———. "Beyond the Boundaries." In *War and the American Difference: Theological Reflections on Violence and National Identity*, 167–81. Grand Rapids: Baker Academic, 2011.

———. "Character, Narrative, and Growth in Christian Life." In *A Community of Character: Toward a Constructive Christian Social Ethic*, 129–152. Notre Dame: University of Notre Dame Press, 1981.

———. "The Christian Difference, or Surviving Postmodernism." In *The Blackwell Companion to Postmodern Theology*, edited by Graham Ward, 144–161. Oxford: Blackwell, 2001.

———. *Christian Existence Today: Essays on Church, World, and Living in Between*. Grand Rapids: Brazos, 1988.

———. "Christians, Don't Be Fooled: Trump Has Deep Religious Convictions." *The Washington Post*, January 27, 2017. https://www.washingtonpost.com/news/acts-of-faith/wp/2017/01/27/christians-dont-be-fooled-trump-has-deep-religious-convictions/?utm_term=.2fec76d66372.

———. "Church as God's New Language." In *The Hauerwas Reader*, edited by John Berkman and Michael Cartwright, 142–62. Durham: Duke University Press, 2001.

———. *A Community of Character: Toward a Constructive Christian Social Ethic*. Notre Dame: University of Notre Dame Press, 1981.

———. *A Cross-Shattered Church: Reclaiming the Theological Heart of Preaching*. Grand Rapids: Brazos, 2009.

———. "Dietrich Bonhoeffer's Political Theology." In *Performing the Faith: Bonhoeffer and the Practice of Nonviolence*, 33–54. Grand Rapids: Brazos, 2004.

———. *Dispatches from the Front: Theological Engagements with the Secular*. Durham: Duke University, 1994.

———. "The End of Religious Pluralism: A Tribute to David Burrell." In *Democracy and the New Religious Pluralism*, edited by Thomas Banchoff, 283–300. Oxford: Oxford University Press, 2007.

———. "Epilogue: A Pacifist Response to the Bishops." In *Speak up for Just War or Pacifism: A Critique of the United Methodist Bishops' Pastoral Letter "In Defense of Creation,"* by Paul Ramsey, 149–182. University Park: The Pennsylvania State University Press, 1988.

———. "Foreword." In *Can War Be Just in the 21st Century? Ethicists Engage the Tradition*, edited by Tobias Winright and Laurie Johnston, xi–xii. New York: Orbis, 2015.

———. "Friendship and Fragility." In *Christians Among the Virtues: Theological Conversations with Ancient and Modern Eth*ics, edited by Stanley Hauerwas and Charles Pinches, 70–88. Notre Dame: University of Notre Dame Press, 1997.

———. *Hannah's Child: A Theologians Memoir*. Grand Rapids: Eerdmans, 2010.

———. *The Hauerwas Reader*. Edited by John Berkman and Michael Cartwright. Durham: Duke University Press, 2001.

———. "Holy Week, Syria, and Christian Ethics." *National Council of Churches*, April 17, 2017. https://nationalcouncilofchurches.us/holy-week-syria-and-christian-ethics-podcast/.

———. "How 'Christian Ethics' Came to Be." In *The Hauerwas Reader*, edited by John Berkman and Michael Cartwright, 37–50. Durham: Duke University Press, 2001.

———. "How I Learned to Think Theologically." In *The Work of Theology*, 11–31. Grand Rapids: Eerdmans, 2015.

———. "How the Holy Spirit Works." In *The Work of Theology*, 32–52. Grand Rapids: Eerdmans, 2015.

———. "How to Be an Agent: Why Character Matters." In *The Work of Theology*, 70–89. Grand Rapids: Eerdmans, 2015.

———. "How to Be Theologically Ironic." In *The Work of Theology*, 147–69. Grand Rapids: Eerdmans, 2015.

---. "How to (Not) Be a Political Theologian." In *The Work of Theology*, 170-90. Grand Rapids: Eerdmans, 2015.

---. *In Good Company: The Church as Polis*. Notre Dame: University of Notre Dame Press, 1995.

---. "Introduction: Lingering with Yoder's Wild Work." In *A Mind Patient and Untamed: Assessing John Howard Yoder's Contributions to Theology, Ethics, and Peacemaking*, edited by Ben C. Ollenburger and Gayle Gerber Koontz, 11-19. Eugene, OR: Cascade, 2004.

---. "Jesus, the Justice of God." In *War and the American Difference: Theological Reflections on Violence and National Identity*, 99-116. Grand Rapids: Baker Academic, 2011.

---. "Making Connections: By Way of a Response to Wells, Herdt, and Tran." In *The Difference Christ Makes: Celebrating the Life, Work, and Friendship of Stanley Hauerwas*, edited by Charlie M. Collier, 77-94. Eugene, OR: Cascade, 2015.

---. *Matthew*. Grand Rapids: Brazos, 2006.

---. "The Ministry of a Congregation." In *Christian Existence Today: Essays on Church, World, and Living in Between*, 111-32. Grand Rapids: Brazos, 1988.

---. "Naming God: A Sermon." In *Working With Words: On Learning to Speak Christian*, 79-83. Eugene, OR: Cascade, 2011.

---. "No Enemy, No Christianity: Theology and Preaching between 'Worlds.'" In *The Future of Theology: Essays in Honor of Jürgen Moltmann*, edited by Miroslav Volf et al., 26-34. Grand Rapids: Eerdmans, 1996.

---. "The Narrative Turn: Thirty Years Later." In *Performing the Faith: Bonhoeffer and the Practice of Nonviolence*, 135-49. Grand Rapids: Brazos, 2004.

---. "The Nonresistant Church." In *Vision and Virtue: Essays in Christian Ethical Reflection*, 197-221. Notre Dame: University of Notre Dame Press, 1981.

---. "The Nonviolent Terrorist: In Defense of Christian Fanaticism." In *The Church as Countercultural*, edited by Michael I. Budde and Robert W. Brimlow, 89-104. Albany: State University of New York Press, 2000.

---. "On Beginning in the Middle." In *The Peaceable Kingdom: A Primer in Christian Ethics*, 50-71. Notre Dame: University of Notre Dame Press, 1983.

---. "On God: Ethics and the Power to Act in History." In *Essays on Peace Theology and Witness*, edited by Willard M. Swartley, 204-9. Elkhart: Institute of Mennonite Studies, 1988.

---. "On Keeping Theological Ethics Imaginative." In *Against the Nations: War and Survival in a Liberal Society*, 51-60. Minneapolis: Winston, 1985.

---. *The Peaceable Kingdom: A Primer in Christian Ethics*. Notre Dame: University of Notre Dame Press, 1983.

---. "Peacemaking: The Virtue of the Church." In *Christian Existence Today: Essays on Church, World, and Living in Between*, by Stanley Hauerwas, 89-97. Grand Rapids: Brazos, 1988.

---. *Performing the Faith: Bonhoeffer and the Practice of Nonviolence*. Grand Rapids: Brazos, 2004.

---. "The Politics of Gentleness." In *Living Gently in a Violent World*, by Stanley Hauerwas and Jean Vanier, 77-99. Downers Grove: InterVarsity, 2008.

---. "Race: The 'More' It is About: Will D. Campbell Lecture University of Mississippi, 2006." In *Christianity, Democracy, and the Radical Ordinary:*

Conversations Between a Radical Democrat and a Christian," by Stanley Hauerwas and Romand Coles, 87–102. Eugene, OR: Cascade, 2008.

———. "Reading James McClendon Takes Practice." In *Wilderness Wanderings: Probing Twentieth-Century Theology and Philosophy*, 171–87. Boulder: Westview, 1997.

———. "The Reality of the Church." In *Against the Nations: War and Survival in a Liberal Society*, 122–31. Minneapolis: Winston, 1985.

———. *Sanctify Them in Truth: Holiness Exemplified*. Nashville: Abingdon, 1998.

———. "Sent." In *Working With Words: On Learning to Speak Christian*, 164–72. Eugene, OR: Cascade, 2011.

———. "September 11, 2001: A Pacifist Response." In *Dissent From the Homeland: Essays after September 11*, edited by Stanley Hauerwas and Frank Lentricchia, 181–93. Durham: Duke University Press, 2003.

———. "September 11, 2001: A Pacifist Response." In *Walking with God in a Fragile World*, edited by James Langford and Leroy Rouner, 121–30. Lanham: Rowman and Littlefield, 2003.

———. *The State of the University: Academic Knowledges and the Knowledge of God*. Malden: Blackwell, 2007.

———. "Suffering Beauty: The Liturgical Formation of Christ's Body." In *Performing the Faith: Bonhoeffer and the Practice of Nonviolence*, 151–65. Grand Rapids: Brazos, 2004.

———. "Taking Time for Peace: The Ethical Significance of the Trivial." In *Christian Existence Today: Essays on Church, World, and Living in Between*, by Stanley Hauerwas, 253–66. Grand Rapids: Brazos, 1988.

———. "The Truth about God: The Decalogue as Condition for Truthful Speech." In *The Doctrine of God and Theological Ethics*, edited by Alan J. Torrance and Michael Banner, 85–104. London: T. & T. Clark International, 2006.

———. *Unleashing the Scripture: Freeing the Bible from Captivity to America*. Nashville: Abingdon, 1993.

———. *Vision and Virtue: Essays in Christian Ethical Reflection*. Notre Dame: University of Notre Dame Press, 1981.

———. *War and the American Difference: Theological Reflections on Violence and National Identity*. Grand Rapids: Baker Academic, 2011.

———. "Which Church? What Unity? Or, An Attempt to Say What I May Think about the Future of Christian Unity." In *Approaching the End: Eschatological Reflections on Church, Politics, and Life*, by Stanley Hauerwas, 98–119. Grand Rapids: Eerdmans, 2013.

———. *Wilderness Wanderings: Probing Twentieth-Century Theology and Philosophy*. Boulder, CO: Westview, 1997.

———. *With the Grain of the Universe: The Church's Witness and Natural Theology*. Grand Rapids: Brazos, 2001.

———. "Witness (with Charles Pinches)." In *Approaching the End: Eschatological Reflections on Church, Politics, and Life*, 37–66. Grand Rapids: Eerdmans, 2013.

———. *The Work of Theology*. Grand Rapids: Eerdmans, 2015.

———. *Working With Words: On Learning to Speak Christian*. Eugene, OR: Cascade, 2011.

———. "'Writing-In' and 'Writing-Out': A Challenge to Modern Theology." *Modern Theology* 26.1 (January 2010) 61–66.

Hauerwas, Stanley, and Charles Pinches. *Christians among the Virtues: Theological Conversations with Ancient and Modern Ethics*. Notre Dame: University of Notre Dame Press, 1997.

Hauerwas, Stanley, and Chris K. Huebner. "History, Theory, and Anabaptism: A Conversation on Theology After John Howard Yoder." In *The Wisdom of the Cross: Essays in Honor of John Howard Yoder*, edited by Stanley Hauerwas et al., 391–408. Eugene, OR: Wipf & Stock, 1999.

Hauerwas, Stanley, and L. Gregory Jones, eds. *Why Narrative: Readings In Narrative Theology*, Eugene, OR: Wipf & Stock, 1997.

Hauerwas, Stanley, and Mark Sherwindt. "The Kingdom of God: An Ecclesial Space for Peace." *Word & World* 2.2 (1982) 127–36.

———. "The Reality of the Kingdom." In *Against the Nations: War and Survival in a Liberal Society*, 107–21. Minneapolis: Winston, 1985.

Hauerwas, Stanley, and Romand Coles. *Christianity, Democracy, and the Radical Ordinary: Conversations between a Radical Democrat and a Christian*. Eugene, OR: Cascade, 2008.

———. "Long Live the Weeds and the Wilderness Yet: Reflections on a *Secular Age*." *Modern Theology* 26.3 (July 2010) 349–61.

Hauerwas, Stanley, and Samuel Wells, eds. *The Blackwell Companion to Christian Ethics*. Malden: Blackwell, 2004.

———. "The Gift of the Church and the Gifts God Gives it." In *The Blackwell Companion to Christian Ethics*, edited by Stanley Hauerwas and Samuel Wells, 13–27. Malden: Blackwell, 2004.

———. "Why Christian Ethics Was Invented." In *The Blackwell Companion to Christian Ethics*, edited by Stanley Hauerwas and Samuel Wells, 28–38. Malden: Blackwell, 2004.

Hauerwas, Stanley, et al., eds. *The Wisdom of the Cross: Essays in Honor of John Howard Yoder*. Eugene, OR: Wipf & Stock, 1999.

Hawksley, Theodora Lucy. *The Ecclesiology of Stanley Hauerwas: Resident Aliens and die Concrete Church*. Durham: Durham University Press, 2007.

Hays, Richard B. *The Moral Vision of the New Testament: Community, Cross, New Creation*. San Francisco: HarperSanFrancisco, 1996.

Healy, Nicholas. *Hauerwas: A (Very) Critical Introduction*. Grand Rapids: Eerdmans, 2014.

Heekuk, Lim. *Christianity in Korea: Historical Moments of Protestant Churches*. Translated by Chung Jujin. Seoul: National Council of Churches in Korea, 2013.

Heidebrecht, Paul C. "Not Engineering, But Doxology? Reexamining Yoder's Perspective on the Church." In *Power and Practices: Engaging the Work of John Howard Yoder*, edited by Jeremy M. Bergen and Anthony G. Siegrist, 117–29. Waterloo, ON: Herald, 2009.

Herdt, Jennifer. "Truthfulness and Continual Discomfort." In *The Difference Christ Makes: Celebrating the Life, Work, and Friendship of Stanley Hauerwas*, edited by Charles M. Collier, 25–42. Eugene, OR: Cascade, 2015.

———. "The Virtue of Liturgy." In *The Blackwell Companion to Christian Ethics, Second Edition*, edited by Stanley Hauerwas and Samuel Wells, 535–46. Malden: Blackwell, 2011.

Hershberger, Guy Franklin. *War, Peace and Nonresistance*. Scottdale, PA: Herald, 1953.

Hess, Cynthia. *Sites of Violence, Sites of Grace: Christian Nonviolence and the Traumatized Self.* Lanham: Lexington, 2009.

———. "Traumatic Violence and Christian Peacemaking." In *The New Yoder*, edited by Peter Dula and Chris K. Huebner, 196–215. Eugene, OR: Cascade, 2010.

Hewitt, Marsha Aileen. "Critical Theory." In *The Blackwell Companion to Political Theology*, edited by Peter Scott and William T. Cavanaugh, 455–70. Malden: Blackwell, 2004.

Hoffmann, Carl. *A Grammar of the Margi Language.* London: Oxford University Press, 1963.

Hoover, Dennis R., and Douglas M. Johnston, eds. *Religion And Foreign Affairs: Essential Readings.* Waco: Baylor University Press, 2012.

Hosler, Jennifer. "Stories from the Cities." http://www.brethren.org/messenger/articles/stories-from-the-cities/?referrer=https://www.google.com/.

Hosler, Nathan. "Blessed Are the Peacemakers, For They Will Be Called Children of God: The Role of Religious Peacemakers in International Conflict Resolution and Peacebuilding." Unpublished master's thesis: Salve Regina University, 2009.

———. "Peacebuilding and the Religious Other: Re-engaging Brethren Practices as a Foundation for Peacebuilding." *Brethren Life & Thought* (Fall 2013) 39–50.

Hovey, Craig. "The Public Ethics of Yoder and Hauerwas." In *A Mind Patient and Untamed: Assessing John Howard Yoder's Contributions to Theology, Ethics, and Peacemaking*, edited by Ben C. Ollenburger and Gayle Gerber Koontz, 205–20. Eugene, OR: Cascade, 2004.

Huebner, Chris K. "Patience, Witness, and the Scattered Body of Christ: Yoder and Virilio on Knowledge, Politics, and Speed." In *The New Yoder*, edited by Peter Dula and Chris K. Huebner, 121–41. Eugene, OR: Cascade, 2010.

———. *A Precarious Peace: Yoderian Explorations on Theology, Knowledge, and Identity.* Waterloo, Ontario: Herald, 2006.

———. "The Work of Reading: Hauerwas, MacIntyre, and the Question of Liberalism." In *Unsettling Arguments: A Festschrift on the Occasion of Stanley Hauerwas's 70th Birthday*, edited by Charles R. Pinches et al., 284–99. Eugene, OR: Cascade, 2010.

Huebner, Harry. "An Ethic of Character: The Normative Form of the Christian Life According to Stanley Hauerwas." In *Essays on Peace Theology and Witness*, edited by Willard M. Swartley, 179–203. Elkhart: Institute of Mennonite Studies, 1988.

Hunter, James Davison. *To Change the World: The Irony, Tragedy, and Possibility of Christianity in the Late Modern World.* Oxford: Oxford University Press, 2010.

Hutter, Reinhard. *Suffering Divine Things: Theology as Church Practice.* Translated by Doug Stott. Grand Rapids: Eerdmans, 2000.

Izuzquiza, Daniel. *Rooted in Jesus Christ: Toward a Radical Ecclesiology.* Grand Rapids: Eerdmans, 2009.

Jennings, Willie James. *The Christian Imagination: Theology and the Origins of Race.* New Haven: Yale University Press, 2010.

Johnson, Roger A. *Peacemaking and Religious Violence: From Thomas Aquinas to Thomas Jefferson.* Eugene, OR: Pickwick, 2009.

Johnston, Douglas M., Jr. "Religion and Foreign Policy." In *Forgiveness and Reconciliation: Religion, Public Policy, and Conflict Transformation*, edited by Raymond G. Helmick and Rodney L. Peterson, 117–28. Philadelphia: Templeton Foundation, 2001.

Jones, L. Gregory, et al., eds. *God, Truth, and Witness: Engaging Stanley Hauerwas*. Grand Rapids: Brazos, 2005.

Just Peace Companion. 2nd ed. Geneva: World Council of Churches, 2012.

Kallenberg, Brad J. *Ethics as Grammar: The Changing Postmodern Subject*. Notre Dame: University of Notre Dame Press, 2001.

Katanacho, Yohanna. "Reading the Gospel of John through Palestinian Eyes." In *Jesus Without Borders: Christology in the Majority World*, edited by Gene L. Green et al., 103–22. Grand Rapids: Eerdmans, 2014.

Katongole, Emmanuel. *Beyond Universal Reason: The Relation between Religion and Ethics in the Work of Stanley Hauerwas*. Notre Dame: University of Notre Dame Press, 2000.

———. "Mission and Social Formation: Searching for an Alternative to King Leopold's Ghost." In *African Theology Today*, edited by Emmanuel Katongole, 121–46. Scranton: University of Scranton, 2002.

———. *The Sacrifice of Africa: A Political Theology for Africa*. Grand Rapids: Eerdmans, 2011.

Katongole, Emmanuel, and Jonathan Wilson-Hartgrove. *Mirror to the Church: Resurrection Faith After Genocide in Rwanda*. Grand Rapids: Zondervan, 2009.

Kenneson, Philip. "Gathering: Worship, Imagination, and Formation." In *The Blackwell Companion to Christian Ethics*, edited by Stanley Hauerwas and Samuel Wells, 53–67. Malden: Blackwell, 2004.

Kerr, Nathan R. *Christ, History and Apocalyptic: The Politics of Christian Mission*. Eugene, OR: Cascade, 2009.

Khalil, Osamah F. *America's Dream Palace: Middle East Expertise and the Rise of the National Security State*. Cambridge: Harvard University Press, 2016.

King, Martin Luther, Jr. "A Time to Break the Silence." In *The Essential Writings and Speeches of Martin Luther King Jr.*, edited by James M. Washington, 231–44. New York: Harper One, 1986.

———. "Where Do We Go From Here?" In *The Essential Writings and Speeches of Martin Luther King Jr.*, edited by James M. Washington, 245–52. New York: Harper One, 1986.

Kreider, Alan. *The Patient Ferment of the Early Church: The Improbable Rise of Christianity in the Roman Empire*. Grand Rapids: Baker Academic, 2016.

Kroeker, P. Travis. "Making Strange: Harry Huebner's Church-World Distinction." In *The Church Made Strange for the Nations: Essays in Ecclesiology and Political Theology*, edited by Paul G. Doerksen and Karl Koop, 92–99. Eugene, OR: Pickwick, 2011.

Langan, John. "The Elements of St. Augustine's Just War Theory." In *The Ethics of St. Augustine*, edited by William S. Babcock, 169–89. Atlanta: Scholars, 1991.

Lederach, John Paul. *The Moral Imagination: The Art and Soul of Building Peace*. Oxford: Oxford University Press, 2005.

Lehenbauer, Joel D. "The Theology of Stanley Hauerwas." *Concordia Theological Journal* 76 (2012) 157–74.

Leiter, David A. *Neglected Voices: Peace in the Old Testament*. Scottsdale: Herald, 2007.

Lindbeck, George A. *The Nature of Doctrine: Religion and Theology in a Postliberal Age*. Louisville: Westminster John Knox, 2009.

Logan, James Samuel. *Good Punishment? Christian Moral Practice and U.S. Imprisonment*. Grand Rapids: Eerdmans, 2008.

———. "Liberalism, Race, and Stanley Hauerwas." *Crosscurrents* (Winter 2006) 522–33.

MacIntyre, Alasdair. *After Virtue*. 3rd ed. Notre Dame: University of Notre Dame Press, 2007.

———. *Three Rival Versions of Moral Enquiry: Encyclopaedia, Genealogy, and Tradition*. Notre Dame: University of Notre Dame Press, 1990.

Majawa, Clement. "The Church's Role in Defining Genuine Democracy in Africa." In *African Theology Today*, edited by Emmanuel Katongole, 99–119. Scranton: University of Scranton Press, 2002.

Maldonado-Torres, Nelson. "Epistemology, Ethics, and the Time/Space of Decolonization: Perspectives from the Caribbean and the Latina/o Americas." In *Decolonizing Epistemologies: Latina/o Theology and Philosophy*, edited by Ada Maria Isasi-Díaz and Eduardo Mendieta, 193–206. New York: Fordham University Press, 2012.

Mangina, Joseph L. "Church, Cross, and *Caritas*, or Why Congregationalism Is Not Enough: A Reply to Stanley Hauerwas." *Pro Ecclesia* 22.4 (2013) 437–54.

Marshall, Ellen Ott. "Conflict, God, and Constructive Change: Exploring Prominent Christian Convictions in the Work of Conflict Transformation." *Brethren Life and Thought* 16.2 (Fall 2016) 1–15.

Martens, Paul. "Universal History and a Not-Particularly Christian Particularity: Jeremiah and John Howard Yoder's Social Gospel." In *Power and Practices: Engaging the Work of John Howard Yoder*, edited by Jeremy M. Bergen and Anthony G. Siegrist, 131–46. Waterloo, ON: Herald, 2009.

Martin, Steven. "Holy Week, Syria, and Chrsitian Ethics (podcast)." https://nationalcouncilofchurches.us/holy-week-syria-and-christian-ethics-podcast/.

Mazarr, Michael J. "The Once and Future Order: What Comes After Hegemony?" *Foreign Affairs* (January/February 2017) 25–32.

Michaels, Jon D. "Trump and the 'Deep State': The Government Strikes Back." *Foreign Affairs* (September/October 2017) 52–56.

Milbank, John. "The Conflict of the Faculties: Theology and the Economy of the Sciences." In *Faithfulness and Fortitude: In Conversation with the Theological Ethics of Stanley Hauerwas*, edited by Mark Thiessen Nation and Samuel Wells, 39–57. Edinburgh: T. & T. Clark, 2000.

———. *Theology and Social Theory: Beyond Secular Reason*. Oxford: Blackwell, 1990.

———. *The Word Made Strange: Theology, Language, Culture*. Oxford: Blackwell, 1998.

Miller, Keith Graber. *Wise as Serpents, Innocent as Doves: American Mennonites Engage Washington*. Knoxville: University of Tennessee Press, 1996.

Miller, Randy. "Resolution Supports Nigerian Brethren, Invites Worldwide Community of Brethren to a Week of Fasting and Prayer." http://www.brethren.org/news/2014/delegates-adopt-nigeria-resolution.html?referrer=http://support.brethren.org/site/MessageViewer?dlv_id=36641&em_id=28981.0.

McCarthy, Eli Sasaran. *Becoming Nonviolent Peacemakers: A Virtue Ethic for Catholic Social Teaching and U.S. Policy*. Eugene, OR: Pickwick, 2012.

McClendon, James William, Jr. *Systematic Theology: Ethics*. Nashville: Abingdon, 1986.

McGann, James G. *The Fifth Estate: Think Tanks: Public Policy, and Governance*. Washington, DC: The Brookings Institution, 2016.

Morgan, Brandon L. "The Lordship of Christ and the Gathering of the Church: Hauerwas Debts to the 1948 Barth-Niebuhr Exchange." *Conrad Grebel Review* 33.1 (Winter 2015) 49–71.

Moya, Paula M. L. "'Racism Is Not Intellectual': Interracial Friendship, Multicultural Literature, and Decolonizing Epistemologies." In *Decolonizing Epistemologies: Latina/o Theology and Philosophy*, edited by Ada Maria Isasi-Díaz and Eduardo Mendieta, 169–90. New York: Fordham University Press, 2012.

Murphy, Nancy. "John Howard Yoder's Systematic Defense of Christian Pacifism." In *The New Yoder*, edited by Peter Dula and Chris K. Huebner, 42–69. Eugene, OR: Cascade, 2010.

Nation, Mark Theissen. "The First Word Christians Have to Say About Violence is 'Church.'" In *Faithfulness and Fortitude: In Conversation with the Theological Ethics of Stanley Hauerwas*, edited by Mark Theissen Nation and Samuel Wells, 19–36. Edinburgh: T. & T. Clark, 2000.

Nation, Mark Theissen, and Samuel Wells, eds. *Faithfulness and Fortitude: In Conversation with the Theological Ethics of Stanley Hauerwas*. Edinburgh: T. & T. Clark, 2000.

Neill, Jeremy. "Political Involvement and Religious Compromises: Some Thoughts on Hauerwas and Liberalism." *Political Theology* 14.1 (2013) 32–57.

Niebuhr, H. Richard. *Christ and Culture*. New York: Harper & Row, 1951.

Niebuhr, Reinhold. *Moral Man and Immoral Society: A Study in Ethics and Politcs*. New York: Scribner's, 1932.

Ollenburger, Ben C., and Gayle Gerber Koontz, eds. *A Mind Patient and Untamed: Assessing John Howard Yoder's Contributions to Theology, Ethics, and Peacemaking*. Eugene, OR: Cascade, 2004.

Park, Joon-Sik. *Missional Ecclesiologies in Creative Tension: H. Richard Niebuhr and John Howard Yoder*. New York: Lang, 2007.

Paul, Herman J. "Stanley Hauerwas: Against Secularization in the Church." *Zeitschrift für Dialektische Theologie, Heft* 59.2 (2013) 12–33.

Pinches, Charles R. "Hauerwas and Political Theology: The Next Generation." *Journal of Religious Ethics* 36.3 (2008) 513–42.

———. "Proclaiming: Naming and Describing." In *The Blackwell Companion to Christian Ethics*, edited by Stanley Hauerwas and Samuel Wells, 169–81. Malden: Blackwell, 2004.

———. "Stout, Hauerwas, and the Body of America." *Political Theology* 8.1 (2007) 9–31.

Pinches, Charles R., et al., eds. *Unsettling Arguments: A Festschrift on the Occasion of Stanley Hauerwas's 70th Birthday*. Eugene, OR: Cascade, 2010.

Raheb, Mitri. *Faith in the Face of Empire: The Bible Through Palestinian Eyes*. Maryknoll: Orbis, 2014.

Rasmusson, Arne. *The Church as Polis: From Political Theology to Theological Politics as Exemplified by Jurgen Moltmann and Stanley Hauerwas*. Notre Dame: University of Notre Dame Press, 1995.

Rauschenbusch, Walter. *Christianity and the Social Crisis*. New York: Association Press, 1912.

———. *Theology for the Social Gospel*. Nashville: Abingdon, 1961.

Reimer, A. James. "Anabaptist-Mennonite Political Theology: Conceptualizing Universal Ethics in Post-Christendom." In *The Church Made Strange for the*

Nations: Essays in Ecclesiology and Political Theology, edited by Paul G. Doerksen and Karl Koop, 80–91. Eugene, OR: Pickwick, 2011.

Reno, R. R. "Stanley Hauerwas." In *The Blackwell Companion to Political Theology*, edited by Peter Scott and William T. Cavanaugh, 302–316. Malden: Blackwell, 2004.

———. "Stanley Hauerwas and the Liberal Protestant Project." *Modern Theology* 28.2 (April 2012) 320–26.

Rivera, Mayra. *Poetics of the Flesh*. Durham: Duke University Press, 2015.

Roberts, Tyler T. "Theology and the Ascetic Imperative: Narrative and Renunciation in Taylor and Hauerwas." *Modern Theology* 9.2 (April 1993) 181–200.

Ross, Rosetta E. *Witnessing and Testifying: Black Women, Religion, and Civil Rights*. Minneapolis: Fortress, 2003.

Ruiz, Jean-Pierre. *Readings from the Edges: The Bible and People on the Move*. New York: Orbis, 2011.

Ryan, Mark. *The Politics of Practical Reason: Why Theological Ethics Must Change Your Life*. Eugene, OR: Cascade, 2011.

Schrock-Shenk, Carolyn, ed. *Mediation and Facilitation Manual: Foundations and Skills for Constructive Conflict Transformation*. 4th ed. Akron, OH: Mennonite Conciliation Service, 2000.

Scott, Peter, and William T. Cavanaugh, eds. *The Blackwell Companion to Political Theology*. Malden: Blackwell, 2004.

Shuman, Joel James. "Discipleship as Craft: Crafting the Christian Body." In *Unsettling Arguments: A Festschrift on the Occasion of Stanley Hauerwas's 70th Birthday*, edited by Charles R. Pinches et al., 315–31. Eugene, OR: Cascade, 2010.

Sider, J. Alexander. "Friendship, Alienation, Love: Stanley Hauerwas and John Howard Yoder." In *Unsettling Arguments: A Festschrift on the Occasion of Stanley Hauerwas's 70th Birthday*, edited by Charles R. Pinches et al., 61–86. Eugene, OR: Cascade, 2010.

———. *To See History Doxologically: History and Holiness in John Howard Yoder's Ecclesiology*. Grand Rapids: Eerdmans, 2011.

Siggelkow, Ry O. "Toward an Apocalyptic Peace Church: Christian Pacifism *After Hauerwas*." *The Conrad Grebel Review* 31.3 (Fall 2013) 274–97.

Spurr, David. *The Rhetoric of Empire: Colonial Discourse in Journalism, Travel Writing, and Imperial Administration*. Durham: Duke University Press, 1993.

Stassen, Glen H. *Just Peacemaking: Transforming Initiatives for Justice and Peace*. Louisville: Westminster, 1992.

Stephens, Bret. "What Obama Gets Wrong: No Retreat, No Surrender." *Foreign Affairs*, September/October 2015. https://www.foreignaffairs.com/articles/what-obama-gets-wrong.

Stewart, Rory. *The Places In Between*. Orlando: Harcourt, 2004.

Stout, Jeffrey. *Democracy and Tradition*. Princeton: Princeton University Press, 2004.

———. *Ethics after Babel: The Languages of Morals and Their Discontents*. Princeton: Princeton University Press, 2001.

Stutzman, Ervin R. *From Nonresistance to Justice: The Transformation of Mennonite Church Peace Rhetoric, 1908–2008*. Scottdale: Herald, 2011.

Stutzman, Paul Fike. *Recovering the Love Feast: Broadening our Eucharistic Celebrations*. Eugene, OR: Wipf & Stock, 2011.

Swartley, Willard M. *Covenant of Peace: The Missing Peace in New Testament Theology and Ethics.* Grand Rapids: Eerdmans, 2006.

Taleb, Nassim Nicholas. *Antifragile: Things That Gain from Disorder.* New York: Random House, 2012.

———. *The Black Swan: The Impact of the Highly Improbable.* New York: Random House, 2007.

Tanner, Kathryn. "Trinity." In *The Blackwell Companion to Political Theology,* edited by Peter Scott and William T. Cavanaugh, 319–32. Malden: Blackwell, 2004.

Tapie, Matthew A. "For He Is Our Peace." In *Reading Scripture as a Political Act: Essays on the Theopolitical Interpretation of the Bible,* edited by Matthew A. Tapie and Daniel Wade McClain, 149–68. Minneapolis: Fortress, 2015.

Taylor, Charles. *Modern Social Imagination.* Durham: Duke University Press, 2004.

———. *A Secular Age.* Cambridge: Harvard University Press, 2007.

Thomson, John B. *The Ecclesiology of Stanley Hauerwas: A Christian Theology of Liberation.* Burlington: Ashgate, 2003.

Toft, Monica Duffy, et al. *God's Century: Resurgent Religion and Global Politics.* New York: W.W. Norton, 2011.

Toole, David. *Waiting for Godot in Sarajevo: Theological Reflections on Nihilism, Tragedy, and Apocalypse.* Boulder: Westview, 1998.

Townes, Emilie M. *Womanist Ethics and the Cultural Production of Evil.* New York: Palgrave Macmillian, 2006.

Tran, Jonathan. "Time for Hauerwas's Racism." In *Unsettling Arguments: A Festschrift on the Occasion of Stanley Hauerwas's 70th Birthday,* edited by Charles R. Pinches et al., 246–64. Eugene, OR: Cascade, 2010.

"Unfinished Business." http://www.brethren.org/ac/2016/documents/business/ub1-vision-of-ecumenism-for-the-21st-century.pdf.

Van der Borght, Eduardus. "Just Peace and the Unity of the Church." In *Just Peace: Ecumenical, Intercultural, and Interdisciplinary Perspectives,* edited by Fernando Enns and Annette Mosher, 40–49. Eugene, OR: Pickwick.

Virilio, Paul. *Speed and Politics: An Essay on Dromology.* Translated by Mark Polizzotti. Los Angeles: Semiotexte, 2006.

Volf, Miroslav. *Exclusion and Embrace: A Theological Exploration of Identity, Otherness, and Reconciliation.* Nashville: Abingdon, 1996.

Wadell, Paul J. "Friendship." In *Unsettling Arguments: A Festschrift on the Occasion of Stanley Hauerwas's 70th Birthday,* edited by Charles R. Pinches et al., 265–83. Eugene, OR: Cascade, 2010.

Weaver, Alain Epp. "On Exile: Yoder, Said, and the Politics of Land and Return." In *The New Yoder,* edited by Peter Dula and Chris K. Huebner, 142–165. Eugene, OR: Cascade, 2010.

Weithman, Paul. "Augustine's Political Philosophy." In *The Cambridge Companion to Augustine,* edited by Eleonore Stump and Norman Kretzmann, 234–52. Cambridge: Cambridge University Press, 2003.

Wells, Samuel. "The Difference Christ Makes." In *The Difference Christ Makes: Celebrating the Life, Work, and Friendship of Stanley Hauerwas,* edited by Charles M. Collier, 5–24. Eugene, OR: Cascade, 2015.

———. *Transforming Fate into Destiny: The Theological Ethics of Stanley Hauerwas.* Eugene, OR: Cascade, 1998.

Werntz, Myles. "The Fellowship of Suffering: Reading Philippians with Stanley Hauerwas." *Review and Expositor* 112.1 (2015) 144–50.

West, Cornel. *Democracy Matters: Winning the Fight Against Imperialism*. New York: Penguin, 2004.

Willard, Mara. "Shaun Casey Talks About Leading the State Department's Faith-Based Office." *Religion and Politics*, March 4, 2014. http://religionandpolitics.org/2014/03/04/shaun-casey-talks-about-leading-the-state-departments-faith-based-office/.

Williams, Delores S. *Sisters in the Wilderness: The Challenge of Womanist God-Talk*. New York: Orbis, 1993.

Williams, Paul D. *War and Conflict in Africa*. 2nd ed. Cambridge: Polity, 2016.

Williams, Reggie L. *Bonhoeffer's Black Jesus: Harlem Renaissance Theology and an Ethic of Resistance*. Waco: Baylor University Press, 2015.

Wilson, Erin K., and Lulca Mavelli. "The Refugee Crisis and Religion: Beyond Conceptual and Physical Boundaries." In *The Refugee Crisis and Religion: Secularism, Security and Hospitality in Question*, edited by Luca Mavelli and Erin Wilson, 1–22. London: Rowman and Littlefield, 2017.

Wink, Walter. *Engaging the Powers: Discernment and Resistance in a World of Domination*. Minneapolis: Fortress, 1992.

Woodard-Lehman, Derek Alan. "Body Politics and the Politics of Bodies: Racism and Hauerwasian Theopolitics." *Journal of Religious Ethics* 36.2 (2008) 295–320.

Woodley, Randy S. *Shalom and the Community of Creation: An Indigenous Vision*. Grand Rapids: Eerdmans, 2012.

World Council of Churches. *Just Peace Companion*. 2nd ed. Geneva: World Council of Churches, 2012.

Wright, Nigel Goring. *Disavowing Constantine: Mission, Church and the Social Order in the Theologies of John Howard Yoder Jürgen Moltmann*. Carlisle, Cumbria: Paternoster, 2000.

Yafeh-Deigh, Alice Y. "The Liberative Power of Silent Agency: A Postcolonial Afro-Feminist-Womanist Reading of Luke 10:38–42." In *Postcolonial Perspectives in African Biblical Interpretations*, edited by Musa W. Dube et al., 417–38. Atlanta: Society of Biblical Literature, 2012.

Yoder, John Howard. *The Christian Witness to the State*. Scottdale: Herald, 1964.

———. *Nonviolence: A Brief History*. The Warsaw Lectures. Waco: Baylor University Press, 2010.

———. *The Original Revolution: Essays on Christian Pacifism*. Scottdale: Herald, 1971.

———. *The Politics of Jesus*. Grand Rapids: Eerdmans, 1972.

———. *The Priestly Kingdom: Social Ethics as Gospel*. Notre Dame: University of Notre Dame Press, 1984.

CPSIA information can be obtained
at www.ICGtesting.com
Printed in the USA
JSHW010923160623
43277JS00002B/65